Upholding Justice

History, Languages, and Cultures of the Spanish and Portuguese Worlds

---

This interdisciplinary series promotes scholarship in studies on Iberian cultures and contacts from the premodern and early modern periods.

TITLES IN THE SERIES

The Mirror of Spain, 1500–1700: The Formation of a Myth
J. N. Hillgarth

Bishops, Councils, and Consensus in the Visigothic Kingdom, 589–633
Rachel L. Stocking

Toasts with the Inca: Andean Abstraction and Colonial Images on Quero Vessels
Thomas B. F. Cummins

A Network of Converso Families in Early Modern Toledo: Assimilating a Minority
Linda Martz

Romans in a New World: Classical Models in Sixteenth-Century Spanish America
David A. Lupher

The Jesuit and the Incas: The Extraordinary Life of Padre Blas Valera, S.J.
Sabine Hyland

Upholding Justice: Society, State, and the Penal System of Quito (1650–1750)
Tamar Herzog

Conflict and Coexistence: Archbishop Rodrigo and the Muslims and Jews of Medieval Spain
Lucy K. Pick

The Origins of Mexican Catholicism: Nahua Rituals and Christian Sacraments in Sixteenth-Century Mexico
Osvaldo F. Pardo

UPHOLDING JUSTICE

Society, State, and the Penal System in Quito (1650–1750)

Tamar Herzog

THE UNIVERSITY OF MICHIGAN PRESS
Ann Arbor

Published in the United States of America by
The University of Michigan Press
Manufactured in the United States of America
⊗ Printed on acid-free paper

2007 2006 2005 2004 4 3 2 1

A CIP catalog record for this book is available from the British Library.

Library of Congress Cataloging-in-Publication Data

Herzog, Tamar.
Upholding justice : society, state, and the penal system in Quito (1650–1750) / Tamar Herzog.
p. cm. — (History, languages, and cultures of the Spanish and Portuguese worlds)
Includes bibliographical references and index.
ISBN 0-472-11375-5 (cloth : alk. paper)
1. Criminal justice, Administration of—Ecuador—Quito—History—17th century. 2. Criminal justice, Administration of—Ecuador—Quito—History—18th century. I. Title. II. Series.
HV7336.Z9Q584 2004
364.9866'13—dc22 2003021684

Acknowledgments

I would like to thank the following people for their help and support:

Nathan Wachtel, my dissertation adviser and a source of inspiration;
Jan Szeminski, who helped me discover the Andes and the early modern period;
José Manuel Pérez Prendes, who taught me about legal history and Iberia;
Francisco Tomás y Valiente, who read, corrected, and gave me good advice;
Juan Pro Ruiz, who discussed different aspects of this work with me and invited me to numerous dinners; and
Mirelle Peytavin, scholar of Spanish Italy who encouraged me to think diachronically about the empire.

Over the years, I was fortunate to enjoy the intellectual support and the friendship of many generous people. I would like to specifically mention Antonio Manuel Hespanha, David Nirenberg, Clara Álvarez Alonso, Magdalena Rodríguez Gil, S. N. Eisenstadt, Sabine MacCormack, Zacarías Moutoukias, Jean-Frédéric Schaub, Jaime Reis, Jacques Poloni, Bernard Lavallé, Michel Bertrand, Bartolomé Clavero, Carmen Iglesias, Thomas Calvo, Carmen Bernand, Jean Pierre Dedieu, Magnus Mörner, Laurence Fontaine, Rafaelle Romanelli, Richard Kagan, David Brading, Fred Bronner, Luis Roniger, Jack Owens, Kenneth J. Andrien, Tulio Halperin Donghi, Marco Belingeri, and my colleagues in Chicago Tom (and Kyle) Cummins, Constantin Fasolt, John Brewer, Michael Geyer, Friedrich Katz, Julius Kirshner, and Steven Pincus.

This work would have been impossible without the constant support of my family and friends. My parents, Rachel and Moshe, and my friends Yuval Erlich, Jorge Díaz Giménez, Laura Lobera Argüelles, Iris Papo, Alejandro Marangoni Bertini, Julio Díaz Sevillano, Lucy Pick, Milada Anna Vachudova, Loredana Lanfranco and Mario Freund, Claude and Claude Hirsch, Isabelle and Claude Hoffmann, María-

Ángeles Cuadrado Ruiz, and Françoise Duscha have my love, gratitude, and appreciation.

Finally, I would like to thank Daniel K. Gullo for translating the original from Spanish, and proofreading the corrected and augmented version, Byron Hamman for helping me revise the footnotes, bibliography, and text, Sean Smith, for preparing the index, and the Social Sciences Division of the University of Chicago for the funding to accomplish this work.

Contents

Abbreviations

AA	Sección de Autos Acordados
AGI	Archivo General de Indias, Sevilla
AGPR	Archivo General del Palacio Real, Madrid
AHN	Archivo Histórico Nacional, Madrid
AHPM	Archivo Histórico de Protocolos de Madrid, Madrid
AHQ	Archivo Histórico Nacional, Quito
AMQ	Archivo Municipal, Quito
ARCSF	Archivo de la Real Congregación de San Fermín de los Navarros, Madrid
BJC	Biblioteca de Jijón y Caamaño, Banco Central, Quito
BN	Biblioteca Nacional, Madrid
BPR	Biblioteca del Palacio Real, Madrid
Ced.	Sección de Cedulario
Cód.	Sección de Códices
Crim.	Sección de Criminales
CSCS	Sección de Consejos Suprimidos—Consejo de Indias
Cuad.	Cuaderno
EC	Sección de Escribanía de Cámara
EP	Sección de Expedientes Personales
EXP.	Expediente
FE	Sección de Fondo Especial
Gob.	Sección de Gobierno
IA	Sección de Incorporación de Abogados
IG	Sección de Indiferente General
LC	Libros de Cabildo
Mat.	Sección de Matrimoniales
Misc.	Sección de Miscelánea
Not. 1	Notaría primera—juicios
Not. 3	Notaría tercera—juicios
Not. 4	Notaría cuarta—juicios
Not. 5	Notaría quinta—juicios
Not. 6	Notaría sexta—juicios
Of.	Sección de Oficios
Pris.	Sección de Prisiones

Resid.	Sección de Residencias
RH	Sección de Real Hacienda
RI	Recopilación de Indias
Test.	Sección de Testamentaría
VM	Sección de Vínculos y Mayorazgos

Formulas for Citing Sources

1. Archive, section, *legajo,* subdivision of the legajo (mostly by *cuadernos*), date.
2. Archive, section, book, date.

Introduction

When I began this investigation some fifteen years ago, I was hoping to answer a simple question: how were early modern forms of government possible? Their institutions were weak, they operated in a climate of material poverty, and they had little or no coercive power with which to enforce their decisions. I soon discovered that the question I was asking was wrong. Today we assume that people obey institutions either because they must, or because they agree with institutional views. When we apply this understanding to the past, we claim that government was possible because it was absolute or because powerful individuals—whose interests coincided with the king's and who were able to command obedience from their clients—collaborated with it. We are thus surprised that an early modern administration could operate in a climate of material poverty. We explain this apparent paradox through further assumptions. We posit—as Michel Foucault once argued—the operation of mechanisms that dissimulated this poverty by presenting government as powerful. Or we posit the existence of a pact between the king and the elites that benefitted both at the expense of the people.[1] In making these claims, we assume that the past is inherently similar to the present.

This assumption is authorized by much of the existing literature. This literature argues that "states"—entities that act in the name of public authority and political community—emerged in the Middle Ages, were reinforced in the early modern period, and came into maturity in the nineteenth century.[2] Although there were noticeable differences between a "medieval," a "feudal," an "early modern," an "abso-

1. M. Foucault, *Surveiller et punir: naissance de la prison* (Paris, 1975).

2. J. Strayer, *On the Medieval Origins of the Modern State* (Princeton, 1970); and C. Tilly, "Reflections on the History of European State-Making," in *The Formation of National States in Western-Europe*, ed. C. Tilly (Princeton, 1975), 7.

lutist," and a "modern" state, all of these structures were states (or protostates) because in all of them a new, specialized, impersonal, and stable government appeared.[3] This was a gradual process. In the beginning, states coincided with, rather than replaced, other political organs capable of acting in the public sphere such as the family, the local community, and the church.[4] Individuals who acted as state makers struggled to eliminate the power of these competing bodies by employing both coercion and negotiation. Their final success led to the appearance of a public administration that not only claimed but also obtained a monopoly over the use of legitimate power. A regime based on law replaced a regime based on justice, nobles lost their power to bureaucrats, and a personal loyalty to the king gave way to an impersonal loyalty to the state. In the administration of criminal justice, a slow transfer took place from a system of private retribution and communal order to a system of state surveillance. The king extended his control to activities previously considered "private," which he now regulated by enacting laws and by appointing professional or semiprofessional bureaucrats to implement these laws. As Michel Foucault once argued, and as many historians who follow him assert, because of material limitations early states employed economic means.[5] Their intervention in society consisted mainly of irregular, exceptional, and highly ceremonial demonstrations. These demonstrations primarily inspired fear. Although early modern administration was successful in dramatizing claims about its effectiveness in society, it was extremely inefficient in all other respects. It was slow, expensive, and corrupt. Communal forms of conflict resolution persisted, complementing and interacting with a deficient royal administration.[6] As residual remains of a previous

3. O. Hintze, "Esencia y transformación del estado moderno," in *Historia de las formas políticas* (1931; reprint, Madrid, 1968), 313–14; H. Schulze, *States, Nations, and Nationalism: From the Middle Ages to the Present,* trans. William E. Yuill (Cambridge, 1996), xi–xii and 3–91; F. Chabod, "Was There a Renaissance State?" in *The Development of the Modern State,* ed. H. Lubasz (New York, 1964), 26–42; A. Musi, "La storiografia politico-amministrativa sull'età moderna: tendenze e metodi degli ultimi trent'anni," in *Stato e pubblica amministrazione nell'Ancien Régime,* ed. A. Musi (Naples, 1979), 11–40; P. Anderson, *Lineage of the Absolutist State* (London, 1974), 15–17; and P. Schiera, "Legitimacy, Discipline, and Institutions: Three Necessary Conditions for the Birth of the Modern State," in *The Origins of the State in Italy, 1300–1600,* ed. J. Kirshner (Chicago, 1996), 31. A summary of these debates can be found in K. H. F. Dyson, *The State Tradition in Western Europe: A Study of an Idea and Institution* (New York, 1980).

4. A. De Benedictis, "Stato, comunità, dimensione guiridica: una riflessione su recenti dibattiti," *Società e storia* 40 (1988): 380–81; C. Mozzarelli, "Introduzione," in *L'amministrazione nella storia moderna* (Milan, 1985), 1: 11–12; and M. Greengrass, "Conquest and Coalescence," in *Conquest and Coalescence: The Shaping of the State in Early Modern Europe,* ed. M. Greengrass (London, 1991), 1–24.

5. Foucault, *Surveiller et punir;* A. Zorzi, "Control social, ordre public et répression judiciare à Florence à l'epoque communale: éléments et problèmes," *Annales ESC* 45/5 (1990): 1169–88; and C. Alberto Garcés, *El cuerpo como texto: La problemática del castigo corporal en el siglo XVIII* (San Salvador de Jujuy, 1999).

period, these communal forms were bound to disappear with the affirmation and consolidation of the state.

This reconstruction (largely intended to explain the genealogy of present-day structures[7]) has been criticized by several historians who question the medieval or early modern existence of states.[8] These historians stress that states were a nineteenth-century invention, inherently tied to contemporary distinctions between private and public spheres. According to them the structures that we tend to identify today with the state were considered equal to a private relationship between individuals.[9] The family, in contrast, was a public institution with an important presence in the political sphere.[10] Because family was the only unit that combined personal relationships with political authority, states were built and imagined as families. Instead of one state, there were many states: the ecclesiastical state, the family state, the corporate state, and so forth. During this period, all activities we identify today as political were in fact judicial. They balanced conflicting interests by dispensing

6. N. Castan, *Les criminels de Languedoc: Les exigences d'ordre et les voies du ressentiment dans une société pré-révolutionnaire, 1750–1790* (Toulouse, 1980); Y. Castan, *Honnêteté et relations sociales en Languedoc, 1715–1780* (Paris, 1974); and C. B. Herrup, *The Common Peace: Participation and the Criminal Law in Seventeenth-Century England* (Cambridge, 1987).

7. J. P. Genet, "Introduction: Which State Rises?" *Historical Research* 65/157 (1992): 122–23, and 128–31; Tilly, "Reflections," 47; O. Hintze, "The Formation of States and Constitutional Development: A Study in History and Politics," in *The Historical Essays of Otto Hintze*, ed. F. Gilbert with assistance of R. M. Berdahl (1902; reprint, New York, 1975), 157–77; T. Ertman, *Birth of the Leviathan: Building States and Regimes in Medieval and Early Modern Europe* (Cambridge, 1997).

8. O. Brunner, *Land and Lordship. Structures of Governance in Medieval Austria*, trans. J. Kaminsky and J. Von Horn Melton (1939; reprint, Philadelphia, 1992); B. Clavero, "Institución política y derecho: acerca del concepto historiográfico de 'estado moderno,'" *Revista de estudios políticos* 19 (1981): 43–57; J. Lalinde Abadía, "Depuración histórica del concepto de estado," in *El estado español en su dimensión histórica*, ed. J. Lalinde Abadía, M. J. Peláez, A. Pérez Martín, E. Rotelli, I. Sánchez Bella, J. Tomás Villarroya, and E. Zurawka (Malaga, 1984), 17–58; A. M. Hespanha, "A historiografia juridico-institucional e 'a morte do estado,'" *Anuario de filosofia del derecho*, n.s. 3 (1986): 191–227; J. F. Schaub, "La penisola iberica nei secoli XVI e XVII: la questione dello stato," *Quaderni storici* 36/1 (1995): 9–10; E. Fasano Guarini, "'État modern' et anciens états italiens: Éléments d'histoire comparée," *Revue d'histoire moderne et contemporaine* 45/1 (1998): 38–40; and G. Chittolini, "The 'Private,' the 'Public,' the State," in *The Origins of the State in Italy, 1300–1600*, ed. J. Kirshner (Chicago, 1996), 35–38 and 42–44.

9. B. Clavero, "*Hispanus fiscus, persona ficta:* Concepción del sujeto político en el ius commune moderno," *Quaderni fiorentini* 11–12 (1982–83): 95–167.

10. Schaub, "La questione," 17–29. Family as a political institution is discussed in J. Costa, *Gobierno del ciudadano*, ed. A. Ubach Medina (1575; reprint, Zaragoza, 1998), 245–395.

justice, that is, by giving each person his or her due.[11] Within such a system, no direct intervention in the normative order was ever allowed, and there was no space for a political action as we know it today.[12]

The question of whether early modern structures were direct precedents for present-day organization has no clear answer. Rupture and continuity are both relative terms, and they can have the meaning we choose to give them. Nevertheless, questioning the paradigm of progress in the study of states has at least two important methodological implications. First, historians who wish to understand early modern states need to approach them anthropologically—by assuming difference and not similarity.[13] Second, historians cannot limit themselves to the study of the royal bureaucracy, and they cannot pretend to reconstruct the state by examining laws in isolation. They must integrate into their analyses organs like the family, as well as a variety of considerations and practices such as social and religious obligations, which were part of the normative order of the early modern period.[14] In short, in these investigations the social and the religious should not be separated from the political.[15]

Although these lessons have been available for at least twenty years, they have found only a limited echo in the writing of Spanish and Spanish American history. Most historians of Spain still adhere to a traditional theory that argues that a state was born in Spain during the reign of the Catholic monarchs because these monarchs centralized the

11. A. M. Hespanha, *Poder e instituições no antigo regime: Guia de estudo* (Lisbon, 1992), 20–35.

12. J. M. Portillo Valdés, "La administración en la reciente historiografía italiana (tema y variaciones)," *Anuario de historia del derecho español* 62 (1992): 645–57.

13. P. Fernández Albaladejo, *Fragmentos de monarquía: Trabajos de historia política* (Madrid, 1992), 13–15 and 86–88; and J. M. Monsalvo Antón, "Historia de los poderes medievales, del derecho a la antropología (el ejemplo castellano: monarquía, concejos y señoríos en los siglos XII–XV)," in *Historia a debate: medieval,* ed. C. Barros (Santiago de Compostela, 1995), 91–92.

14. J. Kirshner, "Introduction: The State Is 'Back In,'" in *The Origins of the State in Italy, 1300–1600,* ed. J. Kirshner (Chicago, 1996), 1–10; J. F. Schaub. "Le Temps de l'ētat: Vers un nouveau régime historiographique de l'ancien régime français," *Quaderni fiorentini* 25 (1996): 127–81; and A. Guery, "L' historien, la crise et l'état," *Annales ESC* 52/2 (1997): 255.

15. J. P. Dedieu, "Procesos y redes: La historia de las instituciones administrativas de la época moderna, hoy," *La pluma, la mitra y la espada: Estudios de historia institucional en la edad moderna,* ed. J. L. Castellano, J. P. Dedieu, and M. V. López Cordón (Madrid, 2000), 24.

administration and took power away from both local communities and nobles.[16] A smaller number of historians sustain that there was no Spanish state, only a Spanish monarchy made of several political entities, each independent of the other and each subjected to the king.[17] Although such an analysis accounts for the "multistructural" character of early modern Spain, it continues to view the monarchy fundamentally as a state, that is, as a public administration that gradually affirmed itself against opposition. The study of the state in Spain thus continues to be associated with the analysis of the royal administration on the one hand and the local elites that resisted or cooperated with it on the other. Prosopography is still popular, as is the social history of both administrators and elites.[18] Scholarship on the administration of justice continues to consider the penal system as a prime manifestation of royal authority. This justice was cruel, and its main purpose was to instill fear.[19] Only on rare occasions do scholars mention the collaboration between a state-run administration of justice and family and communal systems of penal control, systems that survived, we are told, the coming of the state.[20]

The scholarship on Spanish America follows a similar path. It

16. J. A. Maravall, "The Origins of the Modern State," *Cahiers d'histoire mondiale* 6/4 (1961): 789–808; S. De Dios, "Sobre la génesis y los carácteres del estado absolutista en Castilla," *Studia histórica—historia moderna* 3/3 (1985): 11–46; idem, "El estado moderno, un cadáver historiográfico?," in *Realidad e imagenes del poder: España a fines de la edad media*, ed. A. Rucquoi (Valladolid, 1988), 389–408; J. Gil Pujol, "Culturas políticas y clases dirigentes regionales en la formación del estado moderno: Un balance y varias cuestiones," in *Les élites locales et l'état dans l'Espagne moderne du XVIe au XIX siècle: Table ronde internationale (Talence, 13–15 décembre 1990)*, ed. M. Lambert-Gorges (Paris, 1993), 171–92; and J. M. Imizcoz Beunza, "De la comunidad a la nación: Elites locales, carreras y redes sociales en la España moderna (siglos XVIII–XIX)," in *Elites, poder y red social: Las élites del país vasco y Navarra en la edad moderna*, ed. J. M. Imizcoz Beunza (Vitoria, 1996), 193–210.

17. A. Musi, "La storiografia spagnola," in *Stato e pubblica amministrazione nell'Ancien Régime*, ed. A. Musi (Naples, 1979), 103–4; J. Lalinde Abadía, "España y la monarquía universal (en torno al concepto de 'estado moderno')," *Quaderni fiorentini* 15 (1986): 114–15; P. Fernández Albaladejo, "Imperio y administración bajo Carlos V: una reevaluación," in *Hernán Cortés y su tiempo: Actas del congreso Hernán Cortés y su tiempo* (Mérida, 1987), 2: 520–27; and J. H. Elliott, "A Europe of Composite Monarchies," *Past and Present* 137 (1992): 48–71.

18. Musi, "La storiografia spagnola," 115–18; and P. Fernández Albaladejo, "Les traditions nationales d'historiographie de l'état: l'Espagne," in *Visions sur le développement des états européens: théories et historiographies de l'état Moderne*, ed. W. Blockmans and J. P. Genet (Rome, 1993), 228–29.

focuses on royal projects of state building, and it scrutinizes the elites that backed or resisted these projects.[21] This analysis, as exemplified in the works of John Leddy Phelan, H. G. Koenigsberger, S. N. Eisenstadt, and Magali Sarfatti, stresses the consensual nature of the colonial state.[22] Because of its position as a mediator between the court and the subjects, the bureaucracy was able to exhort an enormous influence on society. Following Max Weber, Phelan concluded that the wishes of Madrid were the thesis, local pressures the antithesis, and the solutions adopted by the bureaucrats the synthesis.[23] Among other things, this interpretation implied that in Spanish America there was a distinct (and constantly remarked) difference between law and its application. Law,

19. F. Tomás y Valiente, *El derecho penal de la monarquía absoluta (siglos XVI–XVIII)* (Madrid, 1969); idem, "El derecho penal como instrumento de gobierno," *Estudis* 22 (1996): 249–62; J. L. Heras Santos, *La justicia penal de los Austrias en la corona de Castilla* (Salamanca, 1991); C. Herrero Herrero, *La justicia penal española en la crisis del poder absoluto* (Madrid, 1989); and L. Domengue and A. Risco, *L 'alcalde et le malandrin: Justice et société en Espagne au XVIIIe siècle,* vol. 1 (Toulouse, 2001).

20. T. A. Mantecón Movellán, *Conflictualidad y disciplinamiento social en la Cantabria rural del antiguo régimen* (Santander, 1997). The presence of these tendencies in other European countries has been pointed out by C. Álvarez Alonso, "Tendencias en la investigación del derecho penal histórico: Los casos de Gran Bretaña, Francia e Italia como excusa," in *Sexo barroco y otras transgresiones premodernas.* F. Tomás y Valiente, B. Clavero, A. M. Hespanha, J. L. Bermejo, E. Gacto, and C. Álvarez Alonso (Madrid, 1990) 197–213.

21. B. Bravo Lira, "La noción del estado en la recopilación de 1680," in *La recopilación de leyes de los reinos de las Indias. Estudios históricos-jurídicos,* ed. J. Icaza Dafur (Mexico, 1987), 145–60; J. A. Escudero, "Un 'proyecto de estado' en el siglo XVI y la cuestión indiana," in *Administración y estado en le España moderna,* ed. J. A. Escudero (Valladolid, 1991), 591–96; and S. B. Schwartz, "State and Society in Colonial Spanish America: An Opportunity for Prosopography," in *New Approaches to Latin American History,* ed. R. Grahan and P. H. Smith (Austin, 1974), 3–35.

22. J. L. Phelan, *The Kingdom of Quito in the Seventeenth Century: Bureaucratic Politics in the Spanish Empire* (Madison, 1967); H. G. Koenigsberger, *La práctica del imperio* (1696; reprint, Madrid, 1975); J. Lynch, "The Institutional Framework of Colonial Spanish America," in *Journal of Latin American Studies: Supplement* 24 (1992): 69–81; S. N. Eisenstadt, *The Political System of Empires* (London, 1963); and M. Sarfatti, *Spanish Bureaucratic Patrimonialism in America* (Berkeley, 1966). See also R. M. Morse, "The Heritage of Latin America," in *The Founding of New Societies: Studies in the History of the United States, Latin America, South Africa, Canada, and Australia,* ed. L. Hartz (New York, 1964) 123–77; H. Pietschmann, "El desarrollo estatal de hispanoamérica: enfoques metodológicos," *Chronica Nova* 21 (1993–94): 469–92; and J. M. Pérez Prendes y Muñoz de Arraco, *La monarquía indiana y el estado de derecho* (Valencia, 1989). These conclusions coincide with similar analyses of the early modern British empire: J. P. Greene, *Peripheries and Center: Constitutional Development in the Extended Polities of the British Empire and the United States, 1607–1788* (Athens, 1986); and idem, "Negotiated Authorities: The Problem of Governance in the Extended Polities of the Early Modern Atlantic World," in *Negotiated Authorities: Essays in the Colonial Political and Constitutional History,* ed. J. P. Greene (Charlottesville, 1994), 1–24.

which historians equated with royal wishes, was often ignored, and corruption was rampant. Local interests penetrated government on all levels, leading to a decline, or demise, in royal authority. Poor, distant, and lacking modern mechanisms of control, the colonial state simply could not exist without compromising with local interests. In the eighteenth century, the Bourbons attempted to change this situation and regain control of the Americas by eliminating Creoles from office and by installing a professional bureaucracy in their place. However, these attempts were only partially successful. Considered by locals as a breach in the colonial pact, the reforms led to rebellions and eventually to the independence of the Spanish American states.[24]

In this analysis, the state was once again equated with the royal bureaucracy, and its appearance was tied to a struggle between royal wishes on the one hand and local resistance or local collaboration on the other. Once again, the capacity of state makers to fight against, or manipulate, other political powers was at stake. While laws were harsh, legal practice (that is, the implementation of the law) was flexible and accommodating.[25] This flexibility was explained by the very same phenomenon observed by historians of the state: administrative poverty led to local autonomy. Yet flexibility was also inherent in the legal system itself. This system accommodated local customs and preferred justice and compromise to harsh solutions. Under these circumstances, communal consensus prevailed over personal gain or individual advancement and harmony was preferred over conflict.[26] According to this tradition of scholarship, the state and its laws were not necessarily as tyrannical, arbitrary, or corrupt as they had been perceived by some.[27] They were flexible, accommodating to local needs, and just.

As was the case with scholarship on Spain, and indeed on most other European countries, this analysis of Spanish America was built on several pairs of oppositions: state versus society, institutions and bureau-

23. Phelan, *The Kingdom of Quito*, 336; and P. Marzahl, "Creoles and Government: The Cabildo of Popayan," *Hispanic American Historical Review* 54 (1974): 638.

24. J. L. Phelan, *The People and the King: The Comunero Revolution in Colombia, 1781* (Madison, 1978), xvii–xix; and J. Lynch, "Introduction," in *Latin American Revolutions, 1808–1826: Old and New World Origins*, ed. J. Lynch (Norman, OK, 1994), 5–38.

25. S. M. Arron, "New Direction in Mexican Legal History," *Americas* 50/4 (1994): 461.

26. Ibid., 464, criticizing the contributions of C. Cutter ("Community and the Law in Northern New Spain," *Americas* 50/4 (1994): 467–80); and M. C. Scardaville ("Habsburg Law and Bourbon Order: State Authority, Popular Unrest, and the Criminal Justice System in Bourbon Mexico City," *Americas* 50/4 (1994): 501–25). See also C. Cutter, *The Legal Culture of Northern New Spain, 1700–1810* (Albuquerque, 1995), 40–41 and 148.

crats versus local elites, law versus its implementation, tyranny versus flexibility, public versus private spheres. However, these oppositions cannot be maintained if we seriously engage the aforementioned critiques of the teleological model of the state. If we ignore present-day distinctions between "state" and "nonstate" or "private" and "public," and if we assume that the past was different from the present, another story emerges. This story involves no state builders, as Charles Tilly had led us to believe, and no rigid institutions acting upon and modifying society, as others have described.[28] On the contrary, it reveals an administration whose boundaries and active members were never clearly defined. This administration was by no means separate from society, or truly royal (or public) in character.

In this book, I argue that in early modern Quito there was no clear distinction between officeholders and nonofficeholders. Officers made no distinction between private and public behavior or between private and public ends. The penal system operated through the means of local enforcement and was open to influence through social networks, rumor, and systems of reputation. Justice was not equal to legality, and the legal sphere was not autonomous from other types of knowledge, doctrines, or norms. Because law did not exist independently from the resolution of conflicts law and its implementation were one and the same thing. Instead of spectacular ceremonies of monarchical power, there was an emphasis on routine activities that ensured the public of the presence of a king who, like God, provided the ultimate legitimacy to a system in which he was constantly absent. Within such a framework, it was impossible to draw a clear distinction between society and institutions. There were certainly no people who could be identified as imposing, or attempting to impose, the coming of a Leviathan.

In chapter 1 I introduce these arguments by portraying a system that, in spite of having a set of processes, institutions, and officeholders, remains very different from our time. I argue that the auxiliary staff, whose contribution has been heretofore undervalued, played an important role in the resolution of conflicts. I also demonstrate that the division between professional and nonprofessional justice was unclear and that there was a similarly blurred division of labor between different institutions, instances, and people. In chapters 2 through 7, I question

27. C. Gibson, *Spain in America* (New York, 1966), 109; and S. J. Stein and B. H. Stein, *The Colonial Heritage of Latin America* (New York, 1970), 81.

28. Tilly, "Reflections," 47; and Scardaville, "Habsburg Law and Bourbon Order," 509.

further the traditional image of the administration of justice. I examine how some people became associated with the judicial system (chap. 2), and I elucidate the role of others who did not formally participate in the administration of justice yet who were its most essential components (chap. 4). I reconstruct the social and material conditions that made peace possible, as well as the social considerations that influenced the activities of local agents (chaps. 2, 3, 5, and 6). I examine how Quiteños judged the administration and what they expected it to be (chaps. 6 and 7). Finally, I argue that government was at its best when it did not intervene and that conflict coincided with, rather than destroyed, harmony (chaps. 2 and 7).

My data proceeds from both Spain and Quito. It includes administrative, judicial, and notarial records, as well as correspondence, criminal jurisprudence, laws, and literature. I studied closely some 390 penal cases of first instance, including 179 cases of theft, 66 cases of death, 25 cases of battery, 46 cases of public disorder, 23 cases of illicit love affairs, as well as cases of prison evasions, violations, falsifications, and so forth. I observed why the cases began, who was acting in them and how did they develop. Rather than interested in legal theory, I was interested in the way justice administration actually happened. The material I studied allowed me to look at the way people used, constructed and viewed the administration of justice on both sides of the Atlantic. This administration, I claim, was a communal rather than a state-run enterprise. The penal system guaranteed peace and social cohesion, not legality, and the dominating rules in Quito were social and theological, not legal. These rules proceeded from a source other than the king, and they depended for their implementation on a wide range of agents—some royal and some only to a certain degree. The main preoccupation of those working to instill order was not public interest, but justice: that is to say, the duty to give each one his or her due. People involved in administering justice were never isolated individuals, never impartial, never distanced from society. Social networks first constructed the administration and then influenced it. Not only did this system mirror the wider society but it was also an integral part of it. The administration was public because it belonged to the people of the city, not to a state. This did not happen because of a poverty of means, as argued by Foucault, but because there was no true distinction between a state and a society as we imagine it today.

The implications of these conclusions are far-reaching. They place doubts on our ability to identify a bureaucracy in colonial Spanish America—whether patrimonial or modern, professional or semiprofessional. They question our use of notions such as corruption for an early modern period in which nonpublic interests were at the core of the administrative system. They eliminate the alleged gap between law and practice because it becomes evident that in the early modern period *law* was not the same thing as *legislation*. Laws were revealed only when applied, and *justice* (not *legality*) dominated the judicial sphere. These conclusions also require us to revise our understanding of the sale of office, traditionally identified with the distortion of public order. Needless to say, once we follow this route, we can no longer view the penal system as exemplary and cruel in theory yet deficient (according to pessimists) or simply flexible (according to optimists) in practice. Last but not least, the conclusions of this work will affect our understanding of Spanish American independence, which can no longer be viewed as a breach of a pact between a center and a periphery—such a pact might have never existed.

My aim is to reconstruct early modern structures as they existed in Quito. These structures, I believe, are not indicative of crime or criminality.[29] On the one hand, reconstructing crime from criminal records is problematic because not all crimes were reported and because extrajudicial arrangements were very frequent.[30] On the other, judicial records do not even tell us a clear story about what society wanted to reprimand. Criminal records are products of a long chain of reactions in which many people intervened for different reasons and interests. Indi-

29. I. A. A. Thompson, "A Map of Crime in Sixteenth-Century Spain," *Economic History Review* 21 (1986): 244–67; M. E. Perry, *Crime and Society in Early Modern Seville* (Hanover, 1980); M. C. Scardaville, "Crime and the Urban Poor: Mexico City in the Late Colonial Period," Ph.D. diss., University of Florida, 1977; S. M. Socolow, "Women and Crime: Buenos Aires, 1757–1797," *Journal of Latin American Studies* 12 (1980): 39–54; D. N. Kerr, *Petty Felony, Slave Defiance and Frontier Villainy. Crime and Criminal Justice in Spanish Louisiana, 1770–1803* (New York, 1993); R. I. Sánchez Gómez, *Delincuencia y seguridad en el Madrid de Carlos II* (Madrid, 1994); C. Benavides, *Les femmes délinquantes à Madrid: Justice et société en Espagne au XVIIIe siècle*, vol. 2 (Toulouse, 2000); and V. M. Uribe, "Colonial *Baracunatanas* and Their Nasty Men: Spousal Homicides and the Law in Late Colonial New Granada," *Journal of Social History* 35/1 (2001): 43–72. Historians of crime in other European countries followed the same tendencies, for example, J. A. Sharpe, *Crime in Early Modern England, 1550–1750* (London, 1984; reprint, 1999), 59–101; and R. Williams, "Some Aspects of Summary Justice in Eighteenth Century Rural Berkshire," *Archives* 26/104 (2001): 41–53.

viduals who complained to the authorities, or who initiated judicial prosecution, could be motivated by factors that had nothing to do with crime or its persecution. They could hope, for example, that debtors would pay their debts or that a father would support his children. As Natalie Zemon Davis and others have noted, the narratives elaborated by these people, as well as by criminals, could be at least partially fictional.[31] Criminal records also include the vision and interests of people other than the litigants, such as witnesses, judges, and the auxiliary staff. These records are shaped by a plethora of practices, rules, and regulations—some of which are legal and others of which are not. Criminal jurisprudence is thus complexly refracted by litigants, society, social institutions, and law. Because one factor cannot be easily distinguished from the other, it is impossible to deduce from these records what criminality was like or what society wanted to reprimand. Precisely for this reason, it is essential that historians who use these and other judicial records become familiar with these issues. It is important that they understand the process that led to the elaboration of these records before they proceed to use them as data for their research.

Quito, 1650–1750

Quito provides a context in which to explore all of these issues. In the period between 1650 and 1750, the city underwent important social and

30. These issues had been at the forefront of historians' criticisms of the use of judicial archives to study crime. A. Soman, "Deviance and Criminal Justice in West Europe, 1300–1800," *Criminal Justice History* 1 (1980): 3–28; idem, "L'infra-justice à Paris d'après les archives notariales," *Histoire, économie et société* 3 (1982): 369–75; D. Hay, "War, Dearth and Theft in the Eighteenth Century: The Records of the English Courts," *Past and Present* 95 (1982): 117–60; R. Lévy and P. Robert, "Le sociologue et l'histoire pénale," *Annales ESC* 39 (1984): 400–422; B. Garnot, "Une illusion historiographique: justice et criminalité au XVIIIe siècle," *Revue Historique* 570 (1989): 361–80; idem, "La législation de la répression des crimes dans la France moderne (XVIe–XVIIIe siècle)," *Revue historique* 593 (1995): 75–76; and idem, *Crime et justice aux XVIIe et XVIIIe siècle* (Paris, 2000), 18–22, 41. See also R. B. Shoemaker, "The 'Crime Wave' Revisited: Crime, Law Enforcement and Punishment in Britain, 1650–1900," *Historical Journal* 34/3 (1991): 763–68.

31. N. Zemon Davis, *Fiction in the Archives: Pardon Tales and Their Tellers in Sixteenth-Century France* (Stanford, 1987); and D. Frye, "Telling Histories: A Late Colonial Encounter of 'Spanish' and 'Indian' in Rural Mexico and in the Archives," *Colonial Latin American Review* 3 /1–2 (1994): 115–38. See also S. Songer, ed., *Fact, Fiction and Forensic Evidence: The Potential of Judicial Sources for Historical Research in the Early Modern Period* (Oslo, 1997).

economic readjustments—yet it experienced no major upheaval. As a capital city refounded by the Spaniards in 1534, Quito dominated a province (*audiencia*) that spanned present-day Ecuador, southern Colombia (Cali, Pasto, and Popayán), and various regions in the Amazon basin (Macas, Quijos, Mainas, and Jaén de Bracamoros).[32] The city served as an administrative, religious, and economic center of the province, housing a superior court (audiencia), a royal treasury, two universities, several colleges, and the episcopal seat.[33] There were sixteen convents and monasteries in the city, a large number of smaller churches, and several hospitals. Neither a small provincial town nor an important viceregal center, Quito between 1650 and 1750 provides a good example—doubtless one of many—of what the Spanish American colonial structures looked like.

Situated in a fertile plateau near the volcanic mountain of Pichincha, the city was divided between a traditional center and several surrounding neighborhoods, separated from one another by deep ravines. As in other contemporary Spanish American towns, the center was structured according to a grid plan, with a main square (*plaza mayor*) framed by the cathedral, the bishop's palace, the audiencia, the town council house, and the residences of important citizens. The square served as a marketplace, a favorite area for civic and religious ceremonies, and a meeting place. By the mid–eighteenth century, most streets in the center were paved, and the houses along them were built with a stone foundation and adobe walls. The surrounding neighborhoods, which developed around the center, had a rural or semirural character.[34] At a neighborhood's core was a group of buildings around a parish church; loosely arranged houses with small plots for both subsistence and commercial agriculture expanded outward from this core. The streets were neither straight nor paved, and the quality of neighborhood houses was

32. A. Ortiz Crespo and R. Terrán Najas, "Las reducciones de indios en la zona interandina de la real audiencia de Quito," in *Pueblos de otro urbanismo en la región andina*, ed. R. Gutiérrez (Quito, 1993), 205–61.

33. M. Cicala, *Descripción histórico topográfica de la provincia de Quito de la Compañía de Jesús* (1770; reprint, Quito, 1994), 153–227; and D. Alcedo Herrera, "Plano geográfico e hidrográfico del distrito de la real audiencia de Quito y descripciones de las provincias, gobiernos y corregimientos que se comprenden en su jurisdicción y las ciudades y villas, asientos y pubelos que ocupan sus territorios [signed Madrid, 30 May 1766]," in *Relaciones histórico-geográficas de la audiencia de Quito (siglo XVI–XIX)*, ed. P. Ponce Leiva (Madrid, 1992), 2: 418–65.

34. M. Minchom, *The People of Quito, 1690–1810: Change and Unrest in the Underclass* (Syracuse, 1994), 17–23 and 101–15.

lower than the stone and adobe buildings of the center. The geographical and material distinction between a center and a periphery was also enhanced by social segregation. Wealthier Spaniards lived in the city center, while poor Spaniards, Indians, and those of mixed ancestry (mestizos) lived in the periphery.

The local administration and economy were dominated by a small number of families. It is estimated that seven or eight families controlled some 50 percent of textile mills in operation between 1607 and 1776.[35] In the middle of the eighteenth century, 0.07 percent of the population controlled 30.78 percent of the local rural estates.[36] These families retained their power by intermarriage and by forming a closed social universe dominated by friendship, business relations, and compatronage. In addition to controlling the economy and the administration, these families also controlled the church and the military. Moreover, many members of this group aspired to become part of the nobility.[37] In the seventeenth and eighteenth centuries, a typical member of the elite was a fairly rich man with landed estates and textile mills and both rural and urban residences. He was the owner of a shop or had some commercial contacts outside the city. He belonged to a large extended family that was well established in the jurisdiction, with relatives throughout the province.[38]

Until the late eighteenth century, local elites maintained a fictitious dichotomy between Spaniards and Indians by integrating all other elements such as those of mixed ancestry into one group or another according to the circumstances of the case and the reason for which classification was required.[39] "Indianness" mainly depended not on genealogy and phenotypes, but on sociocultural evaluations that con-

35. K. J. Andrien, *The Kingdom of Quito, 1690–1830: The State and Regional Development* (Cambridge, 1995), 60; and M. Fernández Martínez, *La alcabala en la audiencia de Quito, 1765–1810* (Cuenca-Seville, 1984), 143–45.

36. J. Ortiz de la Tabla, "Panorama económico y social del corregimiento de Quito (1768–1775)," *Revista de Indias* 36/145–46 (1976): 91–95.

37. M. E. Porras, "La élite quiteña en el cabildo, 1763–1805," M.A. thesis, Facultad Iberoamericana de Ciencias Sociales (FLACSO) (Quito, 1987), dact. A summary of this dissertation was published under the title "La élite quiteña a mediados del siglo XVIII," *AFESE* 88/14 (1988): 43–55. See also P. Ponce Leiva, *Certezas ante la incertidumbre: Élite y cabildo de Quito en el siglo XVII* (Quito, 1998), 267–315 and 335–421.

38. D. A. Washburn, "The Bourbon Reforms: A Social and Economic History of the Audiencia of Quito, 1760–1810," Ph.D. diss., University of Texas at Austin, 1984, 10–14. See also C. Borchart de Moreno, "Capital commercial y producción agrícola: Nueva España y la audiencia de Quito en el siglo XVIII," *Anuario de estudios americanos* 46 (1989): 131–72.

sidered the relevance of issues such as office holding, dress, education, way of life, and place of birth.[40] This allowed many people who were not Indians to be categorized as such in spite of their genealogy. We know that the "Indian" population of the city grew during the seventeenth century and then diminished in the next.[41] The number of poor Spaniards and people of mixed ancestry continuously rose during the same period. This led to an eventual distinction between an aristocratic elite, purportedly Spanish, and an urban "pleb" in which poor Spaniards, mestizos, and Indians were all relegated.[42]

The municipal jurisdiction of Quito included some twenty-eight villages, mainly inhabited by Indians and primarily dependent on agriculture.[43] The semirural character of the surrounding neighborhoods and the domination of the city over these villages ensured a continuity between urban and rural space. Some villages of the jurisdiction were practically satellites of the city because of their proximity and because of the subjection of their economic activity to urban needs. Between the various villages and the city were many rural estates, houses, and cultivated lands, most of which belonged to the urban elites. These elites also extended their economic and social control beyond the boundaries of the city and its jurisdiction by owning rural estates, textile mills, and *encomiendas* (control over native labour force) in a vast region that included the jurisdictions of Ibarra, Latacunga, Ríobamba, and Popayán.[44] Despite long-term immigration from the mountain to the coast and from north to south, in the mid–eighteenth century about 65 percent of the population of the province of Quito still lived in areas subjected to the influence of the local elites of the capital. Despite con-

39. E. Ayala Mora, *Resúmen de historia del Ecuador* (Quito, 1994), 41–42.

40. Minchom, *The People*, 153–99; and M. Lucena Salmoral, "La población del reino de Quito en la época de reformismo borbónico: circa 1784," *Revista de Indias* 54/200 (1994): 37–39.

41. M. Minchom, "La evolución demográfica del Ecuador en el siglo XVIII," *Cultura* 8/24B (1986): 478–79.

42. R. Terrán Najas, "La ciudad colonial y sus símbolos: Una aproximación a la historia de Quito en el siglo XVII," in *Ciudades de los Andes: Visión histórica y contemporánea*, ed. E. Kingman Garcés (Quito, 1992), 170–71.

43. The villages included in Quito's jurisdiction in the eighteenth century were San Juan Evangelista, Santa María Magdalena, Chillogallo, Conocoto, Zambiza, Pintac, Sangolquí, Amaguaña, Guápulo, Cumbaya, Puembo, Cotocollao, Pijo, Yaruquí, Quinche, Guayabamba, Machachi, Aloasí, Aloac, Uyumbicho, Pomasque, Lulumbaba, Perucho, Calacalí, Mindo, Gualea, Tumbaco, and Canzacoto. It is estimated that, in 1781, 85 percent of the Spanish population of the jurisdiction lived in the city: Porras, "Elite quiteña en el cabildo," 2–3.

stant miscegenation, some 70 percent of these people were still classified as Indians.[45]

Quito's golden age is often identified with the period before 1650.[46] During this period the city experienced both demographic growth and accelerated urban development. In the middle of the seventeenth century, Quito had some thirty-five hundred citizens and a total population of twenty-five thousand inhabitants, including non-Spaniards, women, and children. The city extended over two hundred blocks, and had some twenty-five hundred houses.[47] This period of growth was followed by a prolonged crisis that continued to the 1720s and 1730s. A period of moderate recuperation then followed, leading, according to various estimates, to an urban population of forty thousand to forty-eight thousand inhabitants in the 1750s.[48]

The transition from the seventeenth to the eighteenth century not only marked a demographic and economic decline but also featured changes in local structures. During the seventeenth century, the power of local *encomenderos* (owners of encomiendas) gradually declined, and their control of the town council (clearly dominant during the sixteenth century, in which as many as 78 percent of the members were encomenderos) substantially diminished.[49] By 1670, only 13 percent of aldermen were encomenderos. Encomiendas, whose numbers were declining, no longer produced as much revenue as before.[50] During this period, textile mills for local and regional consumption tended to replace the encomiendas.[51] Most mills were fairly small, and most of the labor was Indian. Members of the local elite usually owned the mills, which were linked to food-producing estates and sheep ranches.[52] In

44. L. A. Newson, *Life and Death in Early Colonial Ecuador* (Norman, 1995), 182 and 187.

45. Andrien, *The Kingdom of Quito*, 35–36.

46. R. Terrán Najas, "Factores dinámicos en el desarrollo urbano del Quito colonial," in *Enfoques y estudios históricos—Quito agravés de la historia,* ed. P. Aguilar (Quito, 1992), 67–86.

47. D. Rodríguez Docampo, "Descripción y relación del estado eclesiástico del obispado de San Francisco de Quito . . . [1650]," in *Relaciones,* ed. P. Ponce Leiva, 2: 212.

48. J. P. Montúfar y Fraso, "Razón sobre el estado y gobernación política y militar de las provincias, ciudades, villas y lugares que contiene la jurisdicción de la real audiencia de Quito," [13 Septembre 1754]," in *Relaciones,* ed. P. Ponce Leiva, 2: 323–52; and Cicala "Descripción," 223–24. See also Minchom, "La evolución."

49. Ponce Leiva, *Certezas,* 347.

50. J. Ortiz de la Tabla, *Los encomenderos de Quito, 1534–1660: Orígen y evolución de una élite colonial* (Seville, 1993), 116–20 and 138–39.

1602 there were already some sixty mills operating in and around the city of Quito. It is estimated that by 1680 some sixty thousand Indians worked in mills, mostly as free laborers.[53] By 1730, about half of the Indian population of the city was in some way connected to the textile industry.[54] This situation allowed many owners to exploit the Indians working in their mills. Indians, who were theoretically free, were often treated by these owners as slaves.[55] They received their salary in goods and were given advance payments—thereby becoming indebted to owners, who forced them to keep working to pay off their debts. Indian workers were locked in the mills and were often physically abused.

Textile mills and Indian (forced) labor thus sustained the economic growth of Quito in the seventeenth century. Textiles produced in the city were traded as far as Potosí, and Quito's merchants sold and bought products in the fairs of Panamá.[56] This exchange ceased late in the century for a number of reasons. Production in the Peruvian mines declined, the fair system was abandoned, and European textiles reached Peruvian markets directly. These factors triggered an important crisis in Quito, which was followed by economic readjustments and gradual recuperation. By the early eighteenth century, most economic activity was focused

51. J. Ortiz de la Tabla, "Obrajes y obrajeros del Quito colonial," *Anuario de estudios americanos* 39 (1982): 341–65; J. C. Super, "Partnership and Profit in the Early Andean Trade: The Experience of Quito Merchants, 1580–1610," *Journal of Latin American Studies* 2/2 (1979): 265–81 (also published as "Compañía y utilidades en el comercio andino temprano: la práctica de los comerciantes de Quito, 1580–1610," *Revista ecuatoriana de historia economica* 1 [1987]: 59–79); R. J. Bromley, "El comercio precolonial y la transición a un sistema de mercando colonial en la audiencia de Quito," *Revista ecuatoriana de historia económica* 1 (1987): 41–58; R. Rueda Novoa, *El obraje de San Joseph de Peguchi* (Quito, 1988); R. Brines Tyrer, *Historia demográfica y económica de la Audiencia de Quito: Población indígena e industria textil, 1600–1800* (Quito, 1988); R. Terrán Najas, "La historia económica y social sobre la época colonial ecuatoriana: Un balance de la producción historiográfica en los últimos 25 años," *Procesos* 5/2 (1993): 29–52; and C. Büschges, "Crisis y reestructuración: La industria textil de la real audiencia de Quito al final del período colonial," *Anuario de estudios americanos* 53/2 (1995): 75–98.

52. K. J. Andrien, "Economic Crisis, Taxes and the Quito Insurrection of 1765," *Past and Present* 129 (1990): 108.

53. K. Powers Viera, *Prendas con pies: Migraciones indígenas y supervivencia cultural en la audiencia de Quito* (Quito, 1994), 152.

54. Andrien, "Economic Crisis," 118; and Powers Viera, *Prendas,* 146–70.

55. L. Ramos Gómez, "Algunos datos sobre los abusos e injusticias padecidas en 1737 por los indios de los obrajes de la ciudad de Quito," *Revista española de antropología americana* 27 (1997): 153–66.

56. J. Juan and A. Ulloa, *Relación histórica del viaje a la América meridional* (Madrid, 1978), 402–4; and G. Soasti, "Mercaderes y tratantes en Quito durante el siglo XVII," in *Enfoques y estudios históricos—Quito a través de la historia,* ed. P. Aguilar (Quito, 1992), 87–106.

on agricultural production in landed estates.[57] The decline in manufacturing greatly affected the merchants who, instead of exporting textiles to the fleets and Lima, now sold primarily agricultural products (and to some extent textiles) to New Granada (present-day Colombia).[58] At the same time, small-scale textile production units (producing rougher-quality goods) proliferated in the city. Most of these units were based on household industry, and they were owned by women or Indians.[59]

A succession of natural disasters coincided with the economic crisis of the late seventeenth and the early eighteenth centuries: epidemics in the 1690s, the 1720s, and 1743–44; earthquakes in 1645, 1698, and 1750; volcanic eruptions in 1660—as well as many storms and long periods of draught. The accumulated effect was devastating. The volcanic eruptions of 1660, for example, destroyed many buildings, and the epidemics of 1743–44 left about 20 percent of the city's total population dead.[60] Competition from other areas of the province was also mounting. Guayaquil, the main port of the region, entered into an expanding agroexport economy based on cacao, and the southern region, with its capital in Cuenca, gradually separated from Quito, following its own economic and social course.[61]

In the period between 1650 and 1750, Quito thus underwent an important social and economic reorientation. The gap between a "good" and a "bad" society was widening, and residential and economic segregation was becoming clearer. Production in textile mills and

57. M. Miño Grijalva, "La economía de la real audiencia de Quito: siglo XVII," C. Benavides Vega, "Sinópsis histórica del siglo XVII," and H. Arias, "La economía de la real audiencia de Quito y la crisis del siglo XVIII," in *Nueva historia del Ecuador,* vol. 4, *Epoca Colonia II,* ed. E. Ayala Mora (Quito, 1983), 51–229; M. Minchom, *The People,* 64–73; J. P. Deler, *Ecuador: del espacio al estado nacional* (Quito, 1987), 137–62; and M. Miño Grijalva, *La economia colonial. Relaciones socio-económicas de la real audiencia de Quito* (Quito, 1984). See also N. P. Cushner, *Farm and Factory: The Jesuits and the Development of Agrarian Capitalism in Colonial Quito, 1600–1767* (Albany, 1982).

58. Ortiz de la Tabla, "Panorama," 87.

59. C. Borchart de Moreno, "Beyond the Obraje: Handicraft Production in Quito toward the End of the Colonial Period," *Americas* 21/1 (1995): 1–24; and C. Büschges, "Crisis."

60. AHQ, FE, 2 (1646–80), nos. 224, 226, and 227; and A. Lafuente and A. Mazuecos, *Los caballeros del punto fijo: Ciencia, política y aventura en la expedición geodésica hispanofrancesa al virreinato del Perú en el siglo XVIII* (Quito, 1992), 110.

61. J. Estrada Icaza, *El puerto de Guayaquil* (Guayaquil, 1972); M. Hamerly, *Historia social y económica de la Antigua provincia de Guayaquil, 1763–1842* (Guayaquil, 1973); idem, *El comercio del cacao en Guayaquil durante el período colonial: un estudio cuantitativo* (Quito, 1976); L. A. Clayton, *Los astilleros de Guayaquil colonial* (Guayaquil, 1978); and M. L. Laviana Cuetos, *Guayaquil en el siglo XVIII: recursos naturales y desarrollo económico* (Seville, 1987).

participation in long-range commercial networks gave way to an economy based mainly on agriculture and short-distance trade. Having once been "a member of the relatively exclusive club of great Spanish American cities," by the end of this period Quito became a "political, religious, and commercial center exercising control over an agricultural hinterland."[62] Despite these radical social and economic changes there was no major social upheaval or unrest. Overall, the years between 1650 and 1750 were a period of relative calm, characterized by consolidation and readjustment.

62. Minchom, *The People*, 257–60.

CHAPTER ONE

The Penal Administration in Early Modern Quito

The courts of Quito expressed the king's paternal love for his vassals. The king's first obligation, contemporaries argued, was his obligation to maintain his vassals in peace and ensure justice throughout his realm.[1] Public order was dependent on the continuation of the status-quo, and judges, working in the king's name, were expected to punish public sins, correct morals, and suppress scandals. Focused on what they needed to prohibit, rather than on the people who perpetrated the prohibited activity, judges were policemen who forbade acts rather than punished actors.[2]

Concentration on crime, rather than criminals, allowed contemporaries to ignore the judicial process, which legally identified people as criminals and determined their degree of responsibility. This attitude was possible because during the early modern period there was no necessary separation between the pronouncement and the application of the law. Early modern law was dramatically different from present day arrangements. During the early modern period, law consisted of what "nature dictates, divinity ordered, our Saint Mother the Church defended, the people have constituted, the prince established, the city or village ordered, or the custom introduced."[3] Law embodied a system of thought that was expressed in royal and local decrees, doctrine (mainly

1. AHQ, Ced., 2, nos. 83 and 615 from 1633 and 1658, respectively; and AHN, Cód., 488B, no. 112 from 1747.

2. T. Herzog, "The Recopilación de Indias and Its Discourse: The Spanish Monarchy, the Indies and the Seventeenth Century," *Ius Commune* 20 (1993): 150–51.

3. The original text reads: "DERECHO. Lo que dicta la naturaléza, mandó la Divinidad, definió nuestra Santa Madre la Iglesia, constituyeron las gentes, establece el Príncipe, suprémo legisladór en sus dominíos ù ordéna la Ciudad o el Pueblo para su gobierno privado o introduce la costumbre." Real Académia Española, *Diccionario de la lengua Castellana* (Madrid 1726–39), 3: 79–80.

ius commune—medieval-revived Roman law), customs, uses, and social values. This law was not a voluntary or an arbitrary creation. It imitated an order revealed to man rather than decided by him.[4] To some extent, all legal doctrines were theological. They made reference to religious as well as human duties without necessarily distinguishing one from the other.[5] In Quito, for example, lawyers and procurators cited pieces of legislation, legal doctrine, and Christian theology as equally important normative sources. They used the life stories of biblical figures as some sort of a case law, which demonstrated the existence of rights and obligations. For example, litigants made reference to Cain and Abel in order to claim that one was only responsible for his or her own deeds and should not be recriminated for having relatives who were criminals.[6] One brother was good, the other bad; one was punished, the other not. Although the same conclusion could be reached by citing the Roman law, which determined that crimes only incriminate their authors (*Omnia crimina requantur suos auctores*), the Bible was just as effective—or even more effective—for obtaining the same result. The importance of religious texts and the abandonment of Roman and royal law were also evident in libraries owned by lawyers. These libraries included many works of theology and philosophy, genres that outnumbered books on law.[7]

Human decisions about the law did not create the law; they only applied it to specific circumstances. Law was theoretically discovered (and practically created) when judges needed to render a decision in a specific case. It was only when conflicts happened that judges needed (1) to discover the law and (2) to implement it. One activity was not truly differentiated from the other, and there was no distinction between

4. M. García Pelayo, "La idea medieval del derecho," in *Del mito y de la razón en la historia del pensamiento político*, ed. M. García Pelayo (Madrid, 1968), 65–140. See also V. Tau Anzoátegui, "La noción de ley en América Hispana durante los siglos XVI a XVIII," *Anuario de filosofía jurídica y social* 6 (1986): 192–232; idem, "La doctrina de los autores como fuente del derecho castellano-indiano," *Revista de Historia del derecho* 17 (1989): 169–285; and A. Levaggi, "El concepto de derecho según los fiscales de la Segunda audiencia de Buenos Aires (1784–1810)," *Revista chilena de historia del derecho* 13 (1987): 245–59.

5. A. Boureau, "Droit et théologie au XIIIe siècle," *Annales ESC* 47 (1992): 1113 and 1114; and G. Levi, "Reciprocidad mediterránea," *Hispania* 60/1 (2000): 103–26.

6. AHQ, Not. 1, 13: exp. 25 December 1723 from 25 October 1720.

7. The libraries of the magistrate Miguel González Carrasco (AHQ, 3a Not., 3: exp. 9 December 1695), the president Lope Antonio Munive y Axpe (AGI, Quito, 73), and the lawyer Juan de Viniegra (AHQ, 3a Not., 8: exp. 23 June 1705). See also J. Barrientos Grandón, *La cultura jurídica en el Reino de Chile: Bibliotecas de ministros de la real audiencia de Santiago (siglos XVII–XVIII)* (Santiago de Chile, 1992).

what was juridical (pertaining to the law) and what was judicial (pertaining to the courts). Early modern law was above all a mechanism for conflict resolution. This resolution had to be just because it replicated a divine natural order. This order was dictated by God, held by the king (God's lieutenant on earth), and implemented by the king's judges.[8] First and foremost, judges had to listen to their hearts.[9] Their decisions had to be just, or they were not decisions at all.

The idea that judicial decisions were inherently just, or were not decisions at all, influenced the judicial system in a variety of ways. There was no clear typology of offenses, no legal definition of crimes, in the manner we have today. For example, there was no technical distinction between wrongful death, manslaughter, and murder in its various degrees. Individuals were sentenced because they caused death. In their sentencing, all considerations guaranteeing a just solution and all mechanisms that might redeem what had been done were considered pertinent. The accusation consisted of a story relating what had happened. The defense agreed, or not, and analyzed the responsibility of the party and the injury suffered. The judge, balancing these facts, and considering the various interests at stake, rendered a decision. There was no need to determine which law was breached and in what way because what was breached was a norm that was not only legal: it was also moral and social. Judges were not required to explain how they reached verdicts. The verdict either was just, and therefore a valid solution, or was not, and therefore had to be reversed. The legality of the decision was never at stake. Judges did not focus on the observance of certain rules but only on the fitness of the solution. For the same reason, appeals were never technical and never attacked the legal foundation of the decision. Instead, they argued that the decision was unjust. Judges could thus be criticized for following the unjust opinions of lawyers.[10] Contemporaries also demanded that judges decide in "consciousness," even if this consciousness was contrary to the laws. Under such a system it was possible to disregard royal instructions if they were considered

8. J. A. Fernández Santamaría, *The State, War and Peace: Spanish Political Thought in the Renaissance (1519–1559)* (Cambridge, 1977), 31; J. A. Maravall, *La teoría española del estado en el siglo XVII* (Madrid, 1954), 194–99; and idem, *Estado moderno y mentalidad social (siglos XV a XVII)* (Madrid, 1972), 2: 403–37.

9. J. de Mariana, *Del rey y de la institución real,* book 3 (1598; Madrid, 1854), chap. 10, 556.

10. AGI, EC, 911B. Also see T. Campanella, *La monarquía hispánica* (1620; reprint, Madrid, 1982), 77–78.

unjust.[11] Indeed, it was also possible to convict a person in the absence of full proofs of guilt.[12]

Because justice was more important than legality, the administration constantly appealed to notions that were not defined in legislation or in legal doctrine. Most lawyers graduated in "both laws," which is to say, in both Roman and canon law.[13] Those who chose a single career usually preferred to study canon law, which also enabled them to occupy offices in the ecclesiastical hierarchy. Because early modern law regulated the relationships of men with both God and society, universities aimed to teach what was "ethically correct and spiritually pure."[14] Future judges, for example, were trained in theology, philosophy and rhetoric but, until the late eighteenth century, they were not given classes in royal or municipal law. While implementing justice required a profound understanding and a vast theoretical knowledge, the practicalities of being a lawyer or a judge, it was considered, could be grasped by practical training.

Due to these considerations, there was no reason to limit the judicial career to people trained in law. Laymen who were sufficiently informed could be good judges—indeed, many of them were. Most municipal judges and local governors had no legal training, yet their activities were in no way marginal in the judicial system.[15] In Quito, for example, they conducted about half of all judicial proceedings. Although many of them received legal advice, they, not their legal assistants, were respon-

11. I refer here to the famous difference between obeying the law and complying with its instructions: V. Tau Anzoátegui, "La ley 'se obedece pero no se cumple': En torno a la suplicación en las leyes del derecho indiano," *Anuario histórico jurídico ecuatoriano* 6 (1980): 55–110.

12. F. Tomás y Valiente, *El derecho penal de la monarquía absoluta (siglos XVI–XVIII)* (Madrid, 1969), 172 and 200.

13. R. Kagan, *Students and Society in Early Modern Spain* (Baltimore, 1974), 27, 135, and 212; J. M. Pelorson, *Les letrados. Juristes castillans sous Philippe III: Recherches sur leur place dans la société, la culture et l'état* (Poitiers, 1980), 35–57; R. Roldán Verdejo, *Los jueces de la monarquia absoluta, su estatuto y actividad judicial: La corona de Castilla siglos XIV–XVIII* (Laguna, 1989), 75–87; B. Siebzehner, "Hacia la homogeneidad cultural entre España y América: la creación de la universidad de México," *E.I.A.L.* 2/2 (1991): 87–102; and R. I. Peña-Peñaloza, "Principios doctrinarios del derecho penal castellano-indiano: la jurisprudencia," *Revista de estudios histórico-jurídicos* 16 (1994): 87–94. These subjects are treated in greater length in T. Herzog, "Sobre la cultura jurídica en la América colonial (siglos XVI–XVIII)," *Anuario de Historia del Derecho Español* 65 (1995): 903–12.

14. Siebzehner, "Hacia la homogeneidad," 95–96.

15. A. M. Hespanha, "Sabios e rusticos: A violência doce da razão juridica," parts 1 and 2, *Crítica de ciencias sociais* 25 (1988): 31–60 and 26 (1988): 3–98. Spanish translation in *La gracia del derecho: Economía de la cultura en la edad moderna* (Madrid, 1993), 17–60.

sible for making sure that justice would be done. These laymen applied an understanding of justice acquired by going to church and by living in society. Admitting nonjurists as judges was possible on all levels. For example, in 1714 the viceroy of Peru approved the appointment of a nonjurist as magistrate (*oidor*) of the audiencia of Quito (the supreme royal court of the jurisdiction).[16] Although he and others agreed that a legal degree allowed individuals to have a better understanding of justice, they also concluded that a degree in theology was just as useful.[17] The most important task judges faced was to distinguish right from wrong, which is precisely what theologians were trained to do. The true difference between the two careers was practical, not theoretical. In contrast to lawyers, theologians lacked familiarity with the legal practice. They could become perfect judges, though, if they acquired this familiarity. Theologians might become familiar with legal proceedings by apprenticeship in a court. Similar claims were made with regard to philosophy: "although the time he spent in the law faculty was limited, an average discourse illustrated by philosophy needs less time [in a law faculty] in order to learn to decide a proceeding [than those who do not have a philosophy degree], especially if it was accompanied by the practice in the courts . . . after all, law is nothing other than exercising reason, which is what philosophy also does, and having an awake spirit; the natural reason which dominates the matter is more important than the disposition of the laws, or their sophisticated interpretations that only confuse us."[18]

The Council of the Indies fought bitterly against these assertions,

16. This was the decision made in the case Juan Dionisio Larrea Zurbano: see below.

17. T. Herzog, "¿Letrado o teólogo? Sobre el oficio de Justicia a mediados del siglo XVIII," in *Fallstudien zur spanischen und portugiesischen Justiz 16.–20. Jahrhundert*, ed. J. M. Scholz (Frankfurt, 1994), 697–714. This discussion is described in dozens of documents included in AGI, Quito, 106, 143 and 164. See also chap. 2.

18. The original version reads: "aunque fuese limitado el tiempo que cursó la facultad de las leyes, un mediano discurso ilustrado con la filosofía necesita menos tiempo para instruirse en la decisión de una causa, mayormente si con la práctica en la judicatura . . . por no constituir [*el derecho*] en otra cosa, que en dejar obrar la recta razón, propio oficio de la filosofía, y de una capacidad despierta; contrapesando más en cualquier materia la razón natural que la gobierna que la disposición de las leyes, ni sus sofisticadas interpretaciones que la confundan": AGI, Quito, 133, 732. These questions were also explored in Campanella, *La monarquía hispánica*, 77–78; F. Carpintero, "En torno al método de los juristas medievales," *Anuario de historia del derecho español* 52 (1982): 617–26; Roldán Verdejo, *Los jueces*, 75; and J. M. García Marín, "El dilema ciencia-experiencia en la selección del oficial público de la España de los Austrias," *Actas del IV symposium de historia de la administración* (Madrid, 1983), 261–80.

often with little success. In 1714 it failed to convince the king to reverse the decision to appoint nonjurists to the audiencia. In 1755 it again was unsuccessful in blocking the naming of a nonjurist as magistrate of the audiencia charged with defending the interests of Indians (*protector de naturales*).[19] Although demanding that magistrates have a law degree, the council was aware of the fact that such a law degree did not necessarily guarantee juridical preparation. In 1748, it ordered two of its "men of confidence" to examine the qualifications of Manuel de la Vega y Bárcena–a candidate who held a law degree but who was suspected of not being sufficiently informed in legal matters.[20]

The union between pronouncing and applying the law, and the assumption that judicial decisions should be guided by justice and not technical regulation, allowed contemporaries to ignore the judicial procedure that mediated between crime and punishment. The legal procedure (which indeed guaranteed that justice would be done in each case) was never fully regulated. It was partially ordained in the judicial doctrine (mostly of Roman origin), and it was developed by a forensic practice that came into being, over time, as a result of everyday practical solutions. Procedures were copied from one tribunal or from one office to the other, and they were based on experience rather than theoretical learning. Contrary to justice, which depended on judges, procedure was in the hands of the auxiliary staff. Clerks, notaries, and procurators were expected to observe the procedure and to ensure that judges did as well. Justice was thus separated from its actual application. Judicial process was one thing. A just solution was another.

The Penal Process

Processes started either *de oficio* (at the initiative of the court) or *de parte* (at the initiative of the victim or his or her relatives).[21] In both instances, the first act (called *auto cabeza de proceso* in de oficio cases

19. AHN, Cód., 755B, no. 83 from 1755.

20. AGI, Quito, 224.

21. Several royal orders (*cédulas*) established the relationship between the practice of Valladolid, Granada and American courts, for example, AHN, Cód., 690B, 711B, 713B, and 721B, nos. 260, 205, 248, and 29, respectively. Studies of Spanish American penal process include J. Malagón, *Teoría general del derecho procesal en las leyes indianas: Bases para su estudio* (Madrid, 1936); J. Corvalán Meléndez and V. Castillo Fernández, *Derecho procesal indiano* (Santiago de Chile, 1951); and J. M. Ots Capdequi, *Historia del derecho español en América y del derecho indiano* (Madrid, 1967), 167–68. The Castilian penal

and *auto de querella* in de parte cases) consisted of delivering a narrative that included the case's facts. The person who initiated the proceedings, that is, either the judge or the victim (or his or her relatives), presented witnesses who affirmed the veracity of the narrative. When possible, the person or persons who initiated the proceedings also collected material proofs, such as notarized testimonies that the victim indeed died or was wounded, the arms used, or the stolen goods. This part of the procedure, the summary (*sumaria*), was meant to remain secret.

Once the alleged crime was supported by sufficient evidence, the court proceeded to imprison the suspect and sequester his belongings. A judicial official would then take the deposition of the suspect. When considered necessary, this deposition, called "confession" (*confesión*), could be taken under torture. Torture (also called "torment") was a legal practice used in penal proceedings (including inquisitorial ones) in many parts of continental Europe.[22] It was justified by contemporary

process is described in M. P. Alonso Romero, *El proceso penal en Castilla (siglos XIII–XVIII)* (Salamanca, 1982), 159–315; idem, "El proceso penal en la Castilla Moderna," *Estudis* 22 (1996): 199–215; Tomás y Valiente, *El derecho;* J. Lalinde Abadía, *Iniciación histórica al derecho español* (Barcelona, 1970), 758–802; E. Gacto, "Aproximación a la historia del derecho penal español," in *Hispania entre derechos propios y derechos nacionales: Atti dell'incontro di studio Firenze-Lucca, 25–27 de mayo 1989,* ed. B. Clavero, P. Grossi, and F. Tomás y Valiente (Milan, 1990), 1: 501–30; and J. Vallejo, "Historia del proceso, procedimiento de la historia: Diez años de historiografía procesal en España (1979–1988)," in *Hispania entre derechos propios y derechos nacionales: Atti dell'incontro di studio Firenze-Lucca, 25–27 maggio 1989,* ed. B. Clavero, P. Grossi, and F. Tomás y Valiente (Milan, 1990), 2: 885–921. S. Daza Palacios and M. R. Prieto Corbalán, *Proceso criminal contra fray Pablo de San Benito de San Lúcar de Barrameda (1774): Clérigo homocida en el siglo XVIII* (Seville, 1998), contains a detailed description of an eighteenth-century criminal case from the south of Spain.

22. Inspired by Roman law, torture was reintroduced into the Iberian Peninsula in the thirteenth century and was regulated in the *Siete Partidas* (partida 7, title 30, laws 1–9). R. I. Burns, ed., *Las siete partidas,* trans. S. P. Scott (Philadelphia, 2001), 5: 1458–62. Torture is discussed in Alonso Romero, *El proceso,* 244–56; G. Martínez Diez, "La tortura judicial en la legislación histórica española," *Anuario de historia del derecho español* 32 (1962): 223–300; F. Tomás y Valiente, *La Tortura en España* (Barcelona, 1973); idem, "Teoría y práctica de la tortura judicial en las obras de Lorenzo Matheu y Sanz (1618–1680)," *Anuario de historia del derecho español* 41 (1971): 439–85; idem, *El derecho,* 172–75; and "Disertación sobre la aplicación de la tortura a los reos [n.d.]," MS 2886, fol.169, BPR. For a comparative view see P. Fiorelli, *La tortura guidiziaria nel diritto comune* (Milan, 1953); J. H. Langbein, *Torture and the Law of Proof: England and the Ancient Regime* (Chicago, 1977); E. Hanson, "Torture and Truth in Renaissance England," *Representations* 34 (1991): 53–84; C. Vincent, "Justice Criminelle et supplices sous l'ancien régime," *Gavroche* 67 (1993): 11–16; and V. Pinson Ramin, "La torture judiciaire en Bretagne au XVIIe siècle," *Revue historique de droit français et étranger* 72/4 (1994): 549–68.

perceptions of crime, criminals, and guilt. According to these perceptions, there was no clear distinction—although one was gradually emerging—between sin and crime. Those committing an offense were not simply legally wrong—they were morally wrong as well because they acted against the natural (divine) order of things. As persons who rebelled against the natural order, they had to repent their doing before they could be readmitted to society. Because repentance was impossible without acknowledging the crime, obtaining a confession was crucial to the restoration of order. Penance was the (only) way to reenter society, penance required conversion—and conversion depended on the admission of guilt. Confessions, therefore, played a pivotal role not only for probatory ends but also for the correction of criminals.

This reasoning justified torture as a practice that, above all, was directed toward the salvation of the criminal and not toward the protection of the public good. Judges practicing torture explained to the subjects that they were being tortured for their own benefit and warned them to tell the truth, emphasizing that finding out this truth was the sole motivation for judicial torture. These warnings were given four times. The first warning was voiced when the suspect was still outside the torture room, the second one on his way to this room, the third one when entering the room, and the fourth and last one just before the torture session began.[23] Judges discharged their conscience in cases in which torture resulted in death or lesions, claiming that the victims were responsible for their own suffering.

Torture was applied to people who were suspected of wrongdoing if certain indications (*indicios*) of guilt existed against them. According to *Siete Partidas* (the legal code of King Alfonso X of Castile, 1252–84), these indications could include the testimony of a single witness or a *mala fama,* that is, a bad reputation (chap. 6). Insufficient to convict people of crimes, these indications nevertheless suggested the serious possibility of a wrongdoing. In early modern thought, such a possibility merited reprobation in itself. Individuals were not only responsible for their acts; they were also responsible for their public image (*fama*). Those who generated a bad image failed to integrate fully into society. As such, they were guilty of nonsocial behavior, an issue that was independent of the question of whether or not they committed the suspected crime.[24] People who raised

23. A similar ritual is described in A. Morellet, *Abrégé du manuel des inquisiteurs, 1762,* ed. J. P. Giucciardi (Grenoble, 1990), 127–35.

24. Tomás y Valiente, *El derecho,* 181; and idem, "El derecho penal como instrumento de gobierno," *Estudis* 22 (1996): 256–59.

suspicion were thus guilty of a wrongdoing and, as all other criminals, were just as prone to be tortured, confess their crime, and be readmitted to society. This reasoning explained why in exceptional cases torture could be applied to witnesses. Witnesses who did not come forward and share information they had with the judges, or who lied despite knowing the truth, were guilty of an offense. Their behavior was detrimental to the well-being of society, and their activity was prejudicial to the reign of justice. As sinners and criminals they needed to confess their wrongdoing and repent. Torture was as good a tool as any other to achieve this end.

Special professionals carried out the torture sessions in the presence of the investigating judge and a public notary.[25] In seventeenth- and eighteenth-century Quito, officials used the method of *tortura de cordeles*. The subject was stripped naked, and a collar was placed around his or her neck. The official in charge tied two ropes to each of the subject's legs and arms and gradually tightened them. After each tightening, the judge ordered him or her to tell the truth before another tightening would take place. This procedure normally lasted thirty to forty minutes, although there was at least one case in which the judge insisted on its execution for four hours. As the session progressed, the notary registered everything on paper: the physical location, the time, the exchange of words between the judge and the subject, the method applied, and even the cries of pain ("ay, ay, ay," or "Santa María, Jesús"). These records would then be inserted in the penal proceedings.

On occasion, attention to details of formulaic justice was so extreme that a torture session carried out without the presence of a curator (in the case of minors) or a defending officer (in the case of Indians) was annulled and later repeated.[26] In accordance with the idea that torture was only meant to redeem the criminal, the judge insisted in this case that he was worried about defending the rights of the tortured, which included the presence of these representatives. Indeed, contrary to present-day practices, judges were not concerned about the legality of the proofs—there was no theory that condemned proofs that had been obtained illegally.

After the torture session, the subject had to ratify the declaration made under torture. If the subject did, the declaration became part of

25. AHQ, Crim., 16: exp. 5 August 1701; AHQ, Not. 6, 7: exp. 10 May 1731; and AHQ, Not. 6, 8: exp. 27 March 1734.

26. AHQ, Crim., 22: exp. 26 February 1726.

the proofs in the penal proceedings against him or her—or, if the subject was a witness, against third parties. If the subject did not, the declaration carried no effect. Whether people confirmed their confessions for fear of being tortured again, or because they truly recognized their guilt, we do not know. However, in almost all of the cases of torture I have found, people reaffirmed their confessions or testimony after the sessions were over. Those who remained silent during the torture were considered innocent and were usually set free.[27]

The actual practice of torture was also influenced by social and economic considerations. In theory only noblemen, children younger than 14 years of age, pregnant women, and professionals (especially lawyers!) were immune from torture. In practice, the people tortured in Quito almost always belonged to the lower social strata and were non-Spanish. Torture also varied according to the offense. There was a greater tendency to torture suspects and witnesses of rural crimes, especially animal theft (*abigateo*) and road banditry, than other criminals or witnesses. On the one hand, these cases were harder to control, detect, and prove, and they required the application of special investigating and confession-producing techniques. On the other, these crimes were committed on the external boundaries of the Spanish community, which considered itself first and foremost as an urban community. People who committed these crimes were by definition liminal individuals who lived (or worked) in a liminal space. As such, their rejection was greater, as was the need to force their reinsertion into the community. There were specific years in which torture was more common. These years (for example, 1717 to 1731) coincided with periods of a greater preoccupation with the local social order. The more that elites trusted that order prevailed, the less the penal system tended to practice torture—and vice versa.

Overall, torture was not a very common practice. Only eleven people were tortured between 1650 and 1750, a very small number considering how often torture was requested by prosecutors and denied by the presiding or appeal judge. Rather than actually being practiced, torture was primarily mentioned as a possibility or as a threat. Judges made constant allusions to it and even had suspects or witnesses carried to the

27. AHQ, Not. 4, 11: exp. 6 December 1712; AHQ, Crim., 26: exp. 26 July 1731; and AHQ, Crim., 28: exp. 14 May 1736.

torture chamber, with the prior understanding that torture was not immediately to take place.[28]

Once the summary was completed and the confession of the suspect was taken (with or without torture), the judge or the crown attorney (*fiscal*) in cases de oficio, or the victim and his or her family in cases de parte, elaborated a formal accusation. The accused responded to this accusation, and the judge then set a time for both parties to present their proofs. The witnesses of the prosecution ratified the declarations that they had given in the summary, and the accused presented his or her witnesses. This part of the process was called "substantiation" (*sustanción*). When it was finished, the parties summarized their positions and proofs in a document called "it is well asserted" (*bien alegado*) and asked for conviction or absolution. From this moment onward, the case was ready (*en estado*) for sentencing.

Officially, cases de oficio were initiated and then run by the judge. The judge identified the offender, located the witnesses, collected the proofs, and elaborated the accusation. Theoretically, he did so because prosecution was related to royal interest, which had to be defended even in the absence of an action by the victim or his or her family. In practice, however, many actions de oficio involved no royal interest, and an interested party conducted them.[29] Cases de oficio could continue de parte and vice versa without suffering any substantial modification.[30] Because judges initiated processes de oficio, these processes could be adopted in the absence of a specific complaint or when the identity of the criminal was unknown.[31] Victims paid no fees. De oficio proceedings also served to resolve formal difficulties such as the refusal of a husband to give permission to his wife to file a criminal complaint.[32] Processes de oficio were thus more convenient to victims than processes de parte. They required no previous information about the criminal, involved smaller legal obstacles, and demanded no eco-

28. AHQ, Crim., 15: exp. 3 January 1698; AHQ, Crim., 24: exp. 5 March 1728; AHQ, Not. l, 13: exp. 23 December 1723; AHQ, Crim., 16: exp. 5 August 1701; AHQ, Crim., 23: exp. 11 November 1726; and AHQ, Not. 3, 13: exp. 19 February 1722.

29. AHQ, Not. l, 14: exp. 6 September 1725; AHQ, Crim., 4: exp. 25 March 1665; AHQ, Not. 6, 11: exp. 26 December 1738; AHQ, Crim., 6: exp. 4 March 1678; and AHQ, Not. 6, 7: exp. 28 November 1733. For a comparative view see Y. Castan, "Gestion du criminel et protectorat judiciaire dans la France d'ancien régime," *Estudis* 22 (1996): 53.

30. AHQ, Crim., 22: exp. 22 March 1726.

31. Some defendants criticized this use: AHQ, Not. 1, 13: exp. 25 December 1723 from 25 October 1720; and AHQ, Crim., 23: exp. 9 October 1726.

32. AHQ, Crim., 21: exp. 26 January 1723.

nomic investment.[33] These considerations were compelling. The cost of the proceedings could be substantial, depending on the length of the process, the number of declarations that the judges and notaries had taken, and the number of signatures they had placed on the documents. These costs could fluctuate between 10 and 644 pesos, with an average cost of about 30 pesos.[34]

Because of the forementioned advantages, many victims preferred processes de oficio. Most de oficio cases thus dealt with thefts, assaults, and assassinations. De oficio cases multiplied at the end of the seventeenth century and increased substantially again after 1740.[35] Some judges (for example, the magistrates Manuel Rubio de Arévalo, Pedro Martínez de Arizala, and José de Quintana y Acevedo, and the municipal justices José Zenitagoya, Francisco Ante y Mendoza, and Agustín Sandoval Portocarrero) clearly preferred this mechanism, as demonstrated by their frequent use of de oficio proceedings compared with other justices.

Conducting a case de oficio, rather than de parte, could thus aid the victim. Yet, there were other ways by which judges could achieve the same aim. They could declare victims, for example, "notoriously poor" (*pobre de solemnidad*).[36] These declarations gave victims the right to free judicial council and to an exemption from paying the costs of the procedure. From as early as the 1720s onward, there was little or no relationship between this declaration and a true state of destitution. Among those declared notoriously poor in Quito were merchants who owned shops, caretakers who had properties, and citizens who were homeowners.[37] Judges could declare litigants poor without asking for any proof.[38] In most cases, the declaration was simply based on the fact

33. AHQ, Crim., 4: exp. 27 September 1661; AHQ, Crim., 11: exp. 19 March 1687; AHQ, Not. 6, 13: exp. 13 July 1742; AHQ, Crim., 13: exp. 25 May 1694; AHQ, Crim., 21: exp. 3 July 1724; and AHQ, Crim., 35: exp. 6 May 1748.

34. AHQ, Not. 6, 18: exp. 20 August 1750; and AHQ, Crim., 27: exp. 6 October 1733. The cost of justice was studied by J. Lalinde Abadía, "Los gastos del proceso en el derecho histórico español," *Anuario de historia del derecho español* 34 (1964): 249–416.

35. Contemporaries recognized the proliferation of cases de oficio. The notaries of Quito, for example, complained from 1680 onward about this practice, which limited their income: AGI, Quito, 43 and 44, nos. 18 and 4, respectively.

36. Lalinde Abadía, "Los gastos," 402–8.

37. AHQ, Crim., 27: exp. 1 November 1732; AHQ, Not. 1, 14: exp. 6 September 1725; AHQ, Not. 3, 13: exp. 19 February 1722 from 10 December 1721; and AHQ, Not. 1, 12: exp. 18 April 1721.

38. AHQ, Not. 1, 13: exp. 25 December 1723 from 24 December 1719.

that litigants asserted an inability to pay the costs during the proceedings.[39]

Parallel to the ordinary penal process, judges in Quito could also proceed in a "brief and summary" (*breve y sumaria*) manner. In such a case, the judge pronounced the sentence directly after having received a confession, thereby bypassing the elaboration of a formal accusation, the response, the collection of proofs (by both parties), and the allegations.[40] This practice became more common after 1730, yet even then it continued to be exceptional. It was mostly used in cases that merited minor penalties, that ended in absolution, or that involved Indians or mestizos. Judges could also resolve criminal cases by taking an administrative rather than a judicial action; this administrative action was called *vía de proveído* or *de gobierno*. Judges justified taking both summary and administrative procedures by the need to avoid delays and to lower the cost of the proceedings.[41] Yet this way of proceeding was also favored because it allowed the judge total liberty to do as he wished. In the one hundred years between 1650 and 1750, only one litigant criticized this liberty. In 1749, a suspect demanded a plenary process: he asserted that only this process would guarantee his justice and protect him against an arbitrary judicial decision.[42]

Judges and victims could initiate and continue penal proceedings despite the absence of the suspect, or eventually, the accused. When this happened, the suspect or the accused was called to appear before the court in three successive decrees that were published by the town crier (*pregonero*). After each proclamation, the notary accompanying the crier certified that the suspect (or the accused) failed to present him- or herself. Once this ceremony was completed, the court proceeded as if the party were present.[43] Sentences dictated "in rebellion" (*en rebeldía*), which was the term used when suspects failed to appear, tended to be condemnatory. The punishment decreed in them tended to be greater

39. AHQ, Crim., 10: exp. 22 January 1686; and AHQ, Crim., 20: exp. 10 November 1717.

40. Alonso Romero, *El proceso*, 287–30; and Gacto, "Aproximación," 504–7.

41. AHQ, Crim., 13: exp. 28 May 1693; and AHQ, Crim., 31: exp. 8 April 1742.

42. AHQ, Crim., 36: exp. 10 January 1749.

43. "Apuntes de prácticas judiciales, vía ordinaria, ejecutivas y criminal . . . [18th c.]," MS 20.258(28), 11–15 and 23–25, BN; "Explicación teórica del rito y orden de proceder en los juicios [18th c.]," Misc. 001489, 46–47, AMQ; "Practica de la Chancillería de Granada siglos XVII–XVIII [n.d.]," MS 309, 375–82, BN; J. M. Álvarez, *Las instituciones de derecho real de Castilla y de Indias* (1826; reprint, Mexico, 1982), 285–89; and Alonso Romero, *El proceso*, 115–77.

than one dictated against similar convicts who were present at their trials. In many cases, defendants reappeared soon after the judges dictated the sentences and argued that they were unaware of the proceedings. On almost all of these occasions, they were allowed to defend themselves and were able to either reverse the verdicts or obtain lighter punishment.[44] In many cases, however, the absence of the suspect or the accused paralyzed the procedure or even lead to its total abandonment.

Most penal cases began shortly after the crimes were committed. If there was a long delay between the crime and the initial complaint, victims usually explained that they had waited until the suspect was apprehended, the goods were located, or the victim of the assault died. In some cases, victims mentioned attempts to reach an agreement with the aggressors (chap. 7) or noted the need to wait for the judge's return. There were also many cases in which the complaint included a long succession of transgressions, transgressions repeatedly endured until the victim finally decided to request the intervention of the judges.

The duration of proceedings did not depend on the nature of the crime or the number of witnesses. Instead, this length of time varied according to the parties (their will and haste), the availability of judges and officials, the presence of the accused, and other circumstances of the case. It also depended on whether judges followed the normal procedure or acted summarily or administratively. In most cases, the first part of the trial (the sumaria) ended within a few days. The incarceration of the suspect immediately followed. Once the suspect was secured in jail, some time passed before his or her confession was taken. Frequently, the suspect had to ask the judge to take his or her confession in order to speed up the process. Immediately afterward, the judge dictated the period for presenting proofs. This period normally lasted a month for each of the parties and was not easily prolonged. It then took fifteen to twenty days for the parties to produce their final allegations and for the case to be ready for sentence (*estar en estado*). Sentencing followed a few months later. This delay generated many complaints against judges, who were accused of not sentencing cases quickly enough.[45] The judges responded by affirming that this passage of time was involuntary. It was due to "accidents and impediments" such as sickness, overwork, their absence from the jurisdiction, and vacation

44. AHQ, Crim., 10: exp. 8 September 1685.

45. These accusations were frequent in the 1691 inspection ordered by the king (*visita*): AGI, Quito, 72–74. See also Roldán Verdejo, *Los jueces*, 283–90.

days. Judges blamed the parties for deliberately seeking to gain time and to exhaust the patience and resources of their adversaries. Judges also diverted the criticism to the auxiliary judicial staff, whom they accused of failing to prepare the cases for sentencing or forgetting to schedule them. Lastly, judges asserted that the complexity of many penal cases required a thorough study, which implied a longer investment in time and a delayed sentence.[46]

Most penal cases concluded within four to seven months of their initiation. Summary or administrative cases were naturally quicker, producing sentences on the same day or on the following days after a case was initiated. Many processes were dropped for several months and then reinitiated.[47] Although we do not always know why this happened, in some cases delay was caused by a procedure called *recusación*. Recusation was a legal instrument that allowed the parties to ask for the dismissal of the judge, the court clerk (*escribano receptor*), or court notary by accusing him of partiality.[48] Recusation could be motivated by a personal rivalry between the party and the officeholder or by the close ties that connected this officer to the adversaries. People who argued against the participation of a specific officeholder in their case were rarely requested to explain their motivation or supply proofs.[49] It was sufficient to claim that this individual was "hateful and suspicious" (*odioso y sospechoso*). When criticism was directed at a judicial official, the accusation was automatically accepted, and the officer was

46. AGI, Quito, 73–74: The answers (*descargos*) of magistrates Andrés Francia, Gaspar de Luna, Cristóbal Cevallos y Borja, Pedro Salcedo y Fuenmayor, Matías Lagúñez, and Miguel Antonio Ormasa Ponce de León. Manuel Rubio de Arévalo, who investigated President José de Araujo y Río, took a similar stand in AGI, EC, 916A, cuad. 11, 42. See also Roldán Verdejo, *Los jueces*, 283–90; and AHN, Cód., 488B, no. 113: cédula from 2 January 1747.

47. AHQ, Crim., 4: exp. 25 March 1665; AHQ, Crim., 6: exp. 19 December 1676; and AHQ, Crim., 34: exp. 18 February 1746.

48. S. M. Coronas González, "La recusación judicial en el derecho histórico español," *Anuario de historia del derecho español* 52 (1982): 511–615; L. Zarazaga, "Recusación y excusación en el Derecho Indiano," *Revista chilena de historia del derecho* 13 (1987): 117–28; P. L. Rovito, *Respublica dei togati: Giuristi e società nella Napoli del Seicento* (Naples, 1981); and "Notas sobre recusación de jueces [n.d.]," MS 13.297, BN.

49. Exceptions to this rule can be found in AHQ, Crim., 6: exp. 4 March 1678 from 13 April 1682; AHQ, Crim., 4: exp. 27 September 1661; and AHQ, Crim., 25: exp. 28 July 1729. Coronas González believes that Castilian law did not require proof for the recusal of municipal justices but demanded one in all other cases. Coronas González, "La recusación judicial," 587. In Quito it was customary to warn a justice about a forthcoming recusal: AGI, Quito, 142, 161–63: *letter* from Matheu y Villamill from 10 June 1704.

removed. When the person targeted was a judge, either he was removed, or a second judge was appointed to see the case together with him. Although it was practiced only in 4 percent of the cases I studied, recusation could lead to long delays. At times, litigants argued against the involvement of most or even all of the available personnel, thus leading to a stalemate.[50] In 1685, for example, the local governor was faced with the consecutive recusal of five legal experts, the wish of the sixth expert to not take part in the process (*excusa*), and the absence of the seventh and last candidate.[51]

Penal processes could end with an acquittal (*absolución*) or a condemnatory sentence. In theory, there were two types of acquittals: *de la instancia,* which only determined that there were insufficient proofs, and a general acquittal, which was the most common and included a declaration of innocence.[52] There were also cases of conditional acquittal, in which the judge stated that convicts would be acquitted if for a certain time they would not commit any crime.[53] Acquittals were more frequent in sentences delivered by municipal justices than by the royal court. They were also more frequent before 1730 than after and occurred in about 7 percent of all cases.[54]

There were no clear guidelines regarding the proper punishment in cases of conviction. Some crimes were not defined in the laws, and most penal norms either did not specify the punishment for the crimes or the punishment that they established was so harsh that no judge wanted to implement it.[55] Judges thus adopted sanctions that were not stipulated in laws and were called "extraordinary" or "arbitrary."[56] Despite their

50. AHQ, Crim., 6: exp. 4 March 1678. This custom was criticized by the royal council seated in Madrid charged with American affairs (*Consejo de Indias*), who prohibited "vague and repeated recusals": AHN, Cód., 696B, no. 498: cédula from 27 May 1766.

51. AHQ, Crim., 10: exp. 8 September 1685. For a similar case see AHQ, Not. l, 13: exp. 23 December 1723 from 17 March 1721.

52. AHQ, Crim., 15: exp. 3 January 1698; and AHQ, Crim., 27: exp. 20 July 1733.

53. AHQ, Crim., 32: exp. 18 February 1743.

54. AHQ, Not. 1, 14: exp. 10 June 1725; and AHQ, Crim., 28: exp. 14 May 1736.

55. Tomás y Valiente, *El derecho,* 353–405; J. L. Heras Santos, *La justicia penal de los Austrias en la corona de Castilla* (Salamanca, 1991), 265–321; G. Alessi Palazzolo, "Furto e pena: Aspetti del dibattito del tardo diritto comune," *Quaderni fiorentini* 2 (1973): 535–605; and M. P. Alonso Romero and A. M. Hespanha, "Les peines dans les pays ibériques XVIIe–XIXe siècles," *Recueils de la société Jean Bodin* 3 (1989): 198. See also A. Rodríguez Sánchez, "La soga y el fuego: La pena de muerte en España de los siglos XVI y XVII," *Cuadernos de historia moderna* 15 (1994): 13–39.

56. M. Meccarelli, *Arbitrium. Un aspetto sistematico degli ordinamenti giuridici in età di diritto comune* (Milan, 1998).

name, these sanctions were not the result of a free or truly discretionary judicial invention. Nor were they illegal. Arbitrarism was an inherent part of a system that gave judges not only the power to implement laws but also (and mainly) the task of administering justice. A preference for justice over legality instructed judges to ignore what was legal for the sake of preferring what was just, thus making arbitrarism necessary.[57]

The degree to which arbitrary sanctions could become regulated was clearly manifested in Quito, where, during the course of the late seventeenth and eighteenth century, judges practiced a relatively fixed standard of (arbitrary) punishment.[58] The most common sanction they inflicted on criminals was banishment (exile), which normally lasted from one to four years. Banishment was often "voluntary," which meant that the convict could choose where to go. The judges only determined the minimum distance of this destination from Quito. In about half of the cases, judges ordered an "involuntary" banishment by indicating also the place of residence. Involuntary destinations often combined punishment with public service. They included military fortresses, frontier areas, or new settlements that needed the input of new immigrants. From the middle to the end of the seventeenth century, most convicts were banished to Chile, especially to the fortress of Valdavia. In the eighteenth century, most judges preferred to send exiles to Macas and Quijos in the Amazon region. By midcentury, many exiles went to the *Isla de la Piedra,* located in Callao near Lima. Banishment to Guayaquil (the main port of the province of Quito) was also common between 1695 and 1696, 1731 and 1732, and 1740 and 1746. Other possible destinations included Panamā and the new settlements in Esmeraldas and Barbacoas (the northern Pacific coast of the province). These destinations responded to the circumstances of the moment, and in particular to military, economic, or political needs. In the seventeenth century, Chile had to be pacified. In the eighteenth century, new attempts were made to penetrate to the Amazon region, and Guayaquil needed a fresh supply of men in order to resist repeated attacks by pirates. Demand for labor was also growing in Callao, especially in the quarry

57. These issues were studied in a series of articles published by B. Durand, for example, "La détermination de la peine chez les criminalistes catalans du XVIe au XVIIIe siècle: Logique juridique ou effet de mentalités?," *Recueil de mémoires et travaux* 15 (1991): 1–25. See also Garnot, *Crime et justice,* 69–74.

58. For a comparative view see G. Morgan and P. Rushton, *Roughes, Thieves and the Rule of Law: The Problem of Law Enforcement in North-East England, 1718–1800* (London, 1998), 178 and 216.

located in the Isla de la Piedra, and labor was also needed to open a road linking Quito to Esmeraldas. The usefulness of the road itself also depended on the presence of colonists in that region.

Banishment could thus have utilitarian ends. Yet, more than anything else, it transferred the criminal to another jurisdiction. It was believed that criminals would be easier to control in a foreign jurisdiction. The community that received the criminals would be able to apply justice to them without any remorse or hindrance in a way their home community could rarely accomplish. Banishment clearly depended on order being a local affair. Unfit for social life in one place, it was hoped that the criminal might fit into another. The lack of local support might convince the criminal to change his or her activities or might simply disable them. The banishment of criminals also guaranteed that their bad effect would no longer be felt in the original community in which they committed the crime. It was as if by distancing them the (local) crime problem was resolved. This was an efficient solution that required no investment in time, money, or energy.

Whipping was less common than banishment but was still extremely frequent. On occasion, Indian, mestizo, and poor Spanish convicts could also be sentenced to forced labor.[59] Forced labor could include banishment, as was the case in sentences ordering convicts to work in the shipyards of Guayaquil or the quarry of Callao.[60] Other forms of forced labor implied incarceration, as was the case of those who were sentenced to work in textile mills (*obrajes*) or monasteries.[61] In exceptional cases, forced labor only implied the obligation to perform a public duty in Quito, such as building a church. On these occasions, the inhabitants of the city complained that the authorities tolerated crime because they sought economic gain. Labor itself was not a punishment, especially not to those accustomed to manual work. It could not teach criminals a lesson or convince others to avoid crime.[62]

59. Forced labor is described in J. L. Heras Santos, "Los galeotas de los Austrias, la penalidad al servicio de la armada," *Historia social* 6 (1990): 127–40; and S. Kagan, "Penal Servitude in Nueva España: The Colonial Textile Industry," Ph.D. diss., New York University, 1977.

60. AHQ, Crim., 14: exp. 5 August 1695; AHQ, Crim., 22: exp. 4 April 1726; AHQ, Not. 6, 7: exp. 28 November 1733; and AHQ, Crim., 30: exp. 13 July 1740.

61. AHQ, Crim., 31: exp. 10 July 1741 from 11 July 1739; AHQ, Not. 1, 29: exp. 11 May 1748; AHQ, Not. 1, 29: exp. 11 May 1748; AHQ, Crim., 20: exp. 12 November 1717; and AHQ, Crim., 22: exp. 23 May 1728.

62. AHQ, Crim., 15: exp. 24 September 1698; and AHQ, Crim., 22: exp. 4 April 1726.

While banishment, whipping, and forced labor were common, although in different degrees, confinement was extremely infrequent. It was practiced on only eleven occasions between 1650 and 1750, mostly in cases of women.[63] Capital punishment was rarely applied: we know of only twelve cases between 1650 and 1750.[64] The same could be said with regard to monetary fines. For the period between 1650 and 1750 the penal records mention only twenty cases of fines, the majority of which occurred after 1720. Quito's municipal judges did not levy even a single fine between 1729 and 1737. Between 1717 and 1720, and again between 1745 and 1750, there were only two fines, one in each period. A similar situation occurred in the royal court, where only one fine was leveled between 1729 and 1731, in 1733, between 1736 and 1745, and between 1746 and 1750.[65] Furthermore, as much as 50 percent of the revenues from fines could be due to one or two significant sums, the rest of the fines being extremely small.[66]

This economic reality had immediate repercussions on the administration of justice. In Quito, as elsewhere, penal fines were a means to finance different public expenditures.[67] The income fines produced had to pay the salaries of court officers, especially porters (*portero*) and court clerks. Fines also subsidized public works, such as the reconstruction of bridges and jails. After the 1730s, income from fines was also used to compensate victims, particularly in murder and rape cases.[68] Because fines were so scarce and relatively small, they were often insufficient to cover all of these expenses. Officials whose salaries depended on this source of revenue often complained about not being paid. The chaplain of the audiencia, for example, testified in 1713 that

63. AHQ, Crim., 27: exp. 12 December 1732 from 30 May 1738; AHQ, Crim., 27: exp. 18 August 1733; AHQ, Not. 6, 15: exp. 6 October 1746; and AHQ, Crim., 20: exp. 8 September 1717.

64. We do know that many more death sentences were handed down, but it is currently impossible to confirm how many were executed.

65. These figures are mentioned in the judicial reviews (*residencias*) of presidents Dionisio Alcedo y Herrera and Fernando Félix Sánchez de Orellana. AGI, EC, 911B; and AGI, EC, 911C.

66. Accounts of the local governors Francisco de Figueroa (1661–65), Iñigo Aranguren y Aguirre (1676–81), and Diego de Zárate y Murga (1719–21) in their residencias: AGI, EC, 910B, 910C, and 1056B.

67. For a comparative view see H. Benveniste, "Le système des amendes pénales en France à la fin du moyen âge: Une première mise en perspective," *Revue historique de droit français et étranger* 70/1 (1992): 1–28.

68. AHQ, Crim., 26: exp. 5 December 1730; AHQ, Crim., 32: exp. 2 January 1744; and AHQ, Crim., 34: exp. 1 August 1746.

he had only received 180 pesos during his two years of service, instead of the 1,600 pesos that were agreed upon.[69] Bernardo Espinosa de los Monteros, who assisted the crown attorney, expressed a similar complaint in 1691.[70] Yet nothing could be done to improve the situation. The judges insisted that the people of Quito were poor and that the penal system had no means to ensure the collection of fines that were levied.[71] In 1662, the audiencia nominated a person to collect the fines (*receptor de penas*) and promised him 10 percent of the revenues that he gathered.[72] However, this appointment had little or no effect in Quito, where complaints continued about the scarcity of revenues.

Penal sentences could also end with a judicial decree that included instructions (*aprecibimiento*) concerning the future conduct of convicts. For example, judges could order convicts not to associate with criminals or to return home and lead a normal family life with their spouses.[73] These instructions could be accompanied by a suspended sanction that would be implemented in cases of disobedience. Suspended sanctions were also common in cases of recidivist criminals. Such sanctions were at times dictated against people who were not formally convicted but were instead either absolved or pardoned. They indicated that whatever the formal result of the process might have been this time, a specific sanction would be imposed if the behavior was repeated in the future.[74] This last practice was so common that delinquents expected to be forgiven and warned the first time around, and punished only in cases of recidivism.[75] Because judges failed to implement their own threats, many criminals benefited from the same beneficial treatment on second and even third offences.[76]

69. AGI, Quito, 106: decree from 13 June 1713.

70. AGI, Quito, 72.

71. AHQ. Pris., 2: exp. 25 March 1665; AHQ, Gob., 10: exp. 9 November 1707; AHQ, Gob., 11: exp. 5 April 1722; and AHQ, Ced., 2 (1601–60), no. 196: cédula from 1639.

72. AHQ, Ced., 4. no. 12: from 11 April 1661.

73. AHQ, Crim., 4: exp. 6 December 1655; AHQ, Not. 4, 18: exp. 7 February 1730; and AHQ, Not. l, 30: exp. 8 January 1750. Apparently, this practice was also common elsewhere: P. Ortega Gil, "Apercibimientos penales en la práctica criminal de la real audiencia de Galicia (siglos XVII y XVIII), " *Cuadernos de historia del derecho* 3 (1996): 11–41.

74. AHQ, Crim., 23: exp. 9 October 1726; AHQ, Crim., 15: exp. 8 January 1698; and AHQ, Crim., 31: exp. 8 April 1742.

75. AHQ, Crim., 15: exp. 8 January 1698; AHQ, Crim., 24: exp. 2 September 1728; and AHQ, Crim., 27: exp. 20 July 1733.

76. AHQ, Not. 6, 8: exp. 7 April 1734; AHQ, Crim., 31: exp. 10 July 1741; and AHQ, Crim., 31: exp. 18 November 1741 from 15 December 1742.

After the judge handed down sentences, the victims, the crown attorney, or the convicts could appeal against them.[77] Appeal (*apelación,* also called *vista*) was not an automatic right. In order to appeal, the parties needed the authorization of the judge who had decided the case and/or the permission of the appeal instance. The parties could also present a plea (*súplica,* also called *grado de revista*). In contrast to appeals, pleas were presented theoretically to the court that sentenced the case either originally or in appeal. Pleas were the last local instance. After they were exhausted, the only thing a party could do was to address the king and request his intervention.

The distinction between appeals and pleas was not always maintained in Quito, where the terms "apelación" and "súplica" were often used as synonyms. Nevertheless appeals and pleas were almost always different in tone. While appeals typically contained long arguments regarding justice and rightful expectations, pleas were straightforward requests for mercy.[78] Because of this difference, parties who believed that they could substantiate their claims would appeal, and those who did not would plead. The contrast between appeals and pleas also meant that most appeals were presented by crown attorneys or victims who based their arguments on the justice of their cases. In contrast, most pleas originated in convicted defendants who, whether justified or not, simply wished to obtain royal grace.

Appeals and pleas were rarely rejected on formal grounds, such as timing or form.[79] They produced a modification of the original verdict in approximately half of the cases. Clearly, those who addressed the courts several times had a greater possibility for achieving what they wanted than those who did not. A negative appeal did not necessarily mean that a plea would be rejected. The same court that confirmed a

77. S. Aikin Araluce, *El recurso de apelación en el derecho castellano* (Madrid, 1982); Alonso Romero, *El proceso,* 268–80; and Lalinde Abadía, *Iniciación,* 795–802.

78. AHQ, Crim., 14: exp. 5 August 1695; AHQ, Crim., 5: exp. 10 July 1674; and AHQ, Crim., 23: exp. 25 September 1727. For a comparative view see J. Hilaire, "'Supplier le roi': Les voies de recours extraordinaires aux XIIIe et XIV siècles," *Revue historique de droit français et étranger* 74/1 (1998): 73–81.

79. Rejection on formal grounds did happen in three cases: AHQ, Not. l, 15: exp. 27 February 1727; AHQ, Crim., 27: exp. 1 November 1732; and AHQ, Not. 3, 26: exp. 11 October 1746.

sentence in appeal (*vista*) could reverse it after a plea (*revista*).[80] At times, this modification was masked by a discourse that stressed continuity. For example, while confirming the sentence "in its entirety" (*de todo y por todo*), judges specified that this confirmation was made "with the intention that the eight year banishment to Chile would be interpreted as a four year banishment to Guayaquil."[81] Yet, in spite of these good probabilities, the people of Quito rarely appealed or pleaded their sentences.[82] The additional cost of these procedures and their very slow advance (an average of seven months was required for decisions in appeal or plea to come through) may explain this reticence.

Once the process was completed, and the period for appeal and plea had passed, the parties could ask the judges to declare the sentence *pasada en autoridad de cosa juzgada*.[83] This declaration supposedly confirmed the result in a way that prohibited anyone (even the judge) from ever reopening the case. Whether motivated by ignorance or negligence, litigants, mostly convicts, only requested this declaration in fifteen cases.[84]

Processed or convicted criminals could also request a pardon.[85] There were two types of pardons: general and particular. General pardons were announced in Madrid in 1657, 1662, 1707, and 1746 on account of the birth of princes or the coronation of kings. These par-

80. AHQ, Crim., 14: exp. 24 May 1695 from 8 January 1698; AHQ, Crim., 16: exp. 5 August 1701; and AHQ, Not. 3, 13: exp. 19 February 1722.

81. AHQ, Crim., 23: exp. 23 January 1679. Other cases are AHQ, Crim., 20: exp. 12 November 1717; and AHQ, Crim., 32: exp. 2 January 1744. The Council of the Indies also used this type of discourse. AGI, EC, 959: *sentencia de vista* and *revista* in the process concerning the illicit marriage of magistrate Diego Inclán Valdés.

82. *Apelaciones* and *súplicas* were requested in only 12 and 7 percent of the cases, respectively.

83. Lalinde Abadía, *Iniciación*, 795–802; and Alonso Romero, *El proceso*, 262–65.

84. Cases in which it was requested include AHQ, Crim., 26: exp. 5 December 1730; and AHQ, Crim., 27: exp. 10 April 1734.

85. Tomás y Valiente, *El derecho*, 397–405; idem, "El perdón de la parte ofendida en el derecho penal castellano," *Anuario de historia del derecho español* 21 (1961): 55–114; M. I. Rodríguez Flores, *El perdón real en Castilla siglos XIII–XVIII* (Salamanca, 1971); A. M. Hespanha, "Justiça e administração entre o antigo regime e a revolução," *Hispania entre derechos propios y derechos nacionales: Atti dell'incontro di studio Firenze-Lucca, 25–27 mayo 1989*, ed. B. Clavero, P. Grossi, and F. Tomás y Valiente (Milan, 1990), 1: 135–204; Alonso Romero and Hespanha, "Les peines," 201 and 220; and J. L. Heras Santos, "Indultos concedidos por la Cámara de Castilla en tiempos de los Austria," *Studia histórica* 1 (1983): 115–41. See also Congrès National des Sociétés Savantes, *La tact, la répression et le pardon: Philologie et histoire jusqu'à 1610. 107 Congrès National des Sociétés Savantes* (Brest, 1982); AHN, Cód., 752B: decree from 24 August 1632; and BN, MS 2989, fol. 69.

dons freed certain criminals from either legal prosecution or a sentence already dictated against them. Although these royal acts of "grace, favor, clemency, and mercy" were published in Quito, as far as I can tell, in the one hundred years between 1650 and 1750, only three local criminals benefited from them.[86] Rather than obeying the logic of an "economy of grace," which according to Antonio Manuel Hespanha alternated between the king's image as justiciar and the king's portrayal as father and pastor, most pardons in Quito had a clearly utilitarian end.[87] These pardons were arranged during the judges' weekly inspection of the prison (see the following).[88] They were granted to individuals who volunteered to go as soldiers to Chile or, in the eighteenth century, to Guayaquil. Rather than the identity of the criminal, or crime, or general considerations of justice and grace, these pardons depended on the military situation. Local judges made an explicit connection between one thing and the other. They explained that the pardon was required, for example, for "the defense and aid of the city of Guayaquil, which is now threatened by an enemy English squadron which is infesting the South Sea."[89] The idea that a military situation would justify a pardon was sufficiently generalized that in 1686 the city of Quito requested the royal authorities to pardon a citizen whom the town council wanted to help and whom it now presented as indispensable for the defense of the city.[90]

There were also cases of particular pardons. In 1714 the king pardoned Domingo José Basterrechea, a citizen of Quito sentenced to death in absentia for having killed his adulterous wife.[91] Having escaped from the city, Basterrechea traveled to Rome, where he secured absolution from the pope. He then arrived in Madrid and requested

86. AHQ, Ced., 2 (1601–60), nos. 603, 605, 606, and 613; AHQ, Ced., 4, no. 64; and AHQ, Ced., 6, no. 126. The three cases are AHQ, Crim., 4: exp. 30 March 1662; AHQ, Not. 6, 15: exp. 14 September 1746; and AHQ, Crim., 34: exp. 21 June 1747.

87. A. M. Hespanha, "La economía de la gracia," *La gracia del derecho: Economía de la cultura en la edad moderna* (Madrid, 1993), 151–76.

88. AHQ, Crim., 6: exp. 4 March 1678; and AHQ, Not. 6, 13: exp. 17 April 1742.

89. AHQ, Not. l, 17: exp. 3 May 1735 decision from 13 December 1741. The utilitarian use of pardons was also discussed in AHN, Cód., 755B, no. 36.

90. AMQ, LC, 00115: town meeting from 6 June 1686.

91. AGI, Quito, 106: decree of 5 September 1713; AHN, Cód., 756B, no. 48, 222–25, dated 27 September 1713; AHN, Cód., 696B, no. 490, 412–14, decree of 17 January 1714; and AHQ, Crim., 22: exp. 20 October 1724. I describe this case in greater detail in T. Herzog, "Centro, periferia e integración política: el eje Quito-Madrid (siglo XVIII)," *Interpretatio: Revista de historia del derecho* 3 (1995): 140–43.

pardon from the king. After some hesitation, and despite the contrary opinion of the Council of the Indies, the king conceded, instructing Basterrechea to remain outside the limits of the city of Quito and the fifty leagues around it for the next three years. Basterrechea returned to the city in 1724 and regained possession of his properties (which were seized by the royal authorities) and custody over his children.

The Judicial Authorities

Various authorities could handle penal cases originating in the city of Quito and its jurisdiction. They included a royal court (audiencia); a municipal court, which included two ordinary justices (*alcaldes ordinarios*), a local governor (*corregidor*), and his lieutenant (*teniente*); and three justices (*alcaldes* and *provincial*) of the Santa Hermandad.[92] These authorities were not equally active. Among the 390 cases I located in the archives, 152 cases were handled by the alcaldes ordinarios, 149 by the audiencia, 73 by the corregidor and his lieutenant, 8 by the alcaldes of the Santa Hermandad, 3 by its provincial, and 5 by other unidentified judges. The ordinarios and the audiencia were equally active during the period between 1650 and 1750. The corregidor and his lieutenant were more active in the seventeenth than in the eighteenth century. The court of the Santa Hermandad practically stopped functioning at the beginning of the second decade of the eighteenth century.[93]

92. The bibliography concerning these distinct authorities in other American regions is extremely abundant. Some examples are E. Ruiz Giñazú, *La magistratura indiana* (Buenos Aires, 1916); R. Zorraquín Becú, *La justicia capitular durante la dominación española* (Buenos Aires, 1947); idem, *La organización judicial argentina en el periodo hispánico* (Buenos Aires, 1952); J. L. Soberanes Fernández, "La administración superior de justicia en Nueva España," *Boletin mexicano de derecho comparado* 12 (1980): 143–200; idem, "La administración de justicia en la recopilación de 1680," in *Recopilación de Leyes de los Reinos de las Indias: Estudios histórico jurídicos*, ed. F. Icaza Dufor (Mexico, 1985), 165–76; A. García Gallo, *Estudios de historia del derecho indiano* (Madrid, 1972); idem, "Alcaldes mayores y corregidores en Indias," *Memoria del I congreso venezolano de historia*, (Caracas, 1972), 1: 247–31; idem, "Jueces populares y jueces técnicos en la historia del derecho español," in *Justicia municipal y sus aspectos históricos y científicos: Ciclo de conferencias* (Madrid, 1946), 57–61; C. E. Castañeda, "The Corregidor in Spanish Colonial Administration," *Hispanic American Historical Review* 9 (1929): 446–70; and F. Albi, *El corregidor en el municipio español bajo la monarquía absoluta* (Madrid, 1943).

93. A similar phenomenon is documented in some parts of Castile according to M. F. Gómez Vozmediano, "Una corte rural de justicia: la santa hermandad vieja de Almodóvar del Campo," *Cuadernos de historia moderna* 22 (1998): 107–35.

The division of labor between the different courts was unclear. There were no fixed rules for assigning cases, and the audiencia, the municipal ordinary judges, or the local governor and his lieutenant could equally handle penal cases of first instance originating in the city and its rural hinterland. The audiencia was theoretically limited to important cases and *casos de corte,* which included the cases of people worthy of special protection such as orphans, widows, or nobles. However, these limitations were theoretical. In practice, the audiencia intervened in anything that came to its attention. The court of the Santa Hermandad was also theoretically limited in its jurisdiction. This court could only see crimes committed outside settlements in uninhabited lands (*despoblados*). In practice, judges of the Santa Hermandad often got involved in affairs in the villages of Quito or were assigned jurisdiction on matters pertaining to the city (see the following).

The audiencia, the municipal court and the Santa Hermandad judges were all charged with similar missions inside a fairly identical territory. Jurisdiction thus depended not on the identity of the court or judge but on the willingness of the parties. The parties could choose to present their complaints to one judge or another. This choice, which was freely theirs, determined the capacity of the institution to study the case. Once a specific judge began reviewing a complaint, all others were obliged not to intervene. The only exception to this rule was the audiencia, which could instruct lower judges to stop acting and could take hold of matters already studied by them.

The Audiencia

The audiencia was the highest court within the province of Quito. It handled criminal cases originating in the city of Quito and its immediate jurisdiction (five leagues) and it heard appeals for sentences handed down by the provincial and local instances. The audiencia included a president, four magistrates (*oidores*), one crown attorney, and one protector of Indians. The crown attorney was charged with representing royal interests, although he also functioned as a prosecutor and as ordinary magistrate.[94] The protector of Indians was responsible for all

94. S. Gerardo Suárez, *Los fiscales indianos: Orígen y evolución del ministerio público* (Caracas, 1995).

Indian matters, both judicial and administrative.[95] The audiencia functioned as a collegial body. Its decisions were handed out as decisions of the court and never of its individual judges or officeholders.

The audiencia channeled its activities through several different procedures.[96] The most important among them was the *audiencia pública* (also called *audiencia de relaciones*) and the *acuerdo*.[97] The audiencia pública was a public session held daily between eight and eleven in the morning in the presence of the president and all other members.[98] It began with a Mass, which was celebrated behind closed doors. When the Mass was over, the magistrates entered the chamber, where officials, lawyers, and litigants were waiting. They ascended to their seats according to a prescribed order, and the presiding justice called the court clerks and procurators (*procuradores*) to come forward and present the cases. Cases were heard according to a set order. First were appeals coming from the province. Second were new petitions regarding new cases. Third were cases already in progress. Before each matter was discussed, the procurator and the interested party, who often waited in the antechamber, were ordered to enter the chamber. Court clerks read the petitions, and with the permission of the court, the procurator of the party clarified their contents. The magistrates then questioned the procurator or requested that the court recorders (*relatores*) summarize

95. D. Bonnet, *El protector de naturales en la Audiencia de Quito siglos XVII–XVIII* (Quito, 1992).

96. The description that follows is based on the study of penal cases from Quito, as well as legal manuals such as "Práctica de la Chancillería de Granada siglos XVII–XVIII [n.d.]," MS 309, BN; "Ceremonias y estilo de los tribunales del Reino de Navarra [18th c.?]," MS 9910, BN; J. Moriana, "Discursos penales y particulares del gobierno general y político del Consejo Supremo de Justicia de estos reinos de Castilla y León y ceremonial en él [1632]," MS 7467, BN; F. J. Somoza, "La justicia vestida de todas sus autoridades . . . [n.d.]," MS 22.213, BN; and A. A. Ruiz Rodríguez, *La Real Chancellería de Granada en el siglo XVI* (Granada, 1987).

97. Originally, a difference existed between the audiencia pública and the audiencia de relaciones. However, in mid–seventeenth- and eighteenth-century Quito, this difference was completely eliminated, and although sessions were called by one form or another, in practice both audiencias saw the same types of petitions in the same manner and gave similar decisions. Apparently, the same development also happened elsewhere: AHN, Cód., 713B. no. 253 (dated 1582); and "Práctica de Granada."

98. The exceptions were feast days (*fiestas de tabla*): Holy Week, Easter, Christmas, Shrovetide, Ash Wednesday, All Saints, and the feast of Teresa of Ávila. AHQ, Ced., 10, no. 201 from 1747 and *ordinance* no. 25 from the audiencia (of 1563). Congreso del instituto internacional de historia del Derecho Indiano, *Ordenanzas de la Real Audiencia de Quito: V congreso del Instituto Internacional de Historia del Derecho Indiano* (Quito-Guayaquil, 1978).

the circumstances of the case. The decision of the court was immediately given. Each of the magistrates expressed his opinion following a descending order that began with the opinion of the most senior member. The court notary annotated the decision on the petition and later prepared the corresponding decree that was signed by all the magistrates. The last part of the audiencia pública was dedicated to the reading of sentences by the magistrates, who did so according to seniority in office.

Most matters treated in the audiencia pública required a decision concerning what today would be identified as "procedural matters." They included the order to notify an interested party of a certain decision, to request the parties to return the court documents that they had borrowed, and to register a compromise between them. Also common was the appointment of a person to collect the proofs, usually a court clerk, notary (*escribano*), chief constable (*alguacil mayor*), municipal ordinary judge, or magistrate of the audiencia, and the fixing of the period in which the parties could present the evidence.

The audiencia pública was ruled by a strict etiquette.[99] This etiquette determined who could sit and who had to stand up, who could wear a hat and who could not. Lawyers and officials who were not members of the nobility were required to stand up and take off their hats when addressing the magistrates. The places individuals occupied in the chamber also depended on their office and rank. Court recorders were placed before the lawyers, lawyers before the court notaries, and the procurators were at their rear. Some could sit on a chair, while others could only use a bench. A third group had to stand up but could use a table. The litigants either sat down or stood up according to their social circumstances. Nobles, knights of the military orders, and ecclesiastical and secular dignitaries could occupy a preferential place in the area closest to the magistrates, and very often they were allowed to sit down. All other litigants had to stand up behind the procurators. Litigants and officials had to lower their heads before speaking to the magistrates. In some cases, depending on the quality of the person, the magistrates might reciprocate with the same gesture. The magistrates themselves entered the hall according to their office and seniority. They were seated in the same way on a somewhat elevated platform and maintained a

99. Moriana, "Discursos penales"; "Ceremonias y estilo"; and "Práctica de Granada." Also see AHN, Cód., 697B, no. 45.

strict etiquette amongst themselves. They took off their hats when they voted, and they greeted their colleagues by inclining their heads.

Except for attending the audiencia pública, audiencia magistrates also served as *semaneros* and as provincial judges. As semaneros, the magistrates acted as judges on guard. For a week in turn, they received litigants in the afternoon after the official session of the court had terminated. In these sessions, they primarily handled technical decisions meant to ensure the good and rapid administration of justice. Magistrates also took turns acting as provincial judges for terms of three months, meeting litigants three times a week in the afternoons. As provincial judges, the magistrates examined civil cases of first instance originating in the province. The distinction between civil and criminal however was different from what we are familiar with today, depending not on the activity of the offender but on the way the victim wished to proceed. Theft, for example, could be treated as a civil case if the victim was preoccupied with recouping the stolen goods or obtaining a monetary compensation, and not with punishing the thief. Magistrates acting in the provincial court could thus see cases of maltreatment, forgery, disorder, assault, injuries, or theft, all of which we would consider today as criminal cases.[100] The second most important session of the audiencia was the acuerdo. The acuerdo was a plenary meeting behind closed doors and was held two afternoons a week in the presence of all magistrates. It served several purposes: (1) to decide on matters of government and administration, such as opening the correspondence that arrived from Spain, to distribute cases among the judges, to examine the candidacy of notaries, lawyers, and procurators (see chap. 2), and to control the officials of the audiencia; (2) to decide on difficult petitions that originated in the audiencia pública, audiencia de relaciones, the *semanería* (semanero) or the provincial court; and (3) to vote on the verdicts. There were two ways to vote on a verdict: by resolution (*resolución*) or by conference (*conferencia*). Voting by resolution required magistrates to express their opinions as to the guilt or innocence of the accused. Voting by conference, on the contrary, obliged them to justify their opinions. Two votes in agreement, if they constituted a majority, were sufficient to decide the case.

Acuerdos were conducted in a closed session, and their contents were kept in secret by law. Despite clear instructions to take note of the

100. AHQ, Not. 1, 15: exp. 27 February 1727; AHQ, Not. 4, 19: exp. 7 March 1732; and AHQ, Crim., 34: exp. 14 March 1747.

votes of magistrates in a formal yet secret register (*libro del acuerdo*), the judges of Quito never fully complied with this requirement. They only annotated exceptional decisions that were either very important or involved endless debates.[101] In all other cases, they left us with no written record of what had happened during the session. Only the results have survived: the guilt and punishment of the accused or the decision to absolve him or her. This resolution was orally communicated to court recorders, who noted it down and then passed the information to the court notaries. These prepared the corresponding decrees, which were then signed by the magistrates.

Despite its opacity, the division of labor in the audiencia makes it clear that the magistrates' vote in the acuerdo often relied on an elaborated product that a multiplicity of auxiliary agents had created, maybe even invented, before the judges could intervene. In the normal course of activity the allegations, evidence, and declarations were collected by court officials, by a municipal ordinary judge, or by a single magistrate of the audiencia. Although all the magistrates of the court listened to occasional petitions regarding all cases, mainly in the audiencia pública and the semanería, these petitions were mostly procedural. They did not allow the magistrates to become familiar with the cases, nor did they inform them about the allegations or proofs. When cases were finally ready for sentencing, the facts and the proofs were summarized by a court recorder. The court recorder reported the arguments of the parties and analyzed the evidence. This report, which the recorder either handed to the magistrates or read to them, was the first and last opportunity when the magistrates learned the details of the case on which they were about to vote.

This division of labor responded to a theoretical distinction between a preparatory phase called "determination" and the final discussion called "sentencing." Determining (*determinar*) a case consisted of receiving the allegations of the parties and the evidence and verifying whether the allegations were substantiated. This was the work of the auxiliary staff. Sentencing (*sentenciar*) a case involved deciding on the guilt or innocence of the accused and on the punishment that he or she should receive. This was the task of magistrates. The persons who determined the cases were never those who sentenced them. Because sentencing depended on the information supplied, structured, and elab-

101. AHQ, AA, 3 (1684–1717) from 1686.

orated by the auxiliary staff, magistrates had no control over the way truth was translated into legal terms or over how criminals were identified. The information magistrates received necessarily conditioned their understanding of the case to such a degree that it was practically impossible for them to form an independent opinion. Although they pronounced the sentence, their liberty of doing so—once the case was already determined—was limited. The product they discussed in the acuerdo was to a large degree decided before they intervened. Rather than decision makers, magistrates were repositories of an authority, which allowed them to pronounce publicly and give legitimacy to a decision already made by other people.[102]

Contemporary authors recognized this reality. They noted that court recorders "adjusted criminal complaints with the truth and the law in order for the judges to decide them," and they considered court recorders, rather than the judges, to be responsible for the results obtained in the court.[103] Court notaries were "intermediate vehicles, which transmitted to the judge's ears the legal evidence, explanations, acts, the juridical disposition of the cases, and all that was essential in order to sustain, determine, decide, pronounce, and sentence a case."[104] Court notaries also guided the process through its different stages. They controlled its progress, channeled the different actions, indicated the rules, and monopolized all the proceedings until the verdict. This included the writing down of decisions, the interrogation of witnesses, and the preparation of reports. In the words of a contemporary author: "everything is done according to the decision of the notaries, as the judges do not have any other knowledge of the cases or of the suspects than the one the notaries want them to have. As decision makers,

102. J. M. Scholz, "Relatores y magistrados. De la naissance du juge modern au XIX siècle espagnol," in *Les figures historiques de l'administrateur: Institutions, réseaux, pouvoirs en Espagne, en France et au Portugal, 16e–19e siècle,* ed. R. Descimon, J. F. Schaub, and B. Vincent (Paris, 1997), 152–55.

103. Moriana, "Discursos penales," 119; "Memorial sobre el trabajo de relatores del Consejo de Castilla [n.d.]," MS 11.26(7), BN; and Somoza, "La justicia," 16, 113–31.

104. The original version reads: "Vehículos intermedios por donde pasan al oído del juez las pruebas legales, las razones, la confirmación de los hechos, la disposición jurídica de los casos y cuanto constituye el proceso por cuyos méritos se sustancia, determina, falla, pronuncia y sentencia:" "Discurso con una breve idea de los estorbos que en la recta administración de justicia suelen poner los agentes subalternos de los tribunals [attributed to T. González, early 19th c.?]," MSS 20.245(10), 4, BN.

notaries free whom they want, and leave in prison those who do not have sufficient contacts or money."[105]

Notaries were particularly important because they were the official guardians of public memory, both oral and written. They had the right and the duty to issue certificates attesting what had happened in the past. These certificates included not only an enumeration of administrative or judicial decisions but also such diverse things as earthquakes, the state of a building, or a quarrel between two citizens. Testimonies delivered by notaries were considered by definition to be truthful narratives. Notaries were also masters of archives that contained administrative and judicial information, as well as information about testaments, contracts, and all other commercial dealings. These archives were theoretically public, yet they were treated as private property. Officeholders took these archives to their homes and considered them part of their patrimony. Archives had a price and could be bought and sold independently of the notarial office.[106] On occasion, they could justify as much as 20 percent of the price of the office, and offices could change their value according to whether they included some archives, all archives, or even additional archives.[107] The archives themselves were a source of revenue. Parties to penal proceedings who wished to have copies of court records, for example, needed to pay the notary who copied and certified them.[108] It was often the case that, in requesting a copy, the parties established a relationship with the notary, which later guaranteed that they would use him for their other affairs. The papers

105. The original version reads: [las visitas de las carceles] "se hacen al arbitrio de los escribanos, sin tener lo jueces otros conocimientos de las causas ni de los reos que los que los escribanos quieren que tengan, de modo que siendo los árbitros y arbitradores, ponen en libertad al que se les antoja y dejan en la prisión a los que no tienen empeño o dinero." Hipólito de Villaroel, "Enfermedades políticas que padece la capital de esta Nueva España en casi todos los cuerpos de que se compone y remedios que se la deben aplicar para su curación si se quiere que sea útil al rey y al público," cited in T. Lozano Armendares, *La criminalidad en la ciudad de México (1800–1821)* (Mexico, 1987), 68.

106. In 1637 the incoming notary of the provincial court expressed his fear that he would not receive the archives together with the office. In 1655, a colleague of his sold parts of the archives as soon as he obtained control of the office: AHQ, Of., 2: exp. 17 March 1637; and AHQ, Of., 3: exp. 4 March 1655. This practice was prohibited: RI law 17, XVIII, 5.

107. In AGI, Quito, 41, no. 22, the price of the office was 8,000 pesos, to which 2,000 pesos were added if the archives were also purchased. See also AGI, Quito, 43, no. 18; and AGI, Quito, 44, no. 4.

108. AHQ, Of., 1: exp. 11 November 1627.

of the archives also had a commercial value because they could be used to prepare drafts or even to wrap merchandise.

Notarial control over the archives was not only practical, it was also symbolic. In Quito, documents were treated not only as texts but also as objects. Their physical and material possession permitted to control the judicial proceeding. A judge that possessed the records of a trial was also endowed with jurisdiction over the matter. During the legal process, it was more important to have the trial documents than the criminal. The trial could continue in the absence of the accused, but it was completely paralyzed if the file had disappeared. The missing documents could not be replaced by a legal fiction (as happened in the case of absentee suspects) or by the declaration of people who witnessed the trial and knew what had happened. This rule became evident in 1620, when Rodríguez Plaza could not present documents that would demonstrate that he had been convicted and punished for a certain crime.[109] The audiencia refused to hear the testimony of people who had been present in the court or who knew that he had gone to exile. It determined that, unless the documents were produced, Rodriguez Plaza would have to be tried and punished again. Rodriguez Plaza later argued that his misfortune was due to a deliberate act by a notary who disliked him and who either willfully refused to locate the documents or hid them away intentionally.

Because of their control over the archives, notaries were at the very heart of the judicial system. Both the authorities and parties needed their assistance, and both depended on their expertise in the classification, management, and conservation of documents. Expertise was indeed required because controlling archives constantly used by judges, lawyers, and litigants was not a simple task.[110] Notaries had books in which they annotated the identity of people who borrowed the documents (*libros de reconocimiento*). Yet these books were rarely well kept, and the return of documents was rarely inscribed into them. It was often the case that those who borrowed the documents passed them to third parties without the knowledge or consent of the notary. Parties to the proceedings also stole or hid documents, as did the notaries and their auxiliary staff.[111]

109. AGI, EC, legajo 920C.

110. AGI, Quito, 72–74; and the residencias of local governors Francisco de Figueroa and Iñigo de Aranguren y Aguirre: AGI, EC, 910B and 910C.

111. AHQ, Crim., 11: exp. 8 June 1690; AHQ, Of., 13: exp. 18 May 1699, complaint by Ignacio Aybar y Eslava; and AGI, EC, 914B, cuad. 5, 237–51.

The work of notaries, court clerks, court recorders, and procurators was only the tip of the iceberg. By the eighteenth century, Quito's court notaries were no longer the material authors of judicial documents. They delegated this responsibility to their officials and limited their intervention to verifying the contents of documents and signing them.[112] The degree notaries could become dependent on their auxiliary staff was evident at the end of the seventeenth century (1691), during an inspection in the office of Bernardo Espinosa de los Monteros, a provincial notary.[113] The inspector found forty-four types of irregularities in several hundred faulty cases. The documents prepared in this office included illegal abbreviations, and had illegible script. Among other things, this chaos facilitated forgery. The inspector found blank pages with the signature of Espinosa de los Monteros on them. There was evidence that somebody stole such a blank page and used it in order to falsify a document. Responding to these accusations, Espinosa de los Monteros explained that he rarely visited his office. He was simply too busy acting as assistant to the crown attorney. The office was run by his secretary (*oficial mayor*), whom he trusted completely. The work of notaries in Quito, he explained, was divided into two stages.[114] In the first stage, notaries met with the parties and annotated the essence of their wishes or testimony on a simple paper. In the second stage, they proceeded to prepare the formal documents. Because the latter required time, on many occasions the parties and the notary signed blank documents in which their assistants later inserted the required texts. On occasion, assistants had to employ small handwriting or even abbreviations to ensure that the entire narrative would fit into the allocated space between the heading and the signature.

The testimony of Espinosa de los Monteros demonstrates that by the eighteenth century, Quito had notarial offices that existed independently of the officeholder. In many cases the office bore the name of a person who was no longer its owner, was located in the same shop for many generations, and had the same auxiliary staff and archives despite

112. AGI, Quito, 44, no. 11; and AGI, Quito, 43, no. 15, 24.

113. AGI, Quito, 72, 889 and ff.

114. AGI, EC, 910C: residencia of the notaries working during the term of office of local governor Iñigo de Aranguren.

changes in the identity of the notary. Marcos Tofiño was oficial mayor in the office of the court notary under both Alonso Sánchez Maldonado and Lorenzo Bravo. The same thing happened to Jerónimo Cabrera, who worked under Diego Valencia León, Antonio Sánchez Maldonado, and Martín Martínez de Aybar.

Notaries were not the only professionals in Quito who gradually distanced themselves from their original tasks. A division of labor also took place in other offices. Court recorders used assistants who read and summarized the documents and gave the recorders short syntheses of their contents. The recorders used these syntheses to report cases to the magistrates. At the end of the day, the assistants of the subordinates did most of the work. They knew the cases best and were best placed to influence their determination and, hence, their resolution.

The importance of the auxiliary staff and their helpers produced absurd situations in Quito, where magistrates accused this staff for the mistakes that they, the judges, had made.[115] Magistrates asserted that the auxiliary staff was supposed to inform them about these mistakes and, in general, to ensure the correctness of all procedures. Any mistake in the proceedings and any false action was thus the direct or indirect responsibility of notaries and court clerks.[116] But being a notary in Quito was not an easy task. In 1721 Francisco Durango, a public and provincial notary, was prosecuted for "giving testimonies too easily."[117] The accusation was simple: Ignacio de la Escalera, the treasurer of the local church, accused Durango of giving the bishop of Quito, Luis Francisco Romero, a false certificate according to which he, Escalera, had had a love affair with an adulterous woman who was killed by her husband. Apparently, the story was true, but the adulterer was another cleric. Escalera's name was suggested to the notary by the bishop, who was already investigating this cleric with the aim of removing him from office. It was then adopted by a frightened Durango, who could not recall the name of the suspect but who felt obliged to concede to the wishes of the bishop because he placed Durango "under the obligation of the Saint obedience by the virtue of the Holy Spirit." The bishop also

115. C. Dolan, "Entre les familles et l'état: Les procureurs et la procedure au XVIe siècle, " *Journal of the Canadian Historical Association* 10 (1999): 19–36, reveals the existence of similar developments in sixteenth-century France.

116. AHQ, Gob., 4: exp. 1 August 1660: fines levied on Tomás Suárez de Figueroa, Eugenio Farias, Juan de Arce, and Andrés Muñoz de la Concha in 1671 and 1672.

117. AGI, Quito, 131, 425–75; and AGI, Quito, 133, 24.

threatened Durango with excommunication. At the time, Durango could not tell that his declaration was false: seven years had passed since he acted as a clerk in this lawsuit, and the bishop gave him no time to reflect. It was only after he had signed the certificate that he realized his mistake and confessed it to Escalera, who then filed suit against him to the audiencia. Although Durango insisted that the bishop should be censured rather than he, the audiencia and the Council of the Indies disagreed. They found him guilty and suspended him from office. It is therefore not surprising that Diego de Rivera advised his readers in his manual for notaries that it was better to die than to become a notary. Notaries, he said, have one of two options: either they work well and please God or they work badly and please men.[118]

The work of the audiencia was greatly affected by this internal division of labor and the dependence that sprang from it. The responsibility of translating the truth in legal terms—indeed the most important part of the process—was delegated to the auxiliary staff. This delegation was well-known and accepted. Yet, although aware of the practical control that court notaries and recorders had on the development of cases, and although blaming them for their misfortune or thanking them for their success, litigants and judges continued to consider justice as a royal domain, controlled by royal magistrates. Conditioned or unprepared in their decision, knowledgeable or ignorant of the circumstances of the case, royal magistrates were still responsible for ensuring the adoption of just solutions.

The early modern ability to grasp the importance of the auxiliary staff, yet to attribute the result to the judges, was a rational conclusion in a system where the actual process of decision making was less important than the result. At the end of the day, how a decision was reached was less important than the question of whether it was just or not. If a decision was just, then things were functioning as they should. If it was not, then things had to be changed. The roles of the notaries, clerks, and recorders were irrelevant in this respect. Justice and not legality, authority and not decision making, could thus prevail in a system that may falsely appear to us as modern or bureaucratic.

In addition to their judicial activities, the judges of the audiencia were also responsible for performing weekly visits to the prisons of

118. D. Rivera, "Primera parte de escrituras y orden de participación y de residencia judicial, civil y criminal con una instrucción a los escribanos del reino al principio y su arancel [1596]," MS 28.238. 7, BN.

Quito.[119] During these inspections, usually carried out every second Saturday after the audiencia pública was over, the magistrates examined the behavior of the jailers, the legality of arrests, and, in general, the good administration of justice.[120] Visits began with a public session in the presence of all the magistrates, the crown attorney, the notaries, and the procurators. The jailer presented the list of prisoners, the procurators requested their liberty, and the judges decided the cases. Once this stage was over, the visit continued in the prison itself in the presence of one or two magistrates and the jailer. The magistrates inspected the conditions in the prison, as well as interviewed the prisoners to whom they usually recommended that they "use their rights" by presenting petitions according to the normal procedures.[121] During these visits, the magistrates rarely freed prisoners or intervened in order to ensure that they would see a judge.[122] Instead, their most common activity was to pardon criminals who agreed to become soldiers in Chile or Guayaquil or to declare others "notoriously poor" (see the preceding).[123]

Visits to the prisons were highly ceremonial. Governed by a strict etiquette, they were rituals that allowed the judges to demonstrate their jurisdiction and their right to dispense royal justice, especially royal grace. Rather than correcting mistakes, they pardoned criminals and distributed charity. For a present-day observer, these inspections con-

119. This obligation was already mentioned in the *Siete Partidas* (partida 7, title 29, law 8). It was included in ordinance 24 of the *Ordenanzas de la Real Audiencia de Quito* (Quito, 1978), and was also mentioned in a decree of 26 September 1665 in *Anuario histórico jurídico ecuatoriano* 2 (1971): 109. The obligation to visit the prisons was studied in E. Martire, "La visita de cárcel en Buenos Aires durante el virreinato," *Revista Chilena de historia del derecho* 13 (1987): 39–60; B. Bernal Gómez, "Un aspecto más del régimen carcelario novohispano: la visita de cárcel," *Poder y presión fiscal en la América española (siglos XVI, XVII, XVIII): Actas del VI Congreso Internacional del Instituto de Historia del Derecho Indiano* (Valladolid, 1986), 255–79; Lozano Armendares, *La criminalidad,* 167–68; and T. Herzog, "El rescate de una fuente histórica: los libros de visita de cárcel (el caso de Quito, 1738–1750)," *Anuario de Estudios Americanos* 52/2 (1995): 251–61.

120. AHQ, Of., 22: exp. 16 September 1724; and AGI, Quito, 162: certificate of notary Alonso Sánchez Maldonado of 14 August 1704. Records of the inspection visits are also included in special books, called *libros de visita de cárcel,* which can be found in AHQ, Pris., 1: exp. titled visitas de cárcel 1646–49, which covers the period between 10 March 1646 and 3 April 1649; and AHQ, Pris., 2: exp. 24 October 1738 (6 September 1738 to 2 May 1749) and 27 September 1749 (13 September 1749 to 26 May 1759).

121. AHN, Cód., 723B, no.106, 90–91; AHQ, Crim., 14: exp. 24 May 1695; and AHQ, Crim., 32: exp. 7 June 1743.

122. AHQ, Crim., 14: exp. 23 February 1696; AHQ, Crim., 12: exp. 16 November 1691; AHQ, Crim., 14: exp. 16 January 1696; AHQ, Crim., 16: exp. 12 August 1704; AHQ, Crim., 27: exp. 12 December 1732; and AHQ, Crim., 14: exp. 11 January 1697.

123. AHQ, Crim., 4: exp. 30 March 1662; AHQ, Crim., 6: exp. 19 December 1676; AHQ, 4a Not., 26: exp. 10 November 1742; and AHQ, Crim., 12: exp. 16 November 1691.

tain a curious portrayal of the administration of justice in Quito, for they include the most systematic account that we have of imprisonment in the city. They indicate that there were periods of heightened activity in the jail (mainly during the dry season) and periods of relative calm (during the wet months of February, March, and April). Whether this happened because criminal activity or the administration of justice was less frequent during these months, we do not know. We do know that seasons also affected the types of activity most reprimanded by the judges. During some visits to the prison, the presence of many delinquents accused of gambling was recorded. During others, prisoners who owed money to the royal treasury were primarily present.

Some judges sent more people to prison than others. Magistrate José de Quintana y Acevedo, for example, was so prone to this activity that on occasion all of the jail's prisoners had been incarcerated through his orders. Although Quintana y Acevedo continued to send people to prison until 1750, he was most active between 1742 and 1744. Individuals prosecuted by him were mostly thieves and their collaborators. Manuel Rubio de Arévalo was also extremely active, especially in 1739 and 1740. The activities of another magistrate, Pedro Gómez de Andrade, were especially noteworthy in 1748. Overall, the number of prisoners increased between 1739 and 1745 and thereafter slowly descended. The percentage of thieves among prisoners constantly rose.

Jail periods varied dramatically from one case to another. Between 27 September 1738 and 24 September 1740, for example, 120 persons entered the prison. Fifty-four of them were present during only one inspection. This meant that their imprisonment was shorter than 14 days, the time between each visit. One hundred suspects were in prison for three months or less, with an average of 27.5 days. The rest of the suspects spent longer periods in jail.[124] Most of the people belonging to the last group were debtors of the royal treasury who gained freedom only after they paid their debt or arrived at a compromise with the royal officials.

The Municipal Court

The municipal court was charged with maintaining peace inside the city of Quito as well as in the villages within its jurisdiction (the five sur-

124. The exact numbers are ten delinquents (8 percent) were in jail between 100 and 200 days, five (4 percent) between 200 and 300, three (2.4 percent) between 300 and 400, and only two (1.06 percent) between 500 and 550.

rounding leagues). Its justices were expected to be present on the main square (*plaza mayor*) and to guarantee harmony among the inhabitants by patrolling the streets, ensuring the public order, and serving as judges in criminal and civil litigation.[125] The municipal court included the local governor, his lieutenant, and two municipally elected ordinary justices. Although composed of various justices, each theoretically with a different sphere of activity, the court functioned as a pool of authorized judges. No true distinction was made between one judge and another, and the division of labor between them was random. This division depended on who was present and when and where. Once a judge began reviewing a case, he won jurisdiction over it. All other judges were prohibited from intervening unless the presiding judge asked them to do so. Inside the municipal court, cases were transferred from one judge to another on account of sickness, workload, or absence from Quito. Transferred cases continued as if nothing had happened. No explanation was given for the change. One judge simply signed one decision, and another the next.[126]

Proceedings in the municipal court were very similar to those in the audiencia. The parties presented their petitions through procurators, lawyers, or court notaries who were also charged with receiving the evidence and preparing decrees previewed by the judges. By the last quarter of the seventeenth century, most judges (who were usually not trained in law) employed judicial experts (*asesores letrados*) to advise them how to proceed.[127] By the eighteenth century, the employment of experts became such an accepted practice that parties to the proceedings could claim it as their right. By that time, judges were required to hear council even in the absence of readily available experts. Advice became public, and relying on secret council was classified as improper and undignified.[128]

The opinions of legal experts were usually required once the cases were ready for "determination." Like court recorders in the audiencia, legal experts summarized the allegations and discussed the proofs sup-

125. AGI, EC, 915A, cuad. l, 132.

126. AHQ, Crim., 22: exp. 26 February 1726; and AHQ, Crim., 29: exp. 12 October 1737.

127. J. M. Mariluz Urquijo, "El asesor letrado del virreinato del Río de la Plata," *Revista de historia del derecho* 3 (1975): 165–228.

128. AHQ, Crim., 14: exp. 24 May 1695; and AHQ, Not. 1, 15: exp. 27 February 1727. Also see declaration of Francisco Ante y Mendoza in the residencia of Sanchez de Orellana AGI, EC, 911C, 164.

porting them. Yet, unlike court recorders, experts also intervened in the last phase of the process: the sentencing. They ruled whether to absolve or to condemn suspects, and they identified the proper punishment. Legal experts also gave their opinions concerning the imprisonment of suspects and the use of torture. In all of these cases, the experts indicated to the judges what the legal problems were and how they could be resolved.[129] When crimes were considered especially serious or important, experts also served as cojudges and followed the cases from their inception.[130] Judges who did not agree with the experts' opinions could solicit the council of other jurists, but they could not simply ignore the received advice. The capacity of judges to moderate or stiffen the punishment was also restricted.[131]

Because of the obligation to use legal experts, the intervention of municipal judges in sentencing became even more limited than that of audiencia magistrates. By the eighteenth century, municipal penal cases were practically decided by lawyers who did not belong to the royal administration—instead, they were simply nominated on an ad hoc basis by local judges to serve in specific cases as experts.

The Santa Hermandad

Like the audiencia and the municipal court, the Santa Hermandad was also an institution with both policing and judicial powers.[132] It was charged with pursuing, imprisoning, and punishing criminals who committed crimes on roads and in uninhabited areas. Its officials patrolled the countryside in the company of armed groups (*cuadrilleros*) that they recruited and paid. They attended to all needs and were responsible for peacekeeping in the province in the same way municipal judges were responsible for peacekeeping in the city and its villages. Judges of the

129. AHQ, Crim., 20: exp. 8 September 1717.

130. AHQ, Crim., 6: exp. 4 March 1678; and AHQ, Crim., 22: exp. 23 December 1725.

131. AHQ, Crim., 23: exp. 11 November 1726; and AHQ, Not. 6, 15: exp. 13 February 1745 from 14 April 1745.

132. C. M. MacLachlan, *Criminal Justice in Eighteenth-Century Mexico: A Study of the Tribunal of the Acordada* (Berkeley, 1974); and F. Casado Fernández, "El tribunal de la Acordada de Nueva España," *Anuario de estudios americanos* 7 (1950): 279–323. The Castilian antecedent is studied in T. Eugenios Martín, *La santa hermandad vieja de Talavera: Una institución tradicional de vigilancia y justicia en despoblado* (Toledo, 1992); and A. Guillaume Alonso, *Una institución del antiguo régimen: la santa hermandad vieja de Talavera la Reina (siglos XVI y XVII)* (Talavera, 1995).

Santa Hermandad acted mainly against cattle rustlers and in cases of highway robbery. On occasion, they were also charged with reviewing other penal cases, mainly as delegates of the local governors who appointed them as their judicial deputies.

Theoretically, the Santa Hermandad included two justices and a provincial (*provincial*). However, Quito's judicial records demonstrate that only on rare occasions did the provincial take part in the activities of the court. Instead (by the eighteenth century at least) the provincial was an honorary post. It allowed those holding the office to consider themselves judges, and it gave them a vote in the municipal council. But it involved no actual judicial work.[133] Compared with other institutions in Quito, the Santa Hermandad was the least formal of them all. The judges continuously moved around the countryside and they carried out summary legal proceedings without the aid of experts, judicial officers, procurators, notaries, or clerks.

Coordination and Competition

Within the municipal court, cases begun by one judge could be continued by another without causing major interruption. Collaboration between the local governor, his lieutenant, and the municipal ordinary justices was the norm. Most judges recognized the competence of their peers by refusing to take on matters that were already handled by another judge.[134] The audiencia frequently asked the ordinary judges for help. It sent them to verify the information supplied by the parties or requested them to receive proofs in cases pending before the royal court.[135] On their own initiative and without having any legal obligation, municipal judges (both ordinary judges and the local governor) frequently informed the audiencia about the cases pending before them, welcoming its intervention.[136] Orders to change decisions already made—mainly following petitions or appeals by the interested parties—were followed through, as were administrative decrees that summoned

133. AHN, Cód., 757B, no. 3 from 1767.

134. AHQ, Crim., 24: exp. 10 October 1728; and AHQ, Not., 15: exp. 13 February 1728 from 18 December 1745.

135. AHQ, Crim., 4: exp. 2 April 1659; and AHQ, Crim., 30: exp. 13 July 1740.

136. AHQ, Crim., 25: exp. 3 May 1730; and AHQ, Crim., 31: exp. 18 November 1741.

judicial officials, advised them of their duties, instructed them how to execute those duties, or disapproved of their method of work.[137]

Conflicts were the exception and not the rule. Rather than corresponding to true jurisdictional trespasses, on most occasions they were motivated by personal rivalries and were linked to considerations of honor and reputation. Most conflicts occurred when the authority that was audited, or the authority that had exercised control, felt offended or attacked. On these occasions, the legality of the action taken by the judge or against him was not at stake. What mattered was the question of whether or not this action threatened the judge's public image. In 1745, the municipal ordinary justice Juan Ibarguren sought the protection of the audiencia against magistrate José de Quintana y Acevedo. He accused Quintana y Acevedo—who on three different occasions had reversed his decisions—of working against his honor and of limiting de facto his jurisdiction.[138] According to Ibarguren, this massive intervention in his activities as a judge threatened his "representation" as well as the image of all other municipal justices. Quintana y Acevedo claimed his innocence. He explained that the decisions he reversed were incorrect and stated that he had no interest in increasing his workload. He lamented the need to intervene so massively in the work of Ibarguren but attributed it to the fact that Ibarguren sentenced people without obtaining legal advice as other municipal judges did before him. Given this background, it was not surprising that witnesses in Quito applauded President Dionisio Alcedo y Herrera for not having intervened in the work of other judges by modifying their sentences.[139] Ignoring the question of whether or not the cases merited modification, the witnesses agreed that this nonintervention manifested the president's respect of the other judges, which was crucial for the good administration of justice.

Some ministers of the audiencia, for example, Francisco Lōpez Dicastillo y Azcona, Juan de Sosaya, Juan Larrea Zurbano (the elder), and Tomás Fernández Pérez de Hodo, were known for "not leaving the municipal judges in liberty." What was most lamented was the harm inflicted on the public image of the judges and their consequent loss of

137. AHQ, Gob., 4 and 7: exp. 1 August 1660 and exp. 13 August 1723; AHQ, Not. 1, 13: exp. 23 December 1723; and AHQ, Crim., 33: exp. 12 June 1745.

138. AHQ, Gob., 14: exp. 23 September 1745.

139. AGI, EC, 911B, 122.

standing. Some judges bitterly resented not the intervention but the way in which a superior chose to express his disapproval. The more public the disapproval was, the more painful. Bitterness could degenerate into open confrontation.[140] In 1736, the local governor of Quito and the ordinary judge disagreed about the imprisonment of the senior alderman of the city (*regidor decano*).[141] The former rejected the intervention of the latter and interpreted the judge's gesture in favor of the councilman as a rebuff of his authority. The local governor thus proceeded to imprison and punish the judge. The town council's efforts to pacify both parties failed, and the freeing of the senior alderman and the judge was guaranteed only after the audiencia intervened. The intervention, however, only solved the matter legally. The case would finally come to rest only after the judge's honor was also redeemed. After much effort, the members of the town council convinced the local governor that he needed to apologize. In the presence of many people on the main square, the local governor embraced the senior alderman and the judge, called them "my friends," and asked for their forgiveness. It was only after this ceremony was over that the jurisdictional conflict was truly resolved.

Conclusion

The penal courts of Quito used sophisticated mechanisms to transform crimes into criminals. This transformation involved the implementation of a complex penal procedure and the work of a great number of people. Procedural requirements and the division of labor in the courts restricted the freedom of judges, who were literally told how to proceed and who were given the right to sentence an elaborate collaborative product largely decided by their auxiliary staff. Judges were also restricted by what victims and their families wanted. Victims and their families chose whether to prosecute the crime or not and whether to ask for a civil or a criminal redress. They even chose the identity of the judge giving him jurisdiction over the matter.

In the late seventeenth and eighteenth centuries, the assistants of the subordinates were those most able to exert influence on the determina-

140. AHQ, Crim., 31: exp. 13 April 1742.
141. AMQ, LC, 00125: town council meeting from 7 August 1736.

tion of penal cases. Yet litigants and judges insisted that decision making was at the hands of royal delegates and thus the king. Some audiencia ministers were nonjurists and the municipal court, whose judges theoretically had no legal preparation, adopted legal decisions dictated by judicial experts. Conflicts between judges although focused on jurisdiction, were truly centered on questions of public image and honor. As long as things "looked good," everybody seemed content.

This description may lead to the conclusion that in Quito image was preferred to reality. Yet, such an interpretation would fail to account for the distinct logic of an early modern judicial system. Although judges were limited in what they could decide, and although their preparation varied contemporaries who were aware of these conflicts nevertheless believed that the judges were those making the decisions and that image corresponded to reality. Judges made the decisions because it was their duty to administer justice. Justice could never be instituted only or mainly by way of formal procedures, and it required no legal preparation. Formal procedures and legal input could help with the determination of what was just, yet at the end of the day *neither* guaranteed justice. What guaranteed justice were the judges: their persons, their abilities, and their loyalty to the king. This is why selecting the right people for office was so essential, as the next chapter demonstrates.

CHAPTER TWO

Officers of the Law

The people involved in the administration of justice in Quito were appointed by diverse authorities in a variety of ways and held terms for different lengths of time. Some officials were chosen by the king on the advice of the Council of the Indies. Others were selected by him because they were willing to pay the royal treasury substantial sums of money. The city council elected the municipal judges, both ordinary and those of the Santa Hermandad. Members of the auxiliary staff had to pass an exam and then locally purchase the right to exercise their offices. Despite this diversity, all persons who formed part of the justice administration fashioned themselves as delegates of the king. Whether this delegation was direct or indirect, limited or unlimited in scope and time, they all understood that it was ultimately the monarch who commissioned them to execute justice.

Appointment by the King

There were several channels through which individuals could become magistrates of the audiencia or local governors. Until 1682, naming happened by way of a regular appointment, also called a *consulta.* After 1682, some ministers were still appointed in this way, while others purchased their office. Appointment by consulta depended on the recommendation of the Council of the Indies, which was given at the end of a long process. When an office became available because of death or promotion of the previous holder, the council sent its administrative staff to the archives where hundreds of memos (including information about possible candidates) were stored. These memos, called *relaciones de mérito,* were sent by the candidates or by their agents in the court. They described the personal, familial, and professional qualities of each individual and they often included supporting documents or the signature of a notary or clerk attesting that the information supplied in them was correct. Each council member, or each member of the standing committee (*cámara*)—when such a committee existed—chose three candidates and presented their names and qualifications to the council.[1] Although members could present any person as a candidate, councilors were advised to prefer individuals who requested their nomination and who sent memos describing their qualities to the council.[2] The council then collected additional information and requested secret memoranda or oral reports on the candidates—their persons, their families, and their preparation.[3]

When the council finally met to vote, each councilor presented his list. The candidates of the council were then chosen by an open and majority vote.[4] On most occasions, the council proposed three candidates to the king, which it ranked in descending order of recommendation. The clerks prepared a written report (consulta), which included the names of candidates, the council's preference, and (usually) a short description of their qualifications, such as "lawyer of the royal councils," "chancellor of a university," "nephew of such and such person," "promised an office and has not received one yet," and so forth. In most cases, the king selected the candidate most recommended by the council.

The selection process considered the preparation of candidates, the services they had rendered to the monarch, and their family background.[5] This mixture of elements was not an aberration of the system but a constitutive and important part of it. Offices were granted by royal favor (*merced*) to people who deserved them. The council selected and preferred candidates who were loyal to the king and served him well. Loyalty and service could be personal, or they could be inherited.

1. The *Cámara de Indias,* which functioned in 1650–64, 1701–16, and 1717–21, was the body charged with naming people to offices in the Americas.

2. AHN, Cód., 752B, nos. 1180 and 1398 (from 1622 and 1660, respectively).

3. "Discurso sobre que los buenos ministros han de ser buscados y escogidos por más dignos que otros (1644)," MS 2848, fols. 1–26, BPR; and R. Konetzke, *Colección de documentos para la historia de la formación social de Hispanoamérica, 1493–1810* (Madrid, 1953), 2: 630–36: recommendation (*consulta*) of 1676. In 1747 the president of the council informally spoke with several people who knew the candidate in order to verify his suitability for office: AGI, Quito, 224.

4. The practice of secret voting disappeared at the beginning of the seventeenth century. AHN, Cód., 752B, no. 1413 from 1601.

5. R. Roldán Verdejo, *Los jueces,* 41–107.

The loyalty and service of parents or grandparents, for example, were relevant to measuring the obligation that the king had toward a specific candidate. Personal qualifications and proper preparation could also render a person worthy of office. Yet this worthiness was not judged solely from a professional point of view. A good preparation constituted a sign and a promise. It indicated the intention of candidates to serve the king well, and it was this intention, and not the qualifications alone, that made these candidates worthy of office. The same was true in the case of candidates previously employed in royal service. These candidates could be preferred to others because they had already served the king and were prone to do so again. Indeed, the exchange between a loyal servant and a grateful king mattered most in the appointment of magistrates and local governors.

Because past services were important, magistrates could be promoted from one office to the other. In Quito, for example, most presidents, magistrates, crown attorneys, and protectors of Indians were lawyers who worked in one of the royal courts or councils. They usually held a bachelor degree in both canon and civil law, earned at Bologna, Salamanca, Alcalá, Santa Fe de Bogotá, Lima, or Quito.[6] These people were first nominated as protectors of Indians, although some of them were able to gain direct nomination as magistrates. Protectors of Indians became crown attorneys, crown attorneys became magistrates, and magistrates became presidents. Presidents could be sent to another court, promoted to the royal councils in Madrid, or appointed judges of a peninsular chancellery.[7] This promotion pattern was fairly standard, yet individual careers were rarely limited to a single institution or location. It was common, for example, that crown attorneys would be promoted to magistrates in another audiencia, usually of lesser importance. They could then become magistrates in a more important court before being named presidents. Justices of Lima were thus sent as presidents to Quito, and magistrates from Quito continued in their office in the courts in Charcas, Santa Fe, or Lima.

Professional merit and promotion patterns were only part of a larger

6. Among the twelve presidents three had no degree in law, and four studied in Salamanca, two in Quito, and the rest in Bologna or Alcalá. Among magistrates, fourteen obtained their degrees in Lima, eight in Salamanca, three in Alcalá, two in Quito, and the rest in another American or peninsular university. Only eight members of this group held doctorates.

7. Pre-1706 presidents returned to Lima as magistrates (two cases) or earned a promotion to the Council of the Indies (three cases). One president died in Quito without being promoted, and another was promoted to the audiencia of Charcas.

story. Candidates who came from families with a long tradition in royal service were best placed in order to obtain office. There were several reasons why this could happen. First, the families of these individuals had served the king well and therefore merited rewards. Second, because of their contacts with the king and his immediate entourage, members of these families were more likely to be successful in obtaining support for their candidates. The ability to activate social contacts and to establish a relationship either with the councilors of the Council of the Indies or with other influential members of the court was extremely helpful. Candidates had to convince these people that they merited reward, that they were worthy of trust, and that they would be helpful to them in the future. They could do so themselves, or they could draw on the support of their relatives or patrons or even contract the aid of agents already working in the court and familiar with its functioning. Many candidates came to Madrid in order to oversee the process.[8] They spent time and energy in the quest for personal relationships, and they expected certain people to support them because they were tied to them through family networks or through networks of service and patronage. Many such networks predated the quest for office; others were constructed, or reactivated, in order to obtain office. Residence at the court also allowed candidates to obtain precious information about which offices were available where, who was responsible for allocating them, and which strategy would best guarantee success.

Royal allocation of offices thus depended on social and family relations. People who wanted to enter the administration had to insert themselves first in the right social or family milieu and only then seek nomination. This mechanism could lead to a social closure, allowing only a few families (and their friends) to control all offices. Nevertheless, in most cases it led to the consolidation of new alliances. "Old" families constantly recruited new members by intermarrying with them, by collaborating with them, or by calling distant relatives to the court. Through this method, new people were admitted into the administration, although this admission was first social and familial and only later professional.[9] This path for integration guaranteed that those eventually chosen for office would be selected not only because of their indi-

8. "Discurso sobre."

9. J. M. García Marín, *La burocracia castellana bajo los Austrias* (Seville, 1976), 191–206. The relationship between merit justifying royal grace and personal relations was also explored in J. M. Smith, "No More Language Games: Words, Beliefs and the Political Culture in Early Modern France," *American Historical Review* 102/5 (1997): 1435–36.

vidual qualifications—rather, officials were chosen because they were part of a wide-reaching social web. This web connected royal servants to each other, and at the same time it linked them to other important individuals, including the king.[10]

Between 1650 and 1750 twelve presidents, forty-two magistrates, sixteen crown attorneys, and five protectors of Indians held office in Quito.[11] Some of these officers descended from families whose members occupied very distinguished posts, while others were sons and grandsons of simple officers who nevertheless were able to gain the support of some important men. Service that merited compensation and justified nomination or promotion could be won in different ways—depending on whether one was in Spain, in the Americas, or in any other part of the Spanish empire. Most Peninsulars appointed to offices came from families employed in royal service, either in the military or the administration. American-born magistrates (who were present in Quito throughout the seventeenth century but were especially important in the eighteenth) typically descended either from conquistador or encomendero families or from a father already employed in an American audiencia.[12] Once integrated into the sphere of royal service, most nominees (and their families) remained in it. They married inside their group of royal servants, or they chose a partner belonging to the nobility or to families residing at the court. Their children frequently followed their footsteps: daughters married magistrates, and sons took on administrative or legal careers.

While family, social relations, and services rendered were important, economic means seemed much less crucial. Money could perhaps buy friends and relatives and it could perhaps be used to convince the councilors to support a certain candidate. However, among successful nominees were both rich and poor individuals. Wealth was more common

10. AHN, Cód., 705B, 689B, 695B, and 659B, nos. 54, 199, 34, and 35 from 1632, 1643, 1750, and 1747, respectively; and "Discurso sobre."

11. These numbers include numeraries, supernumeraries, and judges from other audiencias who were in Quito on a temporal basis. They exclude temporary officeholders. The numbers of presidents, crown attorneys, and protectors of Indians are reduced because (1) these were offices held by a single person and not by a group of people, as was the case with magistrates, and (2) these offices were often vacant and were exercised by temporary officers. The description that follows is primarily based on the study of relaciones de mérito, consultas of the council regarding nomination, nomination decrees, and information proceeding from the "Notaría," "Testamentaría," and "Matrimoniales," sections of the AHQ.

12. Twelve magistrates were born in the Iberian Peninsula, and twenty-one in the Americas. I have not been able to identify the birthplace of the other nine oidores.

among American-born ministers who often had to manage their appointment from afar. Poverty was more typical of those born in Spain.

The combination of all these factors produced a very diversified judicial world. The following pages present a number of brief biographies of Quito's officeholders. Their cumulative portraits (and chap. 3) give a sense of the social, spatial, personal, and political networks in which officeholders were bound. Consider, for example, the personal and political connections of Juan del Campo Godoy. Campo Godoy served as a magistrate in Quito between 1648 and 1653. Having studied and taught law in Lima, he became a lawyer and served in Lima as protector of the Indians for twenty-five years. Named magistrate of Quito when he was fifty-seven years old, he was promoted to the audiencia of Charcas in 1651, where he died. Campo Godoy was a native of Chile and was descended from conquistador families on both sides. His father, Francisco Campo y Gómez, was native of La Rioja (Spain), a colonel in Chile, and an encomendero. His mother, Isabel Rosa de Godoy, was a native of Chile and an encomendera. Himself the owner of an encomienda, Juan del Campo Godoy enjoyed a very comfortable economic situation. He married María de Larrinaga Salazar, a native of Lima whose father, Doctor Leandro Larrinaga, also descended from conquistadores. Larrinaga was a native of Chile and a member of the town council of Lima. María had several brothers. One of them, Juan, was a knight of the military order of Santiago. Another brother, Luis, was *calificador* (expert on theological issues) of the local inquisition.[13]

Or consider the very similar biography of Antonio Díez de San Miguel Solier. Díez de San Miguel Solier was a lawyer of the inquisition in Lima when he was named first crown attorney (1647) and later magistrate in Quito (1658). He was promoted to the audiencia of Charcas in 1660, where he later died. Díez de San Miguel Solier was a native of Lima and the son of conquistadores on both sides of the family. His father, Juan Díez de San Miguel was a native of Huamanga (Perú) and an encomendero. His mother, María Padilla de la Vega, was a native of

13. AGI, EC, 910A; G. Lohmann Villena, *Los americanos en las órdenes nobiliarias (1529–1900)*, (Madrid, 1947), 1: 74–76; M. A. Burkholder and D. S. Chandler, *Biographical Dictionary of Audiencia Ministers in the Americas, 1687–1821* (Westpoint, CT, 1982), 68; A. Tauro, *Diccionario enciclopédico del Perú, ilustrado* (Lima, 1966), 1: 259; M. Mendiburu, *Diccionario histórico biográfico del Perú* (Lima, 1931), 3: 235; and A. San Cristóbal, *Apéndice al diccionario histórico biográfico del Perú* (Lima, 1935), 1: 286.

Lima. He married Mariana (Josefa) de Bermúdez y de la Torre, a native of Lima. Her father was a member of the local town council. Their first-born son, Juan Francisco, married the daughter of the magistrate Luis Losada Quiñones in 1658. At that time, Juan Francisco was twenty years old, a knight of the military order of Santiago, and chief accountant of the Court of Accounts (*Tribunal de Cuentas*) in Lima.[14]

Antonio Lope de Munive y Axpe, who served as Quito's president from 1678 and 1689, had studied in Salamanca between 1661 and 1663, where he obtained a chair in Roman law (*cátedra de Código*).[15] Having earned a degree in both canon and civil law, he was nominated as a magistrate in Lima in 1665. Munive y Axpe remained in that city until 1677, where he acted in intervals as the governor of Huancavelica (a mining town) and as an investigating judge (*visitador general*) in Chile. After serving over a decade as the president of Quito, he was promoted to "one of the Castilian chanceries" but died on his way to Spain. Munive y Axpe was a native of Vizcaya (Spain), a knight of the military order of Alcántara, and marquis of Valdelirios. His father, Martín Munive, was a knight of the military order of Santiago, count of Peñaflorida, and lord of Molar and Vellón; he had also served as a soldier in France. Munive y Axpe's paternal grandfather—who was a magistrate in the chancery of Granada—died after being nominated as a counselor at the court. His paternal great-grandfather, a knight of Santiago, was a member of the Council of War, secretary of state and war of the Spanish heir to the throne, and occasional ambassador in Flanders, Turin, and England. On his mother's side, Munive y Axpe was the grandson of Andrés Axpe, knight of the military order of Santiago and an American magistrate who died while serving in the audiencia of Charcas. Andrés Axpe's brother was a councilman in the Council of Castile. In 1671, Munive y Axpe married Leonor María de León Garavito y Mexia, a native of La Plata. León Garavito y Mexia was the daughter of Andrés Garavito de León, a magistrate in Charcas, a native of Lima, and a knight of Santiago. Her mother, Constanza María

14. AGI, Lima, 201, no. 4; AGI, EC, 924B; AMQ, LC, 00011: town council meeting of 3 January 1657; and AGI, Quito, 2: consulta of 20 August 1653; AGI, Quito, 3: consulta of 30 July 1660; Lohmann Villena, *Los americanos,* 1: 135–36; and Tauro, *Diccionario,* 1: 486.

15. AGI, Quito, 3: decree of 27 April 1676; AGI, Quito, 4: consulta of 7 May 1686; AGI, Quito, 5: decree of 22 March 1686; AGI, Quito, 34A, and Quito, 72–74; AGI, Quito, 43A; AGI, Quito, 106; AGI, Quito, 2: consultas of 1 July 1656 and 28 March 1664; G. Lohmann Villena, *Los ministros de la Audiencia de Lima (1700–1821)* (Seville, 1974), 182–83 and 271–72; and Mendiburu, *Diccionario,* 7: 383–84 and 8: 43–44.

Mexia, was a native of Lima and a sister of magistrate Diego Cristóbal Mexia. Diego Cristóbal Mexia had obtained his office in Quito in 1656 after he married the niece of the marquis del Prado, who was a lady of company of the wife of the count-Duke of Olivares, the private (*privado*) of King Philip IV. Curiously, Diego Cristóbal Mexia's case was the only occasion between 1650 and 1682 in which the king departed from the regular method of nomination—the king granted the office to Diego Cristóbal Mexia as a donation to the dowry of his spouse.[16] On that occasion, the Council of the Indies protested, arguing that only services and personal qualifications of candidates and their families should matter and not the identity of their wives. This protest went unheard—not only was Diego Cristóbal Mexia appointed to office but he was even promoted to the audiencia of Lima, where he died. Diego Cristóbal Mexia's son soon became count of Sierra Bella, and his grandson, Diego Messia y Torres, married his cousin Ana Munive y Tello. Her brother, Gaspar Munive y Tello, was the local governor of Huanta y Cañete (Perú), marquis of Valdelirios, and councilor of the Council of the Indies and of the Council of State. Ana Munive y Tello also had a sister, Leonor, who married Gregorio de Vega, marquis of Feria.

The king authorized the marriage between Munive y Axpe and Leonor María de León Garavito y Mexia by giving Leonor, in exchange for 4,000 pesos, permission to marry any of the magistrates of Lima.[17] The marriage would have otherwise been illegal because royal instructions ordered that magistrates could not marry women residents in the jurisdiction. León Garavito y Mexia brought a dowry of 78,080 pesos to the marriage, of which 51,000 pesos was paid in cash.[18] The couple had five sons and one daughter, and Munive y Axpe had at least three other illegitimate children. One of his sons became a knight of the military order of Alcántara, while the other inherited the title of marquis from his father. Munive's sons and grandsons followed in his footsteps. Several of them were counselors of the Councils of the Indies, War, and Castile, while others became magistrates in Lima. Munive y Axpe was reputed to be excessively wealthy. Part of this money was his own, and part belonged to his wife. Yet it is clear that his fortune increased during his term in Quito. Apparently, he did well economically because of his involvement in commerce, textile production, and money lending,

16. AGI, Quito, 2: consulta from 1 July 1656.
17. AGI, Quito, 73, 95–96.
18. AGI, Quito, 73, 94–95. See also AGI, Quito, 73, 92–103.

all of which were theoretically prohibited to him by virtue of his office. Among those indebted to Munive y Axpe were his colleagues in the audiencia and other "principal people." The total value of the loans amounted to at least 105,000 pesos. Despite having lost a great deal of money and goods in a shipwreck, upon his death Munive y Axpe still possessed a fortune worth more than 230,000 pesos.[19] Some of the furniture and jewelry he owned were so valuable that they could not be sold in the local market. His library, which contained 1,229 volumes, was sold in parts to the local crown attorney and magistrates.

Tomás Fernández Pérez de Hodo, a native of Lima, was named magistrate of Quito in 1696 after studying in Lima and serving there as a lawyer. He resided in the city until 1718. In 1722 and 1723 he was named first crown attorney of the audiencia of Mexico and then dean of the cathedral of Cuzco.[20] Although the son of Bartolomé Fernández and Isabel Fernández de Vargas, who were "noble Spaniards," Fernández Pérez de Hodo was reputedly poor. He supported his mother and brothers with his salary as a magistrate and on occasions he testified to being unable to pay for his personal expenses.

Manuel Rubio de Arévalo was named magistrate of Quito in 1720, exercising this office until 1748 and again from 1757 to 1565.[21] Between 1743 and 1745 he was named *visitador* (controller), being charged with reviewing the activities of President José de Araujo y Río and presiding over the audiencia. As the most senior magistrate, he again became temporary president of Quito in 1761. Rubio de Arévalo was a native of Seville. He was a doctor in canon and civil law and first worked as a lawyer in the royal councils of Madrid and Seville. In 1716, he became local governor of Albarracín (province of Teruel, Spain). Rubio de Arévalo had a comfortable economic situation. He owned several ranches north of Quito as well as some land in the city. He married Juana Mancheno y Ayala, who was born in Spain to a family from a similar background. The couple had six children. One of them, Benito, studied

19. AHQ, Test., 21: exp. 21 May 1689.

20. AGI, IG, 134; AGI, Quito, 4: consulta of 16 January 1699; AGI, Quito, 130 and 162; and AHQ, AA, 3; Burkholder and Chandler, *Biographical Dictionary,* 118; and M. A. Burkholder and D. S. Chandler, *De la impotencia a la autoridad. La corona española y las audiencias en América, 1687–1808* (Mexico, 1977), 242.

21. AGI, EC, 914A–916C; AGI, Quito, 104: decree of 7 May 1736; AGI, Quito, 133: letter of 6 June 1738; AGI, Quito, 103, 124, and 135; AHQ, Not.[3], 20: exp. 2 October 1737; Burkholder and Chandler, *Biographical Dictionary,* 302; and Burkholder and Chandler, *De la impotencia,* 252 and 416.

philosophy in Quito and was a small-scale merchant who used his father's house as a store. His daughter Teresa married Matías de Santa Cruz, a rich local merchant.

Presidents, magistrates, crown attorneys, and protectors of Indians came from a variety of backgrounds. In contrast were the very similar biographies of most local governors. Appointed by the king, many of them were soldiers, or sons of soldiers, who gained their reputation in wars fought in Europe. They were usually Spanish and frequently had no previous experience in government or judicial functions. A typical case was that of Iñigo Aranguren y Aguirre, who exercised his office in Quito between 1676 and 1681. A native of Spain, and a knight of the military order of Santiago, Aranguren y Aguirre served as a soldier, standard-bearer (*alférez*), master of the field (*maestro de campo*), and infantry captain in the navy, both in Catalonia and Extremadura.[22] While working in Quito, he also acted as temporary treasurer of the royal treasury. Having completed his term of office, he became local governor of Chimbo, an area in the south of the province of Quito.

The Sale of Judicial Offices by the King

In 1682, the king began alternating regular appointments of presidents, magistrates, crown attorneys, protectors of Indians, and local governors with the selling of offices. The sale of judicial offices, also called *beneficio,* allowed candidates to purchase the right to exercise an office for a limited period. Contrary to other sales (see the following), candidates who bought these offices did not acquire ownership over them. They were not allowed to resell the offices or renounce them, as other office purchasers could, and they received nothing of the offices' value once their terms had concluded. This uniqueness was explained by the fact that beneficio involved the sale of judicial offices. These offices had to remain in royal hands because the king could delegate, but not abdicate, his duty to distribute justice. Contrary to other purchases, beneficio could also include a transaction concerning something that was as yet nonexistent: some people purchased the right to exercise an

22. AGI, Quito, 3: cédula of 28 November 1674; AHQ, RH, 42, libro 1677, 18; AGI, IG, 116: relación de méritos; and AGI, EC, 910C: his residencia.

office that was already vacant, while others bought the right to exercise this office when it would become available in the future (*futura*).[23]

The first judicial office sold in Quito, in 1682, was that of local governor. From this date until 1744, fourteen people purchased the office or the right to exercise the office in the future. Only two obtained it by way of a regular grant. Purchases were usually complex economic transactions. They were concluded after long negotiations, in which price and payment terms, as well as the rights and duties of the purchaser, were fixed.[24] In the case of local governors, most purchases were limited to a five-year term, and prices varied between 5,000 and 6,250 *pesos de-a-ocho*. In Quito, at least three of the purchases never materialized, either because the candidates failed to pay for the office or because they were unable to exercise it for different reasons. Two other purchasers (Antonio Bernaldo de Quiros and José Echavarri, marquis of Salinas) were allowed by the special terms of their purchase (which was especially expansive) to resell the office, which they did, choosing freely among candidates who reimbursed them what they had paid.

The sale of judicial offices allowed members of the local elite to gain access to the office of local governor, which beforehand was mainly granted to people born in Spain. For example, the various members of the Sánchez de Orellana clan, who were economically powerful natives of Quito, were governors on several occasions between 1735 and 1743 (see the following). In 1745, this office was purchased by another local elite, Ramón Juachin Maldonado y Sotomayor, who held the governorship until his death in 1748. Maldonado y Sotomayor was a native of Ríobamba (south of Quito), citizen (*vecino*) of Latacunga (south of Quito), and marquis of Lises. He served as a captain and general of the infantry of Quito, captain of the cavalry of Ríobamba, and captain of the guard of the viceroy of Lima.[25] He first exercised the office of local governor of Latacunga between 1729 and 1731 and then became a perpetual alderman in Quito in 1739. In this capacity, he acted occasionally as a representative of local interests (*procurador*), as a commercial

23. A. Moreno Cebrián, "Venta y beneficios de los corregidores peruanos," *Revista de Indias* 36/143–44 (1976): 213–46; and F. Muro Romero, "El beneficio de oficios públicos con jurisdicción en Indias. Notas sobre sus orígenes," *Anuario de estudios americanos* 35 (1978): 1–67.

24. AGI, Quito, 4: consulta from 16 November 1695.

25. AGI, Quito, 106: decree of 15 July 1744; AHQ, Resid., 6: exp. 25 October 1731 and 18 January 1733; AHQ, Not.[3], 37: exp. 15 February 1756; AGI, Quito, 125; AGI, EC, 914C, cuad. 14, 100; and AHQ, Not.[1], 30: exp. 14 February 1748.

judge and deputy (*diputado del comercio*), and as a municipal ordinary justice. Maldonado y Sotomayor was extremely wealthy. In the 1740s, he was considered one of the twenty-three richest people in the city of Quito. He was a landowner, owned textile mills, engaged in loan making, and acted as a wholesale merchant with business dealings in Cádiz and Cartagena. He was the son of Pedro Anastacio Maldonado, a knight of the military order of Alcántara, a marquis, and a landowner who served on five different occasions as an ordinary municipal justice and lieutenant governor in Ríobamba. Maldonado y Sotomayor also had other family members (such as his paternal grandfather) who were local justices, knights, members of military orders, and miners. His mother, María Isidora Palomino Flores, was the daughter of Antonio Saénz Aramburu, the local governor of Ríobamba who was declared a nobleman (*hidalgo*) in 1639. The mother's family included several Castilian nobles, among them Fernando de Valdés, the inquisitor general of Spain, president of the audiencia of Granada, and president of the Council of Castile at the end of the sixteenth century. In the Americas, the members of this family also excelled from the 1660s as conquistadores and soldiers. The mother was also the niece of Martín de Ariolla, president of the audiencia of Quito between 1647 and 1651. Maldonado y Sotomayor's brother Pedro Vicente Maldonado y Sotomayor accompanied the French scientific mission that visited Quito in the 1740s; he obtained some renown for his scientific endeavor, as well as for his project of opening a road from Quito north to the Pacific coast (Esmeraldas). Another brother was a member of the cathedral chapter in Quito. His nephew, Manuel Diez de la Pena, became the local governor of Otavalo (north of Quito) in 1763. Maldonado y Sotomayor first married Francisca Bastarrachea y León and then married Petrona, the daughter of Alonso Zárate y Alarcón, the crown attorney of the audiencia in 1728.[26]

In 1688 and 1695 respectively, the king also began selling the offices of magistrate and president of the audiencia. Thereafter all presidents obtained their nomination by way of purchase. Among magistrates, some purchased their office, while others were still selected or promoted through the more traditional mechanism of nomination through the council's recommendation (consulta). The following magistrates purchased their office: Miguel González Carrasco (1689), Diego de Segura y Lara (1693), Fernando José de Rivas (1693), Lorenzo Lastero Salazar

26. AHQ, Mat., 1: exp. 21 January 1729.

(1706), Juan Bautista Sánchez de Orellana (1711), Juan Dionisio Larrea Zurbano (1711), Juan Romualdo Carfanger y Artienda (1740), Luis de Santa Cruz y Centeno (1746), Juan Romualdo Navarro (1748), Manuel de la Vega y Bárcena (1748), and Gregorio Ignacio Hurtado de Mendoza (1750). It is possible that Cristóbal Cevallos y Borja and Juan de Ricaurte also purchased their offices. These men paid between 6,000 and 20,000 pesos de-a-ocho, depending on the particular conditions stipulated for each candidate and the general conditions in the market. During this period, at least three other individuals entered into the audiencia by purchasing the office of protector of Indians, being promoted later to the office of magistrate. In some cases, this promotion was unplanned. In others, it was specifically stipulated in the terms of the purchase, which indicated that with the sale of the office of protector also came the right to exercise in the future the office of crown attorney or magistrate. Such were the terms of Ignacio Aybar y Eslava (1683), Esteban Olaís y Aroche (1708), and Juan Lújan y Vedia (1724).

Although we have no detailed information regarding the purchase of local governorships or magistracies, the sale of the presidency is richly documented. In 1695, Domingo Eseyza was the first person to purchase the presidency of Quito. Eseyza died soon after the purchase was concluded—before he had occupied the office. However, his contract with the king served as a model for future negotiations. According to this contract, Eseyza would be president for eight years and with this office would gain the title of captain general of the province, that is to say, the title of the highest local military commander. Significantly, if he became incapacitated or died before the end of his term in office, another person could subrogate him–and if not, his heirs would be reimbursed fully or in proportion to the period that he had not served.

After Eseyza's death, the presidency of Quito was sold with the same terms to Juan de Sosaya in 1706, Juan Goyeneche in 1711, José de Araujo y Río in 1732, and Juan Francisco Goeyeneche in 1741. There are some indications that Dionisio Alcedo y Herrera might also have purchased his office in 1729, yet the decrees nominating him to the presidency make no clear mention of a price paid, as they do in similar cases. The price for the presidency fluctuated between 25,000 and 35,000 pesos de-a-ocho, depending on the circumstances and conditions of each candidate and contract.

Juan Goyeneche and his eldest son Juan Francisco Goyeneche (who bought the presidency in 1711 and 1741 respectively) resold it to Santiago Larrayn in 1713 and to Fernando Félix Sánchez de Orellana in 1744. The Goyeneches' involvement in the purchase and subsequent sale of the presidency provides revealing data concerning these kinds of transactions. Juan and Juan Francisco Goyeneche were important members of the court. Juan was a councilor of the Council of Finances (Consejo de Hacienda) and the exchequer of the queen.[27] He was extremely rich, often lending money to the crown. His commercial activities covered the entire Iberian Peninsula and extended to other parts of the empire, such as Quito, where he had at least one business partner: Simón Ontañón y Lastra (chap. 6). His eldest son, Juan Francisco, followed in his footsteps. In the late 1720s Juan Francisco was already the senior councilman (*consejero decano*) of the Council of the Indies and, like his father, made many financial transactions with the crown, as well as commercial dealings with merchants all over the country. Both Juan and his son were generous patrons; both headed an extended social network that connected people living in the province with the royal administration in Madrid.[28] Juan was among the founders of the *Congregación de San Fermín de los Navarros,* where Juan Francisco was also an active member.[29] The congregation was a religious association, which united Navarrese living all over the empire. Theoretically centered on the cult of San Fermín, it was specifically designed to serve as a patronage network. Navarrese, its ordinances stipulated, had to help one another. Rich Navarrese should help the poor, and Navarrese residing in the court should help those who did not.

Although no records survive that would explain how Juan chose Santiago Larrayn to be president of Quito in 1713, and why his son Juan Francisco designated Fernando Félix Sánchez de Orellana in 1744, we

27. Juan Goyeneche and his family are described in AGPR, EP, 476: exp. 46 to 48; AHPM, 16.161, fols. 57–94; *El innovador: Juan de Goyeneche. El señorío de la Olmeda y el conjunto arquitectónico de Nuevo Baztán* (Madrid, 1991); and J. Caro Baroja, *La hora Navarra del XVIII (personas, familias, negocios e ideas)* (Navarre, 1969; reprint, 1985), 82–323.

28. The dedicatory in B. Alcázar, *Crono-historia de la Compañía de Jesús en la provincia de Toledo y elogios de sus varones ilustres, fundadores, bienhechores, factores e hijos espirituales* (Madrid, 1710).

29. P. Sagués Azcona, *La Real Congregación de San Fermín de los Navarros de Madrid (1683–1691): Estudio histórico* (Madrid, 1963); and T. Herzog, "Private Organizations as Global Networks in Early Modern Spain and Spanish America," in *The Collective and the Public in Latin America: Cultural Identities and Political Order,* ed. L. Roniger and T. Herzog (Brighton, 2000), 117–33. Basque networks were also described in J. P. Priotti, "Emigración, redes vascas de negocios y poder en el imperio español (1500–1630): un punto de partida," trans. A. Rodríguez Tomp, *Historias* 42 (1999): 103–13.

do know that both candidates were related to the congregation of San Fermín and, through it, to the Goyeneches. Santiago Larrayn, who classified himself as a Navarrese despite having been born in Chile, was directly related to the congregation through his kinsman Francisco Larrayn. Francisco Larrayn donated different sums of money to the congregation in the 1690s. Together with Juan Francisco Vicuña, he was responsible for a campaign celebrated in Lima in 1727 to collect funds for the congregation.[30] Archival records show that in 1711, when searching for possible candidates for the presidency of Quito, Juan Goyeneche offered the post to both Juan Francisco Vicuña and Francisco Larrayn, who represented the congregation in Lima. Goyeneche first sold the office to the Vicuña family, but when the Vicuña candidate died in 1712, he resold it to the Larrayn family, who named Santiago to the office. Santiago felt grateful to both the congregation and the Goyeneche family. In 1731 when the congregation held a new campaign to collect donations in the Americas, he was the biggest single donor in Quito.[31]

The same could be said with respect to Fernando Félix Sánchez de Orellana, although his case is somewhat less obvious. A few factors connected Sánchez de Orellana to the congregation. In 1733 Fernando's father, the marquis of Solanda, donated money to the congregation.[32] Later that year, Fernando's paternal uncle, Nicolás Sánchez de Orellana, was chosen by the delegates of the congregation to transfer the money from Quito to Madrid. Nicolás's activities as a messenger allowed him to establish a personal relationship with the members of the congregation in the court, and possibly with Juan Francisco Goyeneche himself.[33] Less than a decade later, the Sánchez de Orellanas were able to purchase the presidency of Quito from Goyeneche.

Indications for a possible relationship between the congregation, the Goyeneches, and the presidency of Quito can be found even as early as 1706, the year when Juan de Sosaya purchased the office. Pedro de Sosaya, a kinsmen and a business partner of Juan, was among the

30. "Junta en la que se designa apoderados para limosna en América" from 3 March 1727: ARCSF, América, 1–2.

31. ARCSF, América, 1–4, document no. 1: letter of Pedro Martínez de Arizala to Pablo Escalzo y Azedo, the congregation's secretary, 31 March 1731.

32. ARCSF, América, 1–4, document no. 2: letter of Pedro Martínez de Arizala to the secretary of the congregation, 29 April 1733.

33. ARCSF, América, 1–4, document no. 3: letter of Nicolás Sánchez de Orellana to the secretary of the congregation, 15 March 1734.

Navarrese who contributed to the 1695 collection campaign in Lima. Ten years later, the same Pedro secured the presidency of Quito for himself—or alternatively for his cousin Juan, who took charge of the audiencia at that time.[34] The possibility that the long hand of the congregation operated in this transaction is further supported by the fact that years later Juan de Sosaya married Michaela Ontañón y Lastra, the daughter of the principal business partner of the Goyeneches in Quito (chap 6). Their grandson Francisco Javier Ustarríz eventually married Rosa Sánchez de Orellana, sister of Fernando Félix, who was named president of Quito in 1744 thanks to the intervention of the Goyeneches. These facts, of course, could be accidental; or they could prove the continuing relationship between the presidents of Quito, the Goyeneches, and the congregation of San Fermín.

Unlike other sales of offices, the selling of judicial offices was constantly criticized.[35] Some people in the Council of the Indies accepted it as a necessary evil, and as a sad but required solution to the real economic necessities of the crown. Rather than discrediting the practice, they attempted to control it and to ensure that it would have the fewest possible negative effects. These council members placed special emphasis on the need to ensure that buyers would be individuals worthy of offices and that the price would remain within the reach of suitable aspirants. However, other people within the council disapproved of the sales altogether. According to them, the sale of judicial offices necessarily meant the election of unfit candidates. Experience demonstrated that those most worthy of office would never buy their positions. They would consider such a purchase a dishonor and would expect to be

34. AGI, Quito, 106: decree of 25 May 1706; AGI, Quito, 267: instructions of 11 July 1711; and F. González Suárez, *Historia general de la República del Ecuador* (1890–1903; reprint, Quito, 1970), 835.

35. C. Moscoso y Córdoba, "Discurso en cuanto si es lícito a los reyes vender los oficios de la administración de justicia y que sintió en esto Santo Tomás [n.d.]," MS 2843, fols. 32–53, BPR; and the consulta of the Council of the Indies from 9 November 1693, AGI, IG, 795. See also J. H. Parry, *The Sale of Public Office in the Spanish Indies under the Habsburgs* (Berkeley, 1953); A. Domínguez Ortiz, "La venta de cargos y oficios públicos en Castilla y sus consecuencias económicas y sociales," *Anuario de historia económica y social* 3 (1970): 105–37; F. Tomás y Valiente, *La venta de oficios en Indias (1493–1606)* (Madrid, 1972; reprint, 1982); idem, "Opiniones de algunos juristas clásicos españoles sobre la venta de oficios públicos," *Filosofía y derecho: Estudios en homenaje a José Corts Grau* (Valencia, 1977): 627–49; L. Navarro García, "Los oficios vendibles en Nueva España durante la guerra de sucesión," *Anuario de estudios americanos* 32 (1975): 133–54; and M. Bertrand, "L'état espagnol et ses officiers aux Indes: Le recrutement de la Cour des Comptes de Mexico (1680–1770)," *Mélanges de la Casa de Velázquez* 25 (1989): 119–220.

rewarded because of who they were and what they (and their family) did. Only those who had no other possibility to advance (because they and their family did not merit such a reward) would buy their posts. Having invested money in securing their nomination, their first ambition would be to obtain financial gains. Not only would they be less fit for office, they would also be more prone to corruption. The king's first duty was to guarantee justice, and he could not abandon this obligation in the hands of corrupt and unfit judges. If study and service would not guarantee nomination, how would people be encouraged to do either? If the king sold the offices, how would he reward his loyal subjects? The sale of judicial offices, these people argued, also compelled the king to disobey his own orders. It encouraged applications from candidates whose election was normally prohibited—such as individuals residing or holding properties in the jurisdiction in which they sought nomination. These individuals would offer more money to recompense the king for the illegality inherent in their nomination. In return for this payment, the monarch would issue them a special permit (*dispensa*) that would "dispense" them from compliance with the law. In consequence, the requirements included in the laws would no longer be obeyed. Last but not least, the sale of offices inflated the number of ministers working in the courts. The king, moved by economic necessity, sold offices even in the absence of a vacancy. He added new ministers, called "supernumeraries," to courts above and beyond the normal number of judges each was supposed to have. Courts, which normally held four magistrates, could come to have as many as six or even seven. This proliferation in royal servants was bothersome. A larger number of judges did not guarantee better justice. On the contrary, it was unnecessary, and it inhibited normal (and thus good) judicial administration.

Beyond these theoretical considerations, the Council of the Indies had other good reasons to fight against the sale of judicial offices. Most sales were channeled through royal secretaries, who located the suitable candidates, negotiated with them the terms of the contracts, and transferred their recommendations to the king. This mechanism left the council (and its standing committee, the cámara) with no control over the naming of ministers—which was one of its most coveted privileges. The council also claimed that, like all other administrative tasks carried out by secretaries rather than by councils, the sale of office was a hasty system. No proper nomination could be guaranteed unless the regular rules for candidates' selection were followed. These rules required a long deliberation by many people that ended in a vote. The Council of the

Indies also wished to ensure that merit (understood as social connections and service obligations) rather than financial capacities would determine nomination. This guaranteed the councilors' own position because it protected the administration against the entry of new people who were not connected to it by networks of service and family loyalties. For the councilors, this was also the only way to safeguard the reputation of royal servants, who until then were always "worthy people."[36]

The crown hesitated in its response. On some occasions, it presented the sales as a necessary evil that could not be avoided because of pressing financial needs. On other occasions, it agreed that the practice was prejudicial and attempted to reverse its policies. Following these vacillations, the crown allowed, and even encouraged, the sale of offices in certain periods, prohibited it in others, and then went on to reinitiate the sales.[37] The decision to end the sales was usually accompanied by decrees that canceled all purchases already contracted or that reduced the courts to their original structure by abolishing all supernumerary offices. Because most supernumeraries were purchasers, the elimination of supernumeraries eliminated purchasers. Drastic as it may appear, these measures were not always successfully implemented. Among the numerous readjustments ordered in 1701, 1712, and 1717–18, the first two, for example, had no effect in Quito, where purchasers continued to exercise their offices. It is possible, however, that the third measure (dated 1717) did lead to the revocation of two appointments: that of Juan Bautista Sánchez de Orellana and that of Juan Dionisio Larrea Zurbano.

Historians such as Mark Burkholder and D. S. Chandler have argued that the sale of offices dramatically changed the nature of the administration in the Spanish colonies.[38] The purchase of offices allowed Amer-

36. AGI, Quito, 267. These issues were also discussed in T. Nava Rodríguez and G. Franco Rubio, "Venalité et futuras dans l'administration espagnole au XVIIIe siècle," in *Les figures historiques de l'administrateur: Institutions, réseaux, pouvoirs en Espagne, en France et au Portugal, 16e–19e siècle,* ed. R. Descimon, J. F. Schaub, and B. Vincent (Paris, 1997), 101–2.

37. AHQ, Ced., 5, no. 215 from 1689; AHN, Cód., 487B, nos. 90 and 136 from 1745 and 1742; and AHN, Cód., 696B and 753B, nos. 1 and 212 from 1691 and 1740.

38. M. A. Burkholder and D. S. Chandler, "Creole Appointment and the Sale of Audiencia Positions in the Spanish Empire under the Early Bourbons, 1701–1750," *Journal of Latin American Studies* 4 (1972): 187–206; idem, *De la impotencia,* 33–59; M. A. Burkholder, "From Creole to Peninsular: The Transformation of the Audiencia of Lima," *Hispanic American Historical Review* 52 (1972): 395–415; L. G. Campbell, "A Colonial Establishment: Creole Domination of the *Audiencia* of Lima during the Late 18th Century," *Hispanic American Historical Review* 52 (1972): 1–25; and K. J. Andrien, "The Sale of Fiscal Offices and the Decline of Royal Authority in the Viceroyalty of Peru, 1633–1700," *Hispanic American Historical Review* 62 (1982): 49–71.

ican-born Spaniards, who could not previously achieve nomination to the audiencia, to become magistrates. The crown, fearful of the predominance of Creoles in the administration, reacted by excluding them from most spheres of government by the second half of the eighteenth century. However, a detailed analysis of the data, as well as evidence from Quito, demonstrates that American-born officials were appointed to office in almost similar proportions both before and after the introduction of beneficio. What changed with the sale of offices was the entry of locally born officials who now exercised office in their hometown. Contrary to what had happened in the earlier period, individuals born in Quito could now obtain office in Quito, and the same happened in other Spanish American capitals. Nomination of locals to office was prohibited by law, and in principle, it continued to be prohibited even after the inception of the sale of offices. However, as the Council of the Indies rightly suspected, office purchasers were willing to go a long way to acquire an office in their home jurisdiction. The king, motivated by economic needs, consented to the practice. Many candidates simply paid an additional fee to wave this prohibition in their cases. After purchases began, the American courts were indeed more likely to have local magistrates born, raised, and resident in the jurisdiction.

This development might have been feared in Madrid—some historians have argued that the Council of the Indies was concerned that local officeholders would be less controllable than nonlocal officials. But, if feared in Madrid, it was truly resented in Quito. The entry of elite members to the royal court usually provoked open conflict. At stake was not the division between Creoles and Peninsulars, as has been asserted in the past, but the frictions between rival factions, which were struggling to dominate the local scene. Each faction feared a checkmate, such as an audiencia nomination, by its rivals. This prospect became a reality in Quito in 1712–14 and 1749, when three natives of the jurisdiction purchased offices in the local court. What distinguished these beneficiaries (who were rejected) from other purchasers (who were peacefully received) was that they were descended from wealthy families who resided in the city or its immediate province. These families, it was argued, wished to consolidate their positions by means of a judicial appointment. In their cases, the purchase of office formed part of a family strategy, one that threatened the interests of the rival group(s).[39] Although the struggle against these

39. Burkholder and Chandler, *De la impotencia,* 50.

nominations to the court included the traditional criticism against the sale of office, these general considerations were superceded by other, more particular issues.

The clearest example was the case of the Sánchez de Orellana family. This family pursued a strategy of collective advancement for at least three generations, gradually moving from the outskirts of the province to the capital, and gradually placing their members in improving institutional positions.[40] Antonio Sánchez de Orellana, who initiated this trajectory, was born in Zaruma (south of the province of Quito) to a family of small landowners whose members occupied local judicial offices.[41] When he was thirty years old, Antonio began a gradual economic and social ascent.[42] He moved to Loja, which was a larger and more important settlement. There he became a municipal ordinary judge and lieutenant to the local governor. Appointed master of the field of the local battalion, Antonio walked around the city holding a staff, accompanied by two slaves armed with swords and daggers. In 1694, he received license to explore and conquer the territory of Mainas, an area in the Amazon region that theoretically, but not in practice, was under Spanish domination. By virtue of this license, Antonio became the head of a military expedition. He recruited troops, purchased arms and supplies, and promised to distribute honors, grades, encomiendas, and land among his followers. Antonio invited all people to join the expedition—but he made it a family affair. He arrived in Mainas accompanied by his sons Pedro Javier, Francisco Javier, Miguel, Nicolás, and Antonio Gabriel; his brother Jacinto; his brother-in-law Juan Saldaña; his cousin Manuel Sánchez de Orellana; and other relatives.

We have no information concerning what happened during the expedition. However, we do know that Antonio displayed great riches after the campaign. He founded several churches and charities and, in 1700, purchased the title of marquis of Solanda for the price of 9,000 (or, according to other versions, 30,000) pesos.[43] Antonio then proceeded to

40. T. Herzog, "La empresa administrativa y el capital social: los Sánchez de Orellana (Quito, siglo XVIII)," in *Sociedad, administración y poder en el siglo XVIII: Hacia una nueva historia institucional,* ed. J. L. Castellano (Granada, 1996), 381–96.

41. AGI, Quito, 164: relación de méritos of 1715.

42. A. Anda Aguirre, *Los marqueses de Solanda* (Quito, 1974), 19–52; G. C. Larrea, *Genealogías quiteñas: la casa de Ontañón y sus enlazados* (Quito, 1994); and *Zaruma: cuatro siglos de peregrinaje histórico, 1560–1992 (Memoria XIV Jornadas de Historia Social: Zaruma 27–29.8.1992)* (Quito, 1992).

43. AHN, CS, 8975, 129; AHQ, VM, 3: exp. 3 November 1701; AGI, Quito, 142: relación de méritos of 14 January 1699; AGI, Quito, 164: petition of 1715; and Anda Aguirre, *Los marqueses,* 45–47.

buy the office of local governor of Cuenca (the largest town in the south of the province), which he exercised until 1710, if not later. He also used his fortune to help his brothers. He gave a dowry for Gertrudis his sister, who married Juan Saldaña, one of Antonio's companions in the expedition to Mainas. He also gave a dowry for another sister, María, who married the local governor of Cuenca (he later became the governor of Loja). Antonio financed the pretensions of his brothers Jacinto and Clemente to the local governorships of Cuenca and Loja, and he supported the ecclesiastical careers of his brothers Juan Bautista and Pedro. Having installed himself and his brothers in these and other positions, in 1711 Antonio purchased the office of magistrate for his eldest son Juan Bautista. He also made arrangements for his other twelve sons and daughters. Clemente and José Dionisio became clergymen and worked as canons in the cathedral of Quito or as parish priests. Pedro Javier, Francisco Javier, Miguel, Nicolás, and Antonio Gabriel all became municipal ordinary judges and, in time, local governors in different parts of the province of Quito.

This strategy alarmed the local society and led the audiencia of Quito and many members of the local elite to struggle against the entry of a Sánchez de Orellana to the royal court.[44] In 1714–1717 these people justified the rejection of Juan Bautista in legal terms: the candidate was a minor and had no legal degree. However, they insisted primarily that Juan Bautista was a native of the jurisdiction and that his family literally controlled all of the local governorships. Because of his social connections, as well his ignorance in legal matters, opponents argued that Juan Bautista would have a bad influence on the court. He would adopt improper solutions, leading to endless discussions, and he would cause, or enhance, the formation of local factions.

The king disagreed with these alegations. He insisted that Juan Bautista was a good candidate and asserted that the family connections and lack of a legal degree were irrelevant to his appointment as magistrate. Nevertheless, following a general decree to revoke the sale of judicial offices, the monarch revoked his nomination in 1717.

Despite this defeat, the Sánchez de Orellana family did not give up its hope for a seat in the audiencia. In 1719, Juan Bautista wrote to the

44. AGI, Quito, 102: consulta of 14 November 1711; AGI, Quito, 106: decree of 30 January 1711 and cédula of 13 April 1711; AGI, Quito, 143: letter of Juan Bautista Sánchez de Orellana, 28 December 1717; and the many documents included in AGI, Quito, 164. See also T. Herzog, "¿Letrado o teólogo?"

king and offered to organize a new expedition to conquer territories in the Amazon region that were still under Indian control.[45] Among the conditions he stipulated was the naming of one of his brothers, preferably Pedro Javier, as president of the audiencia of Quito. Only this nomination, he argued, would guarantee the success of the enterprise. The expedition was to be led, controlled, and dominated by the Sánchez de Orellana family.

Although the Council of the Indies rejected this offer, the Sánchez de Orellana family did not lose hope. After the death of Antonio in 1731, the family modified its strategy, and instead of forcing its way into the local society by obtaining royal favor and amassing a fortune, it worked mainly to consolidate its position internally. Pedro Javier, who succeeded his father in leadership, founded an entailed estate (*mayorazgo*) linked to the title of marquis of Solanda in 1740.[46] He then secured the stable employment of his ten sons. He did not distribute them all over the province as his father did—instead he placed them primarily in offices in the capital city. Pedro Javier also had his daughters marry into the most prominent local families, including the Ponce de León (count of Selvaflorida) the Carcelén Pérez de Ubilluz and the Sosaya.

Integrated into local society, recognized by and related to the most important families of the city, the Sánchez de Orellana family became an accepted part the dominant group within the local hierarchy. It was in this capacity, and not in any other, that the family's long-lasting wish to obtain a seat in the audiencia finally came through: Fernando Félix Sánchez de Orellana, marquis of Solanda and heir of his father Pedro Javier, was nominated in March 1745 as president of the court. This nomination was made possible thanks to the purchase of the office and through the mediation of Juan Francisco Goyeneche (who was probably tied to the Sánchez de Orellana family through the congregation of San Fermín—see earlier). But while connections in the court explained the purchase, its local acceptance depended on the dense web of interpersonal relationships that now united the family to the local elite. This, of course, did not mean that the family had no enemies or that these enemies did not try to hinder the Sánchez de Orellana pretension to judicial office. While the majority of the elite now backed this ambition and happily supported this man as president, at least one prominent

45. AGI, Quito, 143: undated letter, 288–92.

46. AGI, Quito, 145, 486–87; AHQ, VM, 3: exp. 3 November 1701; and AHQ, VM, 4: exp. 7 August 1736.

local merchant, Simón Álvarez Monteserín, still threatened to do all that he could to hinder the nomination.[47] He also promised that, if the nomination would go through, he would make the nominee's life miserable.

The acceptance of local purchasers in Madrid and their rejection in Quito was also felt in the case Juan Dionisio Larrea Zurbano, who was nominated together with Juan Bautista Sánchez de Orellana in 1711.[48] Juan Dionisio was the son of Juan Larrea Zurbano, magistrate in Quito from 1684.[49] Juan Dionisio was born in Santa Fe de Bogotá. He was a descendent of an old Vizcayan lineage, whose members had participated in the conquest of the Americas since the early sixteenth century. His father, Juan Larrea the elder, was the grandson of a magistrate in Lima. His mother, Juana Pérez de Manrique, was the daughter of the marquis of Santiago, a magistrate in Lima and president of the audiencias of Charcas, Quito, and Santa Fe. Juan Dionisio was married to María Tomasa Dávalos y Larraspuro, the very wealthy local daughter of General Francisco Dávalos and Magdalena de Larraspuro. In theory, Juan Dionisio was a perfect candidate to purchase an office in the audiencia. He came from the right family, married into the right family, had sufficient merits to justify royal attention, and had sufficient wealth to pay for his benefice. He even had a law degree. Nevertheless, his appointment was met with strong opposition in Quito. What went wrong?

As far as we know, Juan Dionisio's father, Juan Larrea Zurbano the elder, arrived in Quito in 1684 after having served in the audiencia of Santa Fe. His transfer to Quito, which originally was only meant to be a temporary move, was motivated by the proliferation of complaints about his character, especially his inability to collaborate peacefully with his colleagues. This accusation against Larrea Zurbano the elder was dissipated in 1686, when he was found innocent. Nevertheless, the Council of the Indies preferred to leave him in Quito, arguing (among

47. AGI, EC, 914C, cuad. 13, 3: a certificate of the town notary, 13 January 1745.

48. These issues are discussed in great length in Herzog, "Letrado o teólogo?"; idem, "La empresa administrativa"; and idem, "De la autoridad al poder: Quito, los Larrea y la herencia inmaterial (siglos XVII y XVIII)," in *Emigración y redes sociales de vascos en América*, ed. R. Escobedo Mansilla, A. de Zaballa Reascoechea, and O. Álvarez Gila (Vitoria, 1996), 373–83.

49. AGI, EC, legajo 914B, cuad. 7, 147–65. See also F. Jurado Noboa, *Los Larrea: Burocracia, tenencia de la tierra, poder político, crísis, retorno al poder y papel de la cultura* (Quito, 1986).

other things) that he simply had too many relatives and friends in Santa Fe.[50] Larrea Zurbano the elder thus remained in the audiencia of Quito until 1693, when he was allowed to retire with full salary and benefits.[51] As had happened earlier in Santa Fe, he was once again considered a problematic minister in Quito. As early as 1687, the president of the court (Lope Antonio Munive y Axpe) criticized his behavior and requested that he be transferred to another audiencia. The president persistently argued that Larrea Zurbano the elder spent most of his time and energy quarreling with other magistrates or intervening in favor of his friends.[52] In 1691, Larrea Zurbano was personally attacked by José Antonio López de Galarza, a leading member of the local society.[53] In this and the following year, two other citizens accused him of failing to pay them rent.[54] During the same period, a number of merchants complained that Larrea Zurbano the elder suspected that they had bought items that were stolen from his house. Without waiting for the result of the legal proceedings, he attempted to force them to pay the price of these items, which he valued at 3,000 pesos, by making sure that they would be imprisoned until they paid.[55] Around the same time, the lieutenant to the chief constable (*teniente alguacil mayor*) also protested against Larrea Zurbano the elder for beating and imprisoning him without cause.[56]

Juan Larrea Zurbano, father of Juan Dionisio, was not a popular person in Quito. He maltreated litigants and overtly preferred one over another. He threatened people by saying that he would "cut them into pieces and exile them from this world" and maintained close ties with other individuals who were considered undignified companions for a royal judge. There were rumors that he accepted gifts and that he was desperately trying to wed his son (the same Juan Dionisio) into the Freire family, one of the most distinguished families in the region. This family, it was said, rejected the match, which it considered uninteresting. Although Juan Larrea Zurbano the elder routinely denied most of

50. AHQ, Ced., 5, no. 88: cédula of 26 May 1685; and AGI, Quito, 4 and 5: consultas of 15 December 1683 and 12 February 1692, respectively.

51. AGI, Quito, 5: cédula of May 1692; and AGI, Quito, 4: consulta of 12 February 1692.

52. AGI, Quito, 5: letter of the president, 28 February 1687.

53. AGI, Quito, 5: letter of Juan Larrea Zurbano, 28 March 1691.

54. AGI, Quito, 74, 221 and 251: petitions of Josefa Baraona and Gabriel Montesdoca.

55. AGI, Quito, 72, 647–50; and AGI, Quito, 73: declarations by Manuel Montero de Espinosa and Juan Silvestre Guerrero.

56. AGI, Quito, 73, 286–309.

these accusations, he did concede that he had many enemies in the city, naming nine heads of important families among them.[57] He explained that this animosity was unjustified and that it was only due to his practice as a judge. The Council of the Indies, however, thought otherwise. It found him guilty and sentenced him to pay a fine of 1,000 pesos de-a-ocho. It was precisely the conclusion that Juan the elder was a bad minister that led the council to allow him to retire. It agreed that as a retired judge he could no longer do any harm.[58]

Backed by this heritage, as well as by the money his father left him and his wife brought him, Juan Dionisio Larrea Zurbano traveled to Madrid in 1711 to purchase the office of magistrate in Quito.[59] He succeeded in his quest. Yet when he returned to Quito in 1714, the audiencia refused to accept him as a member. The audiencia gave a formal excuse. It suspected that Juan Dionisio secured his office by hiding important facts, such as the fact that he had no legal training. Juan Dionisio requested the intervention of the viceroy, who ordered the audiencia to receive him. The audiencia obeyed, but its magistrates wrote to Madrid, informing its authorities of Juan's ineptitude. As had happened in the case of Juan Bautista Sánchez de Orellana, the more significant accusation against Juan Dionisio was the fact that he had too many relatives and friends in the jurisdiction. Both the audiencia and the local town council, who opposed his nomination as a magistrate, voiced this accusation.

Juan Dionisio agreed that he had many enemies in Quito. He argued that the president and magistrates of the audiencia and the town council were under their influence, and that they opposed his nomination because of a personal dislike. This dislike was tied in part to friendships and animosities previously cultivated by his father. In 1705, the retired and venerable Juan Larrea Zurbano wrote to the Council of the Indies denouncing two of his colleagues: Juan de Ricaurte and Antonio de Ron Bernaldo de Quiros.[60] Both men were popular ministers who had resided in the city for a long time and were considered intimate friends of magistrate Fernando Sierra Osorio. It was Sierra Osorio who led the

57. AGI, Quito, 74, 119–221.

58. AGI, Quito, 4: consulta of 12 February 1692.

59. AGI, Quito, 106: decrees of 2 February 1711 and 8 May 1712; AGI, Quito, 133, 732; AGI, Quito, 145, 92–93 and 103–6; AGI, Quito, 164: different documents; AHQ, Gob., 13: exp. 13 December 1734; AHQ, Test., 32: exp. 2 July 1703; AMQ, 00125: town council meeting of 14 March 1738.

60. AGI, Quito, 128: letter of 28 January 1705.

campaign against Juan Dionisio, first refusing to accompany him when he arrived in the city and then requesting the audiencia not to accept him as a judge. Yet, if his father was guilty, so was he. In the years preceding his nomination, Juan Dionisio constantly complained about different members of the local elite to the authorities in Madrid and Lima. In 1708 and 1709, when he was municipal ordinary judge and temporary local governor, Juan Dionisio fought with magistrates Cristóbal Cevallos y Borja, Tomás Fernández Pérez de Hodo, and Lorenzo Lastero Salazar. He also gave voice to different complaints against President Juan de Sosaya, which initiated an investigation (*visita*) of the activities of the president.[61] Encountering local opposition after his return to Quito in 1714, Juan Dionisio dispatched letters to Madrid denouncing the behavior of magistrates Fernando Sierra Osorio, José Laysequilla y Palacios y Aguilar, and President Lope Antonio Munive y Axpe. He also presented a copy of his law degree. Despite his efforts, he was unable to turn the tide. In 1717, Juan Dionisio's nomination to the audiencia was reversed, probably as part of a larger move to prohibit the sale of judicial offices.

Juan Dionisio refused to accept this solution, and in the following years he constantly wrote to the Council of the Indies and requested his rehabilitation. In 1738, he succeeded in obtaining recognition as an honorary magistrate, with no powers and only half the normal salary. He was then sixty-two years old and "on the verge of dying"—or at least this is what the council believed when it acquiesced to his demands. Juan Dionisio lasted for another twelve years.[62] By 1734, he was so isolated and so hated by a large portion of the local elite and magistrates that he requested that the audiencia be prohibited from ruling on matters related to him or to his relatives to the fourth degree.[63]

Juan Romualdo Navarro, another local purchaser, suffered the same fate.[64] Theoretically, the audiencia rejected his 1749 candidacy because of his inaptitude. Navarro had no legal degree and was related to many people living in the jurisdiction. Nevertheless, once again, behind these formal allegations was a highly complex social reality. Before he was nominated magistrate, Navarro was an infantry captain in Guayaquil

61. AGI, EC, 913A; and AGI, Quito, 267: visita proceedings against Juan de Sosaya.

62. AGI, Quito, 104; and AGI, Quito, 145, 104.

63. AHQ, Gob., 13: exp. 13 December 1734.

64. AGI, Quito, 106: decree of 20 May 1748; AGI, Quito, 224; Burkholder and Chandler, *Biographical Dictionary*, 232–33; and Burkholder and Chandler, *De la impotencia*, 264.

(the main port of the province of Quito), a municipal ordinary justice (1744), and a justice of the Santa Hermandad (1745) in Quito. In this last capacity, he financed the construction of roads and the repair of jails, water conduits, and monasteries. He then bought the office of local governor of Cuenca (south of the audiencia of Quito). However, he renounced this purchase and remained in Quito, having obtained a nomination as magistrate. Navarro was a native of the city and the son of Juan Casimiro Navarro, an important local merchant. His kinship ties made him well placed in the jurisdiction: among his blood and political relatives were many merchants as well as other individuals who formed part of the municipal council. In 1750, the already wealthy Juan Romualdo married Manuela Urquizu, a native of Ríobamba (south of Quito). He, his father, and other relatives and friends formed a compact social network. This network clashed with Fernando Félix Sánchez de Orellana, then president of the court. Fernando Félix Sánchez de Orellana backed the former president, José de Araujo y Río, who was accused of serious misconduct by Navarro and his group (chap. 3). The two rival fractions competed for control of the city for over a decade. Both Sánchez de Orellana's and then Navarro's nomination to the audiencia only exasperated this fight.

Familiarity with the turbulent social scene in Quito led the Council of the Indies to mistrust the information supplied by the audiencia. The council ordered the viceroy to examine the case with detachment and then approved his decision to support Navarro. This decision was based on the conclusion that the candidate was worthy. He had studied theology and philosophy in Quito and then graduated in canon law at the University of Santa Fe de Bogotá. His network of relatives was irrelevant, and its existence was known before he had purchased the office. The purchase stipulated that he would be permitted to hold office despite his roots in local society.[65]

The authorities of Madrid were willing to forgive the local character of candidates who purchased their offices as long as they paid an additional sum. In contrast, the inhabitants of Quito were not so willing to overlook local origins. Purchasers who were members of the local society experienced opposition resulting from the fear that their nomination would upset the local balance of power. The Council of the Indies was thus correct when it pointed out the detrimental effect of nominating

65. AGI, Quito, 374.

locals to the audiencia. But where the council feared its loss of control over Quito, the inhabitants of Quito feared that their rivals might surpass them through nomination. It is therefore essential to distinguish how the authorities in Madrid viewed the sale of office from how local society experienced it. It is also essential to understand that success in purchasing an office was one thing but convincing the local society to approve of it was another. Each one of these steps was essential, yet each required different qualities, mechanisms, and conditions.

While selling offices clearly allowed the nomination of locals to the audiencia (thus importing to it tensions previously existing in society), the relationship between these sales and corruption is less clear. This relationship was pivotal in the arguments of those opposing the practice. Purchasers, they observed, considered their offices an economic investment. They attempted to gain as much money as possible during their terms in office—among other things, by employing illegal and corrupt activities. The simplicity and beauty of this argument has led to its adoption by modern historians. Historians assert—usually with no proof (or need of proof)—that purchasers were necessarily more corrupt than people appointed by royal nomination.[66] Was this true?

To date, we have no proof that this was the case.[67] First, there is no clear evidence that office purchasers were truly of a different background than those who obtained their nomination through royal grace. For example, Felipe Nicolás Fajardo, who bought the right to exercise in the future the office of crown attorney of Quito in 1709, was a Spaniard. He was the son of a minister of the House of Trade (*Casa de Contratación*), the royal institution charged with overseeing all communication and trade between Spain and Spanish America. Holding a law degree, Fajardo was qualified by both personal and family merit, education, and service considerations to be chosen for the office by the king. Fernando José de Rivas, another purchaser, had similar characteristics. Both these candidates were people who typically could have

66. H. Pietschmann, "Burocracia y corrupción en Hispanoamérica colonial: Una aproximación tentativa," *Nova americana* 5 (1982): 23 and 26; and M. González Jiménez, "Corrupciones municipales en Castilla a finales de la edad media," in *Instituciones y corrupción en la historia*, ed. M. González Jiménez, H. Pietschmann, F. Comín, and J. Perez (Valladolid, 1998), 10.

67. M. Bertrand, "La élite colonial en la Nueva España del siglo XVIII: un planteamiento en términos de redes sociales," *Beneméritos, aristócratas y empresarios: Identidades y estructuras sociales de las capas altas urbanas en América hispánica*, ed. B. Schröter and C. Büschges (Frankfurt, 1999), 40.

obtained their office through nomination. Nevertheless, they did not. Maybe they were too impatient, maybe their contacts at the court were insufficient, maybe they simply wanted to serve the king again by giving him payment for something that they merited receiving free of charge. Maybe they were corrupt, but these are all speculations.

Office purchasers could thus be fundamentally similar to people who obtained their nomination by royal grace. We also know—and this is the second point—that the only substantial difference between office purchasers and other nominees was their economic situation. Purchasers tended to be people of some wealth who did not need an additional source of income. For many of them, obtaining an office was the last step in the consolidation of a previously acquired status: office represented the consecration of social achievement. Purchasers were interested first and foremost in the honor attached to office holding, as well as the ability to influence society and to expand their social connections. Nominated ministers, on the contrary, were often poor. Yet they were required to maintain a dignified lifestyle that their salaries could rarely afford.[68] Contrary to most purchasers, ministers nominated by the king were dependent on their salaries to make a living and to secure their own and their loved ones' future. Which of the two sectors—deliberately stereotyped in this description—would more likely be corrupt? I would say the nonpurchasers, those who depended on their office for their income.

Third, during their terms of office, purchasers were not accused of more corrupt practices in comparison with their other colleagues who didn't purchase their offices. Fourth, the hypothetical distinction between the behavior of purchasers and nonpurchasers also disappears once we consider the patrimonial nature of all judicial offices, and not only the "venal" ones. Even offices gratuitously granted by the king were considered property of their possessors. Because of this reality, the office of an audiencia magistrate could not be taken away from an individual without good reason. This became evident in Quito when orders came to abolish the local audiencia in 1718.[69] The decision was motivated by wide-reaching administrative and political reforms that included the erection of a viceroyalty in Santa Fe. Yet even these kinds

68. J. L. Phelan, *The Kingdom of Quito*, 147–49.

69. This issue and others were treated in greated length in T. Herzog, "Las reformas borbónicas a escala humana: La extinción y el restablecimiento de la Audiencia de Quito, 1718–1721," *E.I.A.L*, 7/2 (1996): 133–45.

of measures were not sufficient to justify taking offices away from their possessors. In order to take these offices away, the monarch had to claim that the people who were about to lose their offices had done something to merit their removal. Thus in his decrees terminating the audiencias of Quito and Panamá, the king justified the terminations by accusing the magistrates of being bad ministers. This argument, which was now given primacy, had no role in the deliberations of the council when it decided to abolish the court. Furthermore, when the court was reestablished in Quito in 1722, orders arrived that reinstituted the same (bad) magistrates in their offices.[70] Was there indeed guilt in those who were banished and then reinstalled?

The only magistrate who was purged in the process was Lorenzo Lastero Salazar, who was left out of the court in 1722 because of a pending investigation against him.[71] Resenting this treatment, Lastero Salazar argued that he deserved no punishment. The investigation, he said, was ordered not only against him but also against two of his colleagues, Cristóbal Cevallos y Borja and Fernando Sierra Osorio. Nevertheless, he was not restored to his seat in the audiencia, while they were promoted. The council agreed that the promotion of Cevallos y Borja and Sierra Osorio was a mistake, yet it did nothing to correct this situation by annulling their promotion or by allowing Lastero Salazar to regain his office. The councilors explained that once a promotion was granted, it could not be reversed simply because of a mistake. The charges against the two magistrates were old, and in giving them a promotion, the king had (implicitly) forgiven them. Thereafter, the only possible course of action was to remedy the situation of Lastero Salazar. In order to do so, the Council of the Indies ordered the local authorities to carry out the investigation, which had by now been delayed more than fifteen years. Lastero Salazar was found innocent in 1729, and the council allowed him to reoccupy his seat in the audiencia.

The patrimonial character of nonvenal offices was such that the rights of one holder could contradict the rights of another. In 1722, the crown had to choose whether to reinstate Estéban Olaís y Aroche, who

70. AGI, Quito, 106: cédula of 18 February 1720; AGI, Quito, 129: letter of 6 July 1720; AGI, Quito, 129: letter of 23 April 1720; AGI, Quito, 103: consulta of 27 October 1729; and AGI, Quito, 129: letter of Diego Zárate, 3 February 1722.

71. AGI, Quito, 130: different documents dating from 1724 and 1725; AGI, Quito, 103: consulta of 18 August 1724; AGI, Quito, 104: consulta of 2 December 1729; and AHQ, Ced., 9, book 1727–35, 199: cédula of 15 October 1732.

held the office of the protector of Indians when the court was abolished in 1718, or to prefer Francisco Ramírez de Arellano, who was nominated to this office in the jurisdiction of the city of Quito in 1720 (when there was no audiencia in place).[72] Ramírez de Arellano argued a peaceful possession. Like others who had obtained a property belonging to another, he claimed that when his nomination was issued, there was no reason to assume that Estéban Olaís y Aroche had any rights. He said the nomination was valid and so was his possession of the office. Rejecting his arguments, and stressing that the office belonged to Olaís y Aroche the council promised Ramírez de Arellano that it would consider his candidature for the next available office.

The Sale of Paralegal Offices in Quito

People employed in paralegal offices such as court clerks, notaries, and procurators received their nomination through a two-channel procedure. On the one hand, they had to demonstrate their professional qualifications and receive the title of *escribano de Su Majestad* or procurator. On the other, because offices of court clerks, notaries, and procurators all belonged to the category of "saleable" (*vendibles y renunciables*), they had to purchase the right to exercise their trade.[73] Although these stages were meant to follow one another—only candidates who already proved their worthiness were permitted theoretically to purchase offices—the opposite was often true. It was common for people who purchased offices to then go on to prove that they were qualified for them. This was partially due to practical considerations. Requiring all candidates to pass an exam before they obtained an office seemed a huge waste of time and money. To ensure true competition for vacant

72. AGI, Quito, 129, 158–66, and the letter by Francisco Ramírez de Arellano, 24 April 1722.

73. The best source to understand the rules of the sale of offices remains A. León Pinelo, *Tratado de confirmaciones reales de encomiendas, oficios y casos en que se requieren para las Indias Occidentales* (Madrid, 1630). See also J. H. Parry, "The Sale of Public Office in the Spanish Indies under the Habsburgs," *Iberoamericana* 37 (1935): 74–158; F. Tomás y Valiente, "Ventas y renuncias de oficios públicos a mediados del siglo XVII," in *IV Congreso del Instituto Internacional de Historia del Derecho Indiano* (Mexico, 1976), 725–53; idem, *La venta de oficios en Indias;* V. González Muñoz, *Cabildo y groups de poder en Yucatán (siglo XVII)* (Seville, 1994), 52–132 and the bibliography cited in note 35. For a comparative view see R. Mousnier, *La venalité des offices sous Henri IV et Louis XVII* (Rouen, 1945).

offices, it was vital to allow everybody to present their candidature and to require that only the winners pass a professional exam.[74]

Two qualities were used to measure the candidate's fitness for office: personal and professional. Theoretically, access to paralegal offices was restricted by social and genealogical considerations. Candidates to these offices had to prove their purity of blood, which in late seventeenth- and eighteenth-century Quito mainly meant that they had no Indian, and especially African, roots. They also had to be free men, of legitimate birth, and to possess a good reputation. These characteristics were meant to guarantee that officeholders would be trustworthy—trust being a trait that during this period was determined by inherited qualities and not by personal character or education. Trust was especially important in the case of notaries. When notaries spoke or wrote in their official capacity, they no longer expressed a personal opinion (*fe particular*) but instead spoke for the community as a whole. Their speech was capable of transforming subjective knowledge into public knowledge, considered by definition as objective, neutral, and permanent. By law, their declarations, called *fe pública,* contained the truth. There was no need to prove that such was the case and no way to argue against them. In the case of notaries, therefore, it was essential to verify that they would be people who could incarnate the voice of the community, and the first step in this verification was to guarantee that they were descendants of the right families.[75]

The degree to which these theoretical considerations were met in practice in Quito is unclear. A thorough investigation into the candidates' families required an investment in time and money that both the authorities and the candidates wanted to avoid. As a result, the investigation was fairly limited in many cases.[76] This economy of means was also accompanied by the conviction that the city was small enough to allow for people to discern who was worthy of which treatment without the need for heavy expenses. This impression, which was dominant in the seventeenth century, nevertheless faded away in the next hundred

74. AHQ, Of., 12: exp. 12 February 1695.

75. J. M. Pérez Prendes y Muñoz de Arraco, "Introducción," *El escribano de consejo en la corona de Castilla (siglos XI al XVII)*, E. Corral García, (Burgos, 1987), vii–xii; and J. Luján Muñoz, *Los escribanos en las Indias Occidentales y en particular en el Reino de Guatemala* (Guatemala, 1977), 20–29.

76. AHN, Cód., 758B, no. 99; and AHN, Cód., 720B, no. 58. Although there are indirect references to this practice, the only explicit example of compliance I found is AGI, Quito, 44, no. 11.

years. During the eighteenth century Quileños constantly complained about the proliferation of court clerks, notaries, and procurators who originated in lower social echelons and/or were mestizos. For example, in the mid-1740s witnesses testified that Diego Arias Altamirano, court clerk and provincial notary, was the "the son of a female dressed as a mestiza"—and that this mestiza was actually an Indian.[77] Yet the authorities did nothing against him, nor did they move to ensure that such nominations would be impossible in the future. From the mid–eighteenth century, practically no investigation was carried out concerning the genealogy of candidates.[78]

After the personal requirements were met (or were ignored), eligible candidates had to prove their professional training and pass an exam. Professional training consisted of working in a clerk's, notary's, or procurator's office as a subordinate or an assistant for several years. The exam was conducted in the acuerdo room in the presence of all magistrates. The exam tested the candidates' understanding of legal procedures and ability to handle practical issues. Candidates were presented with real cases that were pending before the court and were requested to analyze them. Procurators had to demonstrate that they were familiar with both the procedures and the legal arguments that could be used. Court clerks and notaries were asked about formulas, the rights of the parties, and procedural issues such as forms of proof, rules to free prisoners, ways to continue a trial in the absence of the suspect, and the legal capacity of minors or slaves.[79]

There was not a single recorded case in Quito of a candidate failing the exam. This means that either failures did not happen or that they were not registered. In notarial manuals, the possibility of failing the exam was discussed. Two solutions were offered in these cases. If failure was due to insufficient training, the candidate could retake the exam later on. If failure was due to other causes, such as inability, he should be barred from office for life.[80]

A candidate who passed the exam could proceed to purchase a suitable office. This purchase was different from the one experienced by

77. AGI, EC, 914B, cuad. 5, 237–51.

78. AHN, Cód., 758B, no. 99.

79. "Cartilla y examen de escribanos en que se contienen todo género de causas civiles y criminales, ordenanzas . . . que pueden servir para los que hablan de semejante asunto, . . . [n.d.]," MS 12.958(3), BN.

80. "Ceremonias y estilo de los tribunales del Reino de Navarra [18th c. ?]," MS 9910, 88–89, BN.

judges because it involved a true patrimonial transmission that allowed purchasers to become possessors of a property that they could resell or donate. The sale of the office was regulated by means of contracts that were a complex economic and ceremonial affair. When the audiencia declared that an office was available for sale, the treasurer and the accountant of the royal treasury estimated its value by collecting information on the prices received in former sales. The president then ordered public announcements to be made indicating an office was now available. In most cases, the town crier (*pregonero*) made thirty such announcements at the rate of one a day. Those who were interested in buying the office put forward their offers. The announcements continued until the authorities considered that they were no longer necessary. On occasion, sixty, ninety, and even as many as three hundred announcements were given for the same office—as many as the president thought necessary. From 1644 onward, the availability of offices in the city of Quito was also announced in other cities, towns, and villages of the province.[81]

After the available office was sufficiently publicized, the president ordered a public auction (*remate y pregón*). This auction was usually held at the door of the audiencia, which overlooked the central square. The town crier, "in a clear and loud voice," repeated the formula for the sale in the presence of a magistrate, the crown attorney, the accountant of the royal treasury, and a notary. Those interested in purchasing the office came forward and made bids. Most bids included a price as well as details on the terms of payment and the conditions of holding the office. These conditions could include the employment of a temporary officeholder, the purchase of an office by a minor, or the holding of more than a single office at a time.[82] When the magistrate presiding over the ceremony decided that no other offers would be forthcoming, he ordered the crier to announce the finishing formula: "is there no one willing to offer a better price? At one, at two, at three; done, done, done."[83] The auction concluded with the ratification of the offer by the best bidder. After the sale was formalized in this way, proofs were sent to Madrid, where the Council of the Indies made the final decision and ratified (or rejected) the purchaser as an officeholder.

81. AGI, Quito, 41, no. 22.

82. AGI, Quito, 43, no. 15, 16.

83. The original version reads: "No hay quién diga más a la una, a las dos, a las tres. Que buena, que buena, que buena."

Offices were usually sold to the candidates who offered the greatest amount of money or the best terms of payment. On occasion, public auctions produced a true haggling session. In 1657 the initial price of 1,000 pesos for the office of court clerk was gradually raised to 1,520 pesos due to the bidding competition between five candidates.[84] The same thing occurred in 1662 with the office of notary of the provincial court (*escribano de provincia*), which rose from 1,500 (its estimated value) to 2,000 pesos (the price for which it was sold) because of the presence of several competitors.[85] Yet even a single candidate with no rivals could improve his offer if the magistrates convinced him to do so.[86]

Bidding for office could be dangerous. In 1670, the office of court clerk was sold to Damián Granja, an absentee candidate.[87] Apparently, Granja submitted an offer in 1668. After the audiencia valued the office at 1,500 pesos (which was 500 pesos more than what he was willing to pay), Granja withdrew the bid. He left the city and established himself in Loja (south of the province). In his absence, and without his knowledge, the court held a public auction, and given that Granja was the only candidate, it accepted his bid despite its being so low. In 1671, because of Granja's continued absence (and lack of payment), the court declared the office vacant, yet it still demanded that he pay its value. Located in Guayaquil, Granja was arrested and his properties seized.

Most purchases were individual, and they identified the person who would exercise the office or gave him the right to nominate somebody else. Nevertheless, in 1645 the town council of Quito purchased the office of provincial of the Santa Hermandad in order to rotate it among its members.[88] This purchase was projected as soon as the king allowed provincials to have a voice and vote in the municipal council.[89] Apparently, the aim of the council was to close ranks: it wanted to make sure no new men entered into it. Francisco Villacís, who advanced the capital necessary for the purchase, was the first alderman to occupy the office. From 1658 onward, the office began rotating among the other aldermen. Finally, in 1681, it was transferred to the king as payment for

84. AGI, Quito, 41, no. 6. A similar case can be found in AGI, Quito, 38, no. 43.

85. AGI, Quito, 41, no. 10.

86. AGI, Quito, 38, no. 59.

87. AHQ, Of., 1: exp. 27 August 1626.

88. Town council meeting of 17 November 1645, published in J. A. Garcés, ed., *Libros de cabildo de la ciudad de Quito, 1638–1646* (Quito, 1960), 329–30.

89. AMQ, Misc., 00005, 111.

the privilege of electing municipal ordinary justices (see the following). Afterward, it fell into the hands of various temporary holders who were named by the president of the audiencia. In 1695, it was fully integrated into the network of "saleable offices."

Offices were auctioned whenever new ones were created, which was fairly rare, or when existing ones were declared vacant. Vacancy could occur when the officeholder died, when he failed to pay the price, or when the confirmation of the purchase from the Council of the Indies didn't arrive on time (within five years).[90] In the case of death, the heirs of the officeholder had the right to receive half of the value of the office, the other half going to the king. In the case of nonpayment or nonconfirmation, no compensation was guaranteed to the frustrated candidate. Because the purchase of office involved an important economic investment, most candidates sought to limit the financial risk that they took. Gradually, candidates introduced a clause into their contracts that allowed them to transfer the office to another individual. This clause, which was exceptional at first, became common practice in both Castile and Spanish America. By the mid–seventeenth century, it was already considered part of the law governing all "saleable offices." Transfer was more advantageous than losing the office because it allowed an individual to conserve two-thirds of the value of the office, instead of only half (in the case of offices declared vacant) or no value at all (in all other cases).

The transfer of offices between individuals was called "renunciation" (*renuncia*).[91] Renunciations consisted of a written document signed in front of a public notary in which the officeholder named one or several people as his successor(s) in office. No special reason need be given.[92] There was no mention of an agreement between the parties (the person who renounced his office and the one who obtained it), a price to be paid, or any other conditions to be fulfilled. Despite this silence,

90. An office purchaser had five years to obtain a confirmation of the sale in Madrid. Vacancy occurred when he failed to request the confirmation or failed to obtain it.

91. J. Rumazo, *Documentos para la historia de la Audiencia de Quito* (Madrid, 1948), 41–45: cédula of 21 February 1689; AHQ, Ced., 2, 1601–60, no. 91, 108: cédula of 14 March 1634; and A. León Pinelo, *Tratado,* vol. 2, chaps. 5–6 and 8–10. For a comparative view see M. Hernández, "¿Y después de las ventas de oficio qué? (Transmisiones privadas de regimientos en el Madrid moderno, 1606–1808)," *Anuario de historia del derecho español* 65 (1995): 705–48.

92. Rumazo, *Documentos para la historia,* 41–45; and AHQ, Ced., 2 (1601–60), no. 91 from 1634.

we know that most renunciations were preceded by long negotiations. Many offices were transferred to sons or sons-in-law as part of their inheritance or dowry.[93] Others were sold in true commercial deals involving middlemen who specialized in these kinds of transactions (*cesionarios*) and a market of potential candidates.[94] In cases where renunciation was practically a private sale, the parties usually reached an oral understanding or signed contracts that were not formalized before a notary. In 1613 Marcos Rodríguez de Gaona, who agreed to purchase the office of the court clerk Alonso Sánchez Maldonado, argued that the clerk (who later changed his mind) should be forced to surrender the office to him. He produced a copy of the notarial act of renunciation in which his name was mentioned. Rodríguez de Gaona claimed that this act was signed after the parties had reached an agreement.[95] He could not, however, produce this agreement. The terms were drawn on paper, but Rodríguez de Gaona said that the only copy was in the possession of Sánchez Maldonado. Because he was willing to pay what he promised, he claimed that Sánchez Maldonado must comply with his part of the deal and allow him to exercise the office. Sánchez Maldonado answered this request by stating that there was neither a deal nor a paper. He had renounced his office to Rodríguez de Gaona because he knew Rodríguez de Gaona wanted to be a clerk. He had hoped that they would reach an agreement at a later date, yet this hope failed to materialize. Because no agreement was reached, he claimed the renunciation should not be enforced. The audiencia, who believed this story, allowed Sánchez Maldonado to keep his office.

Because most terms of renunciations were discussed orally, there are only few complete records of the contents of such transactions. The examples are few, but telling. The first consists of an agreement finalized in 1630 between Andrés Orozco Guzmán and Cosme de Oliva Atienza, in which the first promised to renounce his office of court notary to the second.[96] The second example is a document signed in 1655 by Juan Lorenzo Lucero and Martín Martínez de Aybar. These documents, both dealing with the transfer of the office of court notary, identified the object for sale, the price, the payments, and the identity of

93. AGI, Quito, 38, no. 39; and AGI, Quito, 39, no. 49.

94. AHQ, Of., 1: exp. 24 December 1629; AHQ, Of., 1: exp. 6 April 1633; and AHQ, Of., 4: exp.6 February 1658.

95. AHQ, FE, 1, 1600–1628, no. 35, 45.

96. AHQ, Of., 3: exp. 4 May 1655, 43–45.

the guarantors.[97] In the case dated 1655, Lucero (for whom Antonio Sánchez Maldonado renounced the office in the first place) ceded his primacy to Martínez de Aybar, who was the second person mentioned in the list. Apparently Lucero (who was also the executor of Sánchez Maldonado) did not wish to exercise the office. He thus notified Martínez de Aybar that the office could be his. Martínez de Aybar was happy to comply, and he promised to pay what was agreed upon with the notary to the notary's heirs.

There were two conditions that made renunciations valid. First, the officeholder had to live at least twenty days after the date that he signed the formal renunciation in the presence of a notary. This development, which was fairly late in date, sought to limit the efficacy of transfers between individuals by excluding all transfers carried out on a deathbed. In the aftermath of this legislation, officeholders and their families were forced to estimate when death would arrive. They had to evaluate how long the officeholder could live and when his renunciation should take place. Renouncing too late had bad economic effects because the renunciation could be invalidated if the officer did not live more than twenty days after it was signed. In this case the office would be declared vacant, and half of its value, instead of one-third as in the case of a renunciation, would go to the king. Renouncing too early was just as risky. Those who agreed to purchase the office might want to implement the deal even if the officeholder got better and wished to continue to work. Bad calculations happened again and again. For example, in 1627 Diego Suárez de Figueroa requested permission from the authorities to cancel the renunciation he had made in favor of Diego Rodríguez Urban de la Vega.[98] He explained that when he was sick, his family convinced him to renounce the office because he might die without doing so. He asked the notary Juan del Castillo Figueroa to take care of this issue for him and to find a suitable candidate. Some time later he was notified that the "purchase had been completed." Yet now that he was well again, he wished to continue in his office. His request was denied.

The second condition all renunciations had to meet was the appearance of the persons benefitting from it at the audiencia within sixty days of the renunciation. These individuals would have to claim the office

97. These documents are reproduced in T. Herzog, *Mediación, archivos y ejercicio: los escribanos de Quito (siglos XVII–XVIII)* (Frankfurt, 1996), 168–73.

98. AHQ, Of., 1: exp. 11 November 1627.

and request the court to receive them as office holders. It was usually assumed that the persons named in the renunciation appeared in successive order of precedence. Only when the first person declined the offer to purchase the office would the opportunity fall to the second candidate and so forth.[99]

The next stage in the process fixed the value of the office. The treasurer or accountant of the royal treasury prepared a report that primarily listed the sums received in previous sales. The audiencia then heard the opinions of the interested parties, or their experts, and arrived at a conclusion. This procedure was necessary because in cases of renunciation the king received a third of the value of the office. Yet, while the price fixed by the audiencia determined what the king would receive, it had no effect on the agreement between the officeholder and purchaser. Officeholders and purchasers were bound by the price they agreed upon before the renunciation took place. After the king's third was paid, and even before the officeholder received his full compensation, the office was declared property of the new possessor. It was not considered a royal affair if the new possessor failed to pay his predecessor. It was a debt between particulars. Confirming the transaction in Madrid completed the process. Failure to do so, or a negative response from Madrid, would produce a vacancy.

The sale and transfer of offices never functioned smoothly in Quito. During the seventeenth century, the audiencia consistently set prices too high, prices that almost no one was willing to pay. This problem arose from fixing prices according to precedent. This was a safe mechanism, yet inflexible. It failed to consider, for example, the state of the local economy. Prices were kept at the same level for many years despite constant complaints about a true decline in the value of offices. This devaluation was tied to falling revenues, to a series of natural disasters, and to a general economic recession in the city and province.[100] The pricing of offices also failed to take into account why a certain price was set on a particular occasion. Nevertheless, we know that the terms of sales varied substantially, and that sales that included special subrogation

99. AGI, Quito, 39, no. 28.

100. AGI, Quito, 43, no. 18; and AGI, Quito, 44, no. 4. The audiencia took these factors into account only after the second quarter of the eighteenth century. AHQ, Not. 1, 11: exp. 10 October 1721; and AHQ, Of., 30: exp. 29 January 1742. See also AHQ, Of., 3: exp. 4 May 1655.

clauses or that sold offices to minors, for example, were much more expensive than ordinary sales.

The lack of a clear relationship between price and value produced an endemic vacancy of offices in Quito, especially at the end of the seventeenth century and the beginning of the eighteenth. The offices of court notary and notary of the town council (*escribano de cabildo*), for example, were vacant for the thirteen years between 1667 and 1680. These long-term vacancies resulted from the extraordinarily high prices of the offices in previous auctions, prices that were double the actual value of these offices. (Both offices were bought for 24,000 pesos, yet the value was approximately 15,000 to 18,000 pesos in the first case and 10,000 pesos in the second).[101] Vacancy and price were closely connected. When the audiencia was at last willing to lower the prices to a reasonable level, both offices were immediately sold.

When lowering prices was still insufficient to guarantee the sale of offices, the audiencia resorted to renting them. Offices that were rented remained the property of the king, but their practice was delegated to people who paid an annual fee. Rentals were considered a last resort. The audiencia preferred to nominate temporary officeholders, who although they paid nothing for the right to exercise the offices, nevertheless, left at least some hope for a sale in the future. Yet, the proliferation of vacancies in Quito and elsewhere in the last decades of the seventeenth century (in 1699, the offices of court notary, town council notary, notary of the royal treasury, (*escribano de hacienda*), and two of four court clerks were all vacant) convinced the royal authorities to revise their policies.[102] Starting in 1675, the Council of the Indies authorized and even encouraged the renting of "saleable offices." This decision produced a true revolution in the provision of offices in Quito. After its sanction (especially at the very end of the seventeenth century, and even more so after the reestablishment of the audiencia in 1722), the majority of offices were no longer sold. Instead, they were auctioned off for a leased term. Bidders preferred rent to purchase because it required a smaller investment (usually the annual payment of 5 percent of the value of the office) and a smaller risk

101. AGI, Quito, 33: letter of the crown attorney, 6 February 1673; and related documents in AGI, Quito, 43, no. 15.

102. AGI, Quito, 33: letter of 23 February 1699.

(royal confirmation was not necessary).[103] Offices that were previously the property of the same holders for decades now lost their fixed character. Most rentals covered a three-year period, but many people moved in and out of them even before this term was over. Renters tried to improve their position, find a more profitable office, or simply make a better bid. Only in a small minority of cases did people renew the lease for the same office after their three years were over. This happened primarily with procurators, who had personal obligations to defendants. For example, Antonio de la Muela (1733–39) and Juan Manuel Andosilla (1727–49) were procurators who constantly renewed their offices.

As a result of the renting of offices, the identity of people employed as notaries, clerks, and procurators in Quito continually changed as new people entered or left the market of candidates. Instead of a small group of people exercising the same offices for decades, there was now a dynamic (and larger) pool of officers constantly on the move. This mobility produced important consequences. Officeholders were less identified with their offices compared with the earlier period. They were also less experienced in their work and less familiar with the particularities of their charges and the clients.

The transition from selling to renting offices was very difficult, and officeholders whose offices were declared vacant, and yet unavailable for sale, suffered economic hardship. Their investment (the value of the offices) simply disappeared, and the chances of recouping even a small part of it seemed remote. Wishing to minimize their losses, office owners attempted to guarantee that renters would be members of their households or families. They also asked the authorities to share with them the sums they received in rent.[104] The Council of the Indies initially approved these petitions, yet it changed its policy in the following years. Eventually the council denied the right of office owners to receive any compensation before their offices were sold.[105]

In total, the parajudicial world in Quito included some 160 people between 1650 and 1750. These people constituted a pool of candidates with similar qualifications and similar characteristics. Individuals who were employed as clerks could become notaries, and notaries could

103. AHN, Cód., 684B, nos. 28 and 34, 39–40, and 44–45. Apparently, office rental also became a frequent practice in Madrid: Hernández, "¿Y después," 736.

104. AHQ, Of., 30 and 34: exp. 29 January 1742 and exp. 1 September 1746.

105. AGI, Quito, 104: consulta from 23 August 1734.

become procurators, or vice versa. Pedro de los Reyes and Francisco Díaz de Astayza, for example, were procurators before they each bought a notarial office. Bernave Alarcón Tofino, Miguel Orteja, and Tomás Suárez de Figueroa came to the office of procurator after serving as assistants to one of the notaries. Ambrosio Rueda del Campillo acted as notary and procurator at the same time. Other procurators, such as Juan de Morales and Andrés Muñoz de la Concha, were also qualified to act as notaries, although apparently they did not.

These officers came from a variety of backgrounds.[106] Some were members of the town council of Quito, some belonged to elite families, and still others were associated with merchants, small-time traders, and clerics. The wealthier they were, the better (in terms of income and prestige) the offices they held. The most coveted offices were court notary and notary of the town council. Those employed in these offices were normally the sons of rich families (such as the Valencia León, the Sánchez Maldonado, and the Suárez de Figueroa). Candidates with lesser economic means (such as Juan Duque de Estrada, Francisco Valverde Aguilar, Nicolás Leguia, or Bernardo Espinosa de los Monteros) applied for the positions of provincial court notary, procurator, or court clerk.

Clerks, notaries, and procurators were often engaged in commercial undertakings. This activity was prohibited by law and court notaries such as Andrés Orozco Guzmán and Diego Valencia León were fined by the Council of the Indies for breaking this rule in the 1630s. Valencia León also administrated textile workshops and loaned money. In the mid–seventeenth century, the notary of the town council Diego de la Chica Narváez sold local products in exchange for European goods in the fairs of Panama.[107] He was the owner of textile workshops and farms and was a business associate of several merchants with shops in Quito.

As a group, clerks, notaries, and procurators had little in common—as the following brief biographies reveal. Martín Martínez de Aybar, who bought the office of court notary in 1655 for the price of 24,000

106. The same was noted in Huelva by D. González Cruz, *Escribanos y notarios en Huelva durante el Antiguo Régimen (1700–1801)* (Huelva, 1991), 70.

107. ANQ, Not. 1 (protócolos de Lorenzo Bravo de Pereira, 1699–1701), 626–29. Diego de la Chica Narváez was also studied in G. Soasti, "Mercaderes y tratantes en Quito durante el siglo XVII," *Enfoques y estudios históricos: Quito a través de la historia,* ed. P. Aguilar (Quito, 1992), 97–98.

pesos, held the post until 1663, when it was declared vacant on the news that the Council of the Indies refused to confirm the purchase.[108] A native of Navarre, Martínez de Aybar was a perpetual alderman of Quito, a municipal ordinary justice, and a temporary accountant of the royal treasury on several occasions. Having come to the Americas in 1634 with his uncle (who was the future president of the audiencia of Quito), Martínez de Aybar served as a captain in Buenos Aires and Chile. He married Jerónima de Santisteban y Vestia, a native of Quito and daughter of a wealthy local alderman. Martínez de Aybar was very wealthy, owning both farms and textile workshops. One of his daughters married José Joaquín de Aybar, a relative who was the lord of the palace of Aybar (Navarre) and a knight of the military order of Calatrava. His son Ignacio was a lawyer, a court recorder, and lieutenant governor on several occasions. Named the temporary crown attorney and protector of Indians for the audiencia in 1678–79 and 1687–91, Ignacio first bought the office of protector and then was promoted to that of magistrate, which he exercised until his death in 1708. Ignacio married Rosa Valverde y Contreras, daughter of Francisco Valverde, who was a knight of Santiago and master of the field in Callao (Lima's port). She was also the granddaughter of the magistrate of Lima Sebastián de Alarcón.

The biography of Francisco Gómez Acevedo, court clerk between 1658 and 1662, was somewhat different. A native of Quito, he first married Angela Hurtado de Mendoza and then María de Espinosa y Castañeda, with whom he had eight children. At the beginning of his professional career, his wife accused him of having an adulterous affair with a mestiza woman. Because of his recidivism in adultery, Gómez Acevedo was forced to renounce the office and go into exile.[109] As a moderately wealthy man, Gómez Acevedo collected tithes in the district of Cayambe (north of Quito) and was the owner of a sugar cane farm and distillery. After his debts were paid, some 8,340 pesos were divided among his heirs.[110]

Francisco Dionisio Montenegro was a court clerk in 1685 and a public notary (*escribano público*) from 1686 until his death in 1718. He first married María Álvarez, who gave birth to a daughter who married Ambrosio Rueda del Campillo, notary and procurator in Panamá,

108. AHQ, Ced., 4, no. 26.

109. AHQ, Crim., 4: exp. 30 March 1662.

110. AHQ, Test., 53: exp. 18 August 1722; and AHQ, Not.[3], 7: exp. 16 June 1705.

Lima, and Quito. Montenegro was fairly poor, his daughter earning her living by producing chicha (an alcoholic drink) and textiles at home. Montenegro's fortune changed when he married Cecilia Rosa de Sosa, daughter of the standard-bearer José Sosa. His second wife was fairly wealthy, having inherited several farms outside Quito and a house in the city. At the time of his death, Montenegro was fairly rich. He was the owner of many landed properties and household goods. Among other things, he possessed a farm, a ranch, land plots, and two houses in the plaza of San Francisco in Quito. He had a library with thirteen books, with titles in theology, commerce, law, and notarial practice. Montenegro also seems to have possessed a large collection of documents concerning his family history. However, he was also short on cash, and his property was heavily mortgaged.[111]

Elections in Quito

Municipal ordinary judges and justices of the Santa Hermandad were elected to office by the town council on January first each year. The election ceremony began with a bell calling the local governor and the aldermen (*regidores*) to enter the chamber of the town hall.[112] A priest performed a Mass, and the local governor requested God to illuminate the discernment of the assistants and direct them to a fair election. The governor then verified the presence of all those having a vote in the election or made sure that those who were absent were properly called to the meeting. Afterward, each member of the council took turns voting according to the rank of his office and his seniority in it. The governor had no vote. His role was limited to administrating the act, counting the votes, and declaring the names of those who had been chosen. The pres-

111. AHQ, Test., 32: exp. 22 June 1703; AHQ, Test., 67: exp. 11 November 1729; and AHQ, Not. 6, 8: exp. 21 May 1739.

112. The following description is based on the study of the acts of the city council. The elections of municipal judges were described by J. Solórzano y Pereira, *Política Indiana,* book 5 (1674; reprint, Madrid, 1972), chap. 1; E. Ruiz Giñazú, *La magistratura indiana* (Buenos Aires, 1916), 285–92; C. Bayle, *Los cabildos seculares en la América española* (Madrid, 1952), 107–38; C. Landázurri Camacho, "Estructura y funcionamiento del cabildo de Quito, 1534–1551," *Anuario hístorico jurídico ecuatoriano* 6 (1980): 565–91; González Muñoz, *Cabildo,* 26–45; and O. Cornblit, *Power and Violence in the Colonial City. Oruro from the Mining Renaissance to the Rebellion of Tupac Amaru (1740–1782),* trans. E. Ladd Glick (Cambridge, 1995), 37–91.

ident of the audiencia then confirmed the results, and the council called those elected to the town hall. There, they swore to use their office well and faithfully and received the rod of justice.[113]

In the aftermath of the "Rebellion of the *Alcabalas*," in which the inhabitants of Quito protested against the imposition of a sales tax (1539), the king temporarily suspended the privilege of electing municipal ordinary justices.[114] From 1539 to 1699, when the decision was finally reversed, the city of Quito struggled to regain this right. The town council, the audiencia, the bishop, and even the viceroy of Lima all took part in this struggle, which was especially intense between 1617 and 1699.[115] Many inhabitants of Quito supported these efforts: in 1696 they donated funds to cover the expenses involved in presenting petitions to the crown.[116] The argument Quito invoked was simple. The local election of municipal ordinary judges was important because it signaled the monarch's trust in his subjects. After all, electing judges meant administrating justice for both God and king. In their opinion, the people of Quito merited this trust because they were loyal to the king and served him well. All other cities of the viceroyalty of Perú enjoyed this privilege, and there was no reason to discriminate against Quito. The ability to elect local justices was a matter of "renown, preeminence, credit, and honor." Unless it was granted, Quito would be considered inferior to other cities, which in reality were less important and less loyal.

From the middle of the seventeenth century, the town council was well aware of the economic needs of the crown and so offered to pay a considerable sum in return for the privilege of local elections. It suggested the price of 3,000 pesos in cash or transferring the office of

113. The oath included the obligation to keep the law and the royal decrees, as well as respect the privileges and maintain the secrecy of the town council meetings. AGI, EC, 915A, cuad. 1, 108 and chap. 6.

114. This rebellion was studied by B. Lavallé, *Quito et la crise de l'alcabala (1580–1600)* (Paris, 1992); and idem, "La rebelión de las Alcabalas (Quito julio 1592–abril 1593), ensayo de interpretación," *Revista de Indias* 44 (1984): 141–202. See also T. Herzog, "De la historia y el mito: Las rebeliones de Quito (1592–1765)," *Reflejos* 7 (1998): 72–80; and M. Fernández Martínez, *La alcabala en la audiencia de Quito, 1765–1810* (Cuenca-Seville, 1984).

115. The conflict generated an enourmous amount of paperwork found in municipal records such as the acts of the city council, municipal correspondence (AMQ, Misc., 00053), royal decrees (especially the section of the Cedulario of the AHQ), and different documents included in AGI, Quito, 17.

116. AMQ, LC, 00116: town council meeting of 4 January 1696. At least 121 people participated in the collection, donating amounts between 3 and 500 pesos for a total of 4,629 pesos in favor of this cause.

provincial of the Santa Hermandad to royal hands. This office belonged to the city and was worth some 7,000 pesos. The town also explained that the election of local judges would benefit the crown because it would improve the collection of taxes, economize the salary of the local governor and his assistant (whose presence in the city would no longer be necessary), and increase the value of municipal offices in general.

The administration of justice was hardly ever mentioned. During the hundred years in which the struggle lasted, on only three occasions did the town council mention the belief that a municipally elected judge would be a better justice than an appointed foreign one.[117] In 1699 the king, motivated by the economic donation offered by Quito, ruled in favor of the city and allowed it to elect, once again, municipal ordinary judges.

Between 1650 and 1701, the dates on which the privilege to elect municipal ordinary judges was suspended and recuperated, the council of Quito was only authorized to elect justices of the Santa Hermandad. These elections, carried out each January, were fairly peaceful. In most cases candidates were elected by a majority vote, and at times even unanimously. The number of candidates was often equal to the number of offices available (two). Elections thus consisted of an automatic approval of prechosen individuals. In 1695, there was a lack of sufficient aldermen with the right to vote in the election—only two could participate because the other seven members of the council were debtors of the royal treasury and thus ineligible. In this situation, the council made an exception that "was not meant to serve as a precedent": it allowed the president of the audiencia to nominate the judges.

Only once during the period between 1650 and 1701 did the election provoke an open confrontation between the aldermen. The circumstances were exceptional. In 1668, Fernando Losada Quiñones and Francisco Torres Pizarro, both of whom were sons of audiencia magistrates, were elected to office. Some aldermen feared that their nomination would enable the audiencia to intervene in municipal affairs. They pointed to royal legislation that prohibited this election and insisted that it must be reversed. Under social pressure, both candidates renounced the offices, giving the conflict a rapid and peaceful conclusion.

From 1701 onward, the town council elected both municipal ordi-

117. AMQ, Misc., 00053: letter of the town council, 30 December 1696.

nary justices and justices of the Santa Hermandad. Consensus characterized the first few years. Candidates were elected by either a majority vote or unanimously. The only exception occurred in 1706, when the president of the audiencia canceled the election because several of the people who voted had no right to do so. From 1711 onward, the local governor (who was a passive participant in the elections until then) gradually began controlling the lists of candidates: he forced the council to reelect the justices of the previous year or indicated whom he wanted elected.

In 1732, the participation of aldermen indebted to the royal treasury (and therefore deprived of the right to vote) became a major obstacle to elections. Unlike previous years, in which debtors agreed to refrain from voting, those accused of owing money to the crown now denied the charges. Elections degenerated into conflicts about who owed what. Such questions were not easy to answer. They involved knowing whether or not a debt existed, when it was supposed to be paid, and who was responsible for paying it. The treasurer or accountant of the royal treasury had to clarify these issues. However, the treasurer and accountant, often disagreed and even when they agreed, the town council or some of its members could dispute their conclusion.

In 1735, a discussion concerning the provision of vacant offices in the town council was added to the debate about the identity of debtors. In the past, the audiencia nominated temporary officeholders. However, in September 1734, it decided that offices should be rented.[118] The two municipal ordinary justices and the senior alderman argued against this solution and advocated the continuation of the previous practice. Invoking traditional claims about the need to sell offices rather than rent them, the three men were primarily concerned with the identity of the eight individuals who had succeeded in entering the council in this manner.[119] These eight individuals, they argued, formed a compact social group planned and organized by the royal treasurer (*tesorero de la Caja Real*), Fernando García Aguado. First, García Aguado ensured that offices would be available to rent and then that his relatives and friends would be chosen. In this way, he managed to obtain eight votes

118. The conflict was described in the books of the town council but also left traces in AGI, EC, 927, 62–63; AGI, EC, 911B, 518; and AGI, EC, 914B, cuad. 8, 104–25.

119. These questions are described in greater length in T. Herzog, "Redes personales y capitales institucionales: la real hacienda y el cabildo de Quito a mediados del siglo XVIII," *Fronteras* 4/4 (2000): 113–26.

on a council in which, given his office as treasurer, he was not allowed to participate.

According to the justices and alderman, the suspicion that this is what had happened was reaffirmed in the elections of 1735.[120] The eight new aldermen who obtained their office by rent in 1734 voted in favor of the same candidates; given their numerical superiority within the council, their nominees were elected.[121] The new judges were all related to the treasurer and owed him their election. This guaranteed that they would rule in a way that was favorable to the treasurer. The results of the elections thus clearly benefited the treasurer who was involved in litigation and wanted to ensure the good will of the judges towards his person.

The justices and the alderman criticized the procedure by which aldermen were chosen, as well as the elections that followed. However, while they brought up these issues inside the council, and made some very harsh accusations, they refused to create a public scandal. Despite their bitter opposition, they were willing to behave in a way that would not upset the city or work against the image of civility and consensus. They remained in the municipal hall and witnessed the taking of oath by the new mandatories whom they disliked and whose election they disapproved.

The existence in Quito of two rival groups, one organized by the treasurer and the other formed against him, became even more apparent the following year.[122] The issue was once again the election of municipal ordinary judges. The members of each group masked their opposition, which was motivated by friendship, loyalty ties, and the desire to control the council, with a discourse stressing obedience to the laws. However, their biased understanding of these laws was obvious. One side claimed that the rival faction presented candidates who were debtors to the royal treasury. The other responded by denying the charges and arguing that the lists of debtors presented to the council were deliberately false or simply incorrect.[123] The two justices and the alderman also stated that family ties united the candidates for election with other members of the royal administration. The opposing group

120. AMQ, LC, 00124: town council meeting of 31 January 1735.

121. AGI, EC, 914A, cuad. 1, 152–53. See also "Manifiesto impreso que hace la ciudad de Quito sobre nulidades que intervinieron en las elecciones de los oficiales de justicia de 1735" in AGI, EC, 914B, cuad. 8, 104–25; and the certificate elaborated by the town notary Domingo López Urquía on 2 January 1735 in AGI, EC, 927, 62–63.

122. AGI, EC, 911B, 518–24; and AGI, EC, 915A, cuad. 4, 220–33.

123. AGI, EC, 915A, cuad. 4, 220–36.

undermined this argument by denying the existence of such ties, or at least their importance. Additional arguments included the allegation that the members of the rival group were debtors too. Their candidates could not be elected because there was a legal prohibition against reelecting municipal justices and against electing individuals whose previous time in office was not yet investigated by judicial inspection (*residencia*).

This time the conflict degenerated into "shouting, confusion, and passion" and could only be resolved by the intervention of higher authorities. The viceroy, expressing his opinion that the reelection of municipal judges (which the majority of alderman backed) was indeed illegal, confirmed the minority position and approved the candidates this group had chosen. Yet even before the decision reached Quito, a local solution was already in place. The two men who were elected by the majority of councilmen but whose nomination met with so much opposition resigned their offices, and instead, the president named temporary officeholders.

The struggle inside the council intensified in the following months. New offices became available in the town council, and following the express instructions of the viceroy, the audiencia sold six of them and rented only one.[124] In the aftermath, the treasurer lost his control of the town council, which was now in the hands of the opposing group. Although the members of the other group claimed that they each came to office in order to "serve the king and return the luster to this city," it was clear that they were intentionally grouped together.[125] In 1748, at least one of them openly confessed this fact, explaining that he was "enlisted" by Lorenzo Nates and Lorenzo (Díaz) de la Madrid.[126] The

124. AGI, EC, 915A, cuad. 1, 125: letter of the viceroy to the president of the audiencia, 13 December 1736. Also see the certificate of accountant José Suárez de Figueroa of 2 February 1737 in AGI, EC, 915A, cuad. 1, 65–66.

125. AGI, EC, 915A, cuad. 1, 48: letter of the purchasers to the king, 18 March 1737.

126. AHQ, Not. 1, 29: exp. 27 August 1748. Also see petition of July 1748 in AGI, EC, 916A—*pieza* (piece) 14; and the verdicts of 8 August 1747 and 20 November 1756 in AGI, EC, 964. The commercial activities of Lorenzo (Díaz) de la Madrid are described, for example, in AHQ, Not. 3, 25: exp. 6 July 1742. Lorenzo Nates was an important member of the social network that confronted President José de Araujo y Río in the 1740s: see the next chapter. His commercial dealings are also described in T. Herzog, "Reglas jurídicas e integración social: el comercio (Quito, primera mitad del siglo XVIII)," *Actas del XI Congreso del Instituto Internacional de Historia del Derecho Indiano, Buenos Aires, 4–9 de septiembre de 1995* (Buenos Aires, 1997), 385–87; and in AHQ, Test., 103 and 104: exp. 3 April 1753 and 6 September 1753.

two Lorenzos, who were wealthy merchants, assured him that they would pay the price of the office, as well as take care of any demands placed on him by the exercise of the office. The Lorenzos also promised him that they would take him to the fair in Cartagena and lend him money to purchase goods. They told him that he would not need to do anything while he was a member of the council; they would do everything for him. All they needed were honest people who could represent them and their interests in the municipal sphere.

Each group used different mechanisms to control the city council. In 1734, the treasurer used his institutional position in order to elect people whom he trusted to the council. He first convinced the audiencia to rent rather than sell the offices. He then proceeded to decide who presented the best offers and who would rent the offices. The economic investment of the members of this group was fairly small, and it consisted of an annual rent, equal to 5 percent of the office's value. In 1736, in contast, the people who bought the offices imposed their will (and defeated the treasurer) by virtue of their economic power. Unable to compete with the members of the opposing group on this level, the treasurer employed, once again, his institutional privileges. He identified individuals belonging to the rival group as debtors to the royal treasury and disqualified them from voting in the 1737 elections. In this way, he practically eliminated most of his enemies, including Simón Álvarez Monteserín, José Herrera, Juan José Sánchez de Orellana, Joachin Gómez Laso de la Vega, Tomás Pérez Guerrero, Juan Ponce de León (count of Selvaflorida), and Antonio Pastrana.[127] Help to this group came from an unexpected direction. The accountant of the royal treasury disagreed with the treasurer and determined that only five of the men were truly debtors, for the sixth had paid his debt, and the seventh only owed 40 pesos, which he was not asked to pay because of a mistake by royal officials.[128] This decision was significant because it gave enough votes to the members of the group opposing the treasurer.[129]

In the days preceding the 1737 elections, the new president of the audiencia, José de Araujo y Río, decided to take sides.[130] Following the

127. AGI, EC, 914B, cuad. 5, 118–19: report by Fernando García de Aguado, 23 March 1737.

128. AGI, EC, 914B, cuad. 5, 120–21: report by accountant José Suárez de Figueroa.

129. AGI, EC, 914A, cuad. 1, 31–34: letter of crown attorney Juan Valparda y la Ormasa to the king, 1 March 1737; and AGI, EC, 914A, cuad. 1, 68–71.

130. AGI, EC, 914A, cuad. 1, 1–10, 101–7, and cuad. 3, 72–73.

advice of the treasurer, he named five individuals to the still vacant offices in the town council, and he dictated the list of candidates for the annual election, manifesting his preference for two of them. The president then refused to confirm the election of justices by the majority of aldermen who disobeyed him, and he supported the opinion of the minority who followed his recommendations. He was motivated by his desire, he said, to preserve peace and harmony and to ensure that those elected as justices would be fit for office. This was a nonpartisan position that aimed only at eliminating the power of both bands. However, the members of the group who had obtained a majority in the council, whose decision he had reversed, thought differently. They accused the president of wanting to support the treasurer, his ally, and they resented the implication that the people whom they had chosen were unqualified for office. Their version was not farfetched. The five aldermen whose vote the president confirmed were the five he had appointed to office, and they elected the two sons-in-law of the treasurer. As had happened in the previous year, the two justices elected by the minority of aldermen and approved by the president yielded to social pressure. Despite presidential backing, and despite their allegiance to the treasurer, they renounced their offices, giving a peaceful and quick solution to the conflict.

The 1737 elections thus demonstrated the continuing attempts of treasurer García Aguado to control the town council, this time backed by the president. The rival group, composed mainly of merchants, also won new allies in the accountant of the royal treasury and the crown attorney of the audiencia Juan Valparda y la Ormaza. Valparda y la Ormaza initially directed his attacks at the treasurer, whom he accused of promoting the rent of offices in Quito only because it suited his personal interests.[131] Not only did the treasurer promote rents, he also made sure that no one would be willing to purchase offices. People who wanted to become aldermen now refused to do so, fearing his animosity. The cards were now laid out for a major confrontation. On the one hand was a group of wealthy merchants backed by the accountant and the crown attorney. On the other was the treasurer supported by the new president of the audiencia.

The candidates elected by the majority, yet disqualified by the pres-

131. AGI, EC, 914A, cuad. 1, 31–34: letter of Juan Valparda y la Ormasa to the king, 1 March 1737.

ident from office, were the count of Selvaflorida and Antonio Pastrana. Both were offended by the accusation that they were unfit to be municipal judges, and both sought redress in the months following the 1737 election. In November of 1737, they offered to provide judicial information that would demonstrate otherwise. The president interpreted this move as a preview of the 1738 elections. He rejected the offer by arguing that it was likely to produce "disturbances to the peace" (*disturbios a la paz*). On his own initiative, he conducted an official hearing in November and December that was meant to prove the unworthiness of both men. Araujo y Río collected the declarations of people who he hoped would support his view. Nevertheless, the witnesses he selected refused to comply.[132] They conceded that Pastrana was an "ambitious person," yet they insisted that the count was of "congenial and affable character, without any malicious intentions." Abandoned by people whom he considered his allies, Araujo y Río admitted his defeat. In January 1738, he formally announced that his first year of presidency in Quito convinced him to reconsider his position. He now understood, he said, that both Pastrana and the count were credible people, and he now agreed that they were both worthy of appointment as judges. Araujo y Río could proceed in this way, among other reasons, because he had already managed to eliminate the candidature of both men in the new election, held in 1738.[133]

The elections of 1738 transpired with relative calm. This peace was possible thanks to the elimination of the candidature of Pastrana and the count but also because of a presidential move that kept the decree containing the names of debtors away from the town hall. This decree, which disqualified some of the president's men from voting, was prepared the previous night by the accountant at the house of Lorenzo Nates, one of the leaders of the merchant group.[134] Because its ruling was not taken into account, the town council permitted all its members to vote, and the president, who was content with the results, immediately confirmed them. According to his rivals, the president ensured the obedience of the council to his recommendations regarding the vote by being physically present on-site. He waited outside the door of the hall

132. AGI, EC, 916A, 235–44.

133. AGI, EC, 915A, cuad. l, 109.

134. AGI, EC, 914A, cuad. 4, 125–89, 166; AGI, EC, 914C, 45: letter of President José de Araujo y Río, 18 July 1739; and AGI, EC, 914A, cuad. 2, 115–18: declaration of the notary Diego Arias Altamirano, 5 August 1743. See also AGI, EC, 914B, cuad. 5, 237–51.

in which the aldermen were assembled, virtually guarding it during the election.

The elections of 1739 were a repetition of what had happened in 1737. In late 1738, President Araujo y Río convinced several of his friends (Tomás Pérez Guerrero, Francisco Javier Larrea, Bernardo de León, and Ramón Juachín Maldonado y Solomayor) to purchase the seats still vacant on the town council.[135] Before the elections took place, he pronounced a decree against Pastrana, qualifying him as a debtor of the royal treasury and thus prohibiting his candidature. The smoke announcing an oncoming fire appeared a day before the elections took place, when some aldermen refused to participate in the *venía,* which was the annual visit of the town council to the president. This refusal frustrated the presidential plan to coordinate with the aldermen the identity of next year's judges. The council then disobeyed the instructions of the president and elected people he had not chosen. The president, in response, confirmed the minority vote and disqualified, as a debtor, one of the judges elected by the majority.[136] The conflict regarding the identity of debtors who could not vote in elections grew to such proportions that the audiencia and the viceroy had to intervene.[137] Following the elections, the crown attorney summoned the majority voters (whose vote the president refused to confirm) and declared that the election was null and void. In April 1739, the viceroy censured the steps taken by the president and confirmed the majority vote.

In 1740, debate centered again on the right to vote, as two of the aldermen who voted were also local governors in the province. Because provincial governors were theoretically excluded from membership in Quito's town council it was unclear whether the elections were valid or not. The governor of Macas presented his nomination to office, which specifically allowed him to continue to be alderman in Quito. The (future) local governor of Ríobamba successfully demonstrated that he had not yet taken possession of his office. Thereafter, both men were allowed to vote and the president confirmed this majority vote.

In contrast to the 1730s, from 1740 to 1750 the elections of municipal

135. AGI, EC, 914A, cuad. 2, 153; and AGI, EC, 915A, cuad. 4, 246: declarations of Simón Álvarez Monteserín.

136. AGI, EC, 914A, cuad. l, 108 and 156, and cuad. 2, 159–64; AGI, EC, 914B, cuad. 5, 228–30; AHQ, Of., 29: exp. 10 January 1739; and AHQ, Not. 1, 29: exp. 27 August 1748.

137. AHQ, Of., 29: exp. 10 January 1739: petition of Juan Valparda y la Ormasa, 7 January 1739, and certificate of town notary Domingo López Urquía, 5 January 1739.

ordinary justices transpired without major concerns. In most cases, the local governor supplied a list of candidates and reached an agreement with the council concerning the identity of the judges that would be elected. The aldermen usually respected this agreement and supported it either in a majority vote or in a unanimous decision. The arrival of four new aldermen to the town council in 1745 once again stirred up passions, and some people questioned the right of others to vote. The local governor and the audiencia, however, refused to listen to these allegations.

The issues raised during the elections of municipal justices—the right to vote, the identity of voters, the identity of the elected—should also have affected the elections of justices of the Santa Hermandad. However, such was not the case. The conflicts experienced between 1735 and 1740 focused on the identity of the municipal ordinary justices. Even in years of continuous conflicts, the elections of justices of the Santa Hermandad followed their normal course and were primarily unanimous decisions. The 1737 elections marked this difference most clearly. The open struggle and the mutual accusations between the two groups regarding the election of municipal ordinary justices did not affect the election of the justices of the Santa Hermandad, and members of both factions supported the candidacy of the same people.

Why did the elections of municipal ordinary justices arouse so much passion, and why were the elections of Santa Hermandad justices so consensual? The answer lies in the fact that the two offices were radically different. Municipal ordinary judges became voting members of the local town council. During their term in office, they headed the municipal body and presided over its sessions whenever the local governor was absent. The duties of ordinary judges included administrative and judicial tasks. They managed municipal affairs on their own and had both civil and criminal jurisdiction in the city and villages of its jurisdiction. The justices of the Santa Hermandad, on the contrary, had a different function altogether. Their jurisdiction only covered uninhabited areas (mainly royal roads and the wasteland between settlements), and they were only charged with criminal affairs. Their office was considered a burden. Justices of the Hermandad had to recruit, at their own expense, the troops (*cuadrilla*) that patrolled the countryside with them. They were constantly on the move, forced away from their homes, and engaged in an activity that was unpleasant and dangerous. In short, their office was less honorable, less comfortable, and more expensive. A justice of the Santa Hermandad also had less contact with the affairs and people in Quito and its villages than did ordinary judges. This office, therefore, was less coveted by individuals and less important for the factions to control.

The events of 1732–40 also exemplified the inherent contradiction between the politics of elections and the social ideal of unanimity. In Quito, the wish to maintain and even ceremoniously affirm the omnipresence of peace did not disappear despite the constant recourse to elections. Elections were held, yet votes were unanimous. Unanimity was important because it represented (and ensured) the harmony among the inhabitants of the city. Indeed, unanimity was preserved whenever it was possible. The council unanimously elected the justices of the Santa Hermandad even in times of heated conflict and open debate regarding the identity of the ordinary ones. Concentrating on what was truly important (the election of municipal ordinary justices), and conceding what was less essential, all disputants agreed that peace should not only prevail but should be heralded at least in the elections of justices of the Santa Hermandad. The wish for harmony also explains why the aldermen of the opposition agreed to maintain a posture of agreement in 1735. Avoiding scandal, they remained in the city hall and presided over the oath taken by their rivals. In a similar way, those elected or confirmed against the majority vote resigned on account of social pressure that militated against divisions in 1736 and in 1737.

Desire for peace and harmony did not mask the existence of rivalries. These rivalries were formed inside and outside the institutions (chap. 3). Those participating in the struggle to elect certain individuals as judges argued that they were motivated by loyalty to the king and obedience to the laws. However, the residents of Quito were aware of the fact that the conflict inside the town council was only a reflection of what was happening elsewhere.[138] The elections of municipal ordinary judges thus demonstrated how local institutions could become both players and victims in a global power struggle. This struggle, which I

138. L. Ramos Gómez, "Un ejemplo de la lucha por el poder en Quito," *Cultura* 8 (1986): 117–32; idem, "La estructura social quiteña entre 1737 y 1745 según el proceso contra José de Araujo," *Revista de Indias* 51 (1991): 25–56; and idem, "La pugna por el poder local en Quito entre 1737 y 1745 según el proceso contra el presidente de la audiencia José de Araujo y Río," *Revista complutense de historia de América* 18 (1992): 179–96.

analyze further in chapter 3, had its own logic and its own aims, yet it was often expressed in the wish to secure the nomination of judges who were favorable to one faction or the other.

Municipal ordinary justices and justices and provincials of the Santa Hermandad all belonged to the same group of people, in which lieutenant governors and chief constables also participated. Several people in this group exercised the same office several times, while others were employed in more than a single office. Bartolomé Zarauz y Aldamar was justice of the Santa Hermandad in 1682 and provincial in 1686 and 1690. Nicolás Fernando de la Carrera was justice of the Santa Hermandad in 1678 and 1691 and municipal ordinary judge in 1702 and 1704. Diego Sandoval Portocarrero held the office of justice of the Santa Hermandad in 1663, 1666, and 1669 and was lieutenant of the local governor in 1671.

People belonging to this group were also aldermen. Until the end of the seventeenth century, the provincials of the Santa Hermandad were by definition members of the local town council. In the eighteenth century they were more often members than not. Justices of the Santa Hermandad were aldermen in the seventeenth century, yet after the town started electing municipal ordinary justices in 1701, most of them no longer served on the council. Customarily, at least one municipal ordinary justice was an alderman, and at times both justices were aldermen. Nonaldermen elected to office were at least associated with the town council in other ways. They could be charged with another municipal duty or were relatives or friends of aldermen. Juan de Aguirre Goyzueta, for example, was chief constable, provincial, and lieutenant to the local governor in 1658–59. Juan Francisco Borja y Larraspuro was chief constable between 1705 and 1707 and municipal ordinary justice in 1723 and 1728.

During the seventeenth century, most people elected as local judges were immigrants from the immediate province or from other areas in Spain or Spanish America. By the eighteenth century, this situation was reversed, and most justices were natives of the city. Many of them were economically active as landowners, owners of textile mills, merchants, loan makers, or tax farmers. Simón Álvarez Monteserín and Antonio Laso de la Vega were merchants and tax collectors. Salvador Pérez Guerrero and Ramón Juachín Maldonado y Sotomayor were landowners, loan makers, and merchants. The economic situation of local judges usually ranged from comfortable to wealthy. The poorest among them tended to be the lieutenant governors, who were appointed by the governor. Once again, a series of short biographies serves to illustrate the networks in which justices were caught up.

Diego Sandoval Portocarrero was justice of the Santa Hermandad in 1663, 1666, and 1669 and lieutenant governor in 1671. A native of Quito, he descended on both sides from conquistador families.[139] His father, Diego Sandoval Londoño, was an encomendero and the great grandson of a soldier who died defending the viceroy during the Peruvian civil wars. His mother, Francisca de Loma Portocarrero, was the grandchild of military men who had fought in both Flanders and the Americas and who were employed as local governors in the New World. Captain of the infantry, alderman, and procurator of the town council on several occasions, Diego Sandoval Portocarrero was very wealthy, and his wealth further increased after he inherited the entailed estate of his family. Well connected in the city, his cousins and other relatives also resided in the jurisdiction. He married Ana Noboa Castro y Guzmán, the daughter of an important family from Guayaquil. His son Agustín followed his footsteps. He became justice of the Hermandad in 1709, 1740, and 1744, municipal ordinary judge in 1727, 1738, 1742–43, and 1748–49, and a temporary provincial justice in 1728. Agustín was also a perpetual alderman, a general, and a captain of the local cavalry regiment. His wife, Nicolasa Santa Coloma, was the daughter of a former local governor of Quito and the sister or Andrea, Polonia, and Catalina, all of whom married into the most prominent families of Quito.

Antonio Arias, municipal ordinary justice in 1722, was a Castilian soldier who came to Quito as the proprietary holder of the future right to exercise one of the local governorships (*corregimientos*) of the province. While waiting for the office to become vacant, he worked as a secretary of the bishop, lived in his house, and accompanied him on his visits outside Quito. In 1724, before he had the opportunity to become governor, he was ordered to return to Spain because his wife, who had remained there, had sent for him.[140] Arias had several slaves and servants in his service and gained a bad reputation for mistreating his subordinates and litigants.

Pedro José Bermúdez Becerra was elected municipal justice in 1729

139. AGI, Quito, 14: report of 30 January 1680; AGI, Quito, 73, 228; AGI, EC, 910B: his residencia, inserted in the residencia of Figueroa; and AGI, Gob., 13: exp. 13 December 1734.

140. AGI, Quito, 129: different documents of 1723–24.

when he was sixty-three years old. He was the son of conquistadores, a knight of Alcántara, an infantry captain, and a senior accountant of the court charged with handling the estates of the dead (*juzgado de bienes de difuntos*).[141] Bermúdez Becerra married Rafaela, the daughter of Simón Ontañón y Lastra, a wealthy Spanish landowner and merchant, a knight of the Santiago, an occasional alderman, and a justice of the Santa Hermandad in 1687 and 1695–96.[142] The dowry of Rafaela amounted to some 16,000 pesos. Among Bermúdez Becerra's brothers-in-law were the former president of the audiencia Juan de Sosaya and the local governor of Popayán Fernando Pérez Guerrero, himself a member of an important local family. Bermúdez Becerra's daughter, Teresa, married Bernardo de León, the son of a prominent and wealthy family. In his condition as a wealthy merchant, Bermúdez Becerra lent 20,000 pesos to the government of Cartagena at the end of the seventeenth century, a sum that he did not recover until at least 1713. In 1701 he was accused of murdering his Spanish accountant (*cajero*).[143] In 1729, he again found himself the subject of a criminal case, this time for the forgery of different receipts.[144]

Temporary governors had similar characteristics. José de Marzana, who was named by the president of the audiencia to this office in 1710 and 1711, was previously an ordinary municipal justice (1710) and lieutenant governor (1704–7). While serving as a soldier in Quijos (in the Amazon region), he was made captain of the infantry battalion of Quito. An alderman of Quito and a citizen of that city, Marzana also served as accountant to his friend President Juan de Sosaya (1707–12) and was considered a member of his household. In 1712, he bought the future right to exercise the office of local governor of Quito. It is unclear if he ever exercised this office. In the same year (1712) Juan Goyeneche, who was the proprietary holder of a futura for the presidency of Quito, nominated him as the third candidate for the post behind Lorenzo de Vicuña (who died before taking possession of the office) and Santiago Larrayn (who accepted the position and became president; see the preceding). On this occasion, the Council of the Indies opposed Marzana's

141. AGI, IG, 272: consulta of 28 September 1709; AGI, EC, 1061B; and AHQ, Not. 6, 10: exp. 27 March 1743.

142. AHQ, FE, 5, libro 1687–92, no. 347, 58; AGI, EC, 1061B; AHQ, Test., 68: exp. 23 February 1731, Test., 65: exp. 1 February 1729, Test., 120: exp. 29 December 1759, and Test., 128: exp. 18 September 1762; and AHQ, Gob., 4: exp. 1 August 1660 from 6 March 1684.

143. AHQ, Crim., 16: exp. 5 August 1701.

144. AHQ, Crim., 25: exp. 23 November 1729.

nomination, citing unfavorable reports about his bad character and his prodigious economic activity in Quito. Nevertheless, it allowed Marzana to become a knight of Santiago soon after.

Lawyers and Court Recorders

People wishing to practice as lawyers in Quito were required to have a law degree in canon or Roman law and to spend at least two years working in a legal office (*pasantía*). After this training was complete, they presented themselves to the audiencia and requested to be "received."[145] Individuals who had already obtained recognition as lawyers in another jurisdiction needed to produce their credentials. A new candidate, in contrast, had to present certifications to the audiencia of his university degree and training period (pasantía). The court then reviewed his family and personal qualifications, which (theoretically at least) had to conform to the requirements of legitimate birth, purity of blood, and good reputation.[146] After judging the qualities of the candidate, the audiencia admitted him to an oral exam. The senior magistrate assigned him a lawsuit, which he had to analyze in an oral session that took place a few days later. Having passed this exam, the candidate was received as a lawyer and took the traditional oath promising to use his office faithfully.

Court recorders were also lawyers by training. Yet, like their colleagues practicing the paralegal professions and unlike other lawyers, after they passed the exam they needed to find a vacant office. Theoretically, the office of recorder was granted by royal nomination following the recommendation of the Council of the Indies, very much the same way in which the office of magistrate was allocated in the early period. Nevertheless, in 1722, when the council sought precedents for the nominations of court recorders in Quito, it discovered that its archives contained no information past 1700, except for a single dispatch concerning

145. The following description is based on the study of the section "Incorporación de abogados" of the AHQ. See also "Libro de matrícula de abogados (1733–1829)," *Boletín de la Academia Nacional de Historia* 8/13 (1964): 29–45; and J. Kicza, "The Legal Community of Late Colonial Mexico," *Five Centuries of Law and Politics in Central Mexico*, ed. R. Spores and R. Hassig (Tennessee, 1984): 114–27.

146. AHN, Cód., 715B, no. 117; and "Autos acordados de la Real Audiencia de Quito, 1578–1722," *Anuario histórico jurídico ecuatoriano* 2 (1971): 384.

one of several offices.[147] This led the council to the conclusion that most court recorders in Quito were individuals temporarily appointed by the local audiencia or its president, who on most occasions exercised their offices until their retirement or death.[148]

Between 1650 and 1750, the local legal sphere (composed of lawyers, legal experts, and court recorders) included fifty-seven individuals who moved between one office and another and who on occasion occupied more than a single office at a time. Most members of this group held licentiate degrees obtained in Quito or Lima, although during the seventeenth century the number of native Spaniards with a degree from Spain was quite high.[149] Many lawyers, legal experts, and court recorders were economically prosperous. In some cases, for example the cases of Juan Triunfo Sosaya, Diego Suárez de Figueroa, and Antonio Montesdoca, salaries allowed them to maintain a "decent lifestyle." In others, a family fortune guaranteed economic status. Many lawyers descended from families with a long tradition in the administration of justice or in paralegal professions. On occasion, these families, for example the Ramírez de Arellano and the Suárez de Figueroa, formed true dynasties, with several members of the legal profession in each generation. Several lawyers, such as Pedro Gómez de Andrade and Diego Zárate y Alarcón, were children of audiencia magistrates, while others were relatives of aldermen or participated in the local municipal administration by acting as procurators of the town council, curators of minors, and so on.

Antonio Montesdoca, temporary court recorder in 1679 and proprietary holder of the office after 1681, was a doctor of canon and civil law, a lawyer in the audiencia of Quito, and a priest. When he died in 1703, his property was worth only 917 pesos.[150] Nevertheless, his will demonstrated that his poor economic condition was partially due to his difficulty in collecting his honoraria: at least twenty-two people owed him different sums of money for his professional services. Among his

147. AGI, Quito, 128: from 1716.

148. Ibid.; and AHN, Cod., 695B and 754B, nos. 286 and 104 from 1764 and 1763, respectively.

149. The prosopography of early modern Spanish lawyers was studied by J. M. Pelorson, *Les letrados;* J. Amelang, "Barristers and Judges in Early Modern Barcelona: The Rise of a Legal Elite," *American Historical Review* 89 (1984): 1264–84; and V. M. Uribe, "The Lawyers and New Granada's Late Colonial State," *Journal of Latin American Studies* 27/3 (1995): 517–49.

150. AHQ, Test., 33: exp. 30 July 1703.

personal possessions was a library with forty-nine books, including several titles on theology and law.

Andrés Sánchez de Mendoza was a court recorder from 1685 and a legal advisor to the town council between 1693 and 1699 and between 1700 and 1705. He served as a temporary judge in the audiencia on several occasions in 1699 and as a temporary protector of Indians at least between 1710 and 1711.[151] Sánchez de Mendoza also assisted the officials of the royal treasury and acted as procurator for the town council. It is possible that he served as temporary crown attorney in the audiencia between 1681 and 1691. Sánchez de Mendoza was born in Spain to Antonio Sánchez de Mendoza, a perpetual alderman of Salamanca who also taught at the university. Andrés Sánchez de Mendoza held a licentiate degree and was a lawyer of the Royal Councils. It is unknown why he came to the Americas in 1681, but it is clear that he immediately settled in Quito and began working as a lawyer.

Nobility and Office

In addition to their family, social, personal, and professional qualifications, many judges and judicial officers in Quito held some title of distinction such as nobility, knighthood, or a military rank. The relationship between nobility, war, and office had deep roots in Spanish political theory. Nobles were originally warriors, and as warriors they were the natural protectors and leaders of their communities. They were both loyal and courageous, both trustworthy and able. Although the king could declare that certain individuals were nobles, in doing so he recognized their innate qualities that predated his declaration.[152] Thus, people were not made noble, they were born noble. There was something in them that made them different, indeed better than the other members of society. According to these ideas, choosing nobles for office guaranteed the prevalence of good and loyal servants. It also increased what Pierre Bourdieu once called the "symbolic capitals" of

151. AGI, EC, 911A: residencia of magistrate Tomás Fernández Pérez de Hodo; AMQ, 00053: letter of 8 November 1696; and AGI, Quito, 74, 13.

152. F. J. Somoza, "La justicia vestida de todas sus autoridades . . . [n.d.]," MS 22.213, BN; and Z. Moutoukias, "Réseaux personnels et autorité coloniale. Les négociants de Buenos Aires au XVIIIe siècle," *Annales ESC* 47 (1992): 902.

the administration of justice.[153] Nobility and military rank bestowed honor and reputation and, thanks to them, the recipients were able to command respect and exhort obedience.

During the seventeenth and eighteenth centuries, two local governors, one provincial of the Santa Hermandad, and one municipal ordinary justice were marquises or counts. Nine magistrates, five presidents, three crown attorneys, fourteen local governors, and another thirty-seven individuals belonging to the municipal judicial sphere were knights of military orders.[154] Some of them, for example the protector of Indians Antonio de Ron, Bernaldo de Quiros, crown attorney Ignacio Aybar y Eslava, magistrates Alonso de Castillo Herrera, Miguel González Carrasco, and Pedro Salcedo Fuenmayor, and local governors Gonzalo Rodríguez de Monroy, Miguel de Zatarena Santisteban, and José de Marzana, obtained this distinction before they were appointed to office. Others were granted titles or knighthoods on account of their nomination to office. When petitioning the king to receive this honor, they argued that titles and knighthood were important symbolic tools that would "decorate" them and ensure the "greater grandeur, authority, and decency" of their persons and the administration. The Council of the Indies was usually favorable to these petitions. Although the councilors insisted that these rewards should not be given automatically to all nominees, they nevertheless agreed that knighthood was a suitable "relief" (*aliento*) for royal servants sent to the Americas. These servants had to carry out their activities away from the royal court and favor. Their authority vis-à-vis the local society had to be reinforced, and their obligation toward the king fortified. Both these aims could be achieved, the council said, by granting them a title of nobility or a knighthood. Nobility and knighthood also rewarded these people for their willingness to cross the Atlantic and serve under difficult conditions.[155] Image and efficacy were thus intertwined with considerations of loyalty and

153. P. Bourdieu, "Sur le pouvoir symbolique," *Annales ESC* 32 (1977): 405–11.

154. P. Rizo Patrón, "La nobleza en Lima en tiempos de los Borbones," *Boletín del Instituto Francés de Estudios Andinos* 19 (1990): 129–63. M. J. Álvarez-Coca González, "La concesión de hábitos de caballeros de las órdenes militares: Procedimiento y reflejo documental (siglos XVI–XIX)," *Cuadernos de historia moderna* 14 (1993): 277–97, examines the granting of knighthood in reward for services rendered.

155. AGI, Quito, 4: consultas of 13 October 1689, 26 November 1689, and 29 November 1692; AGI, Quito, 102: consultas of 25 August 1711 and 3 June 1712; and AGI, Quito, 5: consulta of 7 May 1686.

personal reward. Officeholders could become nobles or knights because of their nomination to office, yet at the same time, the association of titled people or knights with the administration reinforced the image of the judicial system and ensured its greater feasibility.

By the eighteenth century, military distinctions were among the symbolic capitals available to officers or brought with them to their positions.[156] Like titles of nobility, military rank proved military excellence and everything else (loyalty, worthiness, trust) associated with it. Nearly 30 percent of justices and officers belonging to the municipal sphere in Quito were generals, captains, or captain-majors. Among them were thirty-two municipal ordinary judges, thirty-one justices of the Santa Hermandad, nineteen people holding more than a single office, fifteen local governors, three provincials, and one lieutenant. Most of these officials obtained their military distinction in Quito, although some came to the city already decorated with military rank. In the first case, these distinctions rarely had any true relationship to war. Quito was located in the American interior, and it had no visible enemies. Military ranks granted in it were, first and foremost, signs of social distinction.[157] They represented a particular personal status, made evident in the uniform and rank. The military honors also conferred legal advantages, embodied in the special military jurisdiction (*fuero*).[158]

156. For a comparative view see A. Morales Moya, "Milicias y nobleza en el siglo XVIII: Apuntes para una sociología de las armas y de la nobleza en España," *Cuadernos de historia moderna* 9 (1988): 121–37.

157. These issues are also treated in J. Velasco, *Historia del Reino de Quito en la América meridional* (1789; reprint, Caracas, 1981), 314–15; M. E. Porras, "La élite quiteña en el cabildo," M.A. thesis, Facultad Iberoamericana de Ciencias Sociales (FLACSO) (Quito, 1987), 65–67; Z. Moutoukias, "Power, Corruption, and Commerce: The Making of the Local Administrative Structure in Seventeenth-Century Buenos Aires," *Hispanic American Historical Review* 68 (1988): 777; and R. Quatrefages, "Le système militaire des Habsbourgs," in *Le premier âge de l'État en Espagne (1450–1700)*, ed. C. Hermann (Paris, 1989): 364–65. The transformation of military ranks into honorary distinction is described in J. Alvarado Planas, "Del trifuncionalismo indoeuropeo y los tres estados: Derecho e ideología de las élites en la Edad Media española," *Anuario jurídico y económico escuriarense* 24 (1992): 421–33; L. P. Wright, "Las órdenes militares en la sociedad española de los siglos XVII y XVIII. La encarnación institucional de una tradición histórica," in *Poder y sociedad en la España de los Austrias*, ed. J. H. Elliott (Barcelona, 1982), 15–56; R. Zorraquín Becú, "El adelantado indiano: título honorífico," in *Memoria del Congreso Venezolano de Historia* (Caracas, 1977), 3: 551–78; and M. Góngora, "Urban Social Stratification in Colonial Chile," *Hispanic American Historical Review* 55 (1975): 421–48.

158. The militias were studied by J. Marchena Fernández, "The Social World of the Military in Peru and Nueva Granada: The Colonial Oligarchies in Conflict, 1750–1810," *Reform and Insurrection in Bourbon Nueva Granada and Peru*, ed. J. R. Fisher, A. J. Kuethe, and A. McFarlane (Baton Rouge–London, 1990), 54–95; idem, *Oficiales y soldados*

Perhaps the clearest relationship in Quito between judicial employment and military rank can be seen in the case of presidents of the audiencia.[159] In 1709, Juan de Sosaya was the first president to acquire the title of military commander (*capitán general*) of the region. Once this happened, all succeeding presidents aspired to obtain the same privilege.[160] In question was not simply the honor and respect of their persons but also their ability to administer justice. These, at least, were the allegations of President Santiago Larrayn, who in 1715 and 1717 confronted the viceroy on this issue.[161] Larrayn argued that he needed the distinction as captain general because it would improve and facilitate his office. He also sustained that it was customary to install presidents of audiencias as military commanders, and he did not see why his case should be different. The king had already recognized him as such, and a refusal by the viceroy to follow these royal orders was a direct attack on his privileges and reputation.

Conclusion

There were many different ways by which individuals could become officeholders. Nomination, purchase, and election all theoretically guaranteed the selection of worthy people. Nomination did because it involved the king and the Council of the Indies. Purchase did (or did not, according to the different stands) because the king sanctioned it. Election also did because it represented the voice of the community, which, on the occasion, was incarnated in the opinion of the aldermen who when united in the council spoke for the entire city. Whatever the process was, those consecrated as officers were delegates of the king. They represented his justice, also identified with divine justice. At the same time, they were also members of families, clans, or rival factions who fought one another and who used judicial appointments as instru-

en el ejercito de América (Seville, 1983), 79–80; and S. G. Suárez, *Las milicias. Instituciones militares hispanoamericanas* (Caracas, 1984), 155–59.

159. This issue is treated in greater length in T. Herzog, "Sobre Justicia, honor y grado militar en la Audiencia de Quito durante el siglo XVIII," *Procesos* 6/2 (1995): 49–57.

160. AGI, Quito, 106: decree of 25 May 1706; AGI, Quito, 102: consulta of 9 June 1706; AGI, Quito, 126: different documents dated 1708; and AGI, Quito, 128, 512–18. See also AGI, Quito, 103: consulta of 16 March 1720; AGI, Quito, 106, 593–94; and MS 2755–39 of 1769, BPR.

161. AGI, Quito, 128, 512–18.

ments in a larger power struggle. This was evident during the elections in Quito, but it was also present in Madrid. One thing did not contradict the other. Unanimity could coexist with elections, and rivalry with consensus.

These characteristics might explain why the preparation, genealogy, services, wealth, and symbolic capital of judges and officials could be radically different from one case to the other. While some judges and officials were rich, were well connected, and had external signs of distinction (title, knighthood, or military rank), as well as family histories that linked them to the king or to the local society, others were fairly marginal members of society who were attached in some way or the other to patrons. There was no necessary correlation between office and personal situation. Minor officials often had larger "capitals" than their superiors. Office could be a means of social or economic promotion to some people. Office could also solidify what one had previously obtained.[162] "Worthy" people were nominated to office, yet appointment to office also made others dignified[163] Worthiness, at any rate, was defined in social and political terms, rather than professional ones. First and foremost, people appointed to office had to be loyal and had to possess sufficient social and symbolic capital to be able to induce obedience as well as respect. What this meant in seventeenth- and eighteenth-century Quito is the subject of the next chapter.

162. T. Hampe Martínez, "Los funcionarios de la monarquía española en América: Notas para su caracterización política, económica y social," *Histórica* 16 (1992), 89–118.

163. Landau came to a similar conclusion regarding English justices of the peace. N. Landau, *The Justices of the Peace, 1676–1769* (Berkeley, 1984), 269–70.

CHAPTER THREE

Officers and Society

In June of 1705, three audiencia magistrates (Juan de Ricaurte, Tomás Fernández Pérez de Hodo, and Fernando Sierra Osorio) entered the chamber of the acuerdo to vote on an appeal regarding a decision made by the president of the court.[1] Before the session was over, Fernández Pérez de Hodo stood up and walked toward the door linking the room of the acuerdo with the public chamber. Ricaurte, who presided, informed him that he could not leave without his permission. Fernández Pérez de Hodo responded with "scandalous words" (*voces escandalosas*), calling his colleague Ricaurte "a cuckold, a grocer, and a potter." Fernández Pérez de Hodo then left the room, entered into the public chamber, and, in the presence of at least twenty people, offended the honor and reputation of Ricaurte. A person named Cristóbal de Jijón, who was waiting in the hall, also joined in verbally and physically abusing Ricaurte. The voices attracted the attention of the president of the court, who came out of his office and sent both magistrates home, suspending them from exercising their office for two years.

The investigation that followed the events clarified their importance, for all witnesses asserted that they were scandalized by the behavior of both magistrates. The seriousness of the conflict, which involved two magistrates, was further accentuated by the fact that it took place in a sacred space (the chamber of the acuerdo and the building of the audiencia) and that it was conducted in public in front of so many people. The entire city, the witnesses argued, was effected by what had happened. When the viceroy attempted to reconcile the parties, Ricuarte refused to accept any redress, insisting that the wrong done to him was incurable. Ricaurte changed his mind only after he was threatened with punishment. Obeying the instructions of the viceroy, he came to the

1. AGI, Quito, 162; and the residencias Juan de Ricaurte and Tomás Fernández Pérez de Hodo in AGI, EC, 911A.

building of the audiencia where, in the presence of several court recorders and lawyers, he took part in a ceremony in which Fernández Pérez de Hodo publicly read a letter expressing his regret and repentance. To make their reconciliation public, both magistrates sat down on the bench wearing their togas.

Historians of colonial Spanish America would agree that this confrontation was not surprising. Many such confrontations happened in many courts all over the continent. They involved magistrates who disliked one another and who, when the debate was heated, lost control over their words and actions—or at least justified their behavior in this way. The question was one of etiquette: namely, who could stand up and leave. This issue was important because of its highly ceremonial nature, involving the affirmation that Ricuarte, because he presided, was superior to Fernández Pérez de Hodo and could order him to remain in the room. But why did Fernández Pérez de Hodo and Ricuarte confront each other? What justified a public explosion in this case?

The investigation that followed the events clarifies some of these issues. Apparently, what Fernández Pérez de Hodo attempted to do was to convince his colleagues not to reverse on appeal a decision already made by his ally the president. He attacked Ricuarte (rather than Sierra Osorio) not only because Ricuarte presided over the session but also because he considered Ricuarte to be his enemy. The same considerations were also true of the president. The president sent both magistrates home because he refused to admit that his friend Fernández Pérez de Hodo was responsible for what had happened. Trying to protect him, he forcefully argued that both magistrates were equally at fault. Ricuarte resented this interpretation and refused to make peace with Fernández Pérez de Hodo. What was at stake was his relationship not only with this single magistrate but also with the president and, through him, the audiencia and city. Cristóbal de Jijón, the witness who attacked Ricaurte, acted according to the same logic. Jijón was a friend of the president and wanted to support him and his ally Fernández Pérez de Hodo. The president was indeed grateful for his intervention and made sure that Jijón, who was jailed following the event, would be released from prison the very same night. Last but not least was Sierra Osorio, present during the initial assault in the chamber of the acuerdo, who testified in a way that clarified his support of Ricuarte. According to his version of events, the responsibility for conflict could only be attributed to Fernández Pérez de Hodo, who behaved very badly. But this interpretation was particularly motivated: we know that Sierra Osorio was a friend of Ricuarte and an enemy of Fernández Pérez de Hodo and the president.

Nothing about the confrontation was innocent or accidental. The positions the parties took and the gestures they adopted were all related to social obligations, obligations that dominated the life of judicial institutions.[2] These social obligations grouped the magistrates into rival factions (*parcialidades*) that actively confronted one another on different issues.[3] For example, in the early 1690s, President Lope Antonio Munive y Axpe and justices Andrés Francia Cavero and Gaspar de Luna were considered allies. They were opposed by their colleagues Matías Lagúñez y Aguilar and Juan Larrea Zurbano the elder.[4] When Lagúñez y Aguilar was promoted to the audiencia of Lima, Larrea Zurbano allied himself with the incoming magistrates Cristóbal Cevallos Borja and Miguel González Carrasco. The three men visited each other frequently, making their association public. During the presidency of Francisco López Dicastillo y Azcona (1703–6), the audiencia was also divided into two groups. One faction allied the president and the magistrates Tomás Fernández Pérez de Hodo, Cristóbal Cevallos y Borja, and Lorenzo Lastero Salazar. The other allied Juan de Ricaurte, Anto-

2. For a comparative view see J. L. Phelan, *The Kingdom of Quito,* 243–319; S. Blank, "Patron, Clients and Kin in Seventeenth-Century Caracas: A Methodological Essay in Colonial American Social History," *Hispanic American Historical Review* 54 (1979): 260–83; J. A. Barbier, *Reform and Politics in Bourbon Chile, 1755–1769* (Ottawa, 1980), 4, 74–75, and 193; M. Bertrand, "Du bon usage des solidarités: Étude du facteur familial dans l'administration des finances de la Nouvelle Espagne, XVIIème–XVIIIème siècle," in *Les figures historiques de l'administrateur: Institutions, réseaux, pouvoirs en Espagne, en France et au Portugal, 16e–19e siècle,* ed. R. Descimon, J. F. Schaub, and B. Vincent (Paris, 1997), 43–58; and J. M. Santos Pérez, "La práctica del autogobierno en centroamerica: conflictos entre la audiencia de Guatemala y el cabildo de Santiago en el siglo XVIII," *Mesoamérica* 21/40 (2000): 69–94. The importance of these issues was also studied in other European territories, for example, R. Mousnier, *Les institutions de la France sous la monarchie absolue, 1598–1789* (Paris, 1974), 1: 85–93; and Y. Durand, ed., *Clientèles et fidélités en Europe à l'époque moderne. Hommage à Roland Mousnier* (Paris, 1981). The role of magistrates as patrons was explored in C. Windler, "Clientèles royales et clientèles seigneuriales vers la fin de l'ancien régime. Un dossier espagnol." *Annales ESC* 52 (1997): 300–304.

3. The relationships between magistrates of the same audiencia were also discussed by T. Calvo, "Les réalités du pouvoir aux confins de l'empire: Le cas de la Nouvelle Galice au XVIIe siècle," in *Les élites locales et l'état dans l'Espagne moderne du XVIe au XIX siècle: Table ronde internationale (Talence 13–15 décembre 1990),* ed. M. Lambert-Gorges (Paris, 1993), 150–51.

4. AGI, Quito, 72–74.

nio de Ron, and Fernando Sierra Osorio.[5] This factionalism explains how Fernández Pérez de Hodo came to insult Ricuarte, why the president intervened in favor of Fernández Pérez de Hodo, and why Sierra Osorio supported, although timidly, the position of Ricuarte.

The situation in the audiencia further deteriorated during the presidency of Juan de Sosaya (1707–15). Juan de Sosaya immediately associated himself with the group that opposed magistrates Fernández Pérez de Hodo, Cevallos y Borja, and Lastero Salazar. He explained that the three men were friends, countrymen, and students of the same college and that their association not only was personal but also had professional repercussions. Because of this association, they were able to coordinate their votes, and by virtue of their sheer number, they controlled the decision-making process of the audiencia. Undermining presidential authority, the three magistrates made it impossible to approve any decision with which they disagreed. Fernández Pérez de Hodo, Cevallos y Borja, and Lastero Salazar responded by accusing the president of being partial to Ricuarte and Sierra Osorio and of intentionally wanting to harm them.[6] They also argued that he was a bad president. They alleged that he continued to engage in mercantile activities, as he had done while still a merchant in Lima and while serving as the local governor of Guayaquil. These activities, mostly contraband, were prejudicial to the royal treasury, and they placed the president in opposition to a large sector within the local society that included many merchants who were allied with Fernández Pérez de Hodo, Cevallos y Borja, and Lastero Salazar.

The new magistrates who came to the audiencia in 1709 (José Llorente and José de Laysequilla y Palacios) were immediately incorporated into the existing groups. The first was considered a "chief enemy" of the president, while the second was taken to be his friend.[7] The presidency of Santiago Larrayn (1715–18 and 1722–28) apparently calmed the passions, yet as soon as new president Dionisio Alcedo y Herrera arrived in the city in 1729, conflict reappeared. Alcedo y Herrera found himself confronted from the first moments of his presidency with a sec-

5. AGI, Quito, 128: letter of 30 December 1704.

6. AGI, Quito, 267; AGI, EC, 913A, 34; AGI, EC, 911B: residencia of José de Laysequilla y Palacios y Aguilar; and AGI, Quito, 130.

7. This period is described in K. J. Andrien, *The Kingdom of Quito,* 166–73; and idem, "Corruption, Self Interest, and the Political Culture of Eighteenth-Century Quito," in *Virtue, Corruption and Self Interest. Political Values in the Eighteenth Century,* ed. R. K. Matthews (Bethlehem, 1994), 273–78.

tion of the local elite that was supported by several magistrates (chap. 6). His precarious situation forced him to ally with magistrates José Llorente, Pedro Martínez de Arizala, and Manuel Rubio de Arévalo. The next president, José de Araujo y Río (1736–43), also followed the same strategy. Upon his arrival in Quito, he immediately censured several magistrates whom he considered his rivals (Manuel Rubio de Arévalo and crown attorney Juan de Valparda y la Ormaza), while he backed others considered his friends (Pedro Gómez de Andrade and Juan Luján y Vedia).[8]

The battle between the magistrates was fought in Quito as well as in Lima and Madrid. The viceroys and the Council of the Indies continuously received information that either approved or disapproved of the character and activities of certain magistrates. Like Pandora's box, once accusations began, it was difficult to stop their momentum. One accusation followed another, and each went slightly further in demeaning the enemy. In the 1640s, President Martín de Ariolla feared the effect of several reports that had been sent to the council by magistrate Jerónimo Ortiz Zapata. Ariolla defended himself by denouncing Ortiz Zapata's activities to the council. Ortiz Zapata realized what was happening and immediately counterattacked by sending the council detailed information against the president. In 1692 the same dynamics opposed crown attorney Juan de Peñalosa y Benavides to President Rodrigo Corro Carrascal. And the same can be seen in the early eighteenth century, in the conflict of (on the one hand) the president and magistrates Tomás Fernández Pérez de Hodo, Cristóbal Cevallos y Borja, and Lorenzo Lastero Salazar with (on the other) Juan de Ricaurte, Antonio de Ron, and Fernando Sierra Osorio.[9] Ironically, even though it was up to the president to pacify the situation in his capacity as the head of the audiencia, most presidents took an active part in conflicts. At times presidents even initiated or encouraged such conflicts. The willingness of Lima and Madrid to listen and act according to these complaints only aggravated the situation and guaranteed the multiplication and intensification of complaints.[10]

As was the case in the conflict between Fernández Pérez de Hodo and Ricaurte, the rivalries that confronted the magistrates were always

8. This period is described in hundreds of documents included in AGI, EC, 914–16.

9. AGI, Quito, 2, various documents from 1651 and 1652; and AGI, Quito, 14: letter of 1672.

10. AHN, Cód., 720B, nos. 131 and 147 from 1636 and 1641.

related to larger conflicts present in society. The magistrates identified with certain people whose interests they wanted to defend and fought against others who they opposed.[11] No one seemed surprised that President Francisco López Dicastillo y Azcona freed one of his friends from jail in the company of thirty or forty of his countrymen (*paisanos*) and afterward took on his case in the audiencia.[12] Nor were witnesses in Quito shocked by the fact that President Lope Antonio Munive y Axpe came to the audiencia only when the interests of his allies were at stake.[13] This behavior was not limited to judges. Powerful individuals also protected their friends to the best of their ability.[14] They interceded in their favor and intervened in judicial processes in order to guarantee that their friends would be freed from prison or receive light sentences.[15] Criminals could thus take refuge in the houses of principal citizens and ask for their protection against judicial persecution. For example, in 1727 a poor woman escaped to the home of the chief constable and convinced him and his wife to intercede on her behalf.[16] Wives and mothers of suspects felt at liberty to present themselves to judges or to write them personal letters pleading in favor of their parties. They "reminded" the officers of the obligations that they had contracted with them and demanded that they continue the exchange of favors, which had begun long before and was expected to continue.[17]

11. AHN, Cód., 715B, no. 135 from 1631; AHQ, Ced., 3 (1612–34), nos. 48 and 118 from 1621 and 1627; MS 2989, fol. 1088: cédula from 1621, BN; and AHN, Cód., 705B, no. 45: decree from 1632. See also J. Perez, "La Couronne de Castille," in *Le premier âge de l'État en Espagne (1450–1700)*, ed. C. Hermann (Paris, 1989), 108–9; H. Pietschmann, "Burocracia," F. Bronner, "Church, Crown and Commerce in Seventeenth-Century Lima: A Synoptic Interpretation," *Jahrbuch für geschichte von staat wirtschaft und gesellschaft lateinamerikas* 29 (1992): 75–89; G. Ramos, "La privatización del poder: Inquisición y sociedad colonial en el Perú," in *Poder y violencia en los Andes*, ed. E. Urbano (Cuzco, 1991), 75–92; S. B. Schwartz, "Magistracy and Society in Colonial Brazil," *Hispanic American Historical Review* 50 (1970): 713–30; idem, *Sovereignty and Society in Colonial Brazil: The High Court of Bahia and Its Judges, 1609–1715* (Berkeley, 1973); Calvo, "Les réalités," 156–57; and A. Baeza Martín, "La condena de españoles a obrajes en Nueva España en 1721: su secuela en la provisión de oficios de las audiencias indianas," *Anuario de estudios americanos* 57/2 (2000): 468–70.

12. AGI, Quito, 162; and AGI, Quito, 142, 369–402.

13. AGI, Quito, 72, 21–23 and 27–28.

14. AHQ, Crim., 4: exp. 18 October 1660; and AHQ, Crim., 12: exp. 16 November 1691.

15. AHQ, Crim., 23: exp. 7 June 1727; and AHQ, Not. 1, 28: exp. 16 September 1746.

16. AHQ, Crim., 23: exp. 20 October 1727.

17. AHQ, Crim., 10: exp. 4 June 1685; AHQ, Crim., 15: exp. 24 September 1698; AHQ, Not. 6, 11: exp. 31 August 1738; and AHQ, Not. 6, 12: exp. 24 November 1739. See also the correspondence between the wife of President José de Araujo y Río and Manuel Rubio de Arévalo, his judge: AGI, EC, 915A, cuad. 3, 161.

Judicial decisions were always interpreted as expressions of social obligations.[18] Litigants expected their friends to vote in their favor and interpreted an unfavorable decision as the confirmation of animosity. This animosity could be deeply resented, even leading to the physical abuse of judges who were classified as personal enemies rather than as neutral arbitrers. The incident involving magistrate Matías Lagúñez y Aguilar can serve as an example. In 1686, a group of Augustinian friars arrived at his house and requested an audience.[19] The members of this group wished to inform the magistrate about a case in which he was the acting judge and in which they were, albeit indirectly, an interested party. Because Lagúñez y Aguilar refused to grant the petition, the hearing degenerated into an open confrontation. Several friars guarded the entrance to the house, while others physically attacked the magistrate. Having beaten the judge, the friars left the house and fled toward their monastery. Lagúñez y Aguilar followed them to the street, invoking the name of the king. However, no one was willing to help him. Shopkeepers entered their stores, shutting the doors behind them. Left on his own, Lagúñez y Aguilar was unable to stop the friars, who reached their monastery safely. Once they were behind closed doors, the friars resumed the attack, stoning the magistrate from the towers of the monastery. Lagúñez y Aguilar, who was already badly beaten, was struck on the head by a stone and left unconscious. His servants carried him back home. Rumor spread in the city that Lagúñez y Aguilar was murdered. The following day, a group of two hundred men organized by the president of the audiencia and led by magistrate Juan Larrea Zurbano the elder (Lagúñez's friend) approached the monastery in order "to seek justice." The friars stoned them, fired rifles at them, and then brought out the Holy Sacrament. The public, which was gathered in front of the monastery, prostrated themselves, and the president ordered them to retreat. Fearing the spread of violence against the magistrates, he ordered guards to be placed in front of the royal palace (where the audiencia resided) as well as at the houses of all audiencia judges.

The aggressors opposing Lagúñez y Aguilar were never identified or

18. For a comparative view see Y. Castan, *Honnêteté et relations sociales en Languedoc, 1715–1780* (Paris, 1974), 94; and J. P. Dedieu, "Procès et interactions: L'analyse des relations interpersonnelles dans les groupes restreints à partir des documents judiciaires," in *Solidarités et sociabilités en Espagne (XVI–XXe siècles): Annales de l'Université de Besançon*, ed. R. Carrasco (Basangon, 1991), 119–39.

19. AGI, Quito, 72, 460–630. The episode was also studied by F. González Suárez, *Historia general*, 801–5.

punished. In the judicial proceedings that followed the event, witnesses expressed their horror and repugnance at what had happened.[20] They censured the authorities for permitting "such a strange" case, with "so many grave consequences," to be dropped without making "many exemplary demonstrations worthy of remembrance."[21] What disturbed the witnesses the most was the degree of violence involved and the insufficient reaction of the authorities. What they took for granted was the fact that a magistrate was censored for his decision that was interpreted as a sign of animosity that merited reprobation.

Quito's magistrates often complained about the custom of interpreting their judicial decisions as signs of friendship or animosity. According to them, this interpretation greatly compromised their activities because they were aware that each decision they made had social consequences. Even the most trivial conclusion generated new social relations because some people felt grateful to the magistrates while others resented them. Juan Larrea Zurbano the elder, Gaspar de Luna, Miguel Antonio Ormasa Ponce de León, Andrés Francia Cavero, Tomás Fernández Pérez de Hodo, and President Dionisio Alcedo y Herrera all argued that their judicial decisions explained why certain people complained against their activities.[22] No one was willing, they said, to acknowledge that an unfavorable decision could still be a just decision. Litigants who were unable to win their case were resentful of justices who did not support their positions. Rather than neutral arbitrers, judges were presented as interested parties. This presentation was ultimately correct: judges eventually became interested parties because their decisions in cases that did not affect them ended up rewarding or punishing them by making or alienating friends.[23]

Some magistrates were especially successful in collecting enemies, such as Jerónimo Ortiz Zapata, Luis Losada Quiñones, and Presidents Francisco López Dicastillo y Azcona and José de Araujo y Río.[24] Other magistrates, on the contrary, were best known for the number of people associated with them. Antonio Diéz de San Miguel Solier was close to many aldermen, and President Lope Antonio Munive y Axpe to several friars. Andrés Francia Cavero and President Munive y Axpe allowed

20. AGI, Quito, 72, 501: declaration of Antonio Ormasa Ponce de León.

21. AGI, Quito, 72, 505: declaration of Antonio de Villacís.

22. AGI, Quito, 74, 119–221; AGI, Quito, 73, 176–78, 322–23, and 386; AGI, Quito, 74, 29–33; AGI, EC, 911A, 86; and AGI, EC, 911B, 121.

23. AGI, EC, 914B, cuad. 8, 264.

24. AGI, Quito, 2; AGI, Quito, 14; and AGI, Quito, 162.

public gambling in their houses, which was enjoyed by locals. Juan Larrea Zurbano the elder and Luis Losada Quiñones maintained a close correspondence with several local merchants. In 1709–10, when confronted with the order to leave the city, Juan de Ricaurte was able to solicit the support of all the provincials of the religious orders, Quito's town council, the bishop, several local governors, and some of the principal townsmen.

The classification of people as friends or enemies depended on many factors. During the early modern period friendship, as well as the opposite condition of animosity, was not solely defined according to an emotional attachment. Instead, friendship and animosity typified primarily the potential for an informal reciprocal exchange between people who interacted with one another.[25] Friendship constructed artificial ties among these individuals. Considered a social as well as a political association, friendship generated loyalties that were neither exclusive nor permanent and that depended on a variety of factors. Those engaged in helping others in litigation, or simply in giving them advice, were considered friends. A public intervention in favor of a person who was attacked, or a discussion regarding precedence in seats in public ceremonies, could be proof, as well as a cause, of new friends and enemies. People willing to serve as witnesses, financial guarantors (*fiadores*), or money lenders were similar. Likewise, business partnership as well as a criminal association justified the creation and maintenance of alliances. Persons who paid the president bribes were thereafter connected to him by their common complicity, which produced friendship. The same was true with regard to contraband associates. The exchange of gifts could affirm the preexistence of friendship as much as it could create it.

25. Friendship as patronage has been the object of many studies focused on France: J. R. Major, S. Kettering, and E. Schalk, "Forum: Fidelity and Clientelage in Seventeenth Century France," *French Historical Studies* 14/3 (1986): 391–446; S. Kettering, "Patronage and Kingship in Early Modern France," *French Historical Studies* 16/2 (1989): 408–35; idem, "Friendship and Clientelage in Early Modern France," *French History* 6/2 (1992): 139–58; S. Kettering, J. R. Major, and A. Jouanna, "Patronage, Language and Political Culture," *French Historical Studies* 17/4 (1992): 839–81; C. Klapisch-Zuber, *La maison et le nom: Stragégies et rituels dans l'Italie de la Renaissance* (Paris, 1990), 76 and 123–33; and A. L. Herman, "The Language of Fidelity in Early Modern France," *Journal of Modern History* 67 (1995): 1–24. Recently, friendship also was taken up by historians of England, for example, S. D' Cruze, "The Middling Sort in Eighteenth Century Colchester: Independence, Social Relations and the Community Broker," *The Middling Sort of People: Culture, Society and Politics in England, 1550–1800*, ed. J. Barry and C. Brooks (New York, 1994), 189–96.

Many of these ties were among those of the same social standing, yet friendship could also exist among people who were hierarchically different. Some people were thankful for a favorable judicial decision. Others were grateful to royal officials for having assigned them a lucrative commission or having given them employment. People were also expected to be loyal to individuals in whose service they were employed or under whose authority they were placed. A clergyman could thus acquire obligations toward the benefactor of his parish, toward the bishop of his diocese, or the head of his monastery. In the same way, students were tied to their professors as well as to their college and university peers.

Despite this diversity, principal among all ties were family ties. Family ties extended to both "real" and adopted members and to blood, political, and fictive relatives such as relatives by marriage and godparents. Individuals who were admitted into a house and who were either raised there or resided there became members of the extended family. Family ties could be powerful even when the degree of parentage was extremely remote or unknown. In the 1740s, for example, Francisco Ante y Mendoza was classified as a member of a certain group because he was the brother-in-law of Diego Donoso. Donoso was married to Teresa Chiriboga, whose sisters were married to Juan and Clemente Sánchez de Orellana. Members of the Sánchez de Orellana family were leaders of the group with which Ante y Mendoza was now associated. In the same way, the wife of President José de Araujo y Río was considered a relative of Judge Juan Dionisio Larrea Zurbano because of their shared surname (Larrea).

Family ties both created and ensured the development and enhancement of social and political relationships. They were often at the core of extensive social networks that connected different people and guaranteed the exchange of services between them.[26] Relatives could share friends, and a relationship with one member of the family often implied

26. J. P. Dedieu and C. Windler, "La familia: ¿Una clave para entender la historia política? El ejemplo de la España moderna," *Studia historica—historia moderna* 18 (1998): 215; M. Bertrand, "La élite colonial," 45–46; idem, "De la familia a la red de sociabilidad," *Revista mexicana de sociología* 61/2 (1999): 116–18 and 124–25; idem, *Grandeur et misère de l'office: Les officiers de finances de la Nouvelle-Espagne, XVIIe–XVIIe siècle* (Paris, 1999); and Z. Moutoukias, "Familia patriarcal y redes sociales. Balance de una imagen de la estratificación social," *Anuario IEHS* 15 (2000): 133–51. See also G. Dalla Corte, *Vida i mort d'una aventura al Riu de La Plata, Jaime Alsina i Verjés, 1770–1836* (Barcelona, 2000); and idem, "La red social frente a la crisis del orden colonial: Compensación judicial y vínculos de parentesco entre Buenos Aires y Cataluña," *Colonial Latin American Historical Review* 9/3 (2000): 347–77.

a loyalty to the entire group. The relationship between family and social ties also survived over time. As Giovanni Levi demonstrated, and as the case of Juan Dionisio Larrea Zurbano (chap. 2) also proves, friends and enemies could be inherited.[27] Like any other capital, they could be conserved or "wasted," augmented or lost.

In Quito, many magistrates were related to one another by descent or marriage. Both Juan Dionisio Larrea Zurbano (in office between 1711 and 1717) and Alonso de Castillo Herrera (1660–75) were sons of audiencia magistrates. Juan Bautista Sánchez de Orellana (1711–17) was the uncle of Fernando Félix Sánchez de Orellana (president 1744–53). The sons and daughters of magistrates Antonio Diéz de San Miguel Solier, Luis Losada Quiñones, Esteban Olaís y Aroche, José de Quintana y Acevedo, and Pedro Gómez de Andrade married one another while their fathers were colleagues in the same audiencia. The wife of President Lope Antonio Munive y Axpe (1676–89) treated the son of Ignacio Aybar y Eslava (protector of Indians and crown attorney between 1693 and 1708) as a member of her family. The daughter of Dionisio Alcedo y Herrera (president between 1729 and 1736) married crown attorney Juan de Valparda (1732–43), who was Alcedo y Herrera's contemporary at court.

Family relations also tied the magistrates to local society.[28] Spanish American legislation prohibited such ties by forcing magistrates to acquire a special license if they wanted to marry women who were born, or were domiciled, in the jurisdiction in which they exercised their office. Yet this prohibition was clearly disobeyed, and/or licenses were easily granted.[29] In 1711, President Juan de Sosaya (1706–12) married Micaela Ontañón y Lastra—the daughter of one of the wealthiest and

27. G. Levi, *Le pouvoir au village. Histoire d'un exorciste dans le Piémont du XVIIe siècle* (Paris, 1989) (originally published as *L'eredità immateriale: carriera di un esorcista nel Piemonte del Seicento* [Torino, 1985]).

28. For a comparative view see Schwartz, *Sovereignty*, 177–80 and 339–41; J. Puente Brunke, "Los oidores en la sociedad limeña: Notas para su estudio (siglo XVII)," *Temas americanistas* 7 (1990): 8–13; P. Rodríguez Crespo, "Sobre parentesco de los oidores con los gropos superiores de la sociedad limeña (a comienzos del siglo XVII)," *Mercurio peruano* 447–50 (1964): 49–61; D. Ripodas de Ardanaz, *El matrimonio en Indias: Realidad social y regulación jurídica* (Buenos Aires, 1971), 35–44; and T. Hampe Martinez, "Los funcionarios, 105–11.

29. RI laws 82 and 83, title XVI, book 2; and R. Konetzke, *Colección de documentos*, 3: 321: cédula of 2 October 1764. I deal with this issue in greater length in T. Herzog, "Identidades colectivas, fronteras comunitarias y derecho: La domiciliación de mujeres de oidores quiteños durante el siglo XVII," *Anuario de historia del derecho español* 67/2 (1997): 1423–31.

best-connected families in Quito. After three years of public courtship, magistrate Miguel Antonio Ormasa Ponce de León (1676–85) received permission to marry María Marqués de Vivaldi, who was the widow of a native alderman of Quito. Juan Larrea Zurbano the elder married a Peruvian lady whose sisters all married and had children in the city. One of the daughters of magistrate Alonso Torres Pizarro (1664–76) married Sebastián Dávila, a local lawyer. Her sister was the wife of the chief constable, while her brother was justice of the Santa Hermandad. The sons of Pedro Gómez de Andrade (magistrate after 1733) and Alonso Zárate y Alarcón (crown attorney, 1721–31) both worked as lawyers in the city. Zárate y Alarcón's daughter married Ramón Juachín Maldonado y Sotomayor, the future local governor of Quito. President Fernando Félix Sánchez de Orellana and justices Juan Bautista Sánchez de Orellana and Juan Romualdo Navarro were descendants of local families whose members occupied different offices of justice and administration.

On the margins of official relationships, at least six other magistrates were accused of publicly maintaining concubines who were natives to the jurisdiction of Quito. Andrés Francia Cavero (1676–90) was associated with the daughter of the audiencia's doorman.[30] Matías Lagúñez y Aguilar (1680–87) shared a lover with the accountant of the royal treasury.[31] According to public gossip, Juan de Ricaurte (1689–1708 and 1722), Tomás Fernández Pérez de Hodo (1696–1718), and Lorenzo Lastero Salazar (1706–18 and after 1723) all maintained sexual relationships with different local women.[32] On occasion, these illicit love affairs degenerated into public scandal. Such was the case in the 1720s, when magistrate Simón Rivera Aguado (1720–33) was said to be involved in a relationship with the wife of Juan de Sosaya, who had been president of the audiencia between 1706 and 1712.[33] Rumors circulated that at least on one occasion Sosaya attempted to wound or even kill his rival, who was saved thanks only to the intervention of the acting president, Santiago Larrayn.

Municipal judges and judicial officers were just as connected with

30. AGI, Quito, 73, 112, 162, and 192.
31. AGI, Quito, 73, 42.
32. AGI, Quito, 130; and AGI, EC, 911A.
33. AGI, Quito, 374.

one another and the local society.[34] In 1676, the provincial and the judge of the Santa Hermandad were father and son, and in 1679 the judge of the Santa Hermandad and the chief constable were brothers.[35] Several families managed to monopolize the administration: Gabriel Yeroví, judge of the Santa Hermandad in 1687, was the father of the municipal ordinary justice in 1710. His daughter Agustina married José Zenitagoya, who acted as municipal ordinary justice in 1734. Similarly, the Villayns, both father and son, were constables in the middle of the seventeenth century. They were related to Bartolomé de Zuleta Reales, who was lieutenant governor between 1674 and 1675. Ramón Juachín Maldonado y Sotomayor, municipal ordinary judge in 1740 and local governor in 1745–48, first married the daughter of Francisco Borja (municipal ordinary justice in 1723 and 1728 and chief constable in 1705) and then married the daughter of crown attorney Alonso Zárate y Alarcón, whose son was a lawyer in Quito.

The situation was similar among notaries. For most of the seventeenth and eighteenth centuries, two families—the Sánchez Maldonado and the Suárez de Figueroa—dominated this profession, extending their influence into other judicial and administrative spheres. The Suárez de Figueroa, for example, owned the office of court notary three times, the office of notary of the town council twice, and the office of court clerk also twice. They also had other members who were legally trained or who were aldermen, municipal justices, and constables. Many offices that were "renounceable and transferable" were transferred from fathers to sons or sons-in-law (chap. 2). One such example was the case of Andrés Orozco the elder, who renounced the office of court notary to his son, who passed it to his son-in-law, Francisco Gómez Cornejo. On at least several occasions, brothers were employed in parallel offices: Juan and Cristóbal Valverde Aguilar were both public notaries in the mid–seventeenth century. The same happened with Diego and Francisco Hernández Marcillo, as well as with Alejo and Juan Bautista Núñez Montesdoca. Family relationships between titleholders and sub-

34. This subject was also studied in M. E. Porras, "La élite quiteña;" P. Ponce Leiva, "El poder informal: Mujeres de Quito en el siglo XVII," *Revista complutense de historia de América* 23 (1997): 98–111; and idem, *Certezas ante la incertidumbre*, 267–315. A comparative view is included in A. Guerrero Mayllo, *Familia y vida cotidiana de una élite de poder: Los regidores madrileños en tiempos de Felipe II* (Madrid, 1993).

35. AGI, Quito, 910C.

ordinates in notarial offices (*escribanías*) were also very frequent. The office of the court notary under Pedro Tomás Sánchez Maldonado (1691–1726) included a senior official (*oficial mayor*) and two of his sons (both of whom were scribes), as well as the adopted son (a third scribe) of the second court notary, Nicolás Andagoya y Otalora, himself a relative of Pedro Tomás.[36]

In order to reproduce this complexity, I summarized some of these family relationships in figures 1 and 2. Rather than being exhaustive, these figures are meant to provide a visual demonstration of the importance of family ties. Indeed, they show that by the middle of the eighteenth century most local officials and justices in Quito, including audiencia magistrates, were related to one another. In these figures, brief summaries of careers follow the names of individuals. The term "ordinario" designates the office of alcalde ordinario, "hermandad" the office of alcalde of the Santa Hermandad, and "lieutenant" that of the teniente corregidor. For the sake of simplification, I have disregarded the ordinary rules used to construct genealogical trees—so, for example, there is no progression in these figures from left to right according to the age differences between brothers, nor are first and second marriages always placed on the same side. Also, some generations are not presented at the same level, while others—for the sake of brevity— are not mentioned at all. Also ignored are connections linking the officers and justices to people employed in other administrative, ecclesiastic, military, and/or financial tasks. Representations of these connections, the social networks in Quito that were so essential to understanding the administration, are depicted later in figures 3 and 4.

Different factors—family ties, mutual protection and help, gratitude, subjection, or business collaboration—thus affected the way people interacted with one another. However, the extent of their influence differed from case to case in accordance with the way these various factors were interpreted and assumed. For example, losing a judicial action could indeed be good cause for making the judge your enemy. However (and as many people argued in Quito), this animosity was justified only if the decision was unjust. Theoretically, if the judge made a just decision, there was no reason to treat him as an enemy and no cause to think that his decision proved the preexistence of animosity between him and oneself. The question, therefore, was not the decision itself but

36. AGI, EC, 914B, cuad. 5, 237–51.

Notaries (Escribanos) and Justices: Quito 1597–1746

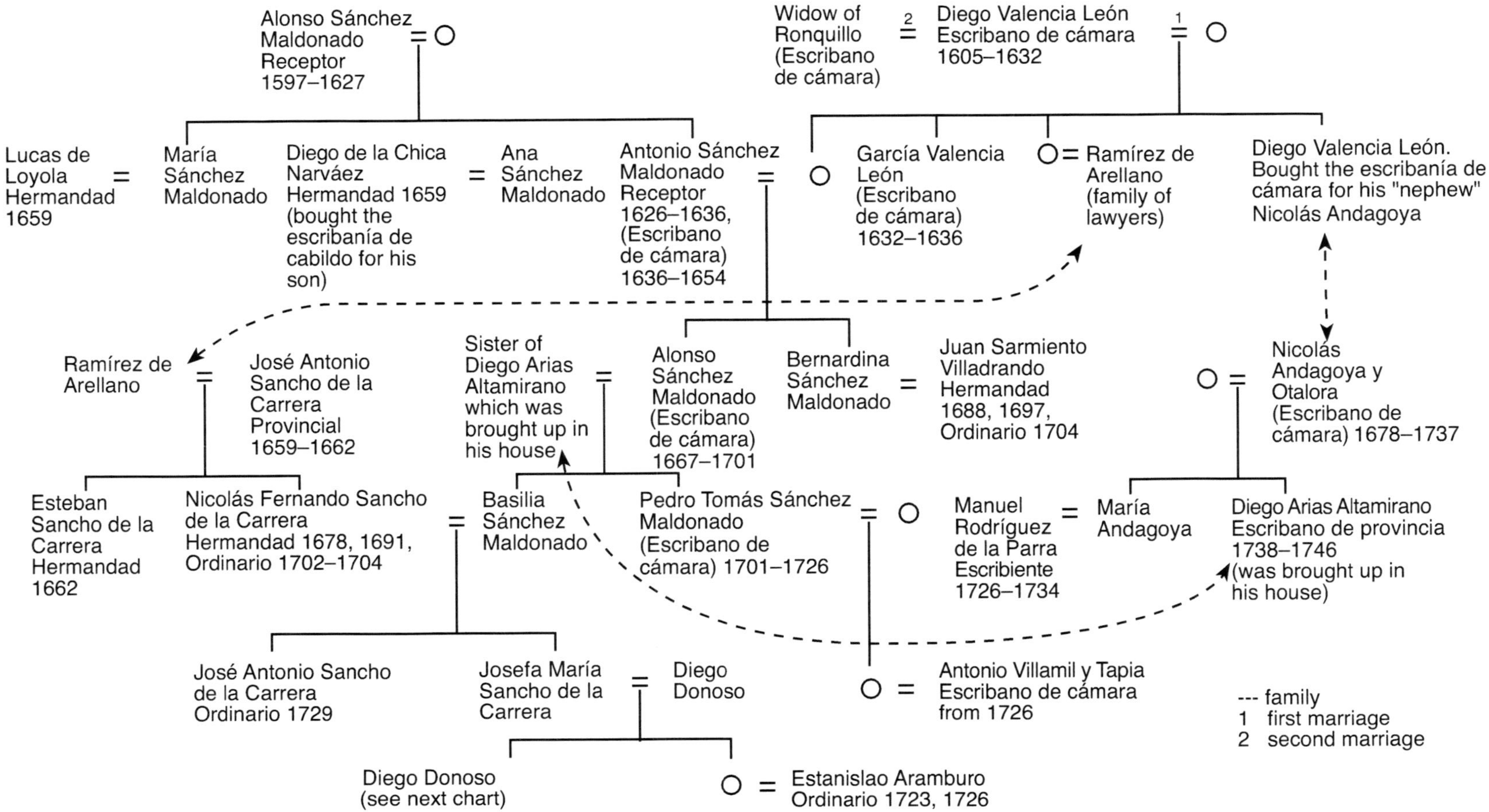

The Administration of Justice: Quito 1660–1753

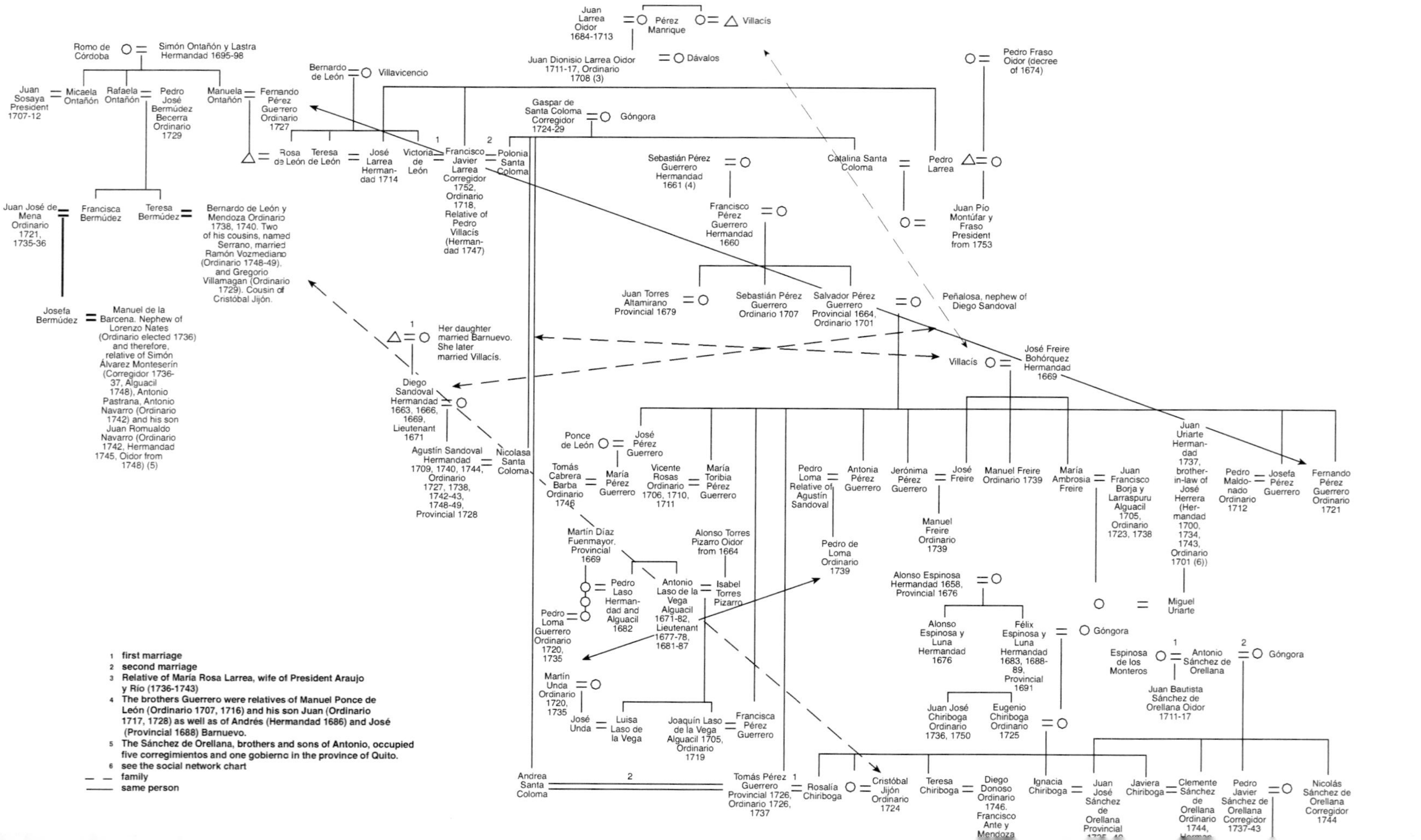

1 first marriage
2 second marriage
3 Relative of María Rosa Larrea, wife of President Araujo y Río (1736-1743)
4 The brothers Guerrero were relatives of Manuel Ponce de León (Ordinario 1707, 1716) and his son Juan (Ordinario 1717, 1728) as well as of Andrés (Hermandad 1686) and José (Provincial 1688) Barnuevo.
5 The Sánchez de Orellana, brothers and sons of Antonio, occupied five corregimientos and one gobierno in the province of Quito.
6 see the social network chart

— — family
—— same person

the way it was interpreted by the party who could feel offended, or not. By the same token, a disagreement about rights and duties, or a discussion about precedence in ceremonies, might or might not be offensive, depending on how it was interpreted. Interpretation depended on context, knowledge, and the predisposition of the parties to take offense. This implies that observing the objective circumstances that tied people to one another (such as noting that they were members of the same family or were confronted on several issues) could be helpful but never conclusive. The fact that a certain objective relationship existed between several individuals never really mattered in and of itself. What truly mattered was that these individuals considered themselves bound by a tie that generated obligations.

Both objective and subjective elements were thus responsible for the social obligations that linked people to one another. This point is well demonstrated by looking at mid–eighteenth century Quito. During this period, the local society (and especially its elite) was deeply affected by an ongoing investigation (*visita*) against the president of the audiencia José de Araujo y Río.[37] The president was charged with a series of offenses, including bribery, contraband trade, limiting the local autonomy, and the imposition of illegal taxes. As soon as complaints against him reached Madrid, it was immediately clear that the city of Quito was divided between the president's supporters and foes. Among those denouncing the activities of Araujo y Río were many leading social figures, including wealthy local merchants tied to the merchant guild of

37. Information on the proceedings against Araujo y Río can be found mainly in AGI, EC, 914A–914C, 915A–915C, 916A–916C, and 964. These proceedings were studied by K. J. Andrien, "Corruption, Inefficiency and Imperial Decline in the Seventeenth-Century Viceroyalty of Peru," *Americas* 41 (1984): 1–20; idem, *The Kingdom of Quito*, 166–80; idem, "Corruption, Self Interest, and the Political Culture," 278–83; L. Ramos Gómez, "Un ejemplo de la lucha," 117–32; idem, "La estructura social quiteña," 25–56; idem, "La pugna por el poder," 179–96; idem, "El 'bien común' como pretexto del presidente José de Araujo para crear una compañía de soldados y prohibir el aguardiente de caña en Quito en 1737," *Revista andina* 11/2 (1993): 381–401; and L. Ramos Gómez and C. Ruigómez Gómez, "La entrada en religión (1739) de Pedro Martínez de Arizala, oidor de la Audiencia de Quito y sus consecuencias," *Revista complutense de historia de América* 22 (1996): 209–37. See also T. Herzog, *Ritos de control, prácticas de negociación: Pesquisas, visitas y residencias y las relaciones entre Quito y Madrid (1650–1750)*, in *Nuevas Aportaciones a la historia jurídica de Iberoamérica*, ed. José Andrés Gallego (Madrid, 2000), chap. 4, point 9, CD-ROM. Araujo y Río was studied by M. Moreyra y Paz Soldán, "El limeño don José de Araujo y Río presidente de la audiencia de Quito y capitán general de Guatemala," *Mercurio peruano* 26/250 (1945): 506–29; and in T. Herzog *Los ministros de la audiencia de Quito (1650–1750)* (Quito, 1995), 46–49.

Lima, with whom the previous president of the audiencia Dionisio Alcedo y Herrera, crown attorney Juan Valparda y la Ormasa, and the accountant of the royal treasury were also associated. A wide range of interests motivated these people, yet they were united in their wish to protect their monopoly on trade. Some of them also wanted to control the local town council and wanted to elect municipal judges of their own liking (chap. 2). Empowered by economic wealth that permitted them to dominate the local scene, in 1736 and 1737 the members of this group wrote to the king and the Council of the Indies requesting that the president be investigated and removed from office. After the investigation began (1743), they took an active part and, led by Simón Álvarez Monteserín, helped the investigating judge Manuel Rubio de Arévalo to collect proofs against the president.[38] By mid-1744, the input of the members of this group in the investigation was such that it often seemed that they, rather than the judge, were in charge of conducting the case.

The group favoring the president included the treasurer of the royal treasury, his clients (chap. 2) magistrates Juan Lújan y Vedia and Pedro Gómez de Andrade, and eventually the incoming president Fernando Félix Sánchez de Orellana. These individuals had some shared mercantile interests (they were all involved to some degree in contraband trade), but their association was mainly focused on their wish to control the local institutions. The members of this group were also bound by their opposition to the powerful merchant guild of Lima, their preference for trade with New Granada, and their support of the local established elite. According to some versions (whose truthfulness cannot be attested) they also allied around their identity as Creoles, in opposition to the members of the rival group, whom they identified as peninsular Spaniards. Rather than employing its wealth, as was the case with the rival group, the association that backed the president benefited from the institutional position of its individual members, which could influence the decision-making process in Quito, although (initially) not in Madrid.

These alliances crystallized around the specific issue of investigating the president. The alliances were continuously formed, reformed, and reshaped according to the circumstances of the moment and the interests at stake. Nevertheless, they demonstrated how the interpretation of a great variety of factors could influence the creation or termination of

38. Eventually, the president was acquitted (1747) and his accusers punished.

social obligations, and how these obligations, in turn, determined the working of the administration. José de Araujo y Río first invoked this issue. As soon as the investigation against him began, he argued that only the people who hated him censored his activities. Because they were his enemies, they were not to be trusted, and their testimony against him should be stricken from the record. Araujo y Río claimed that the crown attorney "publicly encouraged all those discontented with the government and . . . with his genius, he ridiculed all my decisions, or affirmed that they were criminal, thus making them crime, and searching my ruin."[39] The marquis of Maenza, who was another of his enemies, disliked him because Araujo y Río had reported to the Council of the Indies the unwillingness of the marquis to donate money for the military defense of Guayaquil. These incidents were not trivial. According to Araujo y Río, once a confrontation began and animosity was created, it lasted forever. The positions adopted by the parties restructured their relationship in a way that was permanent and that stigmatized them for life. It affected them as much as it affected anyone associated with them.

The claim that the people who complained against him were his enemies, and that they could not be trusted, was of course rejected by those denouncing the activities of the president. They asserted not only that they were telling the truth but also that they were under no social obligation to lie. Rather than members of a group that hated the president, these individuals were simply people who happened to agree on certain facts—facts that happened to be unfavorable to Araujo y Río. According to them, the only social relations that existed between the persons involved in the case were the ones uniting the people who backed the president. All of these people were related to one another, and all of them were willing to lie in order to help Araujo y Río.

Because each party attempted to discredit the other, social networks became central to the debate.[40] These networks—which consisted of

39. AGI, EC, 914C, cuad. 5, 128. See also his allegations in AGI, EC, 916BB—pieza 28.

40. Social networks were studied by J. C. Mitchell, *Networks in Urban Situations* (Manchester, 1969); and J. Boissevain, *Friends of Friends: Networks, Manipulators and Coalitions* (Oxford, 1974). Their use in historical research was discussed in B. Wellman and C. Wetherell, "Social Network Analysis of Historical Communities. Some Questions from the Present for the Past," *History of the Family* 1/1 (1996): 97–121; A.M. Hespanha, "La economía de la gracia," *La gracia del derecho*, 151–76; and Levi, *Le pouvoir au village*. Social networks also extended over large geographical regions and could cover the territory of the empire. See, for example, T. Herzog, "Private Organizations as Global Networks," 117–33.

alliances between a wide range of people who were connected to one another by ties of family, friendship, economic collaboration, institutional and personal dependence, and common origin—were used in order to explain why people testified the way they did. The logic of this explanation was simple: social networks produced obligations, including the obligation to aid friends or to harm enemies. These obligations were sufficiently strong to justify lying in legal proceedings.

The Castilian legal system operating in Spanish America backed such claims. It determined that certain people should not be heard as witnesses in a trial because by definition they were not likely to tell the truth. Among these were relatives, dependents, and slaves of the interested parties, but also their enemies.[41] After they were identified as people connected to the parties by special ties, their testimony could be stricken from the records. This legal instrument was called *tachas*, literally meaning "stains." Tachas were rarely supported by proofs, and legally there was no need to demonstrate that the witnesses had in fact lied. All that was required was to show that the witness's social situation compromised him or her in a way that was likely to affect his or her declaration.

Using the information contained in the tachas, I reconstructed the rival factions in Quito in the mid–eighteenth century in figures 3 and 4.[42] The creation of this visual image necessitated the reduction of a highly detailed narrative into a few basic categories, each defining a different type of relationship. Among the eight categories that I defined are friendship (including simple friendship [*amistad*], close friendship [*amistad íntima*], and godparenting [*parentesco de afinidad*], family ties (both blood and marriage ties), commercial relationships (defined as engagement in a common commercial enterprise), subordination (according to the legal situation of the parties), service (including *criados* or *domésticos*), gratitude (including individuals who had received favors and felt obligated to return them), common residence (those who lived in the same household without being servants or relatives), and an eighth category encompassing all other relationships.

The social network of José de Araujo y Río, as his adversaries presented it, included an alliance between the president, the bishop, a magistrate (Pedro Gómez de Andrade), the royal treasurer (Fernando Gar-

41. Partida III, title 16: "on witnesses," especially laws 8, 10, 12–15, and 20–22.

42. AGI, EC, 914B, cuad. 8, 1–318; AGI, EC, 914C, cuad. 9, 14–81; and AGI, EC, 916B, cuad. 28, 71–96.

The Social Network of President Araujo Rio (1744)

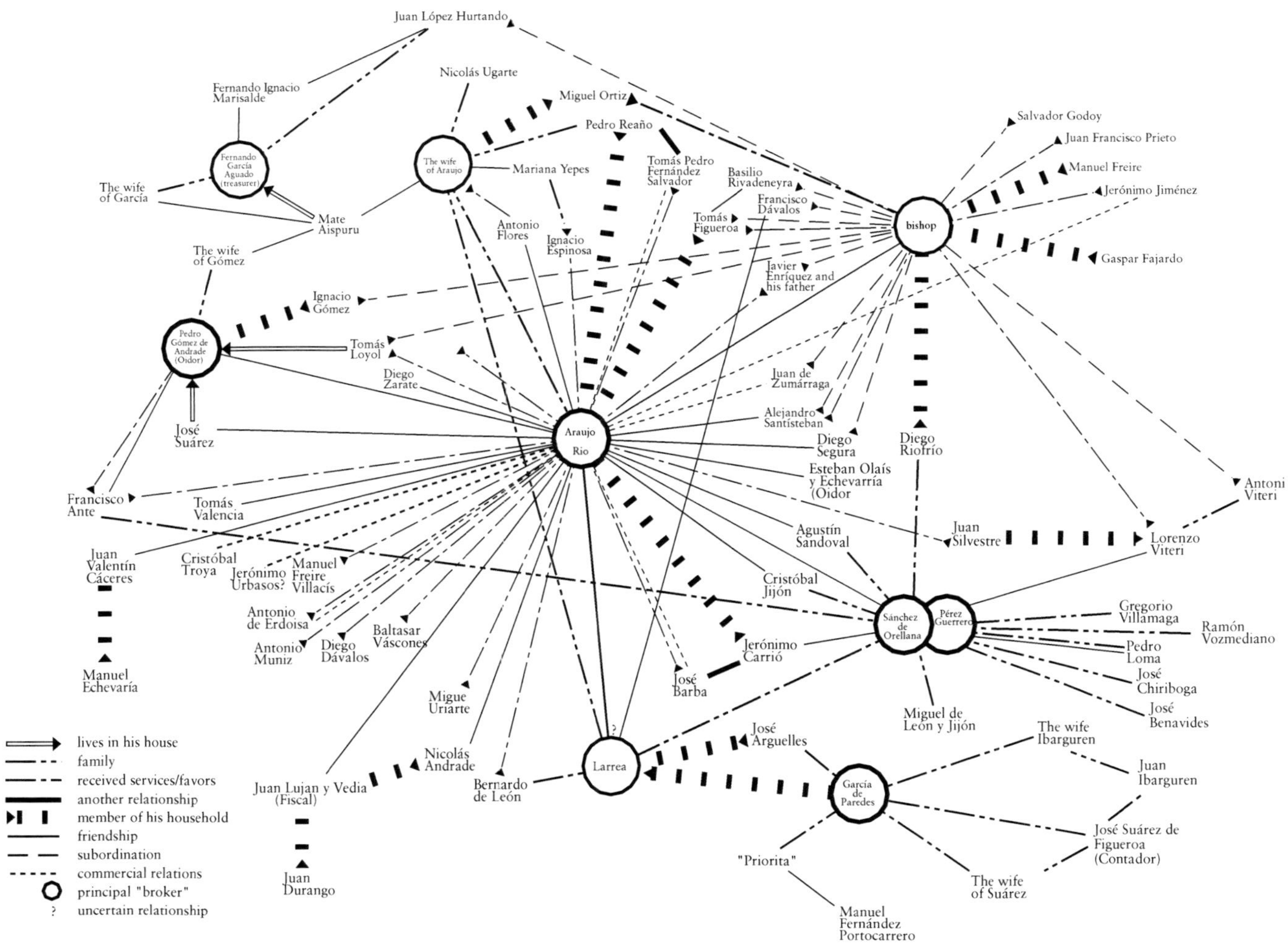

The Opposing Social Network (1744)

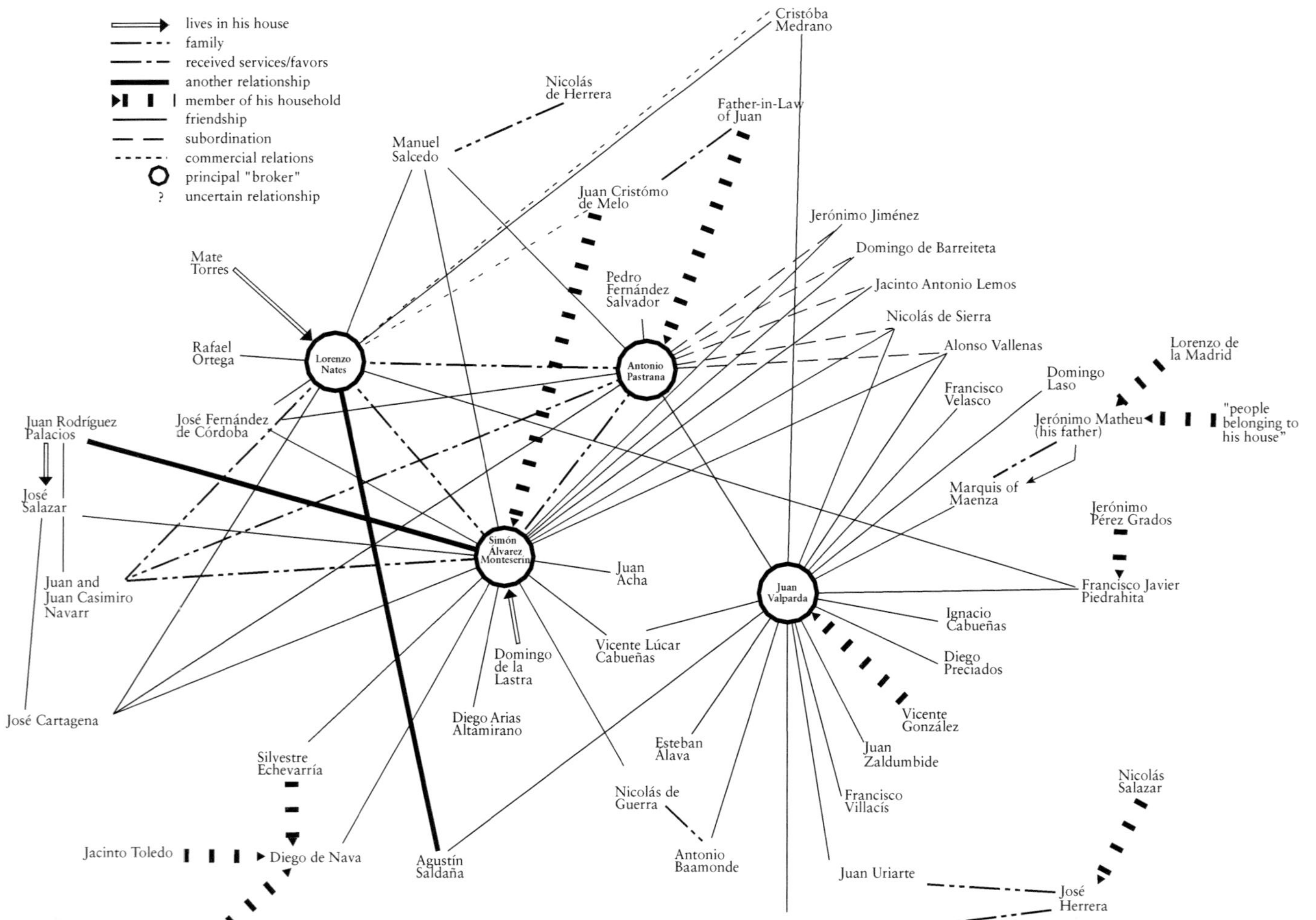

cía Aguado), and members of three of the most important families in Quito (Sánchez de Orellana, Larrea, and Pérez Guerrero). The network was clearly built around the president, who was primarily associated with the other members by virtue of friendship, common origin (*paisanazgo*), gratitude for services rendered, and, to a lesser extent, business association.[43] Some of the individuals belonging to this network acted as "brokers" who supplied it with the loyalty of their own clients. Clients were usually tied to brokers by virtue of subordination (in the case of the bishop) or family relations (in the cases of the Sánchez de Orellana, Larrea, Pérez Guerrero, and García Aguado families). Despite the demarcation of clear spheres of influence, multiple connections also existed between the different brokers and between each one of them and the president. For example, Francisco Ante y Mendoza belonged to the group associated with magistrate Pedro Gómez de Andrade. Yet he was also related to the Sánchez de Orellana and to the Pérez Guerrero families. The same thing was true of many clergymen who were affiliated with the network through both Gómez de Andrade and the bishop but who were also connected to the president directly.[44] Last but not least, several people belonged to this group because of various concurring motivations, for example, both commercial interchange and gratitude (in the case of José Barba) or both subordination and gratitude (in the case of Alejandro Santisteban). The role of female members was mainly restricted to their ability to tie their relatives to the network and to create or consolidate by marriage preexisting ties of friendships, commercial interchange, or subordination.

The social network of José de Araujo y Río, as described by his enemies, included an alliance between some one hundred people who were heads of households and patrons in their own right. It was an "indissoluble league between family-members, friends, service-people, and subordinates." According to the rival camp, its members acted illegally and, given their institutional positions, did not fear judicial or administrative prosecution.

The rival network was dramatically different. According to José de Araujo y Río and his witnesses, it had no single central figure but instead had four separate nuclei that were equally important. These nuclei were formed by three local merchants (Lorenzo Nates, Antonio

43. According to Boissevain, *Friends of Friends*, 28–45 and 147–69, this was a network with a high level of "centrality."

44. These phenomena are classified in the theory of networks as "density" and "rank."

Pastrana, and Simón Álvarez Monteserín), as well as by crown attorney Juan de Valparda. These four men were connected with one other through family and friendship ties, which in the case of merchants also designated commercial collaboration.[45] In contrast to the president's group, this alliance (with the exception of the cluster around the crown attorney) was not based on institutional factors such as subordination or gratitude, nor did it depend on vertical ties. Subordination was mentioned only once in justification for the relationships between Antonio Pastrana and various merchants, on account of his position as deputy of commerce—and even so this subordination was more virtual than real. The office, which gave Pastrana jurisdiction in commercial litigation, was a rotating one that all members of the group exercised in turn. Like the president's network, the merchant network also included brokers, such as Gerónimo Matheu and Diego de Nava. Officially, women acted as consolidators: through marriage, they strengthened the structure of the association. In practice some of them participated in commerce. For example, the wife of Lorenzo Nates, Antonia Monjardín y Ron, was the true merchant in that family.[46] While Antonia was "hard working in commerce and negotiations, earning much money through her work, commerce and other negotiations in which she was occupied, as it was well known in the city," Lorenzo was "a great spender who did not try to increase his wealth. Because Doña Antonia was aware of it, during her life she oversaw the money and the other negotiations of her husband."[47]

The merchant network was numerically smaller than that of the president's group, possibly only including some fifty individuals. Yet, because of its multinuclei structure and the importance of family ties in its construction, it appears it was more coherent and better consolidated than the other group.

Although the legal process against Araujo y Río is extremely helpful in reconstructing the social networks existing in mid–eighteenth century Quito, its true importance lies in the description of how these groups were created and maintained and in the types of obligations that they generated. The process also captures how people described

45. This question, as well as the role of commerce in establishing social ties, is described in greater detail in T. Herzog, 379–96.

46. AHQ, Test., 103 and 104: exp. 3 April 1753 and 6 September 1753.

47. AHQ, Exp. 6 September 1753; idem, 81–83.

these groups and how they fought to demonstrate their importance or prove their inexistence. As I mention earlier, each party stressed the predominance of social networks leading people on the opposing side to lie, and it negated the role of social networks in its own camp—thus assuring listeners that *its* witnesses were telling the truth. As a result of this dynamic, each group was portrayed not by its own members but by the members of the rival camp who wished to discredit the other faction. The relationship between the construction of groups on the one hand and the need to discredit unfavorable witnesses on the other was such that all unfavorable witnesses were immediately inserted into the rival group. People whose testimony was prejudicial to both camps ended up classified as members of both factions. For example, according to one account Jerónimo Jiménez had commercial relations with Araujo y Río and thanked the bishop for having given his brother a parish benefice. According to another account, he was the friend of Simón Álvarez Monteserín and a subordinate of Antonio Pastrana, his relative.

The wish to disqualify unfavorable witnesses not only affected the construction of factions: it also produced an acute awareness of the subjective (and interpretative) elements involved in making friends or enemies.[48] The parties to the conflict thus specified, for example, that it was often impossible to determine who was doing a favor for whom. Manuel (Freire) Villacís was classified as a member of the president's group because Araujo y Río confirmed him as municipal ordinary judge, despite the fact that only a minority of aldermen supported this decision. Yet, according to some witnesses (who belonged to the president's group and who wanted to assure the judge that Villacís was telling the truth), Villacís was quite unhappy about what had happened. He was angry with the president for failing to secure sufficient votes for his nomination and was resentful because this fact exposed him to public criticism. Furthermore, he did not want to be a judge in the first place. Living peacefully on his rural estates, he wished to retire from public life, and he only allowed his candidature to be considered because he wanted to please the president, who begged him to do so.

The awareness that the same act could be interpreted in different and even contradictory ways also occurred on other occasions. Some witnesses questioned the conclusion that all business partners were nec-

48. The following analysis is mainly based on AGI, EC, 914B, cuad. 8 and 9; AGI, EC, 916B—pieza 28; and AGI, EC, 278B.

essarily friends, that all relatives truly loved one another, or that the bishop was, by definition, a friend of all his parishioners. By the same token, many argued that not all decisions favoring a person should be interpreted as signs, or even as guarantees, of friendship. For example, there was no need to feel grateful to a judge who decided the case on its merits and not because of the identity of the parties. The same was true with regard to an administrator who gave a commission to the only available and suitable person. Also questioned was the degree of debt one could have with the president when the decision to favor one was not made by the president alone but by the audiencia as a collegial body. The ability to share or inherit obligations was also discussed. Would harm done to one man necessarily transform all his friends into enemies of his aggressor, or were certain acts "personal" and nontransferable from one group member to another?

The questioners never doubted that relations existed, that they were important, and that they could lead witnesses to lie. Whether or not specific ties existed between certain individuals, it was generally agreed that no person, royal officials included, ever lived on his or her own. Men and women lived in society, and they were affected by social obligations generated by everyday interactions. Each of these interactions created rights and obligations. Some of these obligations were more important than others. They dictated who individuals should love and who not and how they should behave. This reality was not the inversion or corruption of the normal social and institutional system. It *constructed* the system and was an inherent part of it.

Social networks did not only influence officials and judges making a decision or witnesses giving their testimony. They were also crucial in the construction of the institutions and in generating adherence to their orders. Social networks explained (1) how certain people got associated with the administration in the first place (chap. 2).[49] And (2) why others obeyed their orders. People obeyed the magistrates because they were acting for the king and on his behalf. Yet, first and foremost, they

49. J. P. Dedieu, "Une approche 'fine' à la prosopography," in *Les figures historiques de l'administrateur: Institutions, réseaux, pouvoirs en Espagne, en France et au Portugal, 16e–19e siècle,* ed. R. Descimon, J. F. Schaub, and B. Vincent (Paris, 1997), 235–42; and M. Peytavin, "Naple 1610: Comment peut-on être officier?" *Annales ESC* 52/2 (1997): 265–91. Z. Moukoukias, "Negocios y redes sociales: modelo interpretativo a partir de un caso rioplatense (siglo XVIII)," *Caravelle* 67 (1997): 37–55, reaches similar conclusions regarding the role of networks in the structuring of business relations.

obeyed (or opposed) them because of social obligations.[50] As Jorge Juan and Antonio Ulloa noted in the mid–eighteenth century, "the authority of the local judicial governors depends on the power the important townsmen are willing to give to them, whose decision is then emulated by the less important citizens. If the local judicial governor gets along with the townsmen, he is received as an honorable citizen, but if he places himself above them in jurisdiction, or if he wishes to show his superiority by virtue of office, he becomes nothing. He is left with no one who will obey him, and his office becomes practically defunct. If he insists in his intent, they respond by doing their best to jeopardize his activity."[51]

The realization that social networks constructed the administration, influenced its work, and then determined the degree of obedience has far-reaching implications. If we recognize that social networks were both a recognized and an important part of the administrative and social system, and not an aberration of it, then it becomes impossible to speak about institutions as separate from society, and it is no longer viable to portray, as historians have done in the past, a series of phantasmagoric formal rules whose alleged breaking constitutes corruption.[52]

Affirmations that early modern officeholders were corrupt have been under attack for several years. Yet, in the field of Latin American studies this criticism has been limited to discussing the "good" or "bad" effects corrupt practices might have had.[53] Zacarías Moutoukias and

50. P. Bourdieu, "Le capital social: notes provisoires," *Actes de la recherche en Sciences Sociales* 31 (1980): 2–3. This phenomenon was also described in A. Xristóbal Martín, "Amistad, parentesco y patronazgo: Redes vinculares y servidores inquisitoriales en el tribunal de Logroño (siglo XVII)," *Historia social* 17 (1993): 23 and 31. See also Z. Moutoukias, "La notion de réseau en histoire social: un instrument d'analyse de l'action collective," in *Rèsaux, familles et pouvoirs dans le monde ibérique à la fin de l'ancien régime,* ed. J. L. Castellano and J. P. Dedieu (Paris, 1998), 231–45.

51. J. Juan and A. Ulloa, *Noticias secretas de América* (1826; reprint, Madrid, 1988), 438. The *Noticias* were written in the 1740s. These issues are also examined in Bertrand, "La élite colonial," 35–51.

52. S. Poole, "Institutionalized Corruption in the Letrado Bureaucracy: The Case of Pedro Farfán (1568–1588)," *Americas* 38 (1981): 149–71; Andrien, "Corruption, Inefficiency, and Imperial Decline"; and R. Vigil, "*Oidores, Letrados* and the Idea of Justice, 1480–1570," *Americas* 47 (1990): 39–47.

53. Among those questioning the use of corruption in other European settings are J. Hurstfield, *Freedom, Corruption and Government in Elizabethan England* (Camrdidge, MA, 1973), 137–62; and J. C. Waquet, *Corruption, Ethics and Power in Florence, 1600–1770,* trans. L. McCall (Paris, 1984; trans., University Park, PA, 1992), 3–12, 16, and 191.

Horst Pietschmann argued, for example, that corruption introduced into the structures of the Spanish empire a necessary flexibility. Rather than inhibiting good government, it guaranteed this government by allowing economic considerations and commonsense conclusions to prevail.[54] But if we seriously believe in the compenetration of society and institutions, and if we view social networks as a routine mechanism and not an exception, than we can no longer speak about corruption, good or bad.[55] We need to analyze the structures existing in the seventeenth- and eighteenth-century according to early modern, and not contemporary, criteria. Among other things, such an analysis will allow us to appreciate the importance of justice and mutual exchange, not obedience to laws. We must focus on the reasons people behaved as they did and the reasons for which this behavior was admired or criticized.[56] We already know that people had social obligations that were more important than, for example, the duty to tell the truth in judicial proceedings. These obligations, often described as obeying a "law of friendship," caused people to behave in a way that appears corrupt to us.[57] They gave the president of the audiencia gifts, or they helped a friend because he was a friend. Yet these actions were not ones that officeholders took ignoring their obligations, jeopardizing the common

54. Z. Moutoukias, "Power, Corruption, and Commerce," 800; and H. Pietschmann, "Corrupción en las Indias españolas: Revisión de un debate en la historiografía sobre Hispanoamérica colonial," in *Instituciones y corrupción en la historia,* ed. M. González Jiménez, H. Pietschmann, F. Comín, and J. Perez (Valladolid, 1998), 45–49. See also Pietschmann, "Burocracia y corrupción"; and Z. Moutoukias, "Réseaux personnels et autorité coloniale. Les négociants de Buenos Aires au XVIIIe siècle," *Annales ESC* 47 (1992). A summary of some of this discussion can be found in E. R. Saguier, "La corrupción administrativa como mecanismo de accumulación y engendrador de una burguesía comercial local," *Anuario de estudios americanos* 46 (1989): 269–303.

55. A similar criticism was expressed in J. Martínez Millán, "Las investigacione sobre patronazgo y clientelismo en la administración de la monarquía hispana durante la edad moderna," *Studia storica—historia moderna* 15 (1996): 97–98. There are also those who look at the picture from the other direction and view social networks as a mechanism that controlled the corruption of individuals that was endemic to the system: M. González Jiménez, "Corrupciones municipales en Castilla a finales de la edad media," in *Instituciones y corrupción en la historia,* ed. M. González Jiménez, H. Pietschmann, F. Comín, and J. Perez (Valladolid, 1998), 11–12. See also M. Bertrand, *Grandeur et misère.*

56. J. C. Waquet, "Some Considerations on Corruption, Politics, and Society in Sixteenth and Seventeenth Century Italy," *Political Corruption in Europe and Latin America,* ed. W. Little and E. Posada-Carbó (London, 1996), 26–32.

57. B. Clavero, *Antidora: Antropología católica de la economía moderna* (Milan, 1991), 189; and Hespanha, "La economia de la gracia." For a different view see L. Boltanski, *L'amour et la justice comme compétences: trois essais de sociologie de l'action* (Paris, 1990).

good, and only caring for their own advantage, as would be the case with corruption today. Gift giving and the helping of a friend were motivated by social obligations. They obeyed certain known (and well-respected) rules, and they enhanced, rather than weakened, the power of institutions as well as the common good.[58] Take, for example, the case of Antonio Llera, who confessed that he had given President José de Araujo y Río a chest of gold. This gift, he explained, had several concurrent explanations. By giving the president the chest, he recognized him as a superior. He also acknowledged the family relationship that united them, and he thanked the president for a gift that he had given him.[59] His action, which under the current legislation in most countries would be classified as corrupt, was thus embedded in social practices that were considered both legitimate and advantageous because they guaranteed the social cohesion and (ultimately) the public welfare.

This does not mean that a discourse censoring ministers for letting personal ties intervene in their decision-making process did not exist.[60] However, contrary to what most historians have asserted in the past, this discourse was not aimed at replacing an old patrimonial (corrupt) order with a new modern (uncorrupt and legalistic) one. Neither did it recognize the distance between the ideal of impartial judges and the reality of corrupt ones.[61] Instead, it was a discourse concerned with misgovernment. This is why different themes such as illicit trade, oppression of Indians, and gift receiving could be treated under the same rubric of "corruption."[62] This discourse focused on the need to guarantee social harmony by ensuring the predominance of justice. Justice was

58. A. J. Heidenheimer, ed., *Political Corruption: A Handbook* (New York, 1990), 3–14; and C. J. Friedrich, "Corruption Concepts in Historical Perspective," *Political Corruption: A Handbook,* ed. A. J. Heidenheimer (New York, 1990), 15–24.

59. AGI, EC, 914A, cuad. 3, 223.

60. Pietschmann, "Corrupción en las Indias," 34–37; and J. Perez, "El estado moderno y la corrupción, in *Instituciones y corrupción en la historia,* ed. M. González Jiménez, H. Pietschmann, F. Comín, and J. Perez (Valladolid, 1998), 113, 123–124, and 128–129. For a comparative view see W. Prest, "Judicial Corruption in Early Modern England," *Past and Present* 133 (1991): 67–95.

61. J. L. Castellano Castellano and I. Gómez González, "Reflexiones sobre la justicia en el antiguo régimen a propósito de unas cartas a Villena, " *Chronica nova* 22 (1995): 11–28; Perez, "El estado moderno," 128–29; and M. A. Burkholder, "Honest Judges Leave Destitute Heirs: The Price of Integrity in Eighteenth Century Spain," *Virtue, Corruption and Self Interest. Political Values in the Eighteenth Century,* ed. R. K. Matthews (Bethlehem, 1994), 247–69.

62. A. McFarlane, "Political Corruption and Reform in Bourbon Spanish America," *Political Corruption in Europe and Latin America* (London, 1996), 41.

essential because it was the bond that held society together. As Juan de Mariana argued in the sixteenth century, justice was for society what military discipline was for the army, or what the order and structure of pillars was for a building.[63] Without justice, there was no love or respect among men.

Because it was focused on justice, the discourse censoring ministers for making partial decisions was not preoccupied with legality. Those elaborating it were not concerned with obedience to the laws or to some abstract moral criteria. Instead, they wished to ensure that people would be treated according to what they deserved. Indeed, in the early modern period justice was not a guarantee of equality or even impartiality. On the contrary, it implied the obligation to give every person his due, and it legitimized both hierarchy and deference. It acknowledged the need to discriminate between people and the right to treat them according to their estates, abilities, behaviors, and social relations. As Linda Levy Peck and Horst Pietschmann noted, the discourse censuring ministers was mainly engaged in distinguishing what was just (that is, socially acceptable) and what was not.[64]

Because justice required making distinctions, and implementing different solutions for different cases, it could coexist with social strife. Justice did not end the divisions existing in society but on the contrary enhanced them and social harmony was not necessarily contradictory to partisanship.[65] Society was a conglomerate of personal relationships leading to both competition and social cohesion. Take, for example, the elections in the town council. The elections stressed the division of Quito into fractions, yet they were also used as a mechanism to both demonstrate and enhance the general welfare. The ambition was to reach a unanimous decision, and when such a decision was impossible, those elected renounced their offices because of some social pressure. The voting of sentences in the audiencia followed a similar rationale. By nature, voting allowed and even encouraged divisions. Yet sentences were pronounced as if these divisions did not exist and as if the court

63. J. de Mariana, *Del rey y de la institución real*, book 3 (1598; reprint, Madrid, 1854), chap. 11, 559.

64. L. Levy Peck, *Court Patronage and Corruption in Early Stuart England* (London, 1990; reprint, 1993), 5 and 161–207; Pietschmann, "Corrupción en las Indias," 35–38; and idem, "Estado Colonial y mentalidad social: El ejercicio del poder frente a distintos sistemas de valores, siglo XVIII," in *America latina dallo stato coloniale allo stato nazione (1740–1940)*, ed. A. Annino, M. Carmagnani, et al. (Milan, 1987), 427–47.

65. J. A. Maravall, *La teoría*, 115–21.

spoke in a single voice. Indeed, rather than choosing between a pole of legality and a pole of corruption (as would be the case today), early modern actors moved between two equally desirable poles: harmony on the one hand and partiality on the other.

It is thus impossible to speak about corruption in the early modern period. This impossibility is theoretical, but it also has practical motives. Most complaints about the malfunctioning of officers did not develop into judicial procedures, and even when they did, the proofs collected during the investigations usually indicated contradictory conclusions.[66] We can assume, of course, that we, today, can judge who was corrupt and who not, who was telling the truth and who was lying—and this is what many historians have done in the past. We can also adopt the decisions made by early modern judges (who convicted certain people of corruption) and sustain that they were necessarily justified. Yet neither of these solutions is satisfactory. This problem becomes especially complex if we realize that complaints against magistrates could form part of a communication pattern between individuals and authorities and between the authorities among themselves. The case of Araujo y Río is once again revealing. The reason why his rivals denounced him to Madrid, and the way Madrid reacted, had little to do with what he actually did. His rivals were not concerned with the administration of justice or the common good. First and foremost, they wrote to the Council of the Indies because the local society was divided into factions and because they were convinced that the best way to defend their interests was by attacking the members of the other band.[67] The authorities listened to or ignored the testimony according to their own agendas. Sometimes their agenda aimed to guarantee justice, but at other times it was motivated by questions of loyalty and services rendered. The fact that a discourse regarding corruption became central to these dynamics is not surprising. During the early modern period there were no clear rules regarding how royal officials should behave. In the absence of an administrative law the way we know it today, judges could not be accused of not following the letter of the law. As alter egos of the king, neither could judges be accused of making a professional mistake. The only possible method to censure royal officials was by accusing them of being unjust or morally unfit for office. This accusa-

66. AGI, EC, 914A, cuad.3, 135; AGI, Quito, 130, 77; the declaration of Venegas de Córdoba.

67. Pietschmann, "Burocracia," 22; and Levy Peck, *Court Patronage,* 161–207.

tion could be sustained because being just and moral was the religious and social obligation of all men, especially men of authority. It required no special administrative law and no particular definition.

Under such a system, complaints against judges always took on the form of personal attacks against their morality. Although an attack apparently pointed to corrupt practices, it very often embodied criticism that today would be channeled otherwise by pointing to a legal disagreement or by criticizing a judge for making a mistake. The fact that all criticism against judges, even professional criticism, took the form of a discourse regarding corruption was constantly evident in Quito. It was clear, for example, in 1691, when court notary Nicolás Andagoya y Otalora accused magistrate Andrés Francia Cavero of freeing a murderer in exchange for gifts.[68] The magistrate and the municipal ordinary justice that handled the case admitted the irregularity. Yet they explained that this was a pure mistake, which was made not by them but by the audiencia as a whole. It was then made clear that the court notary accused the judge of corruption because there was no other way by which he could proceed. The notary, who could not criticize the audiencia or the judge for making a mistake, could only force an investigation that would review the justice of the case and would decide to reimprison the criminal.

Although the morality of judges became a common means by which to criticize them for their professional mistakes, no one expected judges to be perfect. Judges were part of society, not superior men. They could have a past that according to modern perceptions would make them unfit for office. Magistrate Juan de Ricaurte was suspected of abusing and attempting to poison his wife. His colleague Miguel Antonio Ormasa Ponce de León was investigated for the murder of his concubine's first husband and was eventually convicted for having killed one of the president's slaves who disturbed his peace by playing music.[69] Condemned in 1680 for assaulting a cleric, Juan Triunfo Sosaya was named temporary crown attorney for the audiencia the following year.[70] Bartolomé Zaraus y Aldemar, justice of the Santa Hermandad in 1685, continued in office after he verbally and physically attacked the standard-bearer and the priest of the village of Sangolquí. Pedro Vázquez Feijoo was never punished for having hidden a criminal file

68. AGI, Quito, 73, 246.
69. AGI, Quito, 162; AGI, Quito, 5, no. 201; and AHQ, Crim., 11: exp. 6 December 1688.
70. AHQ, Crim., 8: exp. 26 June 1680.

against one of his relatives while he served as provincial of the Santa Hermandad in 1650.[71] Before they were appointed to office, Pedro Godoy was fined for participating in a brawl, Juan Sarmiento Villandrando was convicted of stabbing the controller (visitador) of the royal treasury, Antonio Navarro and Simón Álvarez Monteserín were convicted of having mistreated a woman, Juan Ibarguren helped a prisoner escape from jail, and Jacinto Sainz de Gaona was convicted for the murder of a lawyer.

Corruption was mainly a discourse of opposition. In the words of Anthony McFarlane, it diagnosed maladies and suggested cures.[72] It was advocated by individuals in order to criticize specific judges, or it was voiced by reformers who wished to modify the structures of the empire. Rather than portraying a reality, this discourse allowed resistance in a world in which opposition was (yet) unheard of.

Conclusion

Royal officials were never lone individuals. They formed part of a group that conditioned their ability to hold office and to exercise it efficiently. Their decisions were motivated by friendship and animosity, and they were defined, first and foremost, by virtue of the relationships that united them with and divided them from other people. These relationships determined their ability to interact with one another and with the population. These relationships also guaranteed their degree of success or failure in judicial matters.

The duty to act in favor of one's friends and against one's enemies dominated the life of local institutions. It was an accepted and widely recognized obligation. Criticized when disruptive of public harmony, it was also a constitutive part of justice making. Corruption in its modern sense did not exist because this behavior was consistent with the public good. It did not contradict a legal or moral code, and it guaranteed that institutions would be properly and effectively run. The analysis of social

71. AHQ, Crim., 10: exp. 4 June 1685; AHQ, Crim., 16: exp. 1 November 1705; and AHQ, Ced., 2 (1601–60), no. 456.

72. McFarlane, "Political Corruption," 43–46. See also I. Kramnick, "Corruption in Eighteenth-Century English and American Political Discourse," *Virtue, Corruption and Self Interest. Political Values in the Eighteenth Century,* ed. R. K. Matthews (Bethlehem, 1994), 55–75.

networks in Quito thus demonstrates the futility of importing modern notions of corruption into an early modern period. They also prove that the distinction between institutions and society was practically nonexistent. Royal officials acted, first and foremost, as members of the local society. They were identified with certain groups and behaved according to the demands of these groups. From their point of view, institutional boundaries the way we think about them today were meaningless. The degree by which this was true is further demonstrated in the following chapter.

CHAPTER FOUR

Society and the Administration of Justice

An important part of judicial activity was carried out in Quito by a variety of people who were not officially or permanently part of the administration. These people were able to obtain jurisdiction because a local authority delegated power to them, frequently on an ad hoc basis. In some cases they helped the administration upon its request; in others they acquired jurisdiction without an administrative prompt. Their aid could be formally sanctioned; or not. Many such people were ordinary Quiteños who in some moment felt the need, or were called, to assist the administration. In some cases their work would be remunerated; in others they might not receive any clear economic benefit. Sometimes they even suffered as a consequence of their intervention. These people acted to ensure the public peace by protecting victims, capturing criminals, and bringing them to trial. They formed what was perhaps the most important part of the justice system: their duties focused on both the prevention of crimes, and the punishment of criminals.

The involvement of the people of Quito in the administration of justice could follow several different routes. A vast number of people acted as temporary officeholders. Protectors of Indians, crown attorneys, and even magistrates could be named locally by the president of the audiencia. Temporary offices were supposed to be exceptional, occurring only when an office was vacant because the new (extralocal) nominee had not yet arrived in Quito. However, given the distance between Quito and Madrid (matched by problems of communication and lengthy procedures in the Council of the Indies) temporary nominations often became permanent—or least covered a long span of time. Many such nominations were semiclandestine. There are no records in the archives clarifying when they were made, by whom, why, and for how long. The Council of the Indies was rarely informed about these nominations, and it often ignored their existence. However, trial records demonstrate their importance. Ignacio Aybar y Eslava and Juan Triunfo Sosaya, for example, acted as temporary protector of Indians and crown attorney respectively, from 1679 to 1781. The president of the audiencia also named temporary local governors whenever the regular governor was absent, was sick, or had died. The audiencia frequently employed, especially in the last years of the seventeenth century and in the beginning of the eighteenth century, cojudges (*cojueces*) either on account of the insufficient number of magistrates in the court or in cases of a judicial tie.[1] People named in this way were ordinary lawyers. They were called by the president to act as protectors, crown attorneys, or magistrates either on a single occasion or for several months or even years. Their nomination could be ad hoc and related to a specific case, or it could be general.[2]

The delegation of judicial authority to people who were not formally part of the judicial system also occurred in the municipal court. The president of the audiencia, for example, named the senior alderman as justice of the Santa Hermandad in 1704 and in 1707. Municipal ordinary justices nominated their friends and relatives to act with them when their impartiality was questioned (when they were "recused") or when they considered that they needed help because the matter was too complex for them to resolve on their own. In these cases, instead of requesting the help of another judge (the second municipal ordinary judge, the local governor, or his lieutenant), municipal ordinary judges appointed as cojudge an alderman, the chief constable, or one of the judicial or parajudicial officers. These appointments followed no formalities, nor were they publicly announced. They appear in trial records without any explanation other than the fact that the judge reviewing the case had decided to call another person to assist him in the task of administrating justice.

Temporality also marked the office of lieutenant governors (*teniente corregidor*), who were appointed by governors and depended entirely on them. The nomination of lieutenants could be ad hoc or general, and it could be revoked at any time. Despite the precariousness of their situation, lieutenants replaced the governor in his judicial tasks. Indeed,

1. AGI, Quito, 15, no.43; AGI, EC, 911A; and AMQ, LC, 00118: town council meeting of 23 March 1707.

2. AHQ, Not. 1, 13: exp. 25 December 1723 from 8 August 1720. The employment of local lawyers as temporary magistrates was also described by T. Calvo, "Les réalités du pouvoir aux confins de l'empire," 152–53.

they did so in most cases.[3] There were also many occasions in which the president or the local governor nominated certain individuals to act as judges on account of the office they exercised. Seventeenth-century local governors of Quito, for example, delegated their judicial authority in criminal matters to one of the justices of the Santa Hermandad in 1664, 1665, 1670, 1686, and 1687.[4] This delegation substantially changed the nature of the justice's office. By law, justices of the Santa Hermandad had jurisdiction only on crimes committed on roads and uninhabited areas. The delegation they received from the local governor allowed them to extend their powers to the city of Quito and to the villages belonging to it. Similarly, the president of the audiencia commissioned certain people to municipal justice. For example, constables Manuel González del Pino and Francisco Javier Piedrahita were both charged with adjudicating criminal and civil matters in the city from 1712 to at least 1744.[5] Other judges named assistants and delegated their jurisdiction to them.[6] This was a common practice among justices of the Santa Hermandad. Functionaries who were named in this way depended on the person who appointed them to office. Not only had he recruited them but he also paid their salaries and was responsible for their behavior (and misbehavior).

Formally appointed officers were thus the tip of an iceberg in a system of judicial control, which permitted the intervention of a vast network of temporary and informal officeholders. In 1679, a judge commissioned the brother-in-law of the complainant to find an accused criminal.[7] In 1724, the chief constable authorized Melchor López to seize goods and imprison suspects. In turn, and on his own initiative, López requested the help of two of his friends, who thereafter became ministers of justice.[8] In 1743, the lieutenant governor charged Cayetano

3. AMQ, LC, 00113, 258; AMQ, LC, 00117 from January of 1700; and AMQ, LC, 00117: town council meeting of 10 February 1701.

4. Town council meetings of 12 February 1664, 12 January 1665, 9 January 1670, 21 January 1686, and 9 January 1687; and "Autos acordados de la Real Audiencia de Quito, 1578–1722," *Anuario histórico jurídico ecuatoriano* 2 (1971): 98, 105.

5. Town council meeting of 26 November 1712.

6. This practice was permitted by law: Ordinance 87 of the Audiencia de Quito, Congreso del instituto internacional de historia del Derecho Indiano, *Ordenanzas de la Real Audiencia de Quito: V Congreso del Instituto Internacional de Historia del Derecho Indiano* (Quito-Guayaquil, 1978), 34.

7. AHQ, Crim., 6: exp. 23 January 1679.

8. AHQ, Crim., 21: exp. 3 July 1724.

Lucero with guarding a criminal.[9] In 1748, Manuel Ponce received a general commission to imprison criminals.[10] Even prisoners were used for judicial missions, and some of them were asked to help locate other criminals.[11]

Temporary appointments were so widespread that it was often unclear who was exercising an office and what was the source of his authority. In 1741, Vicente Cherrez was accused of illegally possessing a knife.[12] Brought before a judge, he explained that he was a temporary officer of justice. His duty consisted of finding and imprisoning criminals, and for that end he was authorized to carry the knife. In order to support his claim, Cherrez produced a letter signed by the ordinary municipal justice who had indeed charged him with this mission. The letter explained that "urgent concerns and occupations" incapacitated the justice from attending to all of his duties and forced him to request Cherrez's help. The audiencia, which considered Cherrez a dangerous man, disapproved of the appointment and suspended his commission.

There were innumerable other cases in which municipal justices sent simple townsmen to execute their judicial orders without informing anyone of their commission and without giving them external signs that would identify them as auxiliaries of the administration. Appointment to office in this semisecret way made it impossible to know who acted as officers of justice and who had to be obeyed. Provisional officers like Cherrez were often attacked, persecuted, or disobeyed because their association with the administration was unknown. When Tomás de Villanueva was accused of resisting justice in 1728, he argued that he had no idea that the people who attacked him were justice ministers.[13] He had no reason to suspect that they were. They were temporary officeholders, appointed by the judge without any publicity, and they carried no signs that would identify them as auxiliaries of the administration.

This situation seemed natural to some people, but others bitterly criticized it. The process through which people could be converted from ordinary inhabitants into officers of justice was discussed in Quito in

9. AHQ, Not. 6, 13: exp. 16 April 1743.
10. AHQ, Pris., 2: exp. 1 January 1748.
11. AHQ, Crim., 32: exp. 16 July 1743 from 29 May 1745; AHQ, Not. 1, 29: exp. 11 May 1748; AHQ, Not. 1, 13: exp. 25 December 1723; and AHQ, Crim., 24: exp. 10 October 1728.
12. AHQ, Crim., 31: exp. 3 February 1741.
13. AHQ, Crim., 24: exp. 29 October 1728.

1741, 1742, and 1746.[14] The subject was the application of the law that determined that both the royal standard-bearer and the senior alderman could act as municipal ordinary justices whenever such justices were absent.[15] Two issues were in question. The first was the need to clarify the type of absence that would provoke such a replacement. The second was the need to decide exactly how the replacement would take place. The senior alderman of Quito Simón Álvarez Monteserín (who was supported by the local council, the crown attorney, and eventually the viceroy) argued that municipal ordinary justices should be replaced whenever they were absent from the city and unable to attend to their duties on the main square. The period of absence and its causes were irrelevant, as was the distance that separated them from Quito. The only thing that mattered was that because of the absence of the justices from the main square, justice could not be carried out with sufficient speed and litigants had no one to listen to them. The replacement of the ordinary justices by the standard-bearer or alderman was automatic. It required no bureaucratic procedure or official announcements. In other words, once the standard-bearer or alderman observed the actual absence of a justice from the square, he could step in and act as a judge. According to Álvares Monteserín this was the only way to guarantee a prompt and continuous administration of justice, which was essential for the maintenance of peace.

The municipal ordinary justices of Quito, the audiencia, and eventually the Council of the Indies disagreed. In their opinion, the only event that would justify the subrogation of judges was their physical departure from the jurisdiction. Absence was not functional: it was organic. As long as the judges continued to be present in the territory (either the city or the villages belonging to it), they could (theoretically) act as judges. Judges who resided on their farms for a prolonged period were still judges, as were those who were chronically ill. Crucially, this argument insisted that the president of the audiencia had to authorize the subrogation of the justices by the standard-bearer or the alderman, and this subrogation had to be formally announced and properly published. Any other solutions were inadmissible, for they would create

14. AMQ, LC, 00126; AGI, EC, 914A, cuad. 2, 41–92; AGI, Quito, 146, 323–97 and 698–721; AHQ, Of., 31: exp. 24 April 1742; AMQ, Misc., 00012, 141; and AHQ, Ced., 10, no. 36.

15. Charles V and Phillip II in 13 May 1535, 11 May 1587, and 31 December 1590. RI law 5, title III, book 13.

anomalous situations that allowed the existence of two substitute justices in the city and two elected justices outside of it. A "secret and private" subrogation would also result in the uncertainty about the identity of judges, which was detrimental to good administration.

The use of temporary officeholders led to problems of identification, as well as to legal uncertainty. Yet perhaps its greatest effect was that it empowered agents who had a limited experience in their office and whose association with the judicial system was short-lived and exceptional in character. These agents, who often misunderstood their tasks, were unable to perform them in an adequate manner. More aware of the public aspects of justice than its internal meanings, these officeholders acted on many occasions according to a superficial image of the administration and justice. For example, in 1735 casual agents carrying out the seizure of goods believed that it was sufficient to collect the property—they felt it unnecessary to inform those present that they were acting according to judicial decree. Nor did they stop to ensure that the properties they seized belonged to the criminal.[16] When a complaint against these agents arrived at the audiencia, the magistrates treated the incident as a misdemeanor. They punished the faulty officers as they would punish any other officer: imprisoning and fining them for their misconduct. There was no reflection on the obligation to teach temporary agents how to behave, or on the need to depend only on regular officeholders.

Temporary agents thus risked their personal liberty and their property by engaging in missions about which they had insufficient information. These agents also endangered their physical and moral integrity. Many of them were insulted or attacked by criminals, either because criminals did not know that they were justice officers or because they *were* aware of it. In spite of these risks, Quito's judicial system rarely had difficulty finding people willing to collaborate with it. Although the reasons for this success were seldom spelled out, willingness to collaborate probably depended on a combination of political, social, and economic factors. Aiding the judicial system was considered a duty: it involved service to both king and community. Collaboration could also be economically interesting: volunteers sometimes received a salary or an honorarium. We know, for example, that in the late seventeenth century magistrate Juan Larrea Zurbano the elder recruited assistants who

16. AHQ, Crim., 28: exp. 11 August 1735.

were paid out of his own pocket. In 1729, the justices offered 100 pesos to the person who would capture a wanted criminal.[17] In 1736, the municipal ordinary judges confessed that they employed several paid informants.[18] Collaboration with the administration of justice also conferred prestige and influence. It enabled people to become closer to powerful individuals (such as judges), and it gave them a greater possibility of using (and misusing) the judicial system for their own benefit. But first in importance was the fact that people living in Quito did not consider the administration of justice to be a distant task executed by other individuals. On the contrary, Quiteños willingly engaged in it at all levels and in all instances, never remaining as mere spectators.

Ordinary inhabitants helped plaintifs uncover the identity of perpetrators, and they defended victims during a crime. They assisted those injured by capturing the people responsible for their suffering, to whom they "gave a lesson" or even punished. Summoned by curiosity and a sense of social solidarity, the inhabitants left their stores, homes, and streets in order to arrive at a crime scene. They did so day or night, either on their own initiative or at the request of the victims or their relatives. They invested time and labor in the collective enterprise of peace making, and their intervention was considered not only legitimate but a duty as well.[19]

The following is a typical example. In 1701, the scribe (*oficial plumero*) Parreño heard people shouting while he was resting in his house at night.[20] He first took no notice, thinking that the noise was probably produced by a group of drunken Indians. However, because he was unsure that this was the case, he ordered his servant to watch the street. When Parreño realized that a crime was being committed, he left his house armed with a sword and dagger. He saw a man running with an unsheathed sword and ordered him to stop. The man begged Parreño to allow him to continue, which Parreño did. A short time later,

17. AHQ, Not. 6, 5: exp. 31 March 1728 from 13 November 1729. See also AHQ, Not. 3, 17: exp. 7 March 1730; AHQ, Crim., 32: exp. 23 February 1743; and AGI, Quito, 131: an announcement from 15 December 1729.

18. AGI, EC, 914C, cuad. 9, 118–25; and AGI, EC, 915A, cuad. l, 131. The use of paid informants was studied by J. L. Bermejo Cabrero, *Derecho y administración pública en la España del Antiguo Régimen* (Madrid, 1987), 27–33; and F. Tomás y Valiente, *El derecho penal de la monarquía absoluta (siglos XVI–XVIII)* (Madrid, 1969), 168–71. See also AHN, Cód., 752B, no. 1343; and AHN, Cód., 724B, no. 206.

19. AHQ, Crim., 31: exp. 22 January 1742.

20. AHQ, Crim., 16: exp. 5 August 1701.

Parreño heard a voice crying, "Someone is being murdered in the ravine." He advanced toward the site, meeting on his way another man who was also armed. An Indian woman led the two to the ravine, where they found a dead body. Two other women—witnesses to the murder—were also present. The first had found the bridge's gate over the brook open, and when she looked below, she saw a group of men fighting. The second was inside her home when she heard the first woman scream, prompting her to step outside with a candle to see what was happening. The two women then realized that down in the ravine two men were assaulting a third. They began to scream, "For the love of God, this is enough." Alarmed by these noises, many people came out of their houses and approached the crime scene. Although it was too late to capture the criminals, or to save the life of the man, the help of the witnesses led to the eventual identification and punishment of the perpetrators.

In at least forty other cases (25 percent of cases of assault) the residents of Quito intervened in a similar manner.[21] At times, the Good Samaritan and the victim knew one another. Yet familiarity was not always necessary. On most occasions intervention came from individuals who accidentally found themselves in the vicinity of a crime and who intervened without knowing the nature of the crime or the identity of the victim.[22] Aid was also given to victims of theft. In 1695, "the people who lived on the street and their neighbors" captured several thieves who were climbing into one of the neighborhood's houses.[23] In 1725, an Indian who was sleeping near the parish of Santa Barbara informed the sacristan that he had heard noises, enabling the priest to capture a thief in flagrante delicto.[24]

After the criminals were under their control, the inhabitants of Quito could choose several possible solutions. They could punish them, hand them over to the judicial authorities, do both, or let them go without further action. In March 1748, Tomás de Aguilar was asleep in his bed in the village of Machache when he heard someone shout, "I am

21. AHQ, Crim., 4: exp. 25 March 1665; AHQ, Crim., 19: exp. 25 January 1716; and AHQ, Crim., 31: exp. 10 July 1741 from 12 July 1738.

22. Examples of cases in which Samaritans knew the victims are AHQ, Crim., 10: exp. 4 June 1685; AHQ, Crim., 23: exp. 7 June 1727; AHQ, Crim., 24: exp. 24 February 1728; and AHQ, Not. 3, 24: exp. 11 June 1743.

23. AHQ, Crim., 14: exp. 5 August 1695.

24. AHQ, Crim., 22: exp. 23 April 1725.

being robbed."[25] He got up and left his house in the company of his daughter, both armed with a staff. Outside, they saw their neighbor Patricio holding onto a young man. The neighbor's wife, Catalina, lay in the street naked, crying that they had been robbed of their clothing. Aguilar's daughter struck the young man on the head with her staff, splitting his skull. Catalina then gave him several blows with her fist, screaming, "you dog of a thief, coming into my house and leaving me naked!" The other neighbors who were present joined in and together they beat the thief before handing him over to the village judge.[26]

On occasion, the incarceration of suspects occurred through a surprising degree of collaboration. In 1739, a tailor brought a fettered Indian in front of the local governor of Quito.[27] He explained that a young man, whom he did not know but met while traveling, asked him to deliver the Indian to the governor, who happened to be visiting the village where he was going. A woman, he said, detained the Indian as he was trying to kill a Spaniard. What followed was a typical case of voluntary assistance to a victim. The Spaniard assaulted by the Indian on the main road shouted. Many people then gathered around him and detained and beat the criminal. A long chain of people then intervened to ensure that the aggressor would be brought to justice. The woman who witnessed the crime handed the Indian to the young man, and the young man asked the tailor to take him to a judge. None of these people knew the victim, and two of them were not even present when the crime was committed. Nevertheless, they all collaborated in making sure that the proper judicial authorities would punish the criminal.

Intervention could also happen *post facto*. In 62 out of the 390 cases I examined, ordinary inhabitants were responsible for the identification of criminals and/or the recovery of the stolen goods.[28] Their intervention was especially important in cases of crimes committed at night, without the presence or the knowledge of the victim.[29] In 1696, the Indian women merchants on the main square of Quito suspected that an unknown man was attempting to sell them stolen goods. Acting together, they seized the man and brought him before the last known

25. AHQ, Not. 1, 29: exp. 11 May 1748; and AHQ, Crim., 13: exp. 25 May 1694.

26. Similar examples are AHQ, Crim., 14: exp. 5 August 1695 from 5 August 1695; and AHQ, Not. 6, 13: exp. 10 February 1743.

27. AHQ, Not. 1, 22: exp. 13 November 1739.

28. AHQ, Crim., 31: exp. 24 January 1743; and AHQ, Not. 3, 28: exp. 22 October 1738.

29. AHQ, Not. 6, 12: exp. 14 January 1740.

robbery victim. The victim recognized the goods as her own and immediately repossessed them. A somewhat similar incident happened the following year when José Torres (who was on duty as night watchman at a land plot) saw three shadows approaching along the royal road.[30] Because they were traveling at night, he suspected that these men were thieves. He ordered them to stop, and called the nearby Indians for help. He was able to capture two of the men, who he handed over to the judicial authorities. His suspicions turned out to be justified. The men were identified as infamous cattle thieves (*cuatreros*), whom the authorities had been looking for.

The ordinary inhabitants of Quito could thus become involved in the administration of justice at all its levels. They not only performed duties as temporary judges or auxiliary officers of justice but also formed part of what we would classify today as the police force. They identified the perpetrators, captured the criminals, and brought them to trial. On many occasions they also acted as ad hoc "judges": they decided on the culpability or innocence of criminals, and proceeded to either absolve them by letting them go or condemn them by punishing them immediately, returning the stolen goods to the victim, or handing them to a judge. Their activities were essential to the functioning of the justice administration in Quito. The number of formal officials who would otherwise take care of these missions was extremely small. The local police force basically included only four people: two chief constables and two lieutenants. The ability of four people to control what was happening in the city and its villages was extremely restricted. Urban order ultimately depended on the collaboration of the inhabitants and on their willingness to engage actively in keeping the peace.

On occasion the system's dependence on social collaboration won official recognition. For example, the most important control mechanism used in Quito was the night patrol (*ronda*).[31] The night patrol

30. AHQ, Crim., 14: exp. 14 February 1697 from 14 January 1697. See also, AHQ, Crim., 14: exp. 24 May 1695 from 25 October 1696; AHQ, Crim., 16: exp. 12 August 1704; and AHQ, Crim., 32: exp. 21 February 1743.

31. RI law 5, title VII, book 8; Ordinances 97 and 103 of the Audiencia de Quito, Congreso del instituto internacional de historia del Derecho Indiano, *Ordenanzas de la Real Audiencia de Quito*. See also the discussion of 1708 and 1716 in AMQ, LC, 00121: town council meeting of 24 March 1716; and "Autos acordados," 348, from 15 July 1708. For a comparative view see R. I. Sánchez Gómez, *Delincuencia y seguridad*, 52–57.

detained and incarcerated criminals.[32] It inquired into the activities of individuals who walked about late at night, and it made sure that no immoral activity took place, such as public dances or extramarital sexual affairs. Judicial, social, and moral in character, the patrol was designed to ensure that the city was as secure and as moral at night as it was during daytime. Its primary actions included dispersing groups of people gathering in the streets, separating amorous couples, and imposing fines on indecent or rowdy behavior.

The night patrol was very much the image of the administration of justice in Quito. On November 1742, an informant (*soplón*) told the municipal ordinary justice that "in the house of the Valverde a Spaniard was having an extra-marital love-affair that had to be stopped."[33] The justice was not keen about leaving his house that night, yet he ordered his slave to summon the members of the patrol. This patrol included an Indian and two brothers who identified themselves as constables (but who had no formal nomination as such). A forth person classified as a constable of the city joined the patrol on his own initiative. The group, also accompanied by the judge, his slave, and the informant, left the house. Except for the informant and the judge, none of the other companions knew why they were summoned that night or where they were going. This secrecy was intentional because the justice feared that members of the patrol would alert the presumed delinquents about its imminent arrival. The patrol first searched a house in the neighborhood of Santa Barbara, and it then proceeded to the domicile of the Espinosa family. The municipal ordinary justice knocked on the door and ordered the people inside to open it. He carried a lantern in his hand and was dressed in a large hat, mantle, and cap. The residents of the house refused to follow the order because they feared that the judge was lying and suspected that the men standing at their door were not part of the night patrol but instead bandits pretending to be the night control.[34] A heated discussion followed, ending in the forced opening of the door and the beating of all the residents. Needless to say, there was no

32. AHQ, Crim., 24: exp. 24 February 1728; AHQ, Crim., 31: exp. 10 July 1728 and exp. 6 September 1741; and AHQ, Crim., 32: exp. 23 February 1743.

33. AHQ, Crim., 31: exp. 13 April 1742; and AGI, EC, 914B, cuad. 6, 100: auto from 3 July 1742.

34. Apparently, some criminals managed to convince people that they were members of the night patrol. This enabled them to enter homes without resistance: AHQ, Crim., 5: exp. 26 July 1671; and AHQ, Crim., 23: exp. 11 November 1726.

Valverde in sight, nor a Spaniard involved in an illegal amorous relationship. No arrests were made, and eventually the judge who organized the patrol was sanctioned for his aggression against the Espinosas. During the proceedings against the judge, no one criticized the Espinosa family for refusing to open their door or for resisting the judge. The informant was not punished, nor were the other members of the patrol.

Night patrols thus included both judicial officers and volunteers. The municipal judge had to use his slave, his house, and his lantern in order to execute the administration of justice, and he organized the patrol against his own preferences. The judge acted on the basis of data obtained from an informant, probably a paid one, who seemed to be the only person who truly controlled the situation. The informant first led the party to Santa Barbara and then indicated the need to search the house of the Espinosas. The rest of the party was kept uninformed because they were considered untrustworthy. The town residents did not identify the patrol as a legitimate police force, and they refused to collaborate with it. This attitude was authorized by the audiencia, who judged it to be a reasonable reaction.

Despite these characteristics, and despite frequent complaints about its faulty execution, the night patrol was the most important and most frequent control mechanism used by the authorities in Quito.[35] It provoked fear among both the innocent and the criminal. News of its approach caused people either to disappear or at least to moderate their activities.[36] The patrol also produced constant (even if small) income for the administration at no economic cost by levying fines on those captured by it.[37]

Collaboration—between officials and volunteers, paid and unpaid individuals, publicly sanctioned and privately organized control mechanisms—also took place on other occasions. The merchants of Quito organized and financed a night patrol of their own called the *ronda del comercio*. This patrol operated in the city between at least 1729 and

35. Residencias of the magistrates Juan Campo Godoy (in 1654) and José de Laysequilla y Palacios y Aguilar (in 1725): AGI, EC, 910A and 911B, respectively; and AGI, Quito, 121: letter from 7 January 1729 registered such complaints.

36. AHQ, Not. 6, 7: exp. 10 May 1731; and AHQ. Not. 6, 15: exp. 11 February 1746.

37. AGI, EC, 910C, 19–21.

1744.[38] It had headquarters, a captain (*rondador mayor del comercio*), and four patrolmen armed with swords and a whistle that they used to alert one another. The patrol policed the streets where the shops of the merchants who financed its activities were found. It operated between seven at night and six in the morning. It guarded the shops, capturing the criminals who attempted to rob them. Patrolmen often extracted confessions and punished suspects immediately by beating them or by confiscating the money or goods they had stolen. On occasion and out of "charity" (*caridad*), the patrol also frequented other streets, helping their residents and shopkeepers to stop crimes.

Successive audiencia presidents complained about this situation, which obliged the authorities to depend on the collaboration of the people. They lamented that although this collaboration was frequent, it was still insufficient. The residents of Quito, they argued, were often too busy to get involved in the administration of justice or were simply unwilling to do so. Because of the lack of a permanent and professional police force, the administration failed in executing its most routine activities. Criminals easily evaded judicial prosecution, either by fleeing the jurisdiction or by taking refuge in sanctuaries.[39] Prison escapes were very frequent.[40] Litigants and judges often abandoned the processes midway because they no longer saw the value in continuing them. People sentenced to exile remained in the city. Many other sentences were not enforced.[41]

The only way to change this situation, the presidents argued, was by instituting a professional corps of auxiliaries. In 1686, President Lope Antonio Munive y Axpe ordered the creation of a company of soldiers whose task would be to impose order in the city and to execute judicial orders.[42] The Council of the Indies objected to this move. In 1690 it determined that Quito did not need a company of soldiers for either judi-

38. AHQ, Not. 6, 8: exp. 6 December 1734; and AHQ, Not. 6, 16: exp. 19 October 1747. The patrol was also mentioned in M. Cicala, *Descripción,* 216. In 1770, the rorda del comercio consisted of two men who were well paid and who patrolled the two streets of the commerce from the beginning of the night to eleven in the morning.

39. AHQ, Crim., 23: exp. 11 September 1726; AHQ, Crim., 27: exp. 20 December 1732; and AHQ, Crim., 34: exp. 12 April 1746.

40. See chap. 5.

41. AHQ, Not. 6, 14: exp. 26 August 1743; AHQ, Crim., 4: exp. 30 March 1662 from 30 March 1662; and AHQ, Crim., 14: exp. 23 February 1696.

42. AMQ, LC, 00115: town council meetings of 5 and 14 October 1686; AGI, Quito, 210: cédula of 11 May 1690; and AGI, Quito, 73, 249.

cial or military tasks and that, at any rate, the royal treasury should not finance such a company. President Francisco López Dicastillo y Azcona raised the same issue in 1704 and 1706. He explained that punishing criminals was impossible in Quito because the judicial system lacked an effective police force. The remedy, he suggested, was the creation of a company of twenty-four or thirty soldiers whose activities would be financed by a new tax on textile mills (*obrajes*).[43] López Dicastillo also asserted that the company could secure the payment of debts to the royal treasury. The authorities in Madrid continued to disagree. Apparently, in 1707 they repeated their refusal to allow the institution of a company when President Juan de Sosaya raised the issue again.[44]

The wish to form a company of soldiers was once again raised in 1726. Writing to Madrid, the audiencia mentioned the habit of using military companies for judicial missions, and it suggested establishing a body of paid constables in Quito. The Council of the Indies continued to resist.[45] Faced with these rejections, President Dionisio Alcedo y Herrera envisioned another solution in 1729.[46] He ordered all grocery shopkeepers (*pulperos*) to participate in a night patrol whose members would be armed and bear insignias of justice. The patrol, he instructed, would "stop crimes, imprison delinquents, and disperse public games and dances." Alcedo y Herrera also named three justices (*alcaldes del barrio*) in each of Quito's five neighborhoods and charged them with prohibiting "crimes and public transgressions." He then wrote to the Council of the Indies, asking for its approval. Alcedo y Herrera explained that the people whom he appointed as justices were of "quality, example, and zeal." To ensure the success of their mission, they used spies, gave rewards to collaborators, and asked the regular night patrol to assist them. The Council of the Indies approved the measures because they were "customary" and carried no charge. Yet this time the members of Quito's town council objected.[47] They asserted that the

43. AGI, Quito, 142: of 30 December 1704; and AGI, Quito, 162: letter of 7 August 1708.

44. AGI, EC, 914C, cuad. 9, 118: the response of José de Araujo y Río to the accusation against him.

45. AGI, Quito, 131: letter of 20 August 1726; and the response of the Council of the Indies, which is inserted in AHQ, Ced., 8, no. 153 from 2 June 1728.

46. AGI, Quito, 131: letter of 31 March 1730 and its accompanying documents; AGI, Quito, 374; and AGI, EC, 91IB, 147–51.

47. Cédula of 4 March 1731 in AHQ, Ced., 9 (1727–35), 119; AMQ, LC, 00123: town council meeting of 16 December 1729; and the letter of Alcedo y Herrera dated 31 March 1730 in AGI, Quito, 131. The existence of similar officials in Quito is registered in 1695 and 1724. AHQ, Crim., 14: exp. 24 May 1695; and AHQ, Not. 1, 13: exp. 25 December 1723 from 8 August 1724.

naming of neighborhood justices during the presidency of Santiago Larrayn (in the second decade of the eighteenth century) had caused social upheaval because those named to office were only interested in their own personal exaltation and thus disturbed, rather than aided, the establishment of public order.[48] Quito was a peaceful city, and the fewer judges it had the better the administration would be.[49] Alcedo y Herrera answered these claims by stating that none of them was true. The city council simply wished to guard its own privileges to name local judges. He even insinuated that some aldermen stood to profit from urban disorder and therefore had no interest in ensuring the peace.

The use of soldiers for judicial tasks was again debated in 1737, when President José de Araujo y Río created a company that he financed by imposing a new tax on grocery shopkeepers.[50] The company included twelve uniformed soldiers and a corporal, all of whom enlisted voluntarily. Its members carried daggers, had written orders, and sounded reveille twice a day. They patrolled the city, guarded its jails, accompanied convicts into exile, and helped the judges whenever necessary.[51] The presence of soldiers in Quito, at least according to the president, prevented crimes because the judicial system was now both feared and respected. Contemporary witnesses disagreed. The company, they said, mainly served the interests of the president. It was stationed in his residence and escorted him on his outings.[52] Rather than preventing crime, the soldiers first and foremost enhanced the dignity and status of Araujo y Río.

The company lasted for eleven months, from February 1737 until January 1738 when it was dissolved by order of the viceroy. The viceroy, like the Council of the Indies before him, insisted that Quito did not need a company of soldiers.[53] The city had no external enemies and could be ruled without a military force. This decision won the support of the local

48. This was not the contemporary view. The witnesses to the residencia of President Santiago Larrayn, for example, Captain Francisco Venegas de Córdoba and Felipe Iriarte, thought that the measure was successful, which is why it was practiced for many years: AGI, EC, 911B, 71 and 88.

49. A. Muro Orejón, *Cedulario americano del siglo XVIII* (Seville, 1956), I, cédula 287; AHN, Cód., 691B, no. 28; and AHN, Cód., 696B, no. 2.

50. AGI, EC, 914A, cuad. 1, 33: letter of 1 March 1737. The company established by José de Araujo y Río was studied by L. J. Ramos Gómez, "El 'bien común' como pretexto del presidente," 381–400.

51. AGI, EC, 914A, cuad. 4, 26–30; and AGI, Quito, 133: letter of 4 October 1738.

52. AGI, EC, 914A, cuad. 3: 15 and 103.

53. AGI, EC, 915A, cuad. 2, 9, 285; and AGI, EC, 914B, cuad. 5, 280: letter of the audiencia, 16 August 1737.

town council and the crown attorney. According to both, Quito was indeed a peaceful and orderly republic. Experience demonstrated that justice could be administered in it without having recourse to a disciplinary force and that the combination of officials and volunteers, judges and inhabitants, was sufficient to guarantee the local peace.[54]

Conclusion

Attempts by successive presidents to institute a paid peacekeeping force in Quito failed because both local society and authorities in Lima and Madrid were convinced that the administration of justice could be sufficiently carried out by a small number of officials, and a great number of volunteers, and temporary officeholders. Quito's records seem to justify this position. Public intervention in the phases of investigation and arrest, and of crime prevention and punishment, were very frequent. These interventions were not only accepted—they were considered by the people to be an obligation. Quito was indeed a peaceful republic—not because there was no crime but because criminality could be handled by a system that joined public with private control, professional with nonprofessional administration, paid with unpaid officers, and ad hoc with ongoing interventions.

This conviction that Quito was an autoregulative space changed only when the local elites felt threatened. Late in 1747, a confrontation between the provincial head and the inspector (visitador) of the order of Saint Francis degenerated into an open conflict between the justices of Quito and the residents of the neighborhoods of San Roque and San Diego.[55] These residents asserted the need to protect the inspector against physical and verbal abuse by his enemies, including the provincial.[56] Armed with sticks and rocks, they made a stand in front of the Recoleta de San Diego (the place where the inspector resided) and prohibited the passage of armed people through the square. The justices of

54. AGI, EC, 914A, cuad. 1, 35–37: letter of the fiscal, 1 March 1737.

55. AHQ, Pris., 2: exp. 1 January 1748; and AHQ, Crim., 25: exp. 12 December 1748. This episode is also studied in P. and A. Costales, *Nos la plebe* (Quito, 1986), 122–25; M. Minchom, *The People of Quito, 1690–1810: Change and Unrest in the Underclass* (Syracuse, 1994), 210–20; and T. Herzog, "De la historia y el mito," 72–80.

56. Residencia of Sánchez de Orellana AGI. EC, 911C, 131: declaration of Francisco Pérez Ubilluz.

Quito were unhappy with this development and decided to intensify the number of patrols in the area. This response met with violent verbal resistance. The people gathering in the square repudiated the authority of the judges (whom according to them "they did not elect") and asserted their ability to maintain peace in the neighborhood: external intervention was unwanted and unnecessary.

Resistance and reaction were both material and symbolic. In question were not only who would control whom but also who would *appear* to be in control. The ability to patrol the streets became a contested issue precisely because patrols were both a practical and a symbolic tool. They were an efficient means of control, true, but above all they manifested the constant presence of authority. This presence was required, the justices argued, because unless it was established the situation could easily degenerate into an open rebellion.[57]

A few weeks were sufficient for this prophecy to come true. The Christmas Day imprisonment of Manuel Parra in 1747 dramatically changed the course of events. Parra, an artisan of mixed-ancestry and a resident of San Roque, was accused of resisting justice. Soon after his arrest, his friends and relatives attacked the prison and, demolishing its doors, were able to set him free. Marching through the city, proclaiming their achievement and celebrating their success, the members of the group also uttered slogans such as "long live the barrio of San Roque, long live the king, death to the corrupt government!" The celebrants included some twenty-five people, although certain eyewitnesses claimed to have seen "almost a thousand." They promised that they would not set down their arms until they were allowed to name a municipal ordinary justice to their liking. They threatened to kill anybody who tried to stop them and they refused to listen to the pleas of the few officials present at the site who attempted to restrain them.

The following morning, the president of the audiencia convened an extraordinary acuerdo and created a company of soldiers whose mission was to restore order. For the first time in one hundred years, the town council agreed that the city needed such a force and was willing to collaborate in order to sustain it. The importance of its collaboration was soon affirmed. On the night of 2 January, the residents of San Roque called the people of the other surrounding neighborhoods to descend upon the center of the city. From an initial nucleus of a dozen

57. AHQ, Pris., 2: exp. 1 January 1748, 53–61.

or so young men, some six hundred to a thousand people gathered in the square of San Francisco. They uttered threats against the ministers of the audiencia, the constable, his assistants, and, according to some witnesses, even "foreigners coming from Spain," "the rich," and the Jews. The crowd then marched toward the house of the president of the audiencia, Fernando Félix Sánchez de Orellana. Sánchez de Orellana left his house armed and escorted by several men (primarily local merchants). Firing into the crowd, they were able to stop the mob's advance. Magistrate José de Quintana y Acevedo then followed and, using the same method, succeeded in dispersing the crowd. All in all, the battle lasted for about an hour and a half. Groups of armed men continued to patrol the city throughout the night to ensure that this "most grave and horrific" situation would not be repeated. This, however, was not necessary—apparently calm returned thereafter.

The judicial investigation that followed the events identified a few of the protagonists, but the judges were unable to locate and punish them. The legal process served, therefore, merely to clarify what had happened. According to different testimonies, the rebels were above all artisans (mainly hatmakers) who resided in the parishes of San Roque, San Blas, San Sebastián, and San Diego and whose association was based on friendship and family ties. Their motivation seemed to lay in a general disapproval of the local government, a disapproval spurred to action when a member of their group (Manuel Parra) was unjustly imprisoned. They targeted the president of the audiencia, Fernando Félix Sánchez de Orellana, because he was a member of a prominent local family who controlled the city economically, socially, and administratively (chaps. 2 and 3). Among other things, he was a well-known moneylender.[58] The threats against the Jews, who were virtually nonexistent in Quito, were thus probably directed at him.

The public that opposed these rebels included all the inhabitants who feared the outburst of violence: mainly the magistrates of the audiencia, the local judges, the town council, and the merchants. Their reaction was conditioned not only by what they saw and heard but also by what they feared might happen. Judges and principal townsmen feared for their lives; merchants were afraid that their shops would be ransacked. These fears led them to ally with one another and to agree, for the first time in local history, that the city needed a company of soldiers.

58. T. Herzog, *Los ministros,* 146.

This company had its headquarters in the audiencia's building and included seventeen soldiers, three officers, and a captain.[59] Its members were armed with swords and had a distinguishing uniform and banner. They sounded the trumpet, accompanied the president on his outings, and participated in public ceremonies. Clearly, although a company now existed, its role was mainly ceremonious. Peace returned to Quito without the intervention of soldiers. And, as happened during the presidency of Araujo y Río, most patrols were still carried out by volunteers (*ronda*), and the most effective police force was still the public, which continued to prevent crime and arrest and punish criminals.

59. AHQ, Pris., 2: exp. 1 January 1748. President Juan Pío Montúfar y Fraso mentioned the existence of this company in 1754 in his "Razón sobre el estado y gobernación política y militar de las provincias, ciudades, villas y lugares que contiene la jurisdicción de la real audiencia de Quito [13 Septembre 1754]," reproduced in *Relaciones histórico-geográficas de la audiencia de Quito (siglo XVI–XIX)*, ed. P. Ponce Leiva (Madrid, 1992), 2: 325. The company was also mentioned in AGI, EC, 911C, 21–22 and 176.

CHAPTER FIVE

The Buildings

The activities of the justice administration in Quito were also influenced by the state of the buildings at its disposal. These buildings were endowed with a symbolic meaning. Because dispensing justice was a divine task, delegated by God to the king and by the king to his servants the judges, the halls of justice were a semisacred space. Those present in this space had to behave differently than they would normally. They had to show their reverence to justice as well as to the king and his delegates. What could easily happen outside the hall—for example, a conflict between two magistrates—should never happen inside it. The fact that it sometimes did, as was the case with the confrontation between Juan de Ricaurte and Tomás Fernández Pérez de Hodo (chap. 3), irritated witnesses.

The halls of justice had to incarnate the presence of both God and king. Yet the environment that produced these results in seventeenth- and eighteenth-century Quito had little to do with dignity the way we understand it today. During this period a sacred environment could be produced even within a ruined structure. The history of the palace of the audiencia (also called *palacio real*) can serve as an example.

The audiencia of Quito originally met in an ordinary house, distant from the main square. The building did not undergo substantial changes in structure or decoration after it was designated as the seat of the court and it was located in an area deemed undignified.[1] In 1612, the court moved to a new location on the main square. Housed again in a private residence, the town council of Quito initially agreed to subsidize "necessary and useful" repairs. Such repairs were never made, for the town council subsequently argued that it did not have sufficient funds

1. "Descripción de la ciudad de San Francisco de Quito (anonymous, 1570–1571)," in *Relaciones histórico-geográficas de la Audiencia de Quito (siglo XVI–XIX)*, ed. P. Ponce Leiva (Madrid, 1992), 1: 209–10. See also, AHQ, FE, 1 (1600–1628), nos. 28 and 29.

and refused to finance the creation of new chambers or invest in the "decency" of existing ones.[2] In the second and third decades of the seventeenth century, a number of people described the building as unworthy and expressed their belief that it needed urgent repairs, possibly even a total reconstruction. This evaluation of the building was by no means exaggerated. We know that the structure suffered from chronic humidity and that, by 1688, the walls of the chambers were in such disrepair that they could no longer support the weight of the paintings hung on them.[3]

The structure itself was collapsing, but its internal decoration was rich and sophisticated. In 1718, when the king shut down the audiencia as part of a plan to redistribute the Spanish American territory, the building was adorned with bells, draperies, carpets, tables, curtains, chairs, and cushions.[4] Many of these objects were made of fine, imported, extremely expensive, and rare materials. The walls were covered with paintings depicting the crucifixion, three portraits of the Virgin Mary, four portraits of saints, and seven portraits of kings. Most of the decorations were hung in the chambers of the audiencia pública and the acuerdo. The latter was slightly more luxurious than the former. It had more tables, furniture, and draperies, as well as carpets in imposing colors such as crimson.

The judges, who returned to the building in 1722 when the audiencia was reestablished, found it completely empty. The pre-1718 decorations had simply disappeared. Some had been left in the hands of Fernando García Aguado, the treasurer of the royal treasury who in 1722 could only account for a few of them.[5] Others were sent to Santa Fe de Bogotá (present-day Colombia), where the audiencia that had jurisdiction over Quito was located between 1718 and 1722. These objects were never returned. Despite repeated petitions, the king refused to allow the court to purchase new ornaments. The town council, who acknowledged its duty to "arrange the palace with the necessary decency as was its obligation," did little to restore the building to its old glory.[6]

2. Town council meetings of 2 December 1614, 16 February 1615, and 20 March 1615. J. A. Garcés, ed., *Libros de cabildo de la ciudad de Quito, 1638–1646* (Quito, 1960), 431, 470, and 478.

3. AHQ, Crim., 11: exp. 19 November 1688.

4. AHQ, Gob., 11: exp. 4 May 1722. These issues were treated at length in T. Herzog, "Las reformas," 140.

5. AHQ, Gob., 11: exp. 4 May 1722.

6. AMQ, LC, 00122: town council meetings of 19 January 1722, 26 January 1722, and 13 March 1722.

Faced with this situation, as well as with the deteriorating state of the structure itself, President Santiago Larrayn ordered some repair work in the late 1720s. These repairs were apparently insufficient to ensure that the building could be habitable again. Because of its "notorious state of ruin," Larrayn—who was supposed to reside in the palace—was obliged to move into a small wooden house that he constructed in the garden.

The repeated flooding of the first-floor offices, and the risk of a total collapse, compelled the audiencia to order a professional evaluation of the building in 1729. The expert who prepared the report affirmed that the situation was indeed serious and expressed his opinion that the structure had to be completely renovated.[7] The two chambers of the audiencia (the audiencia pública and the acuerdo), as well as the chancery and the royal treasury (*Caja Real*), were on the point of collapse. Moreover, two corridors and seven rooms were already in a state of ruin. The expert blamed this structural failure on the cheap materials used in the construction of the building and on the water that saturated its walls. A first aid solution would entail guttering the rainwater, reinforcing certain walls, and strengthening a large part of the cement structure and pillars. The expert estimated the minimum cost of these urgent repairs to be 6,000 pesos de-a-ocho, a considerable sum.

The royal treasury and the city council refused to finance the operation. Faced by the lack of funds, President Dionisio Alcedo y Herrera proceeded to distinguish between the work that he considered essential and the work that he regarded as nonessential. He ordered the repair of the back patio, the two chambers of the audiencia, the chancery, the royal treasury, the chapel, and the three living rooms on the first floor (which he intended to use as his residence). Because of its limited scope, he believed this work could be subsidized by the fines that the court imposed on criminals.

Construction began in June of 1730 when the magistrates collected the first fines. It ended in August that same year. While a great deal of time and money were invested in the restoration of the building itself, comparable sums were spent on decorations. Alcedo y Herrera justified this ornamental expenditure by explaining the need to reinforce both the material and symbolic state of the building. This was especially

7. M. Herrera, "Reconocimiento del estado del palacio," a report dated 11 March 1729, included in the answer of Dionisio Alcedo y Herrera to the accusation, in his residencia. AGI, EC, 911B.

important for the public chamber and the acuerdo chamber, which were "in ruins, without any adornment or repair." He explained that it was essential "not to leave the two principal chambers where the senate administers justice in representation of the prince in the unsuitable condition in which they existed."[8] The final account of the reconstruction demonstrates the importance of—indeed the preoccupation with—symbolic representation. The greatest part of the "indispensable expenditures" (which rose to 730 pesos) was spent on decorations. Very expensive materials were used for decoration, such as fine fabrics, silk, flannels, gold thread, and cedar wood. The work also involved the employment of master carpenters, painters, and spinners.

Proud of his achievement, Alcedo y Herrera wrote to the king in 1732, informing him of his activities and seeking his approval. He attached to his letter a notarized description of the building before and after the 1730 restoration.[9] This description allows us to have a fair idea of what the audiencia building was like, and how contemporaries viewed this palace of justice. According to the description, the building had two floors. The first floor housed the offices of court notaries, the chancery, the royal treasury, and some stores. The second floor included the chambers of the audiencia pública and the acuerdo, the chapel, and the residence and offices of the president. There was thus a clear distinction between a lower level (which was functional and included offices accessible to the public) and an upper level (in which authority and justice resided). The building had a central courtyard that dominated the view of those who entered by the main doorway. Upon entering, they ascended a large stairway that rose to the second level. The structure also included a chapel, with a frontal altarpiece and a rug.

The notaries who prepared the report emphasized the cleanliness of the walls after 1730 and the leveling of the ceilings. They mentioned the paving of the main and secondary courtyards, which would hopefully prevent the accumulation of water and thus reduce the humidity of the walls. The notaries then described with precision the decoration and furniture of the most formal and representative parts of the building: the corridor that led to the halls of justice, the chambers of the audien-

8. The answer of Alcedo y Herrera to the accusation, in his residencia. AGI, EC, 911B, 328, and the order dated 9 July 1732.

9. Report of 14 July 1732 in the residencia of Alcedo y Herrera. AGI, EC, 911B, 348–51. Alcedo also mentioned the building in his letters to the council from 19 July 1732 and 21 August 1732, both found in AGI, Quito, 132.

cia pública and the acuerdo. We thus know that the wood used for the ceilings and balustrade was painted with flowers of various colors.[10] A painted and gilded shield of the royal arms stood at the entrance of the chamber of the audiencia pública, and a gold crown and a golden orb (symbol of royal dominion) topped by a blue cross (symbol of Christianity) stood nearby. Two columns supporting armed Roman statues flanked both sides of the door. The statue on the right carried a scale in his hand and pointed to the inscription *ius suum cuique tribuere* ("law is given to each one accordingly"). The one on the left held a sword and was accompanied by the inscription *Quisquis fecit patitur* ("each one suffers what he has done").[11] Inside the public chamber was a railing, and behind it were two rows of painted wooden chairs for lawyers to sit on. A large wooden table covered in leather with yellow silk and golden nails was placed in the middle of the room. Behind the table stood the dais where the judges sat. The walls were covered with nine large paintings in gilded frames showing scenes of battles won by different Castilian kings from Fernando III to Phillip V. The door was adorned with a velvet and damask curtain. In order to pass from this chamber of the audiencia pública to the acuerdo, one used a painted doorway with a green damask curtain, topped by a painting of Saint Jerome. An office desk covered in leather with crimson silk was placed in the chamber of the acuerdo. Five books lay on top of the desk: the four volumes of the *Recopilación de Indias* (the main Spanish American legal compilation) and the *Ordenanzas en beneficio de los indios* (probably the *Leyes Nuevas,* sixteenth-century laws protecting the Indians). The ordinances of the audiencia were printed on a large parchment canvas over wood, which was mounted on the wall facing the door.[12] Lastly, the chamber of the acuerdo included twelve crimson velvet chairs with gold thread and yellow cushions.

This 1732 description of the audiencia reveals a few important facts. In spite of the restoration, half of the structure still remained in ruins, including its most representative wing that faced the central square. The

10. The residencia of Alcedo y Herrera. AGI, EC, 911B, 403–4.

11. For a comparative view see M. A. León Coloma, *El programa iconográfico de la real chancillería de Granada* (Granada, 1988), 1; and I. Gómez González, "La visualización de la justicia en el antiguo régimen: El ejemplo de la chancillería de Granada," *Hispania* 53/2 (1998): 563–65. In Granada, except for the royal arms, the entrance to the hall of justice had four figures representing justice, fortitude, prudence, and moderation.

12. Acuerdo of 26 November 1732, included in the residencia of Alcedo y Herrera, AGI, EC, 911B.

description is silent concerning the state of the kitchen, the pantries, a room on the first floor, and the entire area previously used for the presidential residence and banquet halls (on the second floor), all of which were probably in a state of ruin. Also noteworthy is the fact that the decoration of the chamber of the audiencia pública was more imposing than that of the acuerdo and that each chamber had a different character. In the former, most paintings made references to the history (and power) of Castilian kings. The statues at the entrance mentioned the obligation of the monarch to impart justice by being both severe ("each one suffers what he has done") and just ("law is given to each one accordingly"). Royal authority thus dominated the room where the public was admitted. But if the audiencia pública was richly decorated and referenced the royal authority, the acuerdo was predominantly functional. As the chamber where the magistrates voted, and where no one else was allowed entry, the necessity of decency was maintained, but less emphasis was placed on opulence. On the whole, only indispensable objects were located in this room: a desk, several chairs, books, and the text of the ordinances of the audiencia. There was only a single external reference: the painting of Saint Jerome, patron of Quito. One could conclude that the audiencia pública was about authority and the king, while the acuerdo was about deliberation guided by both legal and religious duties. This demarcation was new. The information demonstrates that before 1718 both chambers were heavily decorated, and if anything the acuerdo was more elaborate than the public chamber. Furthermore, both chambers possessed paintings of kings and saints before 1718. Indeed, in 1732 the public chamber included some objects that previously were located in the acuerdo.

This difference between the chambers in 1732 could be noticed by anyone allowed entry into the acuerdo. Yet it is possible that this contrast was deliberately highlighted in the notarial report. The authors of the report clearly distinguished what was important from what was not. Rather than simply portraying a building, they chose what to describe and how. For example, the authors did not describe the dais of the audiencia's public chamber, but they mentioned the books and chairs of the acuerdo. They specified the color of certain things, while they ignored that of others. Their report described not only the building but also the authors' vision of it.

The colonial setting was totally ignored. Neither in 1718 nor in 1732 did the chambers include myths, historical references, or inscriptions that were directly related to the European expansion. Except for the laws favoring Indians and the Spanish American legal compilation found in the acuerdo, nothing indicated that this was an American and not an Iberian court. The rest of the images referenced the Old World: European battles, European heritage, European saints, and European legal obligations.

In December of 1735, further structural deteriorations preoccupied the authorities. This time it seemed that the ruined sections threatened the last remaining parts. In order to absolve himself of responsibility, President Dionisio Alcedo y Herrera explained that the deterioration was due to an "extraordinary storm" that pummeled the city. He insisted that the problem occurred in the sections that were not restored in 1730. Nevertheless, his account included a confession that he had not concerned himself with the daily maintenance of the building. Furthermore, what had caused deterioration both before and after 1730 was the inadequate channeling of rainwater. Because rainwater accumulated in the rooms and courtyards, moisture saturated the pillars and walls and led to their collapse. Despite its extensiveness, the work carried out in 1730 did not resolve this problem. Instead of dealing with this central issue, the 1730 renovations made the humidity's visible effects disappear partially and temporarily through the repainting of the walls. The renovations had centered attention on only selected parts of the building, including the two halls of justice and the corridor leading to them. Other parts of the building were totally ignored. The 1730 renovations focused on decoration, rather than on structural issues.

The state of the building was sufficiently dangerous to force Alcedo y Herrera to move out in 1735 and to order the closing down of the first-floor shops. Unable to obtain a viceregal permit to use royal funds for the reconstruction, Alcedo y Herrera called an extraordinary meeting of the audiencia magistrates and the officials of the royal treasury. The only possible solution, the magistrates and officials agreed, was to dismantle the ruined part of the building that faced the main square and preserve the materials for future use. The only dissenting voice came from the royal treasurer, who argued that the building was in no worse condition than it had been before. According to him, its situation did not justify such an extreme measure that would leave the central town square "open and without the audiencia building." The treasurer suggested repairing the outside patio and channeling the water. He concluded that this could be done by investing the reduced sum of 500 to

700 pesos. Because the other members did not support this opinion, Alcedo y Herrera proceeded to implement the decision of the majority. He ordered the constables to safeguard the royal seal, as well as the archives, royal treasury, and chambers while the work took place. The dismantling of the building, which began soon after, was never completed. A lack of money, the coming of winter, and the arrival of a new president (José de Araujo y Río) were all factors in the suspension of repairs.

Despite his failure to substantially improve the state of the building, Alcedo y Herrera celebrated what he considered to be his success. He reported to the Council of the Indies on the "decency" of the chambers, which were now found with the "adornment corresponding to their authority." He insisted that this was the most one could do, in a situation of sparse funding, to a building abused by climate, earthquakes, and forgetfulness.[13] Yet not everyone shared this understanding. José de Araujo y Río, the incoming president, disagreed with the choices that Alcedo y Herrera had made. He criticized Alcedo y Herrera for his failure to obtain any of his original goals, namely the repair of the building. According to Araujo y Río, Alcedo y Herrera's preference for "extremely expensive adornments" instead of investment in necessary repairs was a misguided decision.[14] It produced an intolerable situation in which presidents could no longer reside in the building of the audiencia. Nevertheless, other people in Quito did support the strategy adopted by Alcedo y Herrera, and they discussed the work carried out under his presidency with approval and admiration. These people, who testified during the investigation (*residencia*) of Alcedo y Herrera, emphasized the decency of the audiencia pública, which was now enriched with adornments and beautiful paintings. They considered the chamber "majestic" and "one of the best of the kingdom."[15] As far as they were concerned, the decency and decoration of the principal rooms were more important than the actual reconstruction of a building in decay. At stake was representation, not functionality. It was sufficient to have a grandiose public chamber, even if the rest of the building was

13. Letter, 16 May 1736, of Alcedo y Herrera to the viceroy and the viceregal decision of 5 July 1736, both in the residencia of Alcedo y Herrera, AGI, EC, 911B.

14. This was the charge leveled against Alcedo y Herrera in his residencia. Ibid., 318–19.

15. The opinions of Guerrero Peñalosa, the Count de Selvaflorida, and Alava y Barrientos. Ibid., 39, 44, and 86. The works of the palace were the subject of conversation. Godoy, for example, "heard" and "knew" of them. Ibid., 115.

in ruin. One could ignore the fact that the facade of the building was gone and that those going to the chamber found fallen pillars, corridors without roofs, and abandoned patios. Indeed, the glory of justice could be located in a single room—the public chamber—and as long as this room was dignified, so was justice.

The state of the audiencia building was not substantially modified in the following years. It continued to be partially in ruins, and many of its exterior walls stood at the point of collapse. As far as we know, in the 1730s and 1740s the majority of the building was abandoned; judges and officials used only the chambers of the audiencia pública, the acuerdo, and the royal treasury. President José de Araujo y Río offered to reconstruct the building in 1737. He suggested that an investment of 8,000 pesos would solve the problem once and for all.[16] The Council of the Indies requested a detailed proposal, including an extensive report on the state of the audiencia, the necessary work, its cost, and the possibility of delaying the starting date. Meanwhile it encouraged the president to find another residence—which he did, making his home in the building of the local town council. Nothing came of this proposal: the project fell into oblivion in the following years.

The poor condition of the audiencia building was once again mentioned in 1745, when President Fernando Félix Sánchez de Orellana ordered major restorations. Fines imposed by the court financed this work, and it lasted longer than the renovations ordered by Alcedo y Herrera. Unfortunately, there is no written record describing its extent, except for a brief list of expenditures.[17] According to this list, some money was invested in structural repairs (cementing the walls and ceilings). But, once again, most expenditures were tied to decoration (whitewashing the walls and preparing ornaments for the chapel). In 1746, when "the greater part" of the building collapsed and the audiencia was fearful that "the rest will shortly be ruined because of the poor quality of the cement in the walls," the acuerdo (with the approval of the viceroy and the king) decided to restore the building by using the income from the state monopoly (*estanco*) of alcohol (*aguardiente*).[18]

16. AGI, Quito, 129, 319–26.

17. AHQ, Crim., 33: exp. 5 June 1745. Alcedo y Herrera's efforts lasted 121 days at the cost of 730 pesos. Those carried out by Fernando Felix Sánchez de Orellana took 525 days at a cost of at least 500 pesos. The works are also briefly mentioned in the residencia of Sánchez de Orellana. AGI, EC, 911C.

18. AHQ, Gob., 14: exp. 26 April 1746.

Magistrate José de Quintana y Acevedo was charged with overseeing the work. Unfortunately, no surviving record describes what—if anything—was accomplished. We do know that soon after (in January of 1748) the same funds were reallocated to finance the recruitment of a company of soldiers (chap. 4). The reconstruction project was thereafter abandoned.

Testimonies from the 1750s confirm that, at the end of the day, Alcedo y Herrera was right in assuming that the glory of justice could be sustained by a single beautiful space, the public chamber, and that this glory could be achieved (at least partially) at the price of the chamber being lodged in a ruined building. These testimonies describe a building that was completely in decay yet whose chamber was "decent," "splendid," and even "majestic."[19] The rooms, witnesses said, were full of light and covered with wonderful rugs and expensive cloth.[20] They were decorated with beautiful paintings in silver frames, expensive furniture made of wood with ivory, pearls, precious stones, gold, and silver. The rooms also included wall coverings, rugs, several statues, crystal glasses, mirrors, and porcelain from China and Japan. In the 1750s at least, most of these objects were furnished by the president himself. Because the president (Juan Pío Montufar y Fraso) was extremely rich, he could afford to import them from France, Venice, Germany, and other European countries, as well as from Perú and other parts of the Spanish Americas.

A preference for decoration over reconstruction was also manifest in municipal halls of justice. In contrast to the audiencia, the town council *did* have an income that could cover routine maintenance. And yet just like the audiencia, the town council dedicated most of its attention to the decency of the building, not to its structural-material condition. Municipal ordinary judges received litigants in the town council chamber, which in 1665 had a crimson velvet canopy and a cushioned seat for their use.[21] The chamber was located in the town hall, which was "a good building that had a large stone doorway with gilded ironwork,

19. E. B. Enríquez, *Quito a través de los siglos* (Quito, 1938), 105–25; and C. Gangotena y Jijón, "Cómo era la sala de la Real Audiencia de Quito," *Revista del Museo Histórico* (1945–1946): 72–74.

20. M. Cicala, *Descripción histórico*, 193–94.

21. AMQ, LC, 00013: town council of 19 December 1665.

and in the middle the Royal Arms sculpted out of stone, painted with blue and gold."[22] Precisely because it was considered relatively decent, President José de Araujo y Río (who could not reside in the audiencia, which was in ruins) moved his residence to that building in 1736.[23] On this occasion, the town council carried out several repairs. The dwelling of the priest was improved, rooms, windows, and balconies were redistributed, and the entire building was whitewashed. The town council chamber was divided in two, the roof was restored, and the gutter system repaired. Similar work was carried out in 1739, although on a much smaller scale.[24] In 1748, the poor condition of the roof and the "unsuitability" of the chamber—which lacked a canopy to show "the esteemed honor of such an illustrious congress"—promoted more repairs.[25] Yet while the council ordered the immediate preparation of a new crimson damask, a silver cloth for the table, and the installation of several benches of quality wood covered in crimson cloth, the roof was ignored.

The contradiction between the glory of justice and the physical surroundings in which it was implemented was most evident in cases in which judges received litigants in their private residences. In theory, royal legislation prohibited this practice: all judicial matters were to take place within the courts. Only there, it was reasoned, would the relationship between God, king, and the judges be obvious, and only there would respect for justice be ensured. Nevertheless, the wish to guarantee a rapid, accessible, and somewhat paternal administration also produced the contradictory indication that judges must grant "free hearings" to litigants any time of the day. Because this was the case, magistrates and judges often opened their homes to those requesting judicial intervention. This practice was fairly frequent, and it led to a series of instructions that ordered judges to live in decent conditions,

22. D. Rodríguez Docampo, "Descripción y relación del estado eclesiástico del obispado de San Francisco de Quito . . . [1650]," in *Relaciones histórico-geográficas de la audiencia de Quito (siglo XVI–XIX)*, ed. P. Ponce Leiva, (Madrid, 1992), 2: 212–13. For a comparative view see C. Bayle, *Los cabildos seculares en la América española* (Madrid, 1952), 325–40.

23. Residencia of Alcedo y Herrera, AGI, EC, 911B, 331. See also the letter of the president to the town council dated 28 April 1738: AGI, Quito, 129, 319–26; AGI, EC, 914A, cuad. l, 108, and cuad. 4, 32 and 170; AGI, EC, 914B, cuad. 2, 11–14, and cuad. 5, 259; AGI, EC, 915A, cuad. 2, 11; and the various town council meetings held in August and December of 1736: AMQ, LC, 00125.

24. AMQ, LC, 00125: exp. 27 January 1739.

25. AMQ, LC, 00127: exp. 24 May 1748.

occupying houses that corresponded to their "quality" and to the prestige of their office.

On occasion, the authorities in Quito did demonstrate their awareness that the material condition of the buildings, and not only their decency, was important to the good administration of justice. This happened mainly with regard to the prisons. Quito had two prisons: the public jail (*cárcel pública*) belonging to the town council and located in the town hall and the court jail (*cárcel de corte*) belonging to the audiencia and located in the audiencia's building.[26] During the seventeenth and eighteenth centuries, these jails reflected the buildings in which they were located: although the public jail was in slightly better shape than the court jail, both were at least partially in ruins and considered completely unsafe.

Constructed in 1548, the public jail had iron bars in the windows and was further secured with sixty keys and chains of different sizes.[27] In 1664, it underwent some reconstruction, and the municipal council created a fund to maintain and repair it.[28] In 1731, 1733, and 1736, the council carried out more repairs, yet the building remained in ruins and continued to be unsafe.[29] The court jail underwent a similar succession of repairs. In the 1720s, the audiencia spent some 657 pesos on its structure. Yet in 1729, President Dionisio Alcedo y Herrera complained that the jail was insecure. Its roofs, walls, pillars, and doors had collapsed. There were water leaks everywhere, and the doors were never locked.[30] The jailer only had two iron shackles, six handcuffs, three padlocks, two stocks, and one chain, all of which were very old and easy to open.[31] Alcedo y Herrera estimated that at least 1,000 pesos had to be invested to improve this situation. He immediately applied 340 pesos. New doors, keys, and locks were put in, and the entrance, as well as the

26. Hispanic jails were studied by P. Herrera Puga, *Sociedad y delincuencia en el siglo de oro* (Granada, 1971); M. L. Copete, "Criminalidad y espacio carcelario en una cárcel del Antiguo Régimen: La cárcel real de Sevilla a fines del siglo XVI," *Historia social* 6 (1990): 105–25; E. Troconis de Veracoechea, *Historia de las cárceles en Venezuela (1600–1890)* (Caracas, 1983); R. I. Sánchez Gómez, *Delincuencia y seguridad*, 198–206; and C. Benavides, *Les femmes délinquantes à Madrid: Justice et société en Espagne au XVIIIe siècle* (Toulouse, 2000), 2: 166–92. See also the many articles in volume 16, supplement VII, of *Historia* (1978) dedicated to this subject.

27. AMQ, LC, 00002: town council of 31 December 1548.

28. AMQ, LC, 00013: town council of 15 March 1664.

29. AMQ, LC, 00124: town council of 1 January of these years.

30. AHQ, Pris., 1: exp. 29 July 1732; and AGI, Quito, 132, 617–30: letter of 1733.

31. AHQ, Not. 6, 5: exp. 31 March 1728.

torture chamber, were whitewashed.[32] Alcedo y Herrera also ordered a professional study of the structure. This study pointed out that the jail was made of solid cement and concluded that only the lack of proper care led it to its current state. The experts elaborated a reconstruction plan, which was implemented in July and August of 1733. Seven hundred and ninety-eight pesos were used to replace broken doors, to level and pave patios, to repair the gutters, to reinforce and whitewash the walls, to clean the water system, and to add newer and stronger chains, handcuffs, and iron shackles.[33]

Despite these efforts, securing the prisons continued to be an impossible task. There were at least sixteen escapes from the public jail between 1675 and 1739, and twenty-three from the court jail between 1672 and 1748.[34] Most of these escapes were compound, involving the flight of several prisoners together. Some of them were carefully planned ahead by friends or cellmates. Others happened almost spontaneously, as some prisoners, strangers to one another, took advantage of a circumstance like an open door to facilitate their escape. On occasion, prisoners who noticed that other inmates were planning an escape alerted the authorities or helped them catch those who had managed to flee. In 1688, for example, Alonso Falcón informed the jailers that some prisoners had already escaped. He then volunteered to follow them and bring them back to prison.[35] In 1728, one fugitive declared that when he discovered that his colleagues were planning to evade prison, he passed on the information to his mother so that she could inform the judge. The judge ordered that the prisoners be secured, yet a few days later they escaped, and the informant followed them. In 1745, a general collection of funds was held in the court jail by the convicts to pay the fees of a blacksmith who was charged with preparing false keys and knives necessary for an escape.[36]

Several different escape methods were used. Some prisoners carved

32. Residencia of Alcedo y Herrera, AGI, EC, 911B, 391 and 403–4.

33. AGI, Quito, 132: letters of 19 July 1732, 21 August 1732, and 3 September 1733.

34. The situation was similar in Guayaquil and Cuenca, according to the residencias of their authorities. See AGI, EC, 913A (residencia of Juan de Sosaya as local governor of Guayaquil in 1706); and AGI, EC, 911A (residencia of Francisco Pareja, local governor of Cuenca in 1728). Jailbreaks are also described in J. L Phelan, *The Kingdom of Quito,* 200.

35. AHQ, Crim., 11: exp. 19 November 1688; AHQ, Not. 6, 5: exp. 31 February 1728 from 31 March 1728; and AHQ, Not. 6, 11: exp. 19 August 1738.

36. AHQ, Not. 6, 5: exp. 31 March 1728; and AHQ, Crim., 31: exp. 16 July 1743 from 17 September 1745.

holes in the walls or fled the prison by climbing to the roof and jumping to the street or to a neighboring building.[37] Others used false keys or knives to force their way to freedom.[38] Although evasions were frequent in the late seventeenth and early eighteenth centuries, it was not until the late 1720s that the justices of Quito began to gather systematic information concerning their practice. Perceiving each new escape as an additional episode in a long succession of events, they now argued that escapes must stop and that adequate means had to be found to prevent them. According to the justices, three factors facilitated prison evasions: the negligence of those who were charged with securing the prisons, the audacity of those who were held in them, and the poor state of the buildings. Because the audacity of criminals could not be controlled, the justices stated that the remedy should concentrate on enhancing internal discipline by supervising the activities of the jailers and by ensuring the security of the physical structure of the buildings.[39]

The internal regime of the prisons was now judged lax. Archival records demonstrate that Quito's prisoners entertained themselves by playing cards and drinking.[40] They had constant contacts with the outside world, receiving visitors inside the prison.[41] Although bars separated the jail from the street, prisoners could speak to those passing by and could exchange different objects with them. They could leave the prison in order to take out the trash, bring in food, or help the constables capture criminals. As long as they promised to return promptly, prisoners were allowed to leave the jail in order to take care of their private affairs.[42] This reality was especially absurd given that prison was not a punishment but a precautionary measure that was only meant to ensure that criminals would be present at their trials. There were no books for signing in or signing out prisoners. The wardens of the city and court jail could not normally tell who was a prisoner, when they came in, and when they left. This produced awkward situations in

37. AHQ, Not. 6, 5: exp. 31 March 1728; and AHQ, Not. 6, 5: exp. 31 March 1728 from 9 April 1731.

38. AHQ, Not. 6, 5: exp. 31 March 1728 from 13 November 1729; AHQ, Not. 6, 13: exp. 2 March 1743; and AHQ, Crim., 32: exp. 16 July 1743 from 29 May 1745.

39. AHQ, Crim., 32: exp. 29 July 1732.

40. AHQ, Crim., 6: exp. 4 March 1678 from 13 May 1679; and AGI, EC, 911C, 93.

41. AHQ, Crim., 21: exp. 26 January 1723; and AHQ, Pris., 1: exp. 29 July 1732.

42. AHQ, Crim., 5: exp. 10 July 1674; AHQ, Not. 6, 5: exp. 31 March 1728 from 13 November 1729; AHQ, Crim., 22: exp. 22 March 1726; and AHQ, Not. 6, 12: exp. 20 July 1740.

which escapes from prison were discovered weeks after they happened, and then only because prisoners failed to appear at their trials.[43]

Despite this chaotic situation, in the 1720's the authorities gave most attention to the physical structure of the jails. The court jail, Quito's judges argued, had "weak walls, which could be torn down easily. Innumerous previous escapes left them with many holes, which were only partially repaired."[44] The feeling that the prisons had structural problems that made them unsafe produced a series of repairs in the 1730s in both the public and court jails. Above all, the aim was to ensure security: "the jail of the city being without security, the cells without roofs, and the upper bed-rooms without floors." Repairs were needed in order to "put all of [the necessary] security in two cells, as well as in the doors and locks."[45] Likewise, the court jail, which was "without security and with frequent prisoner escapes," experienced some repairs in 1732; "in addition to its cleanliness [this work], has left the jail strong and secure from that moment . . . having experienced not a single escape by any of its prisoners since then."[46]

This positive appreciation seemed more like wishful thinking. As was the case with the audiencia building, the prison repairs failed to remedy the situation, and escapes continued. In the late 1730s and the 1740s and 1750s, there were numerous new reports about the need to cover roofless cells, to put new floors in the rooms, and to take care of the humidity in the walls.[47] Desperation was mounting. Escapes caused "the most grave and intolerable harm and peril to the public welfare," because they "left crimes without punishment and prisoners free to commit other crimes, which is a scandal to the republic, a detriment to its subjects, and a contempt for authority and respect of Justice."[48] Yet

43. AHQ, Of., 22: exp. 16 September 1724. See also AHQ, Crim., 26: exp. 19 March 1731; AGI, Quito, 74, cuad. 7: the residencia of Diego Inclán Valdés; AHQ, Pris., 1: exp. 7 December 1681; and AGI, EC, 911C, 93.

44. AHQ, Not. 6, 5: exp. 31 March 1728; and AHQ, Pris., 1: exp. 29 July 1732.

45. Residencia of Alcedo y Herrera, AGI, EC, 911B, 562: declaration of Francisco Egas. The original version reads: "estando la cárcel de la ciudad sin seguridad por estar los calabozos sin tejado y los cuartos altos de vivienda sin suelo [los alcaldes la reedificaron] poniendo toda seguridad en dos calabozos, así en puertas y cerraduras."

46. Residencia of Alcedo y Herrera, AGI, EC, 911B, 39: declaration of Joseph Guerrero. The original version reads: "sin seguridad y con fugas frecuentes de reos" and "además de sus aseos se quedó tan fuerte y segura, que desde entonces acá no se ha experimentado que se haya huido ninguno de dichos reos."

47. Residencia de Sánchez de Orellana AGI, EC, 911C: declarations of Francisco Egas Venegas de Córdoba, of Tomás de Cabrera Barba, and the accounts of fines and financial penalties. See also AGI, Quito, 224: declaration of Navarro.

48. AHQ, Pris., 1: exp. 29 January 1732. The original versions read: "gravísimo e intol-

no solution was in sight. In Quito, at least, the decision to remain in prison or evade it depended on the prisoner, and on him alone. Prisoners who wanted to escape could, and those who wanted to stay put remained. Because jails were incapable of detaining prisoners against their will, prisoners whose crimes were not serious or who were integrated members of the local society, with family, friends, and economic interests in the jurisdiction, remained imprisoned. All others escaped. Indeed, the worse the crime, the more dangerous the criminal, or the more socially outcast he was, the less he had to lose by flight and the more likely he was to escape. Jails thus guaranteed only the incarceration of those whom society had nothing (or little) to fear.

Although there are testimonies indicating the occasional presence of females in prison, in most cases women prisoners ended up in the reformatory (*recogimiento*) of Santa Marta. The reformatory was established at the end of the sixteenth century in a two-story building near the cathedral of Quito.[49] It detained women suspected of criminal activity and housed other women who needed refuge, such as orphans, separated women, or those who merited "correction" according to ecclesiastical or lay authorities, their fathers, or husbands.[50] With no independent revenue, the recogimiento depended on alms and charity. Unlike other jails, the reformatory, as its name indicated, imposed strict rules of behavior. In 1617, it had an abbess, a doorkeeper, a sacristan, and nineteen boarders who were forced to work for their living.[51] In 1656, the women of the reformatory were kept in reclusion and cloistered.[52] They were prohibited from meeting anyone except for their lawyers, procurators, and immediate family members. Visits would take place in the presence of a nun appointed by the abbess to supervise the conversation.

In 1703, the reformatory was transferred to a new building. Accord-

erable daño y perjuicio a la causa pública" and "semajante exceso que deja sin castigo los delitos y libres los presos por lo que cometen otros con grave escándalo de la república y detrimento de los súbditos y menosprecio de la autoridad y respeto de la justicia."

49. J. Londoño, *Entre la sumisión y la resistencia: Las mujeres en la audienica de Quito* (Quito, 1997), 271–73.

50. Reformatories were studied by J. Muriel, *Los recogimientos de mujeres. Respuesta a una problemática social Novohispana* (Mexico, 1974); M. D. Pérez Baltazar, "Orígenes de los recogimientos de mujeres," *Cuadernos de historia moderna y contemporánea* 9 (1985): 13–23; Sánchez Gómez, *Delincuencia y seguridad*, 209–12; and M. I. Viforcos Marinas, "Los recogimientos de centros de integración social a cárceles privadas: Santa Marta de Quito," *Anuario de estudios americanos* 50/2 (1993): 59–92.

51. Viforcos Marinas, "Los recogimientos," 76–78.

52. "Autos acordados de la Real Audiencia de Quito, 1578–1722," *Anuario histórico jurídico ecuatoriano* 2 (1971): 65.

ing to some accounts, this move signaled the transformation of the institution from a beneficiary asylum to a true female jail. The aim was to locate a building suitable for this goal. Yet, in 1722 the authorities judged the new structure as "small, uncomfortable, and insecure."[53] Major work was carried out in the building in 1736, costing some 468 pesos and including the reconstruction of at least two ruined rooms.[54] At the end of the 1750s, the reformatory was classified as "secure and clean," even though it did not have even a single handcuff.[55]

Conclusion

The buildings of the justice administration reflected the judicial system in all of its poverty: material poverty (the lack of money), functional poverty (the inability to improve the state of the structures), and ceremonial poverty (the failed struggle to ensure the decency of the courts and prisons). The building of the audiencia was in a state of ruin during most of the seventeenth and eighteenth centuries. Attempts to improve it were unsuccessful in the long run. Renovation gave preference to short-term surface solutions, rather than focusing on the structure itself. The town hall was in a slightly better condition, although on occasion it was also considered indecent. The town jail resembled the court jail: both were in a state of ruin and both were judged completely inadequate to retain prisoners. The same was true to some extent with regard to the reformatory.

However serious these conclusions are, the importance of the questions they raise should not be overestimated. Contemporary witnesses from Quito insisted that what counted was not functionality but decency. It was sufficient to have magnificent halls of justice, even if the buildings themselves were in ruin. Money was better spent on decorations than on eliminating humidity. What mattered was the ability to feel the presence of the authorities, and the glory of God, king, and justice. As long as this could be achieved, all was well—even if the president could no longer reside in the palace, even if the inmates escaped from prison.

53. Viforcos Marinas, "Los recogimientos," 80.
54. AGI, EC, 911B, 550, 553, and 555; and AGI, EC, 914A, cuad. l, 146–50.
55. AGI, EC, 911C, 74.

CHAPTER SIX

Rumor and Reputation

The activities of the Durán family, whose members were stereotyped as infamous cattle rustlers, preoccupied the justices of Quito for over fifty years. Between 1696 and 1745, and especially between 1718 and 1723, the judges of Quito initiated at least twenty-nine legal actions against Rafael, Miguel, two brothers named Marcos, and two others named Juan. On many occasions, the justices had no information against the Duráns except for their bad reputation (*mala fama*). And yet this reputation was sufficient to suspect family members were guilty, without any need to collect evidence.

The circumstances were exceptional. The first half of the eighteenth century was a very difficult time in Quito. According to various accounts, during this period the theft of cattle, mules, and horses was very common.[1] The authorities were unable to remedy the situation because they rarely managed to capture or convict the thieves. Owners were reduced to patrolling their fields and searching for stolen animals. When lucky, they found the animals. Yet this discovery rarely led to the identification and punishment of the thieves. Those holding the animals would argue that they were innocent buyers, and following the chain of sales hardly ever led back to the perpetrator of the crime. Frustration was widespread. As one witness declared in 1746, "these people take away the living of many poor men like myself, and the fact that these cattle rustlers are not punished is a thing to marvel at."[2]

1. Declaration of Polinario Suárez de Figueroa in AHQ, Crim., 14: exp. 24 May 1695. Juan de Espinosa declared in 1718 that some twenty mules were stolen from his ranch: AHQ, Not. 1, 13: exp. 25 December 1723. From 10 March 1718 Captain Felipe Villadrando stated that many mules and horses were stolen from him in the last six years and that all of the ranchers of the area suffered the same problem, AHQ, Not. 1, 13: exp. 25 December 1723 from 8 August 1720. The crime of cattle rustling was studied by A. Levaggi, "El delito de abigeato en los siglos XVII–XIX," *Revista del Instituto de Historia el Derecho Ricardo Levene* 24 (1978): 107–77.

2. The original version reads: "Quita el vivir de muchos pobres como yo y que para estos cuatreros no haya justicia es cosa de admirar." AHQ, Not. l, 28: exp. 12 May 1746, declaration of Pedro Escalante.

It is impossible now, just as it was then, to determine whether the members of the Durán family were indeed cattle thieves. Some witnesses were convinced that this was the case. Several even had evidence that indicated the guilt of a specific member of the Durán family. Nevertheless, many of these proofs were inconclusive, and it was clear that some members of the family were guiltier than others. The Durán story is thus revealing not about crime but about prosecution. It demonstrates how, under specific circumstances, different members of the same family could suffer continuous harassment by the judicial system on the basis of their public image as thieves.[3] As was the case with the moral panic described by S. Cohen and J. Davis, the reputation of the Durán family created a state of opinion that permitted the continuous identification of its members as cattle thieves.[4] Publicity and stereotyping promoted the prosecution of individuals identified as Duráns or associated with them. Prosecution led to further prosecution and eventually confirmed the guilt of the accused. Yet the identification of the Duráns as public enemies did not reassure the inhabitants of Quito. Instead, they panicked by identifying the long hand of the Duráns in

3. For comparison see B. Garnot, "La législation de la répression des crimes dans la France moderne (XVIe–XVIIIe siècle)," *Revue historique* 593 (1995): 90; and P. Piasenza, "Opinion publique, identité des institutions, 'absolutism': Le problème de la légalité à Paris entre le XVIIe et le XVIIIe siècle," *Revue historique* 587 (1993): 97–142.

4. "Societies appear to be subject, every now and then, to periods of moral panic. A condition, episode, person, or group of persons emerges to become defined as a threat to societal values and interests. Its nature is presented in a stylized and stereotypical fashion . . . sometimes the object of the panic is quite novel and at other times it is something which has been in existence long enough, but suddenly appears in the limelight. Sometimes the panic passes over and is forgotten, except in folklore and collective memory. At other times it has more serious and long lasting repercussions." S. Cohen, *Folk Devils and Moral Panics: The Creation of the Mods and Rockers* (Oxford, 1972; reprint, 1990), 9. See also J. Davis, "The London Garoting Panic of 1862: A Moral Panic and the Creation of a Criminal Class in Mid-Victorian England," *Crime and the Law: The Social History of Crime in Western Europe since 1500*, ed. V. A. C. Gatrell, B. Lenman, and G. Parker (London, 1980), 190–213. Related analyses include P. King, "Newspaper Reporting, Prosecution Practice, and the Perceptions of Urban Crime: The Colchester Crime Wave of 1765," *Continuity and Change* 2 (1987): 423–54; R. Muchembled, *Sorcières, justice et société aux 16e et 17e siècles* (Paris, 1987), 207–15; J. Revel and A. Farge, *Logiques de la foule: L'affaire des enlèvements d'enfants, Paris 1750* (Paris, 1988); P. Vanderwood, *Desorden y progreso: Bandidos, policias y desarrollo mexicano* (Mexico, 1981; reprint, 1986); D. Hay, "War, Death and Theft," 117–60; P. Peveri, "'Cette ville était alors comme un bois . . .' Criminalité et opinion publique à Paris dans les années qui precèdent l'affaire Cartouche (1715–1721)," *Crime, histoire et sociétés* 1/2 (1997): 51–73; and P. Rawlings, *Crime and Power. A History of Criminal Justice, 1688–1998* (London, 1999), 24–34.

every aspect of their lives and by blaming them even in cases in which no evidence existed for their involvement. This reaction further impelled the justices to persecute the Durán family, establishing a vicious circle that neither it, the judicial system, nor the people of Quito could easily escape.

The first Durán to appear in the local judicial archives was Marcos, who in 1695 was accused to be a "notorious cattle rustler."[5] Marcos asserted that he had legally bought the animal that was found in his possession. Nevertheless, he affirmed that his brother Rafael and his father, Matías, were indeed cattle rustlers. Despite his denial, his image as a thief persisted. Another victim of theft, who had no particular reason to suspect Marcos, now accused him of having stolen his animals. This accusation was based solely on Marco's reputation and on the fact that the first accusation, which Marcos refuted, concerned a theft that was committed in the same geographical area and at approximately the same time as the second theft. Because of lack of evidence, Marcos was acquitted of both accusations. The judge warned him against buying animals from suspicious people.

During the procedure against Marcos, a search in his father's house discovered a number of horses of uncertain origin that the judges suspected were stolen. Despite this discovery and his son's acknowledgment that he was a thief, the judges acquitted Matías Durán "for the moment" (de la instancia) due to lack of proof. The following year, the owner of the horses appeared in court and denounced Matías. The judges reactivated the legal action, which, as mentioned above, was never truly closed (chap. 1).[6] Matías claimed that he was an innocent buyer. Nevertheless, he was found guilty, fined, and exiled for two years.

The Durán's name reappeared in the archives in 1718, when a shopkeeper denounced Marcos Durán after buying mules from him without knowing that Marcos "had a tendency to sell mules which had an uncertain origin."[7] The witnesses who testified in the process insisted on the Durán's notorious reputation: "because he [Marcos] had a public reputation for being a cattle rustler . . . I heard it being said publicly that

5. AHQ, Crim., 14: exp. 24 May 1695.
6. AHQ, Crim., 14: exp. 24 May 1695 from 24 May 1695.
7. AHQ, Not. 1, 13: exp. 25 December 1723 from 10 March 1718.

the Durán were the rustlers of these mules."[8] One witness even stated that seven months earlier he had seen Marcos climbing the mountain of Pichincha, accompanied by another man. Knowing that Marcos was a thief and suspecting that he was about to commit a crime, he spied on both men throughout the night. In the morning, he saw Marcos descending from the mountain with four pack mules. He managed to catch Marcos and extract a confession. Marcos had just stolen the mules, aided by his brother Rafael. Rafael was the other man the witness had seen, but he escaped capture. In the trial Marcos denied his guilt. Sentenced to questioning under torture by the municipal ordinary justice, he escaped prison while the audiencia reviewed the decision to torture him on appeal. His escape, as well as the absence of his brother Rafael, brought the case to a halt.[9] By this stage, Marcos was already known by the nickname of Charqui Angara, a nickname that was later attributed to all the members of the family. It was indeed suitable for cattle rustlers: *charqui-anca-as* was a Quechua term for a thin bird of prey.

In January of 1720, captain Joseph de Seraín, justice of the Santa Hermandad, initiated a legal action de oficio against Miguel Durán. His motive could not be simpler: a citizen of Quito had spotted Miguel on the main road with goods that this citizen believed to be stolen.[10] Although Miguel escaped and could not be located and questioned the citizen told the judge that he had no doubt that he was a thief. Miguel, like his brother Juan and his nephew, was commonly known as Charqui Angara. All three men were thieves, and they had to be incarcerated if one wanted the "republic to remain free from similar types of people, which it was now infested with." The citizen also explained that he suspected Miguel on account of his notorious reputation, which was justified in this case because, before he fled, Miguel had confessed to the citizen that the horse he was riding was stolen. Soon after, the owner of the horse that had been found in Miguel's possession appeared in court and claimed his property. The process pended for a while, probably due to the absence of Miguel and was then added to another action against him.

In August 1720, Jacinto Cevallos y Velasco, the new justice of the Santa Hermandad, received word about the movements of Rafael

8. Ibid., declaration of Juan de Espinosa. Other witnesses also testified in the same manner.
9. The effect of absence on the process is described in chap. 1.
10. AHQ, Not. 1, 13: exp. 25 December 1723 from 12 January 1720.

Durán. Acting on the basis of this information, he imprisoned Rafael and began a process de oficio against him, accusing him of cattle rustling. The judge willfully took this action: there was no specific complaint against Rafael at that time, and no one had accused him of possessing stolen property. The process was justified only on the basis of Rafael's reputation and the judge's desire "to end all livestock rustling in Quito." Rafael contested the accusation by insisting that his reputation was based on a false rumor. It was not his own but belonged instead to two young men named Marcos Durán, both with the alias Charqui Angara, who had been brought up by his parents. His imprisonment, he complained, was only due to the fact that he was also named Durán. This was not the first time that his brothers' reputation harmed him. In the past he had been incarcerated with his brother Juan when both were accused of stealing potatoes. He was acquitted then and must be acquitted now, which is indeed what happened.

The proceedings held by Cevallos y Velasco clarified the degree the inhabitants of Quito stereotyped the Duráns. At least two citizens declared that after their mules were stolen, they were told that the thieves must be the Charqui Angaras, who lived in San Blas. They immediately sent their servants to search for the animals in the house of the Duráns. Although the search failed to locate the animals, the witnesses were still convinced that the Charqui Angaras were all thieves and infamous cattle rustlers. They were sufficiently confident that this was the case, for when they suffered another robbery, they again sent their servants to look for the Duráns. Interestingly, the witnesses made no distinction between the different members of the family. They did not know, or care to know, their individual names, character, or activities. All they knew was that they had a nickname and a bad reputation—which meant that Duráns were all thieves by association.

In August of 1720, the municipal justices began yet another investigation against Juan, Miguel, and Rafael Durán because "they were notorious cattle rustlers."[11] Once again, prosecution was based solely on the fact that the Duráns as a group were known as cattle thieves. Rafael, the only member of the family present at the proceedings, repeated his earlier defense. He asserted that one must ignore the "disdain produced by the bad reputation, which he has because he belongs to the family of the Durán, alias Charqui Angaras, because reputation

11. AHQ, Not. 1, 13: exp. 25 December 1723 from 25 October 1720.

in itself is a very poor indication, and one must always consider its origin and beginning, which in this case was due to Juan and Miguel Durán, who had been responsible for various similar offenses." The first legal expert accepted this explanation and acquitted Rafael. The presiding judge rejected this acquittal and requested the aid of another lawyer. The first lawyer he chose excused himself from getting involved in the case; he argued that he never consented to give an opinion on criminal matters. Afraid that the municipal ordinary justice would render judgment without the advice of a lawyer, the defendant appealed to the audiencia. We have no information of what happened next.

In March of 1721, a citizen of Quito filed a complaint against Juan Mondragón and Esteban Durán when he was informed that the thieves who had stolen his mules were "two young men called Charqui Angaras, who were imprisoned in the past because of their reputation as thieves and because they possessed stolen cattle." Juan, the father of Esteban, was also included in the complaint because the stolen animals were found in his possession. Juan Mondragón and Esteban fled the city, leaving Juan Durán to face the charges on his own. Juan denied the charges, and the crown attorney requested that he be submitted to questioning under torture. This procedure was necessary, the attorney said, because the Duráns must be corrected: "these thieves were prosecuted for many years by different judges, yet none of them was ever punished, and the crown attorney knows not why." Juan, like Rafael, argued that the bad reputation was not his own but that it belonged to his half brother Marcos, who lived in Ríobamba (a settlement south of Quito). The Durán family, he asserted, had many different members, and the inhabitants of Quito simply confused them all. Reputation, at any rate, was not a trustworthy source of information. It was often "false and untruthful because it originated from ill-intentioned men . . . among the commoners one cannot find truth [and on the basis of reputation] one cannot proceed to punish anyone."

While Juan languished in prison, all the possible legal experts either excused themselves from acting in the process or were contested by the parties (recusación—see chap. 1). A stalemate followed, and for over the nineteen months between June 1721 and February 1723, nothing happened. In 1723, the new municipal ordinary justice attempted to bring the proceedings to a good end. Yet he encountered the same problem as his predecessor: he could not find even one legal expert able or willing to give his opinion on the innocence or culpability of Juan. Faced by this situation, the justice requested the intervention of the president of the audiencia. The president stated that Juan should be questioned under torture. Juan maintained his innocence in the torture session, and he was acquitted soon after. The judge, however, warned him to live honorably and keep a distance from his infamous relatives who were well-known cattle rustlers.

In April of 1721, the municipal ordinary justice Juan Joseph de Mexia began a process de oficio against Miguel Durán, whom he accused of being an "infamous thief and a rustler who did not leave mules nor horses in their pastures . . . and only occupied himself with thefts." Miguel was incarcerated, and a few days later the proceedings were added to older ones pending against him. We do not know what happened next.[12]

In February 1722, a young man (*mozo*) by the name of Jerónimo Durán—barefoot, badly dressed, and of a mestizo origin—was mentioned in a criminal complaint for domestic theft. Being only a secondary figure in this case, we know nothing about his family, reputation, or sentence.[13]

In December of 1723, a magistrate of the audiencia became directly involved in the persecution of a Durán for the first time. The official excuse for his intervention was news that Miguel Durán had assaulted the justice of San Blas.[14] The investigation was meant to clarify the circumstances of the assault. However, it was completely dominated by the question of whether or not Miguel was a thief. Almost all of the witnesses declared that he was. Miguel was known as Charqui Angara and was accustomed to committing crimes. Many mentioned Miguel's notorious family. One witness declared that "he knows that all these Charqui Angaras have a very bad public opinion, and a reputation for being cattle rustlers."[15] Another testified, "Miguel is generally reputed to be a thief . . . and between him and all his brothers they are all famous rustlers."[16] Only one witness limited himself to the question at stake, that is, the attack on the neighborhood judge. He explained that the

12. AHQ, Not. 1, 13: exp. 25 December 1723 from 20 April 1721.
13. AHQ, Not. 3, 13: exp. 19 February 1722.
14. AHQ, Not. 1, 13: exp. 25 December 1723 from 25 December 1723.
15. Ibid., declaration of Xavier de Albaja.
16. Ibid., declaration of Manuel Méndez.

assault took place after Miguel was unable to achieve acknowledgment from the judge that he was a good man and that there was no reason why he should pay for what his brothers had done.[17]

Like the witnesses who testified in the proceedings, the magistrate was also less interested in the assault than in the bad reputation. He ordered the collection of all the penal processes ever attempted or carried out against the Duráns.[18] With this information in hand, the magistrate refused to accept Miguel's explanation that he had assaulted the neighborhood justice in order to defend his honor because the justice uttered "grave words against his credit." Nor was the magistrate interested in listening to Miguel's complaint that he had been mistreated and whipped by the justice. Resolving this issue rapidly by warning the neighborhood justice that his office did not give him the authority to punish criminals, the magistrate proceeded to investigate whether or not Miguel was a Charqui. Miguel defended himself in the same way that Rafael and Juan had done before him. He argued that the reputation originated in a single Durán and that, because of this reputation, "people say that all the brothers are bad without having any reason." Miguel also insisted that he had never before had any dealings with the penal justice system and explained that the Miguel Durán who was accused of theft in 1720 was another man, possibly one of his cousins. We do not know what happened next.

In the 1730s, the justices of Quito centered their attention on the third generation of the Duráns, which included the brothers Miguel, Juan Vásquez Durán, Esteban, and Nicolás Pozo Durán (alias Curibotón, "gold-button"). Magistrate Pedro Martínez de Arizala investigated Nicolás, Esteban, and other individuals de oficio because he suspected their involvement in a theft.[19] Nicolás was the only accused present in Quito, and he confessed the crime after undergoing torture. During the process, the notorious reputation of the family was again at center stage. The magistrate asked Nicolás for the whereabouts of his brothers Esteban and Juan and his father, Juan. The magistrate also investigated Nicolás's involvement in another theft, simply assuming that given his public reputation he could have taken part in it. At this

17. Ibid., declaration of Manuel de los Reyes.

18. This is the origin of the file catalogued in Quito under AHQ, Not. 1, 13: exp. 25 December 1723, including many different penal proceedings against the different Duráns.

19. AHQ, Crim., 25: exp. 5 January 1730.

stage, Nicolás escaped from prison. The case was left pending until 1731 when Nicolás was apprehended and sentenced to whipping.

In April of 1731, a municipal ordinary justice suspected that Miguel assisted Juan, Esteban, and Nicolás in their criminal activities.[20] The reputation of the family, and the fact that two suspicious horses were found near Miguel's residence, were sufficient to justify this conclusion. It was then discovered that Juan and Esteban had indeed left the animals, which were in fact stolen, near Miguel's house. Nevertheless, Miguel denied knowing anything about it or having any part in the affair. The very fact that he was a Durán indicated to the judge that this could not be true: "being an immediate relative of suspected well known thieves is a sufficient indication that the defendant has an intimate friendship and a familiarity with the above said." Friendship and family ties thus made it plausible, even certain, that Miguel aided his brothers in their criminal activities. Miguel argued that the contrary was true. Blood relationship, he said, did not necessarily imply the existence of friendship or a close association: "although they are relatives, because they have a bad reputation as thieves I have kept my distance from them and from the neighborhood of San Blas for over twenty years and I live in the neighborhood of San Sebastián, and I refuse to meet with them because I am a good man who lives of his labor."[21] Miguel also emphasized that his wife's family prohibited him from associating with his relatives because of their bad reputation, a prohibition that he obeyed. Soon after, Nicolás was imprisoned. He affirmed Miguel's innocence, leading to Miguel's acquittal.

The following month, the governor of a small village near Quito captured Esteban Durán.[22] The village had suffered many thefts of cattle, and the villagers were suspicious of all foreigners who passed through the jurisdiction. When they saw three unknown men on horseback, they asked them if they "had committed any crime." Although the men responded negatively, soon after a rumor spread that the three were famous cattle thieves. The village governor searched for and imprisoned them. Juan Durán and his friend Cosme Lomas escaped, yet the villagers captured Esteban Durán. They brought him in front of the magistrate of the audiencia, Pedro Martínez de Arizala, who ordered to collect five pending penal cases against him, including his involvement in several thefts and injuries.

20. AHQ, Not. 6, 7: exp. 19 April 1731.
21. Ibid., Miguel's confession.
22. AHQ, Not. 1, 13: exp. 25 December 1723 of 8 May 1731.

Esteban explained that he had come to the village because he and his brother Juan decided "to leave the city and go to the countryside in order to find work, because [in the city] they were persecuted by the justices."[23] According to his account, they had not stolen the horses; rather, they found them with no owner. Furthermore, he was no cattle thief: "he was not accustomed to accompanying thieves . . . and only casually had communicated with his brothers Juan Vásquez and Nicolás Durán, not for the purpose of committing robbery . . . neither does he become a famous thief because a public rumor (*voz común*) says that he is one. This public rumor is without foundation, because my party has not committed any theft. Because there was once a Marcos Durán, who is now dead, who was a bad man, it has become commonplace to speak of all the Duráns in this way, including my party with no reason." While Esteban and his procurator maintained his innocence, the magistrate insisted that public reputation indicated his guilt: "he had a reputation as a thief throughout the city, and especially in the neighborhoods of Ichimbia and San Blas, through which he was accustomed to walk at night in the company of others, carrying prohibited arms without fearing royal justice, and these antecedents assure me that he [had gone to the village] to commit thefts or robberies to which he was accustomed." The investigation discovered that the horses found with Esteban were in fact stolen. Their owners had been searching for them for days and received news that the thieves were the Charquis. Because Esteban insisted on his innocence, the audiencia sentenced him to questioning under torture. Esteban maintained his innocence throughout the torture session.

In August 1731 Juan Durán was captured, tried, and sentenced to death. On this occasion, he implicated Esteban in another robbery, to which Esteban confessed. Esteban was then sentenced to two hundred lashes and ten years of exile and was forced to watch his brother's execution.

The last piece of information regarding the Duráns dates from 1745. In this year, a municipal ordinary justice accused Rafael Durán and his son Antonio Herrera (both nicknamed Charqui) de oficio for having broken into the house of a local citizen. The accusation against Rafael depended on the evidence against Antonio. Yet this evidence was circumstantial. It consisted of the fact that (1) there had been a theft and

23. Ibid., Esteban's confession.

(2) Antonio was found on the street soon after with instruments that could be used to force open doors or windows. Two legal experts considered these proofs insufficient. A third expert convicted Antonio and sentenced him to a public lashing, to which the municipal ordinary justice added the penalty of exile. His father Rafael was acquitted on account of the lack of evidence.

Four months later, the same justice accused Antonio of yet another theft, which he confessed. The judge again condemned him to exile. The judge's renewed attempt to implicate his father, Rafael, whom he simply called "the Durán" or the "Charqui Angara," failed.[24] It is possible that the same judge initiated two other penal processes against Antonio for his presumed participation in breaking into homes. We also know that in 1748 Antonio was caught in the possession of stolen goods and, fearing judicial persecution, took refuge in the church of San Blas.[25]

Jail records from Quito also demonstrate that different members of the Durán family frequently entered and left local prisons. Between 1729 and 1731, at least four Duráns escaped incarceration, and in 1729, President Dionisio Alcedo y Herrera cited five Duráns among the thirteen suspects most wanted by local judicial authorities.[26]

The end of the Durán era was summarized in a sinister, anonymous, and undated note, which probably was added in 1748 to the records of a 1723 trial:

> They say that Marcos Durán was hung in Pasto. Juan Vásquez and Jacinto Vásquez[27] were hung in this city [Quito]. Esteban Durán is crippled on account of the torture he was given.[28] Nicolás Curibotón[29] was whipped along with the said Esteban, and they killed him [Nicolás] on San Agustín street, and they threw [his corpse] away. Miguel Durán does not appear, and Juan Durán the elder is the one who is now imprisoned. These men belong to the family of the charquis of [the neighborhood of] Ichimbia.

24. AHQ, Not. 6, 15: exp. 13 February 1745.
25. AHQ, Not. 3, 28: exp. 22 October 1748.
26. AHQ, Not. 6, 5: exp. 31 March 1728.
27. Jacinto Vásquez (Durán?) was also mentioned in a letter of President Dionisio Alcedo y Herrera to the Council of the Indies. AGI, Quito, 131: letter of 31 March 1730.
28. The poor state of health of Esteban was described in 1734 when, imprisoned by the town patrol, he was described as "handicapped, with impaired arms and legs." AHQ, Crim., 25: exp. 5 January 1730.
29. Nicolás Durán, alias Curibotón.

The succession of cases initiated by different judges against the members of a single family over some fifty years and four generations demonstrates the importance of reputation to the working of the administration of justice in eighteenth-century Quito. This importance had a legal foundation. The Castilian theory of proof applied in the Americas considered reputation an indication of guilt.[30] Although of itself, reputation could not justify conviction, it did point to the existence of "some guilt," and this indication could justify investigation, as well as prosecution and even questioning under torture. In theory, legal reputation existed once it was (1) public and (2) shared by many people. In practice, reputation was constructed by public perceptions that classified some people as good and others as bad. Good people merited recognition and rewards; bad people merited rejection and punishment. Reputation thus acted as a mechanism of social control. It propagated certain stereotypes, classified individuals on the social ladder according to their alleged behavior, and conferred rights and obligations in the social arena. Uniting the members of society around what was considered worthy, and against what was identified as immoral or indecent, reputation acted at the margin of the judicial system yet in collaboration with it.[31]

Social norms and community control coincided with legal doctrines. Judges were impelled to give reputation both a legal and a social meaning. The visibility and publicity of the Duráns left them no other choice. The judges had to react in this way because the family members were objects of daily conversation and were stereotyped as incarnating a "dangerous class of people." Because of this social reality the legal dis-

30. Scheffer, *Thesis inauguralis de fama* (Altdorff, 1662); F. De la Pradilla, *Suma de las leyes penales* (Madrid, 1639), 63–65; J. P. Lévy, *La hiérarchie des preuves dans le droit savant du Moyen Age depuis la renaissance du droit romain jusqu'à la fin du XIVe siècle* (Paris, 1939), 117; and A. Barrientos García, *El tratado "De iustitia et jure" (1590) de Pedro de Aragón* (Salamanca, 1978), 245–52. The relationship between *indicio* and reputation is also treated in F. V. Callejo y Urbino, "Apología legal de la verdad oprimida contra la calumnia exaltada . . . [1710]," MS 11391, 33, BJC. Indicios are studied in A. Quevedo y Hoyos, *Libro de indicios y tormentos que contiene toda la práctica criminal y modo de sustanciar el proceso* (Madrid, 1632); and M. P. Alonso Romero, *El proceso penal en Castilla (siglos XIII–XVIII)* (Salamanca, 1982), 235–38. See also chap. 1.

31. Reputation was discussed in the special volume dedicated to the subject in *Medievales* 24 (1993). The way reputation affected the working of the administration of justice is also described in C. M. MacLachlan, *Criminal Justice in Eighteenth-Century Mexico: A Study of the Tribunal of the Acordada* (Berkeley, 1974), 42–43; C. Wickham, "Gossip and Resistance among Medieval Peasantry," *Past and Present* 160 (1998): 4–6; and R. S. Shoemaker, "The Decline of Public Insult in London, 1660–1800," *Past and Present* 169 (2000): 97 and 129.

course employed by the Duráns and their procurators fell on deaf ears. Because social and not strictly legal categories were at stake, it was completely impossible to challenge the reputation of the family through legal means, for example, by distinguishing justified from unjustified reputation or one family member from another. Decision making was not truly in the hands of the courts. The family's reputation was established outside the judicial system, and it was outside the judicial system where it could be fought. It was precisely because this reputation was not based on hard core evidence, but linked to internal convictions, that it could survive in spite of concrete proofs against it.

The reputation of the Duráns included both general moral judgments and specific pieces of information, which were often partial or inaccurate. It included information about previous criminal acts or legal convictions, but it mainly consisted of a moral judgment about the character and activities of the members of the family.[32] Commonsense assumptions also operated. It was generally believed that "according to a known rule of law a person who was once bad is [always] presumed to be bad."[33] People who associated with criminals, it was said, were also criminals.[34] As a publicly "shared" opinion, reputation was often limited in its geographic and social range. It could be shared between the residents of certain neighborhoods or among people working in a certain sector, such as animal husbandry, yet all others could ignore it. For example, the witnesses who testified in favor of Miguel Durán in 1731, all of whom resided in the neighborhood of San Sebastián, claimed to know nothing about his infamous reputation. It is therefore possible (although not certain) that what was so evident in San Blas and Ichimbia (where the other Duráns lived) was unknown elsewhere.[35] Likewise, potential victims and livestock owners normally explained that they learned about the reputation of the Duráns only after they had suffered a theft.[36]

32. AHQ, Crim., 4: exp. 10 September 1657; AHQ, Crim., 6: exp. 23 January 1679; AHQ, Not. 6, 5: exp. 10 March 1723; AHQ, Not. 1, 28: exp. 12 May 1746; AHQ, Crim., 4: exp. 18 October 1660; and AHQ, Not. 6, 11: exp. 6 September 1739 from 1 January 1740.

33. AHQ, Not. 6, 15: exp. 17 January 1745. See also AHQ, Crim., 6: exp. 19 December 1676; and AHQ, Not. 1, 30: exp. 8 January 1750.

34. AHQ, Crim., 11: exp. 19 March 1681.

35. AHQ, Not. 6, 7: exp. 19 April 1731. The geographic frontiers of reputation are also mentioned in AHQ, Crim., 22: exp. 23 April 1725; AHQ, FE, 12 (1734–35), 1–11; and AHQ, Crim., 30: exp. 13 July 1740.

36. The relationship between the type of criminal activity and the scope of people who know about the reputation of the criminals was also mentioned in AHQ, Not. 1, 13: exp. 25 December 1723 from 8 August 1720.

Acting as a "certificate of bad conduct," reputation was applied to all Duráns alike, without distinguishing between one Durán and another.[37] It simply stated that the Durán family, or the Charqui Angaras, were all bad. Treated as members of a group and not as individuals, all Duráns suffered the same fate. Neither physical nor social distance guaranteed another outcome. This guilt by association was also applied to those who maintained friendly relations with the members of the family. For example, between 1728 and 1734 the justices of Quito prosecuted Cosme Lomas almost exclusively for his friendship with Nicolás Durán and his subsequent identification as an adopted member of the Durán family.

The placing of all Duráns in the same basket could be explained by the poor early modern means of identification, which made it hard to ascertain the identity of people. It could also be justified by the fact that the names Miguel and Juan, for example, were common among family members, thus leading to a true confusion. Nevertheless, guilt by association was also tied to the nature of reputation itself. Like all other moral and physical characteristics, bad behavior was also transmitted by blood, and as far as early moderns were concerned, character depended on genealogy.

The ability to act de oficio (chap. 1) allowed judges of Quito to initiate penal proceedings against family members even when the only proof against them was their reputation.[38] In the absence of concrete complaints, justices thus undertook campaigns to "rid the land of criminals," explaining their actions by the fact that (1) there were many crimes (2) the Duráns had a bad reputation. Under these circumstances, it is surprising that so many Duráns were acquitted so often: only seven members of the Durán family were ever convicted, thirteen were acquitted, and four fled from justice.[39] Although in many of these cases acquittal was legally justified, a conviction could be expected given the unfavorable climate against the members of the group. Activities tolerated in the cases of other people were not tolerated where the Duráns were con-

37. For a comparative view see the treatment of the brothers Drohmann in D. Sabean, "La conscience et la peur: qui a tué le pasteur?" *Actes de la recherche en sciences sociales* 51 (1984): 41–54.

38. More than three-fourths of the cases against the Durán family were initiated de oficio, with a similar frequency when based on reputation alone.

39. I do not know what happened to the rest.

cerned, and continuous judicial harassment certainly served also as an instrument for evidence gathering.[40]

Miguel's attempt to defend his honor ended up in a process against him as a thief. Clearly, as a member of the Durán family, Miguel had no honor to defend. Truth—the fact that he was not a cattle thief—was irrelevant in his case.[41] The subjective and personal injury he had suffered was not important. The law allowing people to defend their honor only protected the social, public, and objective status people had, not their interior appreciation of self.[42] As some members of the family contended, it became impossible for any of them to lead a normal life. The Duráns could not escape from the bad reputation, and the more the reputation persisted, the more the judicial system intensified its prosecution of them. This vicious circle trapped both the justices and the Duráns, but it also conditioned the behavior of other members of society. The

40. For a comparative view see N. Castan, *Les criminels de Languedoc: Les exigences d'ordre et les voies du ressentiment dans une société pré-révolutionnaire, 1750–1790* (Toulouse, 1980); Y. Castan, "Mentalités rurale et urbaine à la fin de l'Ancien Régime dans le ressort du parlement de Toulouse d'après les sacs à procès criminels, 1730–1790," *Crimes et criminalité en France 17e–18e siècles,* ed. A. Abbiateci, F. Billacois, Y. Castan, P. Petrovitch, Y. Bongert, and N. Castan, *Cahiers des Annales* 33 (1971): 109–80; and J. Brewer, "Law and Disorder in Stuart and Hanoverian England," *History Today* 30 (1980): 23–24. For the Latin American context see E. Tandeter, "La producción como actividad popular: Ladrones de minas en Potosí," *Nova America* 4 (1981): 42–65; M. C. Scardaville, "Crime and the Urban Poor: Mexico City in the Late Colonial Period" (Ph.D. diss., University of Florida, 1977); and G. Domínguez Zoila, "Delito y sociedad en el Nuevo Reino de Granada período virreinal, 1740–1810," *Universitas Humanistica* 8/9 (1974–75): 281–398.

41. A. Pérez Martín, "La protección del honor y de la fama en el derecho histórico español," *Anales de derecho* 11 (1991): 128–29, 144–45; R. Serra Ruiz, *Honor, honra e injuia en el derecho medieval español* (Murcia, 1969), 239; C. Chauchadis, *Honneur, morale et société dans l'Espagne de Philippe II* (Paris, 1984), 163–64; and F. J. Guillamon Álvarez, "El concepto de la honra legal durante el reinado de Carlos III," *Cuadernos de historia* 9 (1978): 457–91.

42. Although honor and reputation were closely related to one another, and could mutually influence one another, honor was objective and depended on membership in a certain group, while reputation (fama) was linked to individual behavior. These issues were explored in C. Büschges, "'Las leyes del honor': Honor y estratificación social en el distrito de la audiencia de Quito (siglo XVIII)," *Revista de Indias* 52/209 (1997): 58–61 and 68–78. See also J. Pitt-Rivers, "Honor y categoria social," in *El concepto del honor en la sociedad mediterránea,* ed. J. G. Peristany (Barcelona, 1968), 21–75; Y. Castan, *Honnêteté et relations sociales en Languedoc (1715–1780)* (Paris, 1974); J. A. Maravall, *Poder, honor y élites en el siglo XVII* (Madrid, 1979); D. Gilmore, ed., *Honor and Shame and the Unity of the Mediterranean* (Washington, DC, 1987); M. Madero, *Manos violentas, palabras vedadas. La injuria en Castilla y León (siglos XIII–XV)* (Madrid, 1992), 31–36; and M. Gautheron, ed., *L'honneur. Image de soi ou don de soi: Un idéal équivoque* (Paris, 1991).

inhabitants of Quito became convinced that the Duráns committed all crimes, and they saw the Duráns' shadows everywhere. They received anonymous clues that the Duráns stole their animals, they watched over the Duráns day and night, and they spied even on their most innocent activities.

Although the Durán family provides an extreme example, the importance of reputation to the working of the administration of justice in Quito was also clear in other cases. About 25 percent of the trials I studied mentioned reputation in one form or the other. Individuals with a good reputation who were accused of having committed a crime could be protected from prosecution or be prosecuted and then acquitted. Suspects who were well reputed could be freed from jail in cases in which other people would have to remain behind bars.[43] A bad reputation, in contrast, facilitated prosecution and conviction. It added weight to the existing evidence, and it allowed justices to claim that beyond the individuality of each case, the prosecution of badly reputed people because of their reputation was justified on its own.[44]

Bad reputation was especially powerful in periods when Quiteños felt that crime was getting out of hand. Between 1656 and 1662, for example, the inhabitants of Quito were mainly preoccupied with the presence of military deserters from Chile, who supposedly led an indolent and criminal life and caused great havoc among the Indians in the outskirts of the city. At the end of the seventeenth century, the people mainly complained about the proliferation of crime in the countryside, believing the judicial system to be incapable of controlling the situation. From the 1720s, these complaints became more frequent, especially with regard to cattle theft. In the 1730s, the inhabitants of Quito criticized judges for allowing thefts in shops and homes. On all these occasions, individual criminals were no longer at the center of judicial activity. Instead, the justice administration was concerned with the appearance of a "dangerous class of people." Once such a class was identified—for example, "deserters" or "those who did not leave a house, door, key, or balconies safe"—the system had to react against its members.[45] This

43. AHQ, Crim., 14: exp. 23 February 1696; AHQ, Crim., 25: exp. 28 July 1729; and AHQ, Not. 3, 28: exp. 22 October 1748.

44. AHQ, Crim., 6: exp. 19 December 1676 from 29 October 1676.

45. AHQ, Crim., 20: exp. 8 September 1717. A similar perception was mentioned in AHQ, Not. 1, 13: exp. 25 December 1723 from 17 March 1721.

reaction was mainly based on reputation, not hard facts. Examples are not wanting. In 1748, the lieutenant to the local governor began a campaign against "many thieves active in the region."[46] He published a decree inviting the inhabitants to denounce recent thefts and promised to pursue them energetically. In a similar way, several merchants denounced various thieves in 1748. Under these circumstances, recidivism was considered the rule, not the exception, and criminals were classified according to their friendship and family ties, not their individual activities. Reputation was applied to these "dangerous people," and its uses changed according to the different groups that were stereotyped as dangerous in each given moment. In the beginning of the eighteenth century, dangerous people were identified as cattle rustlers and highway robbers. It the following decades, attention centered on thieves. It therefore should not surprise us that between 1695 and 1730 the members of the Durán family were stigmatized as cattle rustlers and that, after 1730, they became urban thieves.

Bad reputation was used at specific times and against specific criminals. Yet, it was also invoked against certain types of people. Individuals who suffered from a bad reputation tended to be of similar socioeconomic, ethnic, and family backgrounds.[47] They often originated in the lowest social strata. Also vulnerable were foreigners, people of mixed ancestry or of illegitimate birth, and those working in daily nonpermanent jobs (*jornaleros*). The use of a nickname also served as an indication that the person was not sufficiently respected, thus making him vulnerable to bad reputation.[48]

Perhaps the most interesting feature of reputation in Quito was the fact that it was always presented as a "notorious piece of information." This gave reputation the stature of a higher category of evidence. Legally, things that were classified as "public and notorious" (*público y notorio*) (1) required no proof (2) could not be disproved, that is to say,

46. AHQ, Not. 1, 29: exp. 11 May 1748; and AHQ, Crim., 36: exp. 9 September 1748.

47. For comparion see C. B. Herrup, *The Common Peace: Participation and the Criminal Law in Seventeenth-Century England* (Cambridge, 1987), 4, 81, and 198; and F. Dabhoiwala, "The Construction of Honor, Reputation and Status in Late Seventeenth- and Eighteenth- Century England," *Transactions of the Royal Historical Society* 6 (1996): 201–13.

48. According to Pitt-Rivers, the use of nicknames was frequent in cases that involved notorious reputations because the names denoted a disdain for these individuals. Pitt-Rivers, "Honor y categoria social," 41.

they continued to be considered "true" even if there was evidence to the contrary.[49] Reputation was thus presented as something substantially different from simple gossip (*labios que corrían*) and rumor. While the latter included subjective knowledge, which was neither substantiated nor refuted, reputation identified a general public opinion because it included information that theoretically was held by the community as a whole and was therefore true by definition.[50] In some ways, reputation was a superior rumor of sorts, which managed to cross from a zone of uncertainty, typical of rumor, to a zone of assurance, typical of a full judicial proof, indeed of the strongest category of proof, the public and notorious.

The difference between rumor and reputation can be exemplified by the following story. Sometime in the late 1720s, Juan de Goyeneche, councilor of finances (*consejero de hacienda*) and treasurer of the queen, requested the recently named president of the audiencia of Quito, Dionisio Alcedo y Herrera, to carry a pack of diamonds to Quito.[51] The diamonds were an overdue payment to the widow of a business partner of Goyeneche, Juana Romo de Córdoba. By the time Alcedo y Herrera reached Quito, he could not account for the diamonds. Juana Romo de Córdoba was already dead, and her three daughters, who could not agree on a fair division of their inheritance, bitterly fought one another, both socially and judicially. The accumulation of these factors was grounds for a major social scandal. Rumors proliferated about the whereabouts of the diamonds, and the entire city speculated about who was guilty for their disappearance.

Rumors concerning the diamonds circulated in casual conversations between friends and relatives. When the people of Quito visited the sick, when they greeted one another because of the coming holidays, or when they requested the bishop permission to deliver a Mass, they discussed the most recent information regarding the affair. They asked questions, listened to answers, analyzed them, and then discussed it further with other people. Motivated by curiosity, those engaged in circulating rumors also attempted to help their friends or injure their ene-

49. C. Ghisalberti, "La teoría del notorio nel diritto comune," *Annali di storia del diritto* 1 (1957): 403–51; Lévy, *La hiérarchie des preuves*, 32; and A. Carboni, "La notorietà del delitto nelle riforme eclesiastiche medioevali," parts 1 and 2, *Studi sassaresi* 27 (1957): 5–55; 28 (1959): 49–99.

50. J. A. Maravall, *La teoría*, 252. For a comparative view see R. L. Rosnow and G. A. Fire, *Rumor and Gossip: The Social Psychology of Hearsay* (New York, 1976), 4 and 42.

51. AGI, EC, 1061B.

mies. Alcedo y Herrera, for example, argued that because the diamonds were not in the boxes that he had brought with him to Quito, they must have been included in the luggage that he had sent to Jerónimo Urbasos. This hypothesis involved Jerónimo Urbasos in the messy affair and led both Urbasos and his relatives to actively engage in circulating contrary rumors that placed the diamonds with Alcedo y Herrera or that explained their disappearance by a theft executed by magistrate Simón Rivera y Aguado. Josefa del Corro also played a similar role. As a friend of the wife of Juan José Mena, who was related to the husband of one of the interested parties (Rafaela Ontañón y Lastra, married to Pedro José Bermúdez Bezerra), she had the obligation to circulate rumors favoring this party. Likewise, no one seemed surprised that enemies of Alcedo y Herrera spoke against him.

In order to support your friends, or to annoy your enemies, it was sufficient to let your imagination go. The party backing the president, for example, argued that Alcedo y Herrera had sent the diamonds by mail. Because the diamonds did not arrive, the courier (*chasqui*) must have handed them over to one of the heirs. This presumption was based on a simple fact: the courier was seen in the vicinity of Quito a few days before his entry into town. Was it not possible that he arrived in the capital under the veil of secrecy, visited one of the heirs, gave her the diamonds, then left and reentered? This theory, which began as a pure suspicion, was thereafter transmitted as a fact. The people it accused reacted by circulating a contrary rumor. This rumor agreed with the facts but gave them a different reading. The courier had indeed lied about his arrival in Quito, but he had given the diamonds secretly to Alcedo y Herrera, not to the heirs. This conclusion was based on the same hypothesis, also adding to it the fact that Alcedo y Herrera arrived in Quito poor but thereafter lived in comfort, which his economic situation could not justify.[52] Similarly, the party backing the president found it easy to explain why magistrate Simón Rivera Aguado would get involved in the matter and steal the diamonds. His position as a magistrate enabled him to do so, and his love affair with one of the heirs (Micaela Ontañón y Lastra) provided him with a motive.[53]

Prepared to circulate rumors, the inhabitants of Quito nevertheless

52. A similar rumor appeared against the suspect in AHQ, Not. 1, 26: exp. 21 August 1744.

53. The love affair is described in AGI, Quito, 374: investigation of April 1729 and the reports of Dionisio Alcedo y Herrera from 25 September 1729 and 20 November 1730.

refused to give them judicial meaning. A typical example was the information supplied by Pedro José Bermúdez Bezerra, husband of Rafaela Ontañón y Lastra, who was one of the daughter-heirs. Bermúdez Bezerra stated that his relative Juan José Mena said that when Josefa del Corro visited his (Mena's) wife, she told him (Mena) that she had overheard that Rafaela's sister Micaela punished and then sold a slave who had seen the diamonds in her possession. When the judge investigating the case interrogated Corro, she could no longer recall the identity of her informants. She stated that, while speaking with friends, she asked them what they knew about the case, informing them also about what she "had heard said." Corro thus claimed that she had nothing to tell the judges. She could not act as a witness in an investigation or a trial because she was but a mere participant in a long chain of rumors, whose origin and foundation were beyond reach.

Corro was not alone in her refusal to give weight to the information she had circulated. Mena also informed the brother of Bermúdez Bezerra of another rumor: that magistrate Simón Rivera Aguado had taken the diamonds from the courier who had brought them to the audiencia building. Mena received this information from the municipal justice Jacinto Antonio Lemos, who heard it from his father-in-law, Jerónimo Urbasos, who heard it from Fray Francisco, Guerrero. Yet, when Guerrero was asked to trace the origin of the information, he stated: "[It was] a vague voice that I heard . . . and I judged [the case] on the basis of this voice . . . this [the one I made] was not an affirmative proposition, nor an absolute one . . . rather, it supposed that this might be true . . . the voice I heard was common; I do now know whose voice it was, or where it came from, because I had not inquired about it, nor do I remember who I heard it from; because I did not care, nor did I have any curiosity to find it out. This is the truth of the matter, and if one tries to present it differently, I will no longer recognize it . . . . Indeed, I cannot be certain where I heard it, from who, nor how, nor when, because all this was part of small and vulgar conversations, which are very accidental to my person . . . and which I never seek out."[54]

A long chain of transmissions thus broke down with Fray Guerrero, who could not (or did not want) to explain where, when, how, and from whom had he heard the information that reached the interested

54. AGI, EC 1061B, cuad. 6, Doc. 6, 59–60: declaration of Fray Francisco Guerrero.

parties. Guerrero pretended that his words had no importance because he himself gave them none. Contrary to other types of verbal exchanges, rumors, he said, were hypothetical rather than affirmative, casual rather than intentional. In short, they could have a social but not a legal meaning. The difference between the social and the legal sphere was clearly laid out. Many inhabitants got socially involved in the scandal, either out of curiosity or because of the wish to support their friends and relatives or to injure their enemies. Yet, although willing to engage in them socially, they refused to give the rumors a judicial reading.

The transformation of social knowledge into judicial knowledge thus depended not only on the nature of the information and its origins, as Guerrero argued, but also on the willingness of those engaged in circulating rumors to give them importance. A comparison between the diamonds' case and the case of the Duráns makes this issue clear. The witnesses who declared that the Duráns were thieves based their opinions primarily on rumors. However, contrary to their colleagues caught up in the case of the disappearing diamonds, they were willing to go a step further and affirm that what they said was an absolute truth by claiming that their individual knowledge was in fact a public knowledge of a higher standing. The people involved in the diamond affair did exactly the opposite. They refused to acknowledge the rumors they themselves circulated, and they denied them a stature that would raise them to the level of truth and make them institutionally (and judicially) meaningful.

The character of each case could explain this difference in attitude. The Duráns were members of a marginal family. They lived in the outskirts of the city, had originated in another region, were of mixed ancestry, and were extremely poor. Confirming the veracity of the rumors against them had no social cost. On the contrary, for both the authorities and the people of Quito the transformation of the Duráns into dangerous public enemies was a convenient tool. The affair of the diamonds was totally different. It involved the president of the audiencia, one of its magistrates, and many members of the local elite. Accusing any of them of misconduct—or, even worse, of having committed a crime—could have important consequences. It is thus clear why many people refused to do so. Yet the same people were curious about what had happened, and they wished to help their friends. The compromise was to accuse certain people of misbehaving in a way that was socially, but not judicially, meaningful. Accusations were never openly made. They were insinuated, hinted at, made into rumors.

President Dionisio Alcedo y Herrera resented this difference between rumor and fact, and between social and judicial meaning. Yet, contrary to what he implied when he spoke about the diamonds, this difference was one of the most enduring characteristics of the justice administration in Quito. There are many other examples of people declaring off the record what they were unwilling to affirm in judicial proceedings.[55] Off the record, most people would go a long way to support their friends or to injure their enemies. On the record, they did so only occasionally. Their refusal had nothing to do with the fear of committing perjury. Under the Castilian legal system, people who declared on the basis of rumor, or who invoked a public opinion, were not held responsible if the information turned out to be false. In question therefore were not the legal consequences of their acts but the difference between the social and the judicial arena, indeed the difference between rumor and reputation.

While the justices of Quito attempted to trace the origins of rumors that spread in the case of the diamonds, and wished to transform them into judicial information, the authorities of Madrid refused to follow this path. Arguing that "rumors did not amount to any evidence," the Council of the Indies stated that there was no way of knowing what had happened to the diamonds. Because this was the case, Dionisio Alcedo y Herrera, the new president of Quito, must be held responsible. Although no one could accuse him of theft, he clearly failed to deliver the diamonds over to the heirs. Regardless of the reason why this had happened, he should compensate the heirs. This solution, which was legally justified, could be adopted given Madrid's social and geographic distance from Quito. In contrast to what happened in Quito, in Madrid one could ignore the social pressure created by the proliferation of rumors and could evaluate the case according to its merits—and thereby implement a correct legal solution. This did not mean that the decision of the council was free of ulterior motives. The sentence against Alcedo y Herrera implied that, despite the fact that the diamonds did not reach their destination, Juan de Goyeneche no longer

55. In another case, dated 1731, the crown attorney of the Council of the Indies asked his informants if "lo que extrajudicialmente informaban, judicialmente lo depondrían." He received a negative answer: AHN, Cód., 756B, no. 48.

owed anything to his creditors in Quito. He had paid his debt at the moment he gave the diamonds to the president, and it was now the president (who had lost them or stole them—it made no difference) who had to pay the heirs. The condemnation of Alcedo y Herrera thus favored Goyeneche, who was a member of the Council of Finance and the treasurer of the queen and whose son Francisco was the most senior councilor in the Council of the Indies (which rendered the final judgment).

The adoption or rejection of rumors according to the needs and interests of the moment was a common phenomenon. The same happened with regard to reputation. Procurators, for example, used reputation when it was beneficial to the defendant, and they refused to consider it if it was prejudicial.[56] Similarly, crown attorneys at times argued that certain crimes justified prosecution solely on the basis of reputation, yet at other times they asserted that "there is not a worse or less trustworthy witness then reputation, because it usually comes from very false beginnings, and from malevolent and a slanderous people, who are in no way honest."[57] President Dionisio Alcedo y Herrera, who suffered so greatly on account of rumors, used both rumors and reputation to justify many de oficio processes.[58] Similarly, magistrates who invoked reputation to prosecute criminals were resentful whenever the same strategy was applied to their cases. They especially rejected the use of rumors to prove their involvement in illicit love affairs with local women. Tomás Fernández Pérez de Hodo argued that "if any such rumor had spread, it was due to the easiness in which ordinarily similar voices appear in this city, [voices] that had been qualified as false."[59] Yet the inability to control rumors, or to stop the generation of a certain reputation, was considered in itself a misdemeanor. Juan Ricaurte convinced his judge that a rumored love affair with a servant was false. Nevertheless, Ricaurte was sanctioned because he failed to dismiss the servant, thus neglecting to do what was required in order to dissipate the rumor.[60]

56. AHQ, Crim., 16: exp. 5 August 1701; AHQ, Not. 6, 15: exp. 14 September 1746; and the legal proceedings against the Durán family mention above.

57. AHQ, Crim., 27: exp. 10 April 1734; and AHQ, Not. 6, 17: exp. 10 July 1748.

58. AGI, Quito, 131, 649–70: exp. 5 April 1731.

59. AGI, EC, 911A. The response of magistrate Miguel Antonio Ormasa Ponce de León was similar in AGI, Quito, 74. He qualified rumor as "prueba falsa y sujeta a lo incierto y mentiroso."

60. AGI, EC, 911A.

Conclusion

The history of the Duráns and the tale of the missing diamonds demonstrate the relationship between social and judicial information. The manipulation of categories of proof such as reputation and rumor allowed the people of Quito to influence the working of the judicial institutions. It also permitted the system to respond to pressures coming from outside. The administration of justice was never an autonomous sphere. Rather, it depended on and influenced other social control mechanisms. Yet information obtained or circulated socially might or might not become legally meaningful. Its success or failure in influencing the result of judicial proceedings depended on the identity of the parties, the offense, and the period. Most importantly, it depended on what the inhabitants of the city were willing to do and the weight they were willing to give to their words.

CHAPTER SEVEN

Ceremony and Image

In January of 1737 the president of the audiencia, José de Araujo y Río, was sick in bed when he received a petition from Antonio Ulloa. Ulloa was one of two naval officers charged by the king of Spain to accompany the French scientific mission that visited the viceroyalty of Peru between 1736 and 1744.[1] Refusing to read the petition, Araujo y Río immediately returned it to the sender. The president demanded that Ulloa change the address from *Vuestra Merced* (which was an address between equals) to *Señoría* (which was an address to a superior). Ulloa, who was offended by the response, presented himself at the palace. He forced his way into the chamber and bedroom of the president and ridiculed him in the presence of at least seven witnesses. The president ordered a house arrest, which Ulloa resisted, explaining that Araujo y Río "was not his judge."[2] The following morning, Araujo y Río sent for Jorge Juan, the second Spanish naval officer. The president hoped the officer would recognize his superiority. After Juan refused to do so, the president initiated a penal investigation against both officers and ordered their arrest. Ulloa and Juan resisted, wounding two constables and taking refuge in the sanctuary of the Jesuit college.

Unable to resolve the dispute on their own, the parties wrote to the viceroy and to the king, each party asking for approval of its own behavior and for censure of the behavior of its rival. The Council of the Indies considered the matter grave and worthy of a quick response. Nevertheless, the king, who initially supported this interpretation (he

1. N. Gómez, *La misión geodésica y la cultura de Quito* (Quito, 1987); A. Lafuente and A. Mazuecos, *Los caballeros del punto fijo: Ciencia, política y aventura en la expedición geodésica hispanofrancesa al virreinato del Perú en el siglo XVIII* (Quito, 1992); and L. Ramos Gómez, *Época, génesis y texto de las Noticias Secretas de América de Jorge Juan y Antonio de Ulloa* (Madrid, 1985).

2. AGI, EC, 914B, cuad. 5, 68–115; and Ramos Gómez, *Época, genesis y texto*, 70–81.

had even named a judge to investigate the case), subsequently changed his mind and asserted that there was no point in intervening. The affair, he concluded, was petty and of no consequence. It could be resolved by simply expressing royal disapproval of the actions of both parties.[3]

For a student of the justice administration in Quito, this event is significant for its highly theatrical nature and for the role of ceremony and law in its development.[4] The central question was the social decorum involved in writing. Decorum was important, because external conduct was considered a sign of internal belief. Ceremony, including verbal exchange, reflected reality, and as a reflection of reality it was of great concern to those affected by it. A claim of equality or superiority where equality or superiority did not exist was considered "serious disrespect," disrespect that could only be motivated by pride and the lack of self-restraint. Such attitudes had severe repercussions in a society that worshiped prudence and moderation.[5] The claim that the president was not "their judge" and had no jurisdiction over the mariners was as serious. It implied that his authority was limited and that there were people in Quito who were not under his control. Within a hierarchical social system, this was an extremely dangerous conclusion.

The importance of decorum and jurisdiction led to their definition in customs and laws. However, these definitions were often contradictory. Officially, all people had to address presidents of audiencias and their magistrates as Vuestra Merced, *del consejo de Su Majestad,* or *Alteza.*[6] However, in Quito a local custom dictated that people call magistrates Vuestra Merced and presidents Señoría.[7] This contradiction between law and custom allowed both Araujo y Río and Juan and Ulloa to legally justify their position. But, whether formally justified or not, the

3. AGI, EC, 916A, cuad. 29, 101–18 and 224–90. See also, AGI, Quito, 105: consulta from 10 October 1742.

4. R. E. Giesey, *Cérémonial et puissance souveraine: France XVe–XVlle siècles* (Paris, 1987), 69–70. See also C. Chauchadis, *La loi du duel: Le code du point d'honneur dans l'Espagne des XVIe–XVIIe siècles* (Toulouse, 1997).

5. J. Solórzano y Pereira, *Política Indiana* (1674; reprint, Madrid, 1972), 5.8.7 and 5.8.10; and M. Herrero García, *Ideas de los españoles del siglo XVII* (Madrid, 1966).

6. AHQ, Ced., 1: tit. 13, cédula 14; and AHQ, Crim., 11: exp. 6 December 1688.

7. President Juan de Sosaya, for example, was treated in this manner by magistrate Tomás Fernández Pérez de Hodo. AGI, EC, 911A. Royal legislation legitimized this practice at the end of the eighteenth century. AHN, Cód., 759B, no. 43 (from 1771); and AGI, Cód., 714B, no. 125 (from 1778). Doppagne described how forms of courtesy generalize, leading to the creation of new forms of address that impede the leveling among those who are of an unequal status. A. Doppagne, "La expresión de la cortesía," in *Actas del III congreso internacional de hispanistas* (Mexico, 1970), 288–89.

confrontation between the two parties ran deeper than that. At its center was a profound disagreement about the social position occupied by the two naval officers in Quito. Ulloa and Juan were delegates of the Spanish king. They came to Quito under royal orders, orders that instructed them to accompany and facilitate the work of a French scientific mission. The mariners, like all other members of the expedition, argued that as personal envoys of the French and Spanish kings they could not be touched because they were judicially and legally superior (or at least exterior) to the local system. Formally external, in practice they behaved as if they were members of the local society. They maintained a close relationship with the local elite, in whose houses they resided and who supplied the expedition with both social and economic support.[8] In some cases, the members of the expedition obtained local employment and made marriage arrangements. Many of them were (almost) permanent, rather than transient, members of society. The claim that the authorities in Quito had no jurisdiction over the expedition was therefore particularly problematic. As one witness later concluded, "it was necessary that these people . . . although especially recommended by his majesty, would recognize at least some superior who could correct them if they committed a crime . . . and although in the beginning the city criticized the proceedings of the said president . . . after the initial fervor was over, all prudent people recognized that he did not deviate in the slightest from a judicial way of acting, attempting to maintain the necessary respect to his person and representation."[9]

Subjection to hierarchy was a public affair. As Norbert Elias argued, in early modern societies rank was established through public display.[10] Individuals occupied the social position that other persons were willing to give them—that is to say, social rank was fixed through actions that met with no opposition. In such a system, it was essential to observe the

8. AHQ, Not. 1, 24: exp. 16 December 1740. See also Gómez, *La misión*, 69–76.

9. The original version reads: "Se hacía preciso que dichos sujetos . . . aunque especialmente recomendados por Su Majestad, tuviesen de reconocer algún superior de quien fuesen corregidos en caso de delinquir . . . , aunque en la ciudad se moralisase por entonces sobre el proceder de dicho señor presidente . . . después pasado aquel fervor reconocieron todos los prudentes que no se desvió un punto de lo judicial, procurando mantener el respecto debido a su decoro y representación." AGI, EC, 914A, cuad. 2, 133–35: petition of José Suárez y Figueroa.

10. N. Elias, *La société de la cour* (Paris, 1969; reprint, 1985), 84. See also J. C. Schmidt, *La raison des gestes dans l'occident médiéval* (Paris, 1990). For the Spanish example see C. Lisón Tolosana, *La imagén del rey: Monarquía, realeza y poder ritual en la Casa de los Austrias* (Madrid, 1991), 132–35.

way people behaved in order to ensure that they made no implicit claim for a status that they did not deserve. By the same token, it was crucial to have one's status recognized and admitted by all. Because of this logic, unless the inhabitants of Quito and the two Spanish mariners recognized the president as their superior, his superiority did not exist. For exactly the same reason, the mariners had to contest this claim of superiority and publicly defy it by asserting their equality.

Each position taken, each movement, and each gesture represented these needs. The president was not content with the simple imprisonment of Ulloa. Instead, he ordered the municipal ordinary justice to accompany Ulloa to his house. This order ensured that the act of imprisonment would be public and would be understood by all spectators. Ulloa, for his part, openly declared that he would gladly return to his home to eat and rest but that he refused to comply with the presidential order to be under house arrest. Publicly demonstrating his disobedience, Ulloa (who was also ill) spent the entire afternoon strolling along the principal streets and the main square. To ensure that the president would be aware of what was happening, he approached his residence.

In this struggle for supremacy and recognition, the participation of the public, although passive, was indispensable. The public had to witness both the act of submission and the act of disobedience. The presence of the public transformed the conflict from a minor into a major incident. During the initial confrontation, a peaceful and negotiated solution was still possible. The detention of Ulloa and later Juan could end without a trial and without the intervention of the Council of the Indies or the king. Araujo y Río confessed that all he wished to do was "contain" Ulloa and that he had no desire to punish him. The president did not change his mind until the next afternoon, after his attempt to reason with Juan failed. Only then did he realize that strong action had to be taken in order to safeguard his status in Quito. By that time, he had not only suffered two public defeats: news of the conflict had spread throughout the city, "making" response necessary. The action Araujo y Río took, initiating criminal proceedings against the two officers, was perfect for a number of reasons: (1) it placed him in a position of superiority vis-à-vis the two men—despite their protests, he was indeed their judge— and (2) it qualified the two men as delinquents. Abandoning the symbolic-theatrical arena, which led to his defeat, Araujo y Río turned the discussion to legal and procedural grounds.

Law, however, was not a separate field. Turning to the law could be a good response to a situation that was getting out of hand precisely because law was embodied with symbolic and theatrical meaning. Law was a source of authority because it represented divine and royal wisdom. Its intervention had the power of a mediating force, almost a peace-making entity. In the first act of the conflict (at the palace), Ulloa forced his way into the president's room. The confrontation, which was characterized by rapid movements (the sudden entrance of Ulloa and the reaction of those who were present in the room) and by the use of foul language, changed its nature after "law" was invoked. Ulloa claimed that the president was not his judge, and both parties began what was apparently a calm scholarly debate about jurisdiction. Ulloa produced a copy of his commission as a naval officer. The municipal ordinary justice read the certificate and concluded that it did not exempt Ulloa from regular jurisdiction. Ulloa then sustained that perhaps such an exemption was included in the regulations of the marine. In order to prove his point, he needed to produce a copy of the regulations. Because this copy was at his home, he suggested that he go there accompanied by the municipal ordinary judge. Ulloa was willing to go home with the judge in order to produce the regulations. Nevertheless, he refused to do so when ordered to remain under house arrest.

This function of the law was not exceptional. Law had a similar effect in the third act, when Ulloa and Juan took refuge in the Jesuit college. Although both men were still physically reachable, after they were inside this ecclesiastical institution, the ministers of justice could no longer touch them. Immune from imprisonment, Ulloa and Juan continued to attack the ministers and even injured two of them. This aggression had no response because the law prohibited the ministers from responding.

Ceremonies like the ones mentioned in the preceding formed an integral part of the administration of justice. They were intended to guarantee the social prominence of judges and judicial officials by affirming their relative position in the city. Considered a faithful reflection of the social world, these ceremonies created and maintained a nonverbal discourse that demanded the passive participation of the spectators.[11] The awareness that the public was watching, interpreting, and evaluating led to many conflicts, such as the one experienced between Araujo y Río

11. For a comparative view see A.Garapon, "Justice rituelle el justice bureaucratique," *Annales de Vaucresson* 29 (1988): 103–15.

and the two Spanish mariners. It also produced a dense legislation that was meant to codify people's behavior.

The daily life of magistrates, judges, and officers was regulated closely. Regulation began even before individuals took possession of their offices. Presidents, magistrates, and local governors entered Quito in a public ceremony.[12] The town council and the audiencia, who were notified about the nominees' imminent arrival, were charged with preparing a reception that began outside the city limits. Magistrates and members of the town council received the presidents, and the town council accompanied the local governors. The reception ceremony was spread out over several days and took place in different locations. Presidents, magistrates, and governors spent time in various rural estates around the city, eating, drinking, and getting familiar with local scenery and local society. They then entered the city in a public ceremony, which was carefully staged. The authorities who were equal or subordinate to the arriving officials waited for them at the city's limits and escorted them to the main square and to their future places of residence. In the case of the president, this ceremony was followed by three days of bullfighting and two days of plays and fireworks, during which banquets of ice cream and sweets were offered to participants. In 1728 and 1736, the president entered the city on the back of a saddled horse.[13] In 1736, drums and trumpets were used to announce the president's arrival at the town square.[14] In the case of the local governors, the reception ceremony was simpler, limited to the offering of a single banquet in the city.

Reception ceremonies were fairly expensive.[15] For example, in 1661, 1707, and 1744 the cost of hospices outside the city alone was estimated to be some 240, 500, and 600 pesos respectively. In 1736, the price of the horse and saddle was 350 pesos.[16] Local municipal revenues (*proprios*)

12. The following description is based on the study of the town council records and relevant decisions voted on by this body (*autos acordados*), especially the receptions of the corregidores and presidents between 1661 and 1744.

13. AMQ, LC, 00123: town council meeting of 16 November 1728. The same occurred in 1744.

14. AMQ, LC, 00123: town council meeting of 7 September 1736 and 16 November 1736.

15. AMQ, LC, 00012, 00118, and 00126: town council meetings of 10 July 1661, 10 February 1707, and 29 December 1744, accordingly. See also AMQ, LC, 00012 and 00017: meetings of 10 July 1661 and 26 April 1704. For a comparative view see S. G. Flinchpaugh, "Economic Aspects of the Viceregal Entrance to Mexico City," *Americas* 52/3 (1996): 345–65.

16. AMQ, LC, 00123: town council meeting of 16 November 1728.

were insufficient to cover these expenses, and on many occasions the execution of the ceremony depended on donations from private individuals who fought for the privilege to pay these costs. Although the interest for doing so was never openly confessed, it was probably tied to the fact that financing the ceremony was one of the most important forms of participating in it.[17] Participation was a privilege that could only be granted to worthy people. Individuals participated in the ceremony according to their "nobility, authority, honor, and splendor."[18] Paying the costs thus confirmed the status of those taking part in the event. At the same time it established the distance between them and other people living in the city. Among those participating were the alderman, who (by definition) were "powerful people of the republic" and of "prime authority, and representation."[19] Among those who could not participate were the plebs and other unimportant people. Because the aldermen already enjoyed public recognition, and participated in the event by virtue of office, they rarely had an interest in paying the costs of the event. The plebs, of course, had no money to donate, nor were they interested in obtaining recognition. It was mainly those in the middle, between these two groups and yet with pretensions of belonging to the first of the two, who most contributed to the receptions. Among them were merchants, who usually paid for the fireworks, and ranchers, who supplied the bulls for the bullfights.[20] The public reception of ministers thus responded to two distinct rationales. On the one hand, it honored the new office holders and placed them within the local social hierarchy. On the other, it was an instrument that allowed locals to demonstrate and confirm their status within the community.

After the reception was over, the officeholder presented his letter of nomination and took an oath before the body that he was about to enter and in the place where he was about to exercise his office. Municipal ordinary justices, Santa Hermandad justices (who were residents of the city and had no need to ceremoniously enter it), and local governors

17. M. Fogel, *Les cérémonies de l'information dans la France du XVIe au XVIII siècle* (Paris, 1989), 243 and 428. The economic cost of prestige is also studied in Elias, *La société,* 43–44 and 47–61.

18. AMQ, LC, 00117 and 00118: town council meetings of 26 February 1704 and 10 February 1707.

19. AMQ, LC, 00121, 174–77.

20. AMQ, LC, 00012, 00116, and 00118: town council meetings of 7 December 1661, 8 December 1661, 23 October 1691, 2 August 1697, and 10 February 1707.

took their oaths in front of the town council and in the town council hall.[21] Magistrates and presidents took their oaths in the chamber of the acuerdo in the presence of the other ministers. Although not open to the public, oath taking did involve the presence of the auxiliary staff of these institutions, such as court recorders, notaries, and procurators. It ceremonially indicated the newly established relationship between the new officer and the physical and social space where he was to exercise his office. Every detail was strictly regulated. In the audiencia, an open missal was placed next to the royal seal, which was brought from the chancery. At the sight of these symbols of authority (both religious and royal authority), the future justice read out loud a formulaic oath containing the promise to uphold the law and royal interests, to maintain the court's deliberations in secret, and to refuse bribes. The last sentences fused the alliance between king and God: "If I should do such things, God shall help me . . . and if not, [God] shall take action against me . . . amen."[22] Following the oath, the new officer took physical possession of his office: the magistrates sat upon their bench, and the municipal ordinary justices and local governors received their rods.

The ceremonial veneration of magistrates and judges continued after they were received in office. One common practice was to accompany the presidents and the magistrates on their outings—an act that again demonstrated respect for their persons as well as confirmed the importance of those participating in the ceremony. On occasion, the wish to be venerated was such that presidents like José de Araujo y Río were criticized for creating a company of uniformed and armed soldiers whose only mission (according to his rivals) was to escort him and his wife throughout the city (chap. 4). Although he denied these charges, years later Araujo y Río narrated with pride how the inhabitants of Quito accompanied him when he entered or left the city. This behavior, he said, demonstrated their love, admiration, and respect for his person. In 1744 he was received by both the "nobles and the humble people [*plebe*]" and was accompanied to his house. When his wife left the city, she received homage from all of the nobility and the "secular and ecclesiastical corps."[23]

21. A. Van Gennep, *The Rites of Passage* (Chicago, 1908; reprint, 1960).

22. The original version reads: "si así lo hiciera Dios todo poderoso me ayude . . . y si no, me lo demande . . . amen." AGI, Quito, 129, 297–99. The oath of ordinary municipal justices is described in AGI, EC, 915A, cuad. 1, 108. See also R. Roldán Verdejo, *Los jueces*, 111–21.

23. AGI, EC, 914C, cuad. 11, 47; and AGI, EC, 916B, cuad. 28, 590.

Other ministers, who were less fortunate than Araujo y Río, complained about the lack of attention. In 1711, magistrate Juan Dionisio Larrea Zurbano (junior) grumbled against his colleagues of the audiencia for failing to greet him when he arrived in the city. He accused them of disobeying "customary urbanity," and he asserted that this was not a simple negligence but an intentional and violent act meant to humiliate him.[24] The offense, he argued, was not only his. It reflected on the entire justice administration and even the king. Because respect was reciprocal, and because it honored both those greeting and those receiving attention, the failure to greet him had damaged the reputation of the negligent party as much as it did his own.

Presidents also had the right to be accompanied by the magistrates from their place of residence (usually one of the rooms in the audiencia building) to the public or acuerdo chamber. In 1704, some ministers accused President Francisco López Dicastillo y Azconza of abusing this privilege. According to their complaint, he had moved his place of residence only to secure a longer route. This move, which they interpreted as intentional, was resented because they felt that it was specifically planned in order to denigrate them by forcing them to accompany him for a longer distance than usual.[25] López Dicastillo y Azconza, they argued, was known for inventing new ceremonies and increasing his demands for honor and recognition. In 1705, for example, he received the public seated under a canopy (*dosel*).[26] This custom, "which was never practiced by his predecessors, and not even by the viceroy," was interpreted as yet another attempt to demonstrate his superiority and another rupture of the acceptable ceremonial order.

Clothing was also strictly regulated. Judicial officers and judges, including the aldermen, municipal justices, constables, notaries, lawyers, procurators, magistrates, crown attorneys, and protectors of Indians, all wore a special uniform, which was determined according to their offices as well as their personal attributes (i.e., nobility).[27] This uniform consisted of a long black vestment, normally made of silk, that stretched to the heels, a decoration around the neck (*golilla*) made of cardboard covered in silk (obliging the bearer to keep his head erect),

24. AGI, Quito, 164: his undated report to the viceroy.

25. AGI, Quito, 162: testimony of the notary Sánchez Maldonado.

26. AGI, Quito, 162.

27. AMQ, LC, 00126: town council meeting of 4 March 1746 and the letter from the viceroy to the audiencia, 12 October 1745.

and a cap.[28] Judges also carried a staff (*vara*), which normally was as tall as a man and had a cross on one end—thus imitating, although not perfectly, the royal scepter.[29] The magistrates of the audiencia dressed similarly. They had a vestment of the same length and color that included a cuff that fell from the shoulders over the back. This uniform was called a *garnacha* or *toga*.

The regulation of clothing was a normal practice in a society that used similar methods to distinguish between Spaniards and Indians, nobles and commoners, and so on.[30] Yet, the regulation of clothing also had a functional end. It identified the judicial officers in and outside the office, and it distinguished them from the rest of society by creating a visual social code that, among other things, disregarded the individual financial situation of each official.[31] Dress codes also obeyed political, commercial, and religious interests. They prohibited the use of certain colors or fabrics that came from enemy countries, they discouraged the use of "indecent" dress, and they criticized luxury leading to excessive expenditure.[32]

Because uniforms were endowed with symbolic meaning, they could become the object of disagreement, resentment, and open confronta-

28. "Noticia del origen y principio del uso de las golillas en España . . . [n.d.]," MS 2850, fol. 241, BPR; and E. Ruiz Guiñazú, *La magistratura indiana* (Buenos Aires, 1916), 326–27.

29. B. Bravo Lira, "Símbolos de la función judicial en el Derecho Indiano," in *Poder y presión fiscal en la América española (siglos XVI, XVII, XVIII): Actas del VI congreso del Instituto Internacional de Historia del Derecho Indiano* (Valladolid, 1986), 235–54. See also C. Bayle, *Los cabildos seculares*, 259–63.

30. Indians, for example, were prohibited from using certain fabrics: AMQ, LC, 00012: town council meeting of 18 August 1660. See also D. Roche, *La culture des apparences: Une histoire du vêtement XVIIe–XVIIIe siècle* (Paris, 1989), 14 and 108–10; and P. Civil, "Corps, vêtement et société: Le costume aristocratique espagnol dans la deuxième moitié du XVIe siècle," in *Le corps dans la société espagnole des XVIe et XVIIe siècles*, ed. A. Redondo (Paris, 1990), 307–19.

31. AHN, Cód., 696B, no. 86 from 1766; and L. Navarro García, "Honra, pobreza y aislamiento de los oidores indianos," *Temas americanistas* 1 (1982): 15. A decree from 1716 criticizes the use of expensive coaches and dress by people who should not use them on account of their office, "siendo justo hacer distinción de las que pueden usar de ellos por su decencia." R. Konetzke, *Colección de documentos*, 3: 124–34.

32. AHN, Cód., 696B, no. 86 from 1766; AHN, Cód., 758B, no. 30 from 1707; Konetzke, *Colección de documentos*, 3: 124–34; AHN, Cód., 684B, no. 26: cédula from 1682; and "Consulta del Consejo de Castilla a Fernando IV sobre exceso de lujo y prágmatica de él motivada por la consulta," MS 5563, BN. See also M. Fogel, "Modèle d'Etat et modèle social de dépenses: les lois somptuaires en France de 1485 à 1660," *Prélèvement et redistribution dans la genèse de l'Etat moderne: Actes du colloque, 1984* (Fontevrault, 1987); and idem, *Les cérémonies*, 415–16. The relationship between dress and religious precepts was discussed by Roche, *La culture*, 13.

tion. In 1705 and 1706, the magistrates of the audiencia could not decide whether they should accompany the royal standard wearing a cap (the local custom) or a hat (the practice in Lima).[33] Those who supported the first view asserted that any change in the ceremony would cause a public scandal; that is to say, it would bring about the demise of moral order. Their opponents, on the contrary, argued that wearing a hat was more respectable and that there was no reason not to do so if such was the practice in Lima.

The importance of dress is best exemplified by the case of the garnacha, the special garment reserved for audiencia magistrates and presidents who were trained in law. The garnacha confirmed the professional training of its bearers (a law degree), and it gave them the rights of career magistrates.[34] Once granted, it could not be taken away without a solid reason. Aware of the implications of wearing a garnacha, President José de Araujo y Río requested a license to use this uniform in 1735, which as a purchaser of the office he was not entitled to wear.[35] Like all other purchasers (and contrary to individuals who obtained their nomination by way of grace [merced]), Araujo y Río was not a career judge. The king had no obligation toward him other than to allow him to serve the office that he had bought. In theory Araujo y Río was not entitled to promotion or to hold another office after his term ended. Despite having a law degree, Araujo y Río was treated like all other president-purchasers whose academic qualifications played no role in their nomination. He was not allowed to vote in legal matters, and he could not use the garnacha.

Unwilling to conform to this situation, Araujo y Río first secured recognition of his law degree and thus of his right to vote in legal matters. He then requested a royal permit to wear a garnacha. His justification could not be simpler: he claimed that all he wanted was to look the same as the other magistrates who voted in legal matters as he did. However, some members of the Council of the Indies suspected from the first moment that much more than appearance was at stake.

33. AHQ, AC, 3 (1684–1717), 96 and 114. Public scandal is discussed in C. Leal Curiel, *El discurso de la fidelidad: Construcción social del espacio como símbolo de poder regio (Venezuela siglo XVIII)* (Caracas, 1990), 203–9.

34. AGI, Quito, 33, 16: letter of Antonio de Castro; and AGI, Quito, 4: consulta of 1699.

35. The petitions of Araujo y Río and the responses of the council can be found in AGI, Quito, 106: decree from 7 March 1735; AGI, Quito, 104: consulta from 14 March 1735; AGI, EC, 916A, cuad. 29, 128–29: letter of Araujo y Río, 1740; and AHN, Cód., 753B, no. 182: from 1735.

The wearing of a garnacha was not necessary for voting, and, according to the councilors, it should be reserved to people who deserved it. These apprehensions led to a compromise. Araujo y Río was allowed to use the garnacha under the condition that it would not change his legal situation and would not grant him any rights that he did not already have.

Despite this warning, after he obtained the right to use a garnacha Araujo y Río began claiming other privileges that were associated with this dress. Among other things, he requested appointment to another office after his term in Quito. The Council of the Indies reminded him that the permit he received was exceptional and that it did not modify his rights. However, aware of the symbolic implications of wearing or not wearing a garnacha, and unwilling to punish the president by taking this dress away from him, the council allowed Araujo y Río to continue to wear the garnacha and to enjoy the honor and status it conferred even after he completed his term in office.

Araujo y Río was not the first magistrate to invoke the relationship between dress and office. Already in 1736, Juan Dionisio Larrea Zurbano asked the Council of the Indies to declare his "state as a *togado,*" that is to say, his status as a person who once wore a toga (garnacha).[36] His was not a question of fashion or dress. What Larrea Zurbano requested was a public recognition that he deserved treatment as a magistrate for the rest of his life because he once was one and once wore the uniform of magistrates. The Council of the Indies was not surprised. It agreed that it was customary to give people who once served as magistrates the treatment of togados, even if they no longer wore a garnacha. No formal declaration was thus needed for Larrea Zurbano to be considered togado. Armed with this answer, Larrea Zurbano presented himself at the audiencia and the town council, where he received the honors, privileges, and prerogatives of an audiencia magistrate.[37]

The image of the judicial system, and its members, also depended on other factors. For example, President Dionisio Alcedo y Herrera managed to promote an exceptional reception of his person and activities in both Quito and Madrid. His image as a highly successful administrator of justice originated in his presidency, and endured afterwards—to be adopted even by modern historians.[38] Vis-à-vis Madrid, this image was

36. AGI, Quito, 145, 103–6: his letter, studies by the council on 9 May 1736.
37. AMQ, LC, 00125, dated 14 March 1738.

generated by a succession of reports, sent by Alcedo y Herrera, informing the metropolitan authorities of his most trivial decisions. In 1729, he notified the Council of the Indies about the flight of several famous criminals and the legal orders dispatched to find and imprison them.[39] In 1736, he sent news about a homicide and about the penalty given to the perpetrator.[40] Alcedo y Herrera justified these reports by asserting that these cases were exceptional. Yet nothing about them truly explains the nature of their importance and why the council might need to be involved.

In this correspondence, Alcedo y Herrera presented himself as a savior. The state of things had been disastrous before his intervention and glorious thereafter. He alone was responsible for this improvement, which he designed, ordered, and executed. Painting a somber picture of what Quito was like before he became president, Alcedo y Herrera argued that the city suffered from "repeated crimes of perfidy, murders, and robberies." After he arrived, he gave rapid and efficient orders that in fifteen days established "public peace by restraining the audacity of the hooligans."[41] The many scandals and disorders that were previously permitted were now prevented: "I have been able to establish a peaceful and tranquil republic . . . without having experienced [either] a murder or robbery in the space of the five months that have passed since I gave these decrees."[42]

The information Alcedo y Herrera sent to Madrid was inaccurate. Neither was the city in a state of chaos before he came nor did his orders eliminate crime. Indeed, Alcedo y Herrera wrote to the council only three months after the new measures were implemented, and in this period at least one well-known robbery took place.[43] Alcedo y Herrera also exaggerated his own role and intentionally undervalued the contribution of other local actors.

38. C. M. Larrea, *El presidente de la Real Audiencia de Quito don Dionisio de Alcedo y Herrera* (Quito, 1961); and R. Terrán Najas, "Sinopsis histórica del siglo XVIII," in *Nueva historia del Ecuador*, vol. 4, *Epoca Colonia II*, ed. E. Ayala Mora (Quito: 1983), 4: 263–300, especially 280–82.

39. AGI, Quito, 145, 583: letter dated 22 April 1729.

40. AGI, Quito, 133: letter dated 1 February 1736.

41. AGI, Quito, 131: letter dated 3 February 1729.

42. AGI, Quito, 131: letter dated 31 March 1730 and the accompanying documents.

43. The measures were undertaken during December 1729. The letter was written in March 1730. The robbery was dealt with by the audiencia: AHQ, Crim., 25: exp. 5 January 1730.

While the letters he wrote to the Council of the Indies defined the image of Alcedo y Herrera in Madrid, his local reputation depended on the publicity and ceremonial nature of his acts. More than any other president before or after him, Alcedo y Herrera published his decisions by town criers, drums, and trumpets. He wrote to the other authorities of Quito, both local and ecclesiastical, announcing his decisions to them and explaining their rationale.[44] During his term in office, banishment and public executions were carefully staged. Contrary to past practice, Alcedo y Herrera did not permit convicts to travel alone to their destinations, nor did he allow them to be accompanied only by the local governor. Instead, he gathered the convicted individuals, and once their numbers justified a public act, he ordered a ceremony to be performed on the main square. Those sentenced to banishment left the square and exited the city together, accompanied by guardsmen purposefully recruited to that end. The convicts wore chains, handcuffs, shackles, and padlocks. The spectacle, which must have been impressive, remained fixed in the memory of witnesses.[45]

The execution of two money forgers was also carefully planned. The convicts were hung and later burned on the main square before public spectators. Alcedo y Herrera presided over the act in person and was in charge of its implementation. After the execution, the criminals' instruments (the die stamp and seal) were publicly destroyed. Alcedo y Herrera then published an order instructing all the inhabitants to present their coins for inspection. The scene communicated "a solemn horror and a great remedy" (*de grave terror y de mucho remedio*) to the audience, and witnesses agreed that in the aftermath of this affair nobody dared to falsify money.[46]

The execution of the infamous cattle rustler Esteban Durán, a spectacle planned by Alcedo y Herrera, also caught the attention of the public (chap. 6).[47] The president went in person to the prison and brought the convict to the main square "with great ceremony" (*con gran sol*). He then took off Durán's sword and handed him over to the magis-

44. His letters of 1729 and 1730 in AGI, EC, 911B.

45. Declarations of Joseph Guerrero y Peñalosa, of the Count of Selvaflorida, and of Eugenio Estrada y Ulloa, all in the residencia of Alcedo y Herrera, ibid., 39, 42–43, 121–22, 391, and 402.

46. Ibid. See also the declarations of Francisco Egas, Lorenzo Nates, Lorenzo Madriz, and Manuel Jerónimo de la Cerda, ibid., 80, 102, 106, and 151.

47. Declaration of de la Cerda, ibid., 151. We know that the person hung was Juan and not Esteban Durán.

trates of the audiencia. The magistrates substantiated the case and condemned Durán to death in the presence of the public. His execution was a "great example for the entire city" (*gran ejemplo a toda la ciudad*).

On all these occasions, there was a direct relationship between what was spectacular and what was recorded. Between 1730 and 1735 there were at least four other executions in Quito, yet none of them were worthy of public memory.[48] Clearly, it was the theatrics and the personal intervention of the president that were recalled, not the executions themselves. The same was true with regard to banishment. In total, the witnesses who evaluated the performance of Alcedo y Herrera mentioned the banishment of very few people, probably eight to ten individuals in seven years. Yet, in spite of the small number, and in spite of the fact that we know that other people were also similarly punished before and after the presidency of Alcedo y Herrera, witnesses in Quito were convinced that these proceedings were exceptional. They agreed that the president's actions, which they clearly remembered, diminished the "scandals and crimes" in both the city and the province.[49] They identified the local administration of justice with the person of Alcedo y Herrera, and they attributed to him all its activities. One witness even stated, "It has been seen and heard that after he left the government several people have walked about publicly asking for the canonization of the said señor on account of his happy, just, and peaceful government."[50]

Although carefully planned at times, the image of the justice administration or its individual officers was also a byproduct of their activities, and it reflected the people's familiarity with the judicial system as well as their expectations, hopes, and fears. People became familiar with the judicial system because they were employed in it as permanent, temporary, or casual agents. Information about the system could also be obtained by having been a victim or perpetrator of a crime or by observing the activities of judges and officers as a bystander. Rumors also contributed to what people knew, or imagined, concerning the

48. AHQ, Not. 6, 8: exp. 20 January 1734; and AGI, Quito, 133: letters of Alcedo y Herrera from 2 January 1736 and 31 March 1730.

49. Declarations of Joseph Suárez de Figueroa and Eugenio Estrada y Ulloa in the residencia of Alcedo y Herrera, AGI, EC, 911B, 154–55 and 121–22.

50. The original version reads: "Ha visto y oído que después que dejó el gobierno han andado varias personas pidiendo públicamente para la canonización de dicho señor en aplauso de su feliz, justificado y pacífico gobierno." Declaration of Suárez de Figueroa: ibid., 156. Only two witnesses complained against Alcedo y Herrera during his trial: ibid., 122 and 149.

administration of justice.[51] Rumors allowed the inhabitants of Quito to discuss the most recent crimes and to express their opinions about the proper punishment. Any information, or opinion, was interesting in this respect. Quiteños discussed the fact that several aldermen were exiled, that a dispute occurred between others, or that the provincial of the Santa Hermandad was imprisoned.[52] In 1730, the murder of Manuel Freire, a man "of very good character, poor and burdened with a wife, and eight young children," captured public attention.[53] The hour when it took place, the instrument of the crime, the identity of the perpetrator, and the judicial response were all public knowledge. Similarly, the death of Juan de Encalada did not fade quickly from public memory.[54] The witnesses in the residencia of President Lope Antonio Munive y Axpe remembered it and criticized the president for the way he proceeded. They reported (wrongly) that the guilty party was acquitted.[55]

Pieces of information concerning the justice administration were everywhere to be found. The presence of judicial officers, identified among other things by their clothing, indicated that something worth attention was happening.[56] The presence of the town crier (*pregonero público*) was just as significant. Most criers were professionals and well-known to the public, occupying the office for many years. Francisco Vicente, for example, held this office between 1668 and 1692, while Juan Pallo held it between 1725 and 1748. Criers proclaimed the coming of public punishments. They read edicts announcing the escape of and search for criminals, and they pronounced decisions proceeding from Quito, Lima, and Madrid.[57] Their announcements were highly ritual-

51. For comparison see R. Boyer, "People, Places and Gossip: The Flow of Information in Colonial Mexico," *La ciudad y el campo en la historia de México: Memoria de la VII reunión de historiadores mexicanos y norteamericanos* (Mexico, 1992), 143–50; and L. R. Corteguera, "The Painter Who Lost His Hat: Artisans and Justice in Early Modern Barcelona, " *Sixteenth Century Journal* 29/4 (1998): 1034–35.

52. AGI, Quito, 162: letter of the town council, 8 October 1705; AGI, EC, 911A, 40–43, 137–40, and 145–51; and AGI, EC, 911A, 98–103 and 111–14. See also AHQ, Crim., 16: exp. 5 August 1701; and AGI, EC, 1061B.

53. AHQ, Crim., 26: exp. 5 December 1730. See also AGI, EC, 1061B, 99, 101, and 104.

54. AHQ, Crim., 10: exp. 8 September 1685.

55. AGI, Quito, 72: residencia-visita of the president.

56. AHQ, Crim., 6: exp. 4 March 1678.

57. The description that follows is based on the study of many different announcement ceremonies. The announcement of residencias was studied by J. M. Mariluz Urquijo, *Ensayo sobre los juicios de residencia indianos* (Seville, 1952). Municipal criers were studied in Bayle, *Los cabildos seculares,* 274–77. See, for example, AHQ, Gob., 8: exp. 17 October 1687; AGI, Quito, 72: testimony of 15 April 1692; AGI, Quito, 123 and 130: letters of the audiencia from 23 July 1722 and 8 August 1726.

ized ceremonies that were supervised by court clerks.[58] Criers read or repeated texts that called the listeners to pay attention to them. Criers did so "in a clear and loud voice" in the presence of many people. Reading usually took place between ten and eleven in the morning, on Sundays.[59] During the seventeenth century, most announcements took place on the main square, especially near the audiencia and the town council building. By the end of the century, ceremonies were also performed in other parts of the city center, mainly the commercial streets.[60] By the mid–eighteenth century, announcements extended to the peripherical residential areas.[61] As the geographical area covered by the criers expanded over time, so did the ritual. Mid–seventeenth-century readings tended to be simple pronouncements of edicts. In 1684, the use of drums and trumpets to call the public to attention was recorded for the first time. The use of percussions became generalized thereafter, and from 1725 onward people referred to it as "publication in the mode of war" (*usanza de guerra*).[62] When Quito had a company of soldiers (1737 and 1748) (chap. 4), its members also participated in the spectacle, giving it an additional touch of importance.[63]

The activities of criers were slightly different in Indian villages belonging to the jurisdiction of Quito. In most cases, publication took place just before or after Sunday Mass. This assured the authorities that sufficient people would be present, and it allowed the government and the justice administration to enjoy the protection of the Church.[64] All residents of the village were called to gather, and contrary to what habitually happened in the capital, listeners in villages were expected to react immediately to the contents of the announcement by giving signs that they understood what they had heard. The reading or recitation of the text in Spanish was immediately followed by its translation into Quechua.

Public punishment was another means by which the inhabitants of

58. AGI, EC, 914A, 38–41: certification of Agustín Capilla of 8 March 1737.

59. AGI, EC, 910B, 15 (from 1679); and AGI, EC, 911A, 7 (from 1711).

60. AHQ, Gob., 8: publication of 23 April 1692; AGI, EC, 911B, 11: publication of 1 January 1725; and AGI, EC, 911B, 12: publication of 1 July 1737.

61. AGI, EC, 914B, 204–5: publications from 23 and 26 February 1737; and AHQ, Crim., 25: exp. 12 February 1748 from 3 January 1748.

62. AGI, EC, 910C, 52: from 24 September 1684; AGI, EC, 911B, 11: from 20 January 1725; and AHQ, Not. 6, 5: exp. 31 March 1728 from 13 November 1729.

63. AGI, EC, 914A, cuad. 1, 28–41: publication of 8 March 1737; and AHQ, Crim., 25: exp. 12 February 1748 publication of 3 January 1748.

64. AGI, EC, 910B, 15; AGI, EC, 911B, 270; and AGI, EC, 910C, 64–65 and 71–76: the residencias of the local governors Francisco de Figueroa, Diego Nava y Aguilar, and Iñigo de Aranguren y Aguirre, respectively. For a comparative view see Fogel, *Les cérémonies.*

Quito could obtain information about the administration of justice. Public punishment was relatively frequent and attracted the attention and assistance of many spectators. Punishments were carried out primarily on the main square and in the principal streets of the city. Ranging from execution to public display, these punishments were highly theatrical in nature. Executions began with the preparation of convicts in jail.[65] Convicts were separated from other inmates and were held incommunicado in the chapel in the company of various priests. After several days of reflection, they were led outside the prison in procession. Riding mules, with their hands and feet bound together and rope tied around their necks, the convicts were preceded by a town crier who announced their crimes. A number of ecclesiastics followed the convicts. The procession, which began on the main square, covered the "public and customary streets" before it returned to the square, where the execution took place. After the execution, the body of the convict was either buried or quartered and hung at the scene of the crime.[66]

Although less spectacular, whipping was the most common form of public punishment in Quito. Convicts sentenced to whipping were also publicly displayed in a procession and were preceded by a town crier who announced their crimes. Another public punishment was shaming (*pena de vergüenza*), which could take the form of a procession or the placement of the convict in a large collar on the main square.[67] In the latter case, convicts remained in the collar two to four hours during the morning, which was the busiest time of day. The collar was permanently left on the square as a reminder of the presence of justice as well as its might.[68] In

65. AHQ, Not. 6, 8: exp. 6 December 1734; and AHQ, Ced., 9 (1727–35), 227: letter of Alcedo y Herrera , 12 May 1734. Public executions were studied by D. Sueiro, *La pena de muerte, ceremonial, historia, procedimiento* (Madrid, 1974). For a comparative view see M. Foucault, *Surveiller et punir;* J .A. Sharpe, "Last Dying Speeches: Religion, Ideology and Public Execution in Seventeenth-Century England," *Past and Present* 107 (1985): 144–67; M. Bée, "Le spectacle de l'exécution dans la France d'Ancien Régime," *Annales ESC* 38 (1983): 843–59; L. Masur, *Rites of Execution: Capital Punishment and the Transformation of American Culture, 1776–1865* (New York, 1989); and P. Spierenburg, *The Spectacle of Suffering: Execution and the Evolution of Repression from a Pre-Industrial Metropolis to the European Experience* (Cambridge, 1984).

66. AHQ, Crim., 5: exp. 10 July 1674; and AHQ, Not. 6, 9: exp. 7 September 1735.

67. AHQ, Crim., 14: exp. 14 January 1697; AHQ, Crim., 21: exp. 11 May 1724; AHQ, Crim., 23: exp. 3 January 1727; and AHQ, Crim., 36: exp. 9 September 1748.

68. The use of permanent structures to remind viewers of judicial might was described in A. González Blanco, *Horcas y picotas en La Rioja* (La Rioja, 1984); and C. Bernaldo de Quirós, *La picota y figuras de delincuentes* (1907; reprint, Madrid, 1975).

extreme cases, the authorities had the heads of convicts shaved or their back or cheeks marked.[69]

Although publicity was important, so was secrecy, which was just as carefully planned, regimented, and staged. Like publicity, secrecy also contributed to the generation of images concerning the administration of justice.[70] Theoretically, the first part of all criminal cases (the sumaria) was secret. Also secret was the entire procedure when involving people of "quality." The acuerdo had a book in which the president annotated secret information.[71] This book was considered sufficiently important for people to quarrel over the right to have copies of its keys.[72] Royal legislation firmly ordered judges to keep their votes secret in hopes that secrecy would free them from social pressure and allow them to vote according to their conscience.[73] Secrecy guaranteed an appearance of consensus because decisions that were delivered by the audiencia or the town council were always publicly presented as unanimous, never mentioning the existence, or content, of a dissenting opinion.

The image of the justice administration that resulted from all these practices was clearly laid out in the residencias and visitas, which were judicial instances that allowed local inhabitants to express their opinions on judicial affairs. On these occasions, the criteria the inhabitants used were fairly simple. They reviewed the performance of judges and concluded that the failure to achieve peace, which they considered a realistic goal, necessarily pointed to negligence. If crimes continued, it was because criminals were not punished properly, because they were treated with too much compassion or because the justices refused to use

69. AHQ, Not. 6, 7: exp. 10 May 1731; and AHQ, Not. 6, 13: exp. 2 March 1743 from 25 January 1743. This subject was also studied by A. Redondo, "Mutilations et marques corporelles d'infamie dans la Castille du XVIe siecle," in *Le corps dans la société espagnole des XVIe et XVIIe siècles*, ed. A. Redondo (Paris, 1990): 185–99.

70. For a comparative view see L. Marin, "Logiques du secret," *Traverses* 30–31 (1984): 60–69.

71. AHQ, Crim., 8: exp. 26 June 1680; AGI, EC, 911B: residencia of Alcedo y Herrera—accounts of penalties; AHQ, Crim., 21: exp. 26 January 1723; and AHQ, Crim., 22: exp. 20 October 1724.

72. AMQ, LC, 00121: town council meetings of 6 December 1718 and 9 December 1718; and AHN, Cód., 702B, no. 399: cédula from 16 April 1703

73. AHQ, Ced., 4, no. 469: cédula from 15 February 1677; and AGI, EC, 914B, cuad. 5, 237. Also see AHN, Cód., 710B, no. 256: cédula of 25 August 1600; AHN, Cód., 705B, no. 45: letter from the king to the archbishop of Granada; and AHN, Cód., 752B, no. 1218: decree of 9 September 1669. Secrecy was also used in the councils of the court: "Ordenanzas de la Cámara de Indias de 1609," MS 2987, 241–45, BN; and AHN, Cód., 691B, no. 35: cédula from 9 September 1669.

exemplary punishment.[74] Criminals not only broke the law, they also acted with contempt for royal justice or without fear of it. To the social wrong inherent in each crime, which injured the victim but also the community and the king, were thus added the sins of (1) disrespect of legitimate authority and (2) the attack against the natural order of things. Because crime and sin were closely associated in this way, judges had to be harsh on those who did not respect the rules of cohabitation. This was a theoretical claim, but also one focused on efficacy. It was generally believed that in order to be effective, judges had to be feared. Judges who were feared were also judges who were respected and obeyed and who managed to reduce crime.

The fear of judges was not only actual: it was also ceremonially invoked by people who intimately knew the judicial system, such as lawyers or notaries. Juan Triunfo Sosaya, a lawyer of the audiencia and occasional lieutenant to the local governor, fled justice in 1680 after he became involved in a brawl.[75] Presenting himself to the authorities after the victim had already recuperated, he explained that because "truth suffers much doubt," and because he was afraid of prosecution, he preferred to disappear. Alejo Núñez Montesdoca, a court notary, decided to forge the power of attorney that he had been accused of losing in 1732 "because of his great distress and fear due to the gravity and circumspection of the court, and because he was involved in such a grave deed".[76] Repeat offenders who wished to terrorize their victims claimed that they belonged to the night patrol, and victims invoked the imminent arrival of justice in order to scare away their attackers.[77]

Judges answered that the expectation of eliminating all crimes was unrealistic. To the chronic lack of information and personnel was added the "extraordinary artifice and imagination with which criminals almost always made fun of the zeal of those who worked in a Christian manner to hinder the excesses of their licentious way of life."[78] Judges

74. AHQ, Crim., 6: exp. 19 December 1676; AHQ, Crim., 20: exp. 29 April 1722; AHQ, Not. 6, 17: exp. 10 September 1748; AHQ, Not. 3, 26: exp. 10 June 1746; AHQ, Not. 1, 28: exp. 12 May 1746; AHQ, Not. 3, 26: exp. 22 September 1747; and AHQ, Crim., 12: exp. 16 July 1691.

75. AHQ, Crim., 8: exp. 26 June 1680.

76. AHQ, Crim., 27: exp. 20 October 1732.

77. AHQ, Crim., 35: exp. 6 March 1748.

78. The original version reads: "Artificial e imaginación extraordinarias con que [los reos] casi siempre burlan del ferveroso conato de los que cristianamente andan a estorbar los excesos de su licenciosa vida." AGI, EC, 911C, 164–65: declaration of Francisco Ante y Mendoza.

were too easily accused of tolerating crime. No one appreciated the fact that they used paid informants and were constantly present in the streets of the city in an honest attempt to establish peace. No one knew that they also levied administrative fines, ordered different people to be (extrajudicially) lashed, or warned many others to correct their behavior. Crime and the image of crime were not one and the same. Crimes appeared more frequent and more menacing than they really were, and despite all complaints, Quito was a safe and well-ordered city: "Evil tongues . . . exaggerated the punishments which the criminals merited for their crimes, and as a result, in the proceedings [reviewing the activities of judges] instead of applauding the judges, witnesses criticize them."[79]

Along with the demand that judges act against criminals was the contradictory expectation that they would not intervene. The judicial system was at its best, witnesses asserted, when its sheer image was sufficient to prevent crime without the need for its actual intervention. Like a dormant giant whose presence reassured the public, judges were expected to intervene only on exceptional occasions when no other solution was possible. Parties to a conflict were supposed to reach a compromise without involving the authorities. People had to be tolerant of one another, and they had to work out their differences on their own.[80] Victims of crime were expected to tolerate continuous acts of aggression against them and were to attempt to stop them by different means before they were morally authorized to denounce the aggressor to the judges.[81] Those who requested the intervention of judges too quickly or too frequently earned a bad reputation. Many victims filed criminal complaints only after they abandoned the hope of reaching a negotiated solution. Wives denounced the long-term concubinage of their husbands when they refused to contribute to the dowry of their

79. The original version reads: "Exageran los castigos que por sus culpas merecen [los delincuentes] y de allí nace que en las pesquisas, sólo tenga lugar la queja sindicante al juez y no el aplauso que se merece." Ibid., 155.

80. AHQ, Crim., 4: exp. 27 September 1661; and AHQ, Not. 6, 15: exp. 2 March 1746. These issues were also treated in G. Haslip-Viera, *Crime and Punishment in Late Colonial Mexico, 1692–1810* (Alburquerque, 1999). For a comparative view see R. S. Shoemaker, *Prosecution and Punishment: Petty Crime and the Law in London and Rural Middlesex, c.1660–1725* (Cambridge, 1991), 316.

81. AHQ, Crim., 4: exp. 30 March 1662; AHQ, Not. 3, 26: exp. 10 June 1746; AHQ, Not. 3, 26: exp. 7 March 1747; AHQ, Crim., 5: exp. 17 March 1671; and AHQ, Crim., 6: exp. 19 December 1676. For a comparative view see Y. Castan, "Gestion du criminel et protectorat judiciaire dans la France d'ancien régime," *Estudis* 22 (1996): 53–54.

daughter.[82] Likewise, robberies were denounced only when the thieves, who promised to return the stolen goods, failed to do so.[83]

Solving crime without the help of the authorities was the obligation of both victims and perpetrators. It was also the moral duty of all other social members. This conclusion explains why spectators intervened at a crime scene to help victims (chap. 4). And it also explains why witnesses could legitimately assist delinquents in their attempts to escape justice. By giving this assistance, witnesses were not necessarily helping criminals avoid the social consequences of their acts. On the contrary, on many occasions their help was conditioned on the promise of the perpetrator to comply with his or her duty toward the victim. After the perpetrator did, or promised to, there was no longer a need to appeal to the authorities, and it was plausible, or at least permissible, to help the criminal escape.[84]

Only when these mechanisms of social control failed could the inhabitants of Quito request the help of judicial authorities. This often happened when the criminal was an outsider, beyond communal control. Judges were also called to intervene when the victim was hierarchically inferior to the aggressor and thus incapable of forcing the latter into compromise. Judges could intervene when the crime was far too scandalous or horrible to be solved inside the community. The judicial system could be called upon when its intervention was the most efficient method to receive satisfaction or when victims needed public recognition that a crime had been committed (i.e., when the stolen goods belonged to a third party who now claimed them from the victim or in cases of violation).[85] Formal complaints to judges could be motivated by the wish to coerce a rival into complying with his or her duties. Creditors pressured their debtors to pay their debts by threatening them with judicial action.[86] On occasion, those involved in lawsuits defended themselves by accusing their rivals of a criminal offense. This was particularly frequent in battery cases, where the complaint of one side usually produced the complaint of the other. In a similar way, husbands accused of assaulting their wives initiated criminal proceedings against

82. AHQ, Not. 26: exp. 7 March 1747.
83. AHQ, Not. 28: exp. 23 August 1748.
84. AHQ, Crim., 5: exp. 26 July 1671.
85. AHQ, Crim., 4: exp. 7 April 1659; AHQ, Crim., 15: exp. 3 January 1698; AHQ, Crim., 22: exp. 4 April 1726; and AHQ, Crim., 34: exp. 7 October 1747.
86. AHQ, Crim., 22: exp. 13 April 1726.

their spouses for adultery.[87] In all these cases, the initiation of formal criminal procedures was strategically motivated. The judges were called to intervene when it was convenient to the parties, and their presence was virtually ignored when other methods, which were considered more effective, could be adopted. In short, the initiation of criminal procedures was a possible, not a necessary, course of action. It often served to achieve goals other than the punishment of criminals.

Judges and judicial officials were often used as mediators.[88] In 1725, the local governor received a complaint that justified opening a criminal investigation.[89] However, convinced that the parties in the conflict (who were neighbors) did not truly desire a formal legal process, he decided to attempt reconciliation. After his initial effort failed, he performed a phony ceremony of confiscation of the property of the accused, which he hoped would compel the aggressor to come to an understanding with the victim and avoid scandal. It was only when this second attempt failed that he was obliged to initiate a formal judicial hearing.[90] In 1746, the protector of Indians requested the local governor to "use his superior authority" to reconcile the parties and unite them in friendly terms as an arbitrator and not a judge.[91] In 1723, in yet another case, the municipal ordinary justice initiated penal procedures against a woman accused of mistreating her neighbor. Although he elaborated the neces-

87. AHQ, Crim., 5: exp. 26 July 1671; AHQ, Crim., 23: exp. 7 June 1727; and AHQ, Not. 6, 18: exp. 20 August 1750.

88. B. Garnot, "L'ampleur et les limites de l'infrajudiciaire dans la France d'ancien régime," in *L'infrajudiciaire du moyen âge à l'époque contemporaine: Actes du colloque du Dijon, 5–6 octobre 1995*, ed. B. Garnot, 69–76 (Dijon, 1996); and idem, "Justice, infrajustice, parajustice et extrajustice dans la France d'ancien régime," *Crime, histoire, société* 4/1 (2000): 103–20. See also A. Merchán, *El arbitraje: Estudio histórico-jurídico* (Seville, 1981); J. Vallejo, "Amor de árbitros: Episodio de la sucesión de Per Afán de Ribera el viejo," *Fallstudien zur spanischen und portugiesischen Justiz 15. bis 20. jahrhundert*, ed. J. M. Scholz (Frankfurt, 1994), 212–69; T. A. Mantecón Movellán, "Desviación, disciplina social e intervenciones judiciales en el antiguo régimen," *Studia historica—historia moderna* 14 (1996): 223–43; idem, *Conflictualidad y disciplinamiento*, 278–83; and idem, "Meaning and Social Context of Crime in Preindustrial Times: Rural Society in the North of Spain, 17th and 18th Centuries," *Crime, histoire et sociétés* 2/1 (1998): 60, 65–68. For a comparative view see D. Oberwittler, "Crime and Authority in Eighteenth Century England: Law Enforcement on the Local Level," *Historical Social Research* 15/2 (1990): 2–34.

89. AHQ, Not. 1, 14: exp. 6 September 1725.

90. Presidents also acted in this way, for example, in AHQ, Crim., 10: exp. 4 June 1685; and AHQ, Crim., 24: exp. 10 November 1729.

91. AHQ, Not. 1, 28: exp. 23 November 1746. See also AHQ, Crim., 24: exp. 10 February 1729.

sary decrees, he also asked the constable to attempt reconciliation.[92] Unaware of the fact that such a reconciliation was indeed reached, the judge dictated a sentence. The parties appealed to the audiencia, requesting it to ignore the sentence given by the judge and give force to the extrajudicial resolution. The audiencia proceeded to examine whether both women freely reached the compromise or they were coerced to accept it. After it determined that the former was true, it adopted the compromise and annulled the decision of the judge.

The fear that parties to a conflict would be subjected to social and institutional pressure to renounce a formal legal action and consent to an extrajudicial arrangement was not unusual. In 1693, an Indian woman complained that two constables and the protector of Indians forced her to come to terms with the murderer of her husband.[93] Although the compensation she was offered was too small, not even covering the expenses of the funeral, the constables strongly suggested to her that she should be content with receiving at least some money, and they threatened "to cause her trouble" if she disagreed.

Judges who intervened in cases that were already settled by the parties justified their intervention by arguing that the compromise was not free. Rarely invoking a public interest that demanded protection, they pretended to accept extrajudicial arrangements as long as they truly satisfied the parties. However, their willingness to admit that victims truly pardoned their agressors diminished over time. This attitude, especially common in the eighteenth century (in about half of the cases the decision of the victim "to forgive" the aggressor was ignored by the judges), brought about changes in the wording of extrajudicial agreements. Thereafter, these arrangements were presented as voluntary, and victims went a long way to convince the authorities that they truly forgave the criminals. They explained that they wanted to die with a free conscience, that they were willing to reach a compromise because of the family ties that united them with the aggressors, or that they would reach a compromise because they lived in the same neighborhood.[94] The monetary arrangement, and in fact all other practical arrangements that were included in the act of "forgiving," were silenced, forgiveness almost always presented as both disinterested and free.

92. AHQ, Crim., 21: exp. 26 January 1723.

93. AHQ, Crim., 13: exp. 28 May 1693.

94. F. Tomás y Valiente, "El perdón de la parte ofendida en el derecho penal castellano," *Anuario de historia del derecho español* 21 (1961): 55–114.

It is impossible to estimate the frequency of extrajudicial arrangements in Quito. Many such arrangements were oral, and having been reached outside the courts, they left no written record. They were mentioned in the official documentation only when they ran into trouble or were ignored by the judges. Indeed, a failure or an unexpected complication was necessary in order for modern historians to learn about them.[95] When everything proceeded as planned, the agreement was not registered at all, or it appeared in notarial acts rather than in judicial documentation.[96] We do know, however, that extrajudicial compromises were especially frequent in cases of theft because victims agreed to withdraw their legal action after they received back the stolen goods.[97] Also frequent were extrajudicial arrangements in cases of violation, when marriage between the aggressor and the victim often silenced the affair.[98]

The judicial system was an essential component of the local order not only when it acted but also when it did not. The need to support a system that was at its best when it did not intervene brought about a great investment in ceremony. Yet, contrary to what was argued by Michel Foucualt, most ceremonies were not spectacular or menacing.[99] On the contrary, and as Michelle Fogel noted, their most important feature was their repetitiveness.[100] One such repetitive ceremony was the residencia, that is, the judicial inspection carried out at the end of the term of most royal officials.[101] According to most historians, these inspections were meant to guarantee the proper functioning of the administration.[102] However, they also consisted of repetitive rites,

95. AHQ, Crim., 6: exp. 19 December 1676; AHQ, Crim., 24: exp. 15 July 1729; and AHQ, Crim., 31: exp. 11 October 1742.

96. A. Soman, "L'infra-justice à Paris d'après les archives notariales," *Histoire, économie et société* 3 (1982): 369–75.

97. AHQ, Crim., 23: exp. 20 October 1727; and AHQ, Not. 3, 28: exp. 23 August 1748.

98. AHQ, Not. 3, 16: exp. 6 November 1732; AHQ, Not. 1, 19: exp. 22 March 1737; and AHQ, Not. 6, 15: exp. 11 February l746.

99. Foucault, *Surveiller et punir.*

100. Fogel, *Les cérémonies.*

101. These issues were treated in greater length in T. Herzog, *Ritos de control, prácticas de negociación: Pesquisas, visitas y residencias y las relaciones entre Quito y Madrid (1650–1750),* in *Nuevas Aportaciones a la historia jurídica de Iberoamérica,* ed. J. A. Gallego (Madrid, 2000), chap. 2, CD-ROM.

102. Mariluz Urquijo, *Ensayo sobre los juicios;* R. S. Chamberlain, "The Corregidor in Castille in the sixteenth Century and the Residencia as Applied to the Corregidor," *Hispanic American Historical Review* 23 (1943): 222–57; L. Zumalacarregui, "Visitas y residencias en el siglo XVI: Unos textos para su distinción," *Revista de Indias* 7 (1946): 917–21; L. García Valdeavellano, "Las Partidas y los orígenes medievales del juicio de residencia,"

marking, but also creating, a jurisdictional space that otherwise was hardly noticeable.

A residencia began when the judge (often a newly arrived mandatory) and the notary charged with its execution announced the commencement of the inspection by sending decrees to the villages of the jurisdiction (in the case of residencias of local mandatories) or the provincial capitals (in the case of magistrates, presidents, and crown attorneys). The decrees stated that a residencia would soon begin, and they encouraged the inhabitants to inform the judge about the proceedings of the inspected official. The judge of the residencia prepared a questionnaire and received declarations from people whom he selected or who presented themselves voluntarily in order to complain before him. The judge then presented an accusation (*cargos*) that the inspected official could contest (*descargos*) by supplying his own witnesses. The sentence dictated was approved by the audiencia in cases of local officials (i.e., the local governor and municipal judges) or by the Council of the Indies in all other cases.

Most judges commissioned to execute residencias were newly arrived mandatories, sent to replace the officials whom they inspected. This practice was illegal and indeed the Council of the Indies often wished for another solution.[103] However, the naming of successors continued, often transforming residencias into occasions of confrontation between new and enthusiastic officers and older and more experienced ones. Residencia judges reprimanded the officials for activities that were well received, or at least tolerated, locally.[104] They acted without sufficient familiarity with the local society and offended the sensibilities of many people on whom their success in office depended. Precisely because inspectors were to remain in the city and collaborate with at least some of the people whom they censured, or simply disregarded,

Boletín de la Real Academia de la Historia 153 (1963): 205–46; B. González Alonso, *El corregidor castellano (1348–1804)* (Madrid, 1970): 181–96; idem "El juicio de residencia en Castilla I: Origen y evolución hasta 1480," *Anuario de historia del derecho español* 48 (1978): 193–247; A. R. Caro Costas, *El juicio de residencia a los gobernadores de Puerto Rico en el siglo XVIII* (San Juan 1978); and M. Ponce, *El control de la gestión administrativa en el juicio de residencia al gobernador Manuel González Torres de Navarra*, 2 vols. (Caracas, 1985), 1: 33–390.

103. RI law 25, XV, 5; AHN, CSCI 20.686: consulta of 6 July 1758; AHN, CSCI 20.686: "Paper" of the Duke of Alba of 30 November 1760; and the discussion in AHN, CSCI 21.686: different documents of 1756–58.

104. AGI, EC, 910B: residencia of Francisco de Figueroa.

residencia judges occasionally hesitated in their proceedings. Not wanting to provoke a conflict that would hurt them, they performed a light inspection. They made formal accusations that included disobedience to rules of etiquette and to official duties but rarely touched upon criminal or immoral activities.

The need to maintain good relations with the local society thus led residencia judges to perform investigations that, above all, portrayed the administration of justice in Quito as a fairly successful enterprise. Although some problems were located and even corrected, all of them were minor. The conclusion was always the same: overall, the officials were good professionals, and the administration was in a good shape. Residencias of local administrators clearly demonstrate this point. Local governors were inspected along with other local administrators, such as the municipal judges, judges of the Santa Hermandad, notaries, procurators, constables, and jailers.[105] Witnesses who testified in these residencias usually portrayed the administration in an impersonal way. They pointed to its failure or success without necessarily identifying the people responsible for it—or, in contrast, they assumed that all officials were equally guilty. This enabled members of the local society to imag-

105. The following description is based on the study of residencias of local governors who functioned in the province of Quito from data currently available at AGI and AHQ. They include the residencias of Pedro Ortiz y Cevallos of Ibarra (AHQ, Resid., 1: exp. 4 September 1653); Luis de Torres Altamirano of Cuenca (AGI, EC, 910B: exp. of 1655); Francisco de Figueroa of Quito (AGI, EC, 910B: exp. of 1666); Manuel de la Torre y Verna of Guayaquil (AGI, EC, 958: exp. of 1674); Tomás Felix de Argandoña of Guayaquil (AHQ, Resid., 2: exp. 21 February 1680); Íñigo de Aranguren y Aguirre of Quito (AGI, EC, 910C: exp. of 1680); Alberto Fernández Montenegro of Otavalo (AHQ, Resid., 2: exp. 27 April 1683); Juan José de Saavedra Bustamante of Loja (AGI, EC, 910C: exp. of 1683); Martín de (Velasco) Araizú of Otavalo (AHQ, Resid., 2: exp. 14 July 1684, 23 December 1684, and 28 December 1684); Juan Bautista Bardasí of Loja (AGI, EC, 910B: exp. of 1692); Sebastián Manrique of Otavalo (AHQ, Resid., 3: exp. 19 July 1694); Alberto Fernández Montenegro of Latacunga (AHQ, Resid., 4: exp. 3 June 1705); Juan de Sosaya of Guayaquil (AHQ, Resid., 4: exp. 25 March 1706); Francisco Pareja of Cuenca (AGI, EC, 911A: exp. of 1723); Antonio de Aguirre of Cuenca (AHQ, Resid., 5: exp. 20 October 1722 and 3 November 1724); Juan Aumada of Guayaquil (AHQ, Resid., 6: exp. 11 December 1730); Ramón Juachín Maldonado y Sotomayor of Latacunga (AHQ, Resid., 6: exp. 25 October 1731); Juan de Ojeda y Escamilla of Jaén de Bracamoros (AHQ, Resid., 6: exp. 23 August 1732); Diego de Nava y Aguilar of Quito (AGI, EC, 911B: exp. of 1734); Juan-Joseph Sánchez de Orellana of Otavalo (AHQ, Resid., 6: exp. 15 December 1735); Francisco de Villasuso y Contera of Ríobamba (AHQ, Resid., 7: exp. 8 September 1737, 18 September 1737, 21 September 1737, and 12 December 1738); Carlos Prudencio de Guzmán of Jaén de Bracamoros (AHQ, Resid., 7: exp. 12 November 1739); Matías Dávila of Cuenca (AHQ, Resid., 8: exp. 20 December 1745); Juan Martín Pérez de Anda of Latacunga (AHQ, Resid., 8: exp. 26 February 1746); and Joseph de Clemente y Mora of Guayaquil (AGI, EC, 911B: exp. of 1753).

ine the administration as a durable machine that was independent of the individuals that incarnated it in a certain moment or in certain activities. As Ernst Kantorowicz argued for the king, the administration had two bodies: a corporeal and temporary one and a symbolic and permanent one.[106]

This portrayal of the administration distorted the inspections because it led to the elaboration of similar accusations against all mandatories. In the residencia of Francisco de Figueroa, for example, all aldermen were accused of not attending the meetings of the city council, all judges of the Santa Hermandad were blamed for not inspecting the countryside, and all curators of minors were charged with not attending to the duties of their office.[107] Of course, the persons cited in this way could prove that their practices were different. Yet, regardless of their individual responses, their luck was collective. Either they were all guilty or they were all innocent. Aldermen accused of not attending town council meetings and who had a royal order allowing them to do so were nevertheless fined in the same way as their colleagues who had no such permit. The same happened to aldermen who could not attend the meetings because they were ill.

The insistence on the collective rather than the individual nature of office was also evident when residencia witnesses spoke about the activities of collegial bodies such as the town council. They described these bodies as animated organs, with an agency and a will of their own. In the residencia of Íñigo de Aranguren y Aguirre, for example, the town council was accused of having elected relatives for the office of provincial and judge of the Santa Hermandad.[108] However, in the proceedings that followed, it became clear that not all aldermen were present in the session and not all of them voted in favor of this decision. Nevertheless, they were all equally censured.

Residencias thus created an image of an administration that was communal rather than individual. They maintained that this administration persisted over time. Successive residencias produced similar information and even identical accusations. Both Francisco de Figueroa (1660) and Íñigo de Aranguren y Aguirre (1680) were blamed for appointing a lieutenant who was native of the jurisdiction and for per-

106. E. H. Kantorowicz, *The King's Two Bodies: A Study in Medieval Political Theory* (Princeton, 1957).

107. AGI, EC, 910B.

108. AGI, EC, 910C, 15–16.

mitting illegal card games. They both responded in the same way and were both equally absolved. A similar case occurred with the judges of the Santa Hermandad in 1666 and 1684. Although it is possible that some problems persisted over time, it is also plausible that what persisted over time was their image, as well as the image of the administration.

The administration was thus collective and enduring. It was also a fairly modern institution, if judged by the types of offenses treated in residencias. Judges and officials were mostly accused of offenses such as not attending meetings, not being available, or not obeying the rules of etiquette. These accusations assumed that there was a fixed body of functions, routine meeting places, ordinary working hours, and clear work ethics. Nevertheless, none of this was true. We know that in Quito the division between officeholders and nonofficeholders was not obvious (chap. 4), meeting places were not always fixed (chap. 5), there were no clear work ethics (chap. 3) or working hours.

Perhaps the most important contribution of residencias was their insistence on the omnipresence of the administration. This insistence found expression primarily in the public announcements that marked their commencement. Each announcement was an act of communication between Madrid and the residents of Quito. It established that the king was present despite his absence, and it proclaimed his care for his vassals on the one hand and his control over royal officials on the other. This care differed according to whether the listeners were Spanish or Indian. In Spanish settlements, individuals were called to testify, and their opinions were valued according to their estate, stature, office, and character. In contrast, in Indian villages residencia judges recorded the voice of the Indians as a whole. This treatment of Indians as a community, and not as individual vassals, was clear from the first moment. The publication of the decrees announcing the residencia in Indian villages was usually followed by a demand to receive an immediate response. On many occasions, the people gathered indeed responded, collectively (and ceremonially) affirming that they had nothing to declare against the mandatory.[109] This affirmation was annotated on the decree, and it later served as evidence.

109. This happened, for example, in the villages of San Tomás de Mangasi and San Jerónimo de Pintaj on 22 and 26 May 1735 (AGI, EC, 911B: residencia of Diego de Nava y Aguilar, 270) and in the village of Xirón on 30 May 1728 (AGI, EC, 911A: residencia of Francisco Pareja, 51).

The treatment of Indians as communities rather than as individuals continued even in exceptional cases where particular Indians testified as witnesses. The examples I found are from the province of Quito, but they are nevertheless telling. Indian witnesses, whom a residencia judge in Guayaquil interviewed in the late 1740s, included the governors and six individuals from each one of the eight villages of the jurisdiction.[110] The judge recorded the opinions of the governors and then took the testimonies of the six individuals in a collective declaration, which they all signed. Although most of these individuals identified themselves as "Indios Ladinos," that is to say, as acculturated Indians who spoke Spanish, the judge insisted on their "Indianness," which was best exemplified by the use of Quechua and the mediation of translators. He even forced one of the witnesses, who protested that he did not speak Quechua but only Spanish, to use a translator.[111] A similar thing happened in the residencias of Juan José de Saavedra Bustamante (1683) and Juan Bautista Bardasí (1692), who were local governors of Loja.[112] On both these occasions, an Indio Ladino who lived in the city gathered and then interrogated several Indians. Among them were the Indian governor of the city, caciques of Indian migrant groups (*forasteros*) residing in the city, caciques of Indian villages, and two Indian natives of the jurisdiction. Although these witnesses were at least to some degree Hispanicized, they were compelled to act "as Indians." Once again, the judge insisted that they testify in Quechua despite their protests that they spoke Spanish. In addition, rather than responding to the general questionnaire, these witnesses were only asked about matters pertaining to Indians.

The decrees announcing the commencement of residencias and the activities that followed them thus defined a social space that included—and at the same time distinguished—Spaniards and Indians. The same decrees and activities also marked a geographical space. Inspectors attempted to guarantee that the publication ceremony would happen all over the jurisdiction on the same day, or at least the same week. This required organization, planning, and coordination that included the early elaboration of decrees, the use of many different emissaries, and so forth.

110. AGI, EC, 911B: residencia of Joseph de Clemente y Mora, 91–171.

111. Ibid., 122.

112. AGI, EC, 910C: residencia of Juan José Saavedra y Bustamante, 166–79, 220–41, and 352–500; and AGI, EC, 910B: residencia of Juan Bautista Bardasí, 101–10 and 134.

This effort of coordination was especially noteworthy in residencias of magistrates and presidents of the audiencia.[113] Despite the enormous territorial jurisdiction of the province, the bad state of the roads, and the poverty of communication networks, decrees announcing these residencias were sent all over the territory.[114] In some cases—such as the residencias of magistrates Diego Inclán Valdés and José de Laysequilla y Palacios y Aguilar and of President Dionisio Alcedo y Herrera—decrees were read everywhere (Quito, Jaén de Bracamoros, Cuenca, Otavalo, Ibarra, Chimbo, Ríobamba, Pasto, Quijos, Cali, Ambato, Latacunga, Loja, Zaruma, Puerto Viejo, Popayán, and Guayaquil) on the same day. This effort at integration gave all settlements belonging to the jurisdiction the same importance and reminded the listeners that they formed part of a larger unit.

Despite the wide diffusion of the decrees, most residencias were carried out only in the capital city. Residencias thus represented, above all, the vision of the capital and, within it, the opinion of a restricted group of people, usually about thirty men selected by the judge. This limited social and geographical coverage conflicted with the ceremonial effort to integrate the entire province and the entire population in the process.

Rather than simple inspections of particular officials (which indeed were far from being satisfactory, as many historians have observed in the past), residencias thus insisted on the routine activities that royal institutions were supposed to perform; duties that were not always realized in practice. They celebrated the collective, permanent, and embracive character of these institutions, and they presented them as modern, that is to say, as having clear rules. Residencias mainly cen-

113. The following description is based on the study of eleven residencias currently available in AGI and AHQ. They include the proceedings against Juan del Campo Godoy (magistrate,1648–53), AGI, EC, 910A; Diego Inclán Valdés (magistrate,1663–79), AGI, EC, 910B; Miguel Antonio Ormasa Ponce de León (magistrate,1679–87), AGI, EC, 910C; Lope Antonio de Munive y Axpe (president, 1678–89), AGI, EC, 910C; Francisco López Dicastillo y Azcona (president, 1703–6), AGI, Quito, 162; Tomás Fernández Pérez de Hodo (magistrate,1696–1718), AGI, EC 911A; Juan Ricaurte (magistrate,1689–1718 and again from 1722), AGI, EC, 911A, and AHQ, Resid., 5: exp. 14 April 1712; José de Laysequilla y Palacios y Aguilar (magistrate,1708–18), AGI, EC, 911B; Santiago Larrayn (president, 1715–18 and 1722–28), AGI, EC, 911B; Dionisio Alcedo y Herrera (president, 1728–36), AGI, EC, 911B; and Fernando Félix Sánchez de Orellana (president, 1745–53), AGI, EC, 911C, and AHQ, Resid., 9: exp. 20 December 1753.

114. The state of the roads is treated in greater length in T. Herzog, "La configuración histórica del espacio: caminos y correos en la Audiencia de Quito (siglos XVII y XVIII)," in *Actas del XI Congreso Internacional de Ahila (Liverpool, 17–22 de septiembre de 1996)* (Liverpool, 1998), 1: 413–27.

sored officials who failed to arrive at a compromise with local society or with local reality and/or who undermined the image of the administration as a collective, efficient, modern, and embracive enterprise. Magistrate Tomás Fernández Pérez de Hodo, for example, was accused of fomenting divisions within the court and of continuously acting in favor of friends and against enemies.[115] Although he was not the only person to do so (chap. 3), his activities in this respect were (apparently) unusual in their scope and in the degree of antagonism that they produced. The residencia of Fernández Pérez de Hodo thus reveals his failure to comply with the local code and his inability to accumulate sufficient friends among the people who were in a position to influence the results of the inspection. The case of President Juan Pío Montúfar y Fraso was similar.[116] Although accused of a number of misdeeds—such as contraband trade and marriage without license with a native of the jurisdiction—he was first and foremost censored for his social behavior. Most of his colleagues resented him, and a number of the local elites, to which he also belonged, felt directly threatened by his presence at the court. Convicted and fined, his residencia judge nevertheless expressed the conviction that Montúfar y Fraso was a "benign, and generous person, who loved the good order of the republic, and who spent much money favoring the poor and religious orders."[117]

The residencia of Montúfar y Fraso demonstrated that residencias were not meant to be truly inquisitive processes. Rather, they were designed to project a good image of the administration and lead to social cohesion. As mentioned in the preceding, the judge who censored the president, condemned and even fined him, also felt the need to redeem his image by assuring his readers that he was a good man and a good Christian. This compromise, which presented the tenure of Montúfar y Fraso as both a failure and a success, was the end result of a long confrontation between the judge and the heirs of the president, who accused the judge of willfully seeking to condemn their relative. As a future local governor of Canta (Perú) and an outsider (*forastero*), the judge, they said, had nothing to lose by behaving in this way. He did not care what would happen in the city after he left. He advised the president's enemies of the proceedings and tolerated their misbehavior.[118]

115. AGI, EC, 911A: residencia of Tomás Fernández Pérez de Hodo, 34–80 and 81–84.
116. AHN, CSCI, 20.260: residencia of Juan Pío Montúfar y Fraso, I, 248–59.
117. Ibid.: sentence of 21 October 1762, I, 351.
118. Ibid., I, 292.

Only interested in his personal advancement, the judge provoked severe tensions between the inhabitants of Quito. His actions, the heirs said, should not be tolerated because they were against the interests of the entire community. A good residencia pacified the jurisdiction; it did not send it into flames.

Because of this logic, it should not surprise us that most residencia judges approved of the actions of those they inspected either immediately or after receiving their declarations. They announced that they were "good, correct and uncorrupt (*bueno, recto y limpio*) judges, worthy of royal honors and grace." In cases of doubt, judges requested the opinion of the Council of the Indies, who reserved the right to decide the case.

Rather than a method to censor judges or to guarantee the correct administration of justice, residencias were, above all, a political and symbolic tool. In a world where personal confrontations dominated and where the actual penetration of the administration was not always guaranteed (or desired), and in a jurisdiction that was divided between Spaniards and Indians and between urban and rural settlements, residencias created the administration as it was expected to be. This administration (1) existed equally all over the territory, (2) was communal (3) persistent over time, (4) was socially responsible, and (5) was professionally controlled by the king. None of these factors, heralded in the residencias, had a clear existence in the outside world. Indeed, like the king's two bodies, the royal administration persisted and was good despite the changes in its personnel and despite the mistakes or inabilities of its individual members.

The role of the residencias in creating an almost mythical administration was perhaps best exemplified in residencias of viceroys.[119]

119. These conclusions are based on the study of declarations of witnesses from the province of Quito in four residencias, two proceeding from Peru and two from the viceroyalty of New Granada. They included the inspection against Melchor de Liñán y Cisneros (1678–81) in AGI, EC, 541B, 38–70; 541C—pieza 4, 205–52, 314–47, and 387–415, and 541C—pieza 5, 1–26, 27–47, and 143–171; Melchor de Navarra y Rocafull, Duke of la Plata (1681–89) in AGI, EC, 454B—pieza 7; Jorge Villalonga (1719–23) in AGI, EC, 799B—pieza 80, 801A—piezas 122 and 123, and 801C—pieza 152; and Sebastián de Eslava (1740–49) in AGI, EC, 808B—pieza 30, 809A—pieza 31, and 809B—piezas 60–67. The issue is discussed in greater length in T. Herzog, "La presencia ausente: El virrey desde la perspectiva de las élites locales (Audiencia de Quito, 1670–1747)," in *Monarquía, imperio y pueblos en la España moderna, Actas de la IV reunión científica de la Asociación Española de Historia Moderna, Alicante, 27–30 de mayo de 1996*, ed. Pablo Fernández Albadalejo (Alicante, 1997), 819–26.

Viceroys were ministers who replaced the king as his alter ego in areas such as the Americas, where the monarch's absence was continuous. Yet, from the perspective of the local elites of Quito who were asked to declare in residencias of viceroys between 1670 and 1750, these mandatories were just as absent. These elites were unable to supply details about the viceroy or his activities. What they knew was acquired by accident, such as having been in the same city as the viceroy or having traveled with him to America. Witnesses in Quito could not tell what the viceroy was like or how he discharged his duties. This feeling of remoteness, almost disinterest, was especially noteworthy during the periods when Quito belonged to the viceroyalty of New Granada (1718–22 and from 1739 onward). During this time the inhabitants of the province of Quito argued that as people who resided in a marginal area, distanced and disconnected from the center of the viceroyalty, they could not be expected to know anything relevant to the inspection.[120] This feeling was strongest in the south of the province, which was connected to Lima socially, economically, and politically and which most resented the subjection of Quito to New Granada.[121]

Despite these affirmations, none of the witnesses in Quito doubted that (1) the viceroy existed and (2) he was a good mandatory. As was the case with God or the king, no proof was needed. Faith was sufficient.

Conclusion

The administration of justice was a highly visible enterprise, and the inhabitants of Quito believed they had sufficient information to understand and judge its performance. Nevertheless, ideas regarding its success or failure could be manipulated. This was successfully done by President Dionisio Alcedo y Herrera, yet manipulation was also structured into most judicial demonstrations. These demonstrations ranged from public ceremonies to public punishments. They involved secrecy, ceremonies like public inspections of royal officials and a discourse invoking the fear of justice. The visibility of justice was also supported by rules of conduct, dress, and decorum, which carefully defined the

120. AGI, EC, 799B—pieza 80, 39–42; and AGI, EC, 801A—pieza 123, 49–51.
121. AGI, EC, 809B–piezas 65 and 66.

place of individuals inside (and outside) the system. Ceremony was never simply about ceremony. It was an affirmation of who people were, what their nature was, and how they related to the rest of society.

Justice was considered a latent mechanism. Its very existence, in itself somewhat mythical, was supposed to dissuade criminal activity. If this failed, criminal activity had to be resolved mainly by employing extrajudicial arrangements. Recourse to justice was legitimate only when communal efforts failed. This recourse, at any rate, was often dominated by considerations that had little to do with the wish to punish criminals. Instead, such recourse gave expression to, and also was influenced by, other interests.

These factors demonstrate that the early modern administration of justice was a system radically different from what we had once supposed. It was a system that made intentional efforts to appear present where it was absent, efficient when it was not. These efforts were not exceptional, nor were they necessarily linked to a fearful image. They were quotidian, ordinary, and continuous, and they invoked the need to achieve social peace and cohesion. Rather than the omnipresence of the king, the administration of justice in Quito confirmed the omnipresence of community and the preference of compromise over ruthless vindication.

CHAPTER EIGHT

Conclusion

The administration of justice in early modern Quito was an open system that had no clear boundaries with respect to society. It was never clear, or known, who was an officeholder and who was not. Judges obtained their nomination by merit (determined primarily by the services rendered by their family) and through their connections at the court in Madrid. Officers acted according to interests that were both "public" and "private." They felt bound by social obligations that determined how they should behave and what positions they should adopt. Their decisions reflected the limited knowledge they had (what the notaries, clerks, and court recorders chose to present to them), and it was conditioned by their social and familial obligations. This conditioning should not be read as a sign of corruption; rather, it was an inherent trait of a system that did not distinguish social or political from institutional spheres.

The placement of officers in society was not only personal but also ideological. Judges considered reputation as relevant to their work, and they attempted to transform rumors into facts when this suited their goals. The resolution of conflicts could follow judicial, governmental, or extrajudicial paths. Enforcement relied on informal public participation more than formal policing. Law, as applied in the courts of Quito, was centered on considerations of justice, and the Bible and Christian theology served as its most fundamental sources.

The willingness of the people to participate in and contribute to the establishment of peace was perhaps the best example of this penetration between justice and society. People who walked along the street felt sufficiently involved in their community to assist the victims of crimes or to risk physical well-being in order to prevent crime. These people not only helped their friends and neighbors but also intervened to favor people whom they did not know. They collaborated with one another, and with the administration, by handing over criminals or by supplying information or help that would lead to an arrest. The distribution of responsibility among so many people, some officially belonging to the justice administration and some not, demonstrates that the people of Quito did not consider justice to be a matter external to them or to be an issue that was the responsibility of a professional corps of officers.

Perhaps the most striking character of the administration was its absence: that is, it rarely intervened, and its intervention was considered exceptional by definition. Society, it was continuously argued, was self-regulatory. Peace could be guaranteed by the people, or through social mediators, without the intervention of the king. This implied that royal intervention was not only exceptional: it was also a sign of society's failure to control itself.

Sustaining a system that was at its best when it did not intervene required an investment in ceremony. However, ceremony was not necessarily spectacular, as Michel Foucualt has led us to believe. Most ceremonies were repetitive rather than extraordinary. Such repetitive ceremonies included inspections that demonstrated that the administration existed, was enduring, was modern, and functioned smoothly. Such ceremonies also included the quotidian work of officers dressed in a certain manner, of criers who published decisions, and of many other manifestations of order's presence—even omnipresence. Judicial buildings contributed to this effort. Although they hardly permitted any effective or quotidian administration, these buildings attested to the glory of justice and generated respect and admiration for judges, king, and God.

The penal justice was not a public enterprise. Rather, it was an enterprise "of the public." This character of the system was not only due to the survival of communal forms of control. Nor can it be interpreted as the simple consequence of material limitations as historians have tended to argue. Although both factors should be considered, it is important to emphasize that the structures, forms, and methods of justice never separated institutions from society. On the contrary, they continuously maintained a flow between different types of actions, different levels of activity, varying rationales, and multiple actors. As a result, the cases and verdicts we historians study may appear to us as "legal"—that is, they obey a certain procedure and are pronounced in the name of the king (chap. 1). However, close examination reveals that they were not completely or truly legal. As Simon Robert has noted, we should be "very cautious in forming views as to the nature of apparently court-like institutions, and in reaching conclusions about the purposes for which parties approach them."[1] In seventeenth- and eighteenth-century Quito, social considerations were more important than the rules of law, and justice primarily reproduced ceremonial and ritual requirements. Justice was never a vague moral idea or an abstract legal concept. It was translated and retranslated into concrete social realities.

These conclusions might be read as a denunciation of a particular situation, city, and time. However, this was not my intention. For, although they describe the legal structures of the past, these conclusions primarily seek to re-examine the work of historians. If we ignore present-day distinctions between private and public, if we assume difference, and if we are willing to ignore the modern divide between institutions and society, imaginary formal structures simply disappear. Such disappearances are not limited to Quito—they are attested everywhere in early modern Europe. Tomás Mantecón Movellán has argued that old regime discipline in Cantabria (Spain) was not a unilateral result of state imposition but rather a product of regulation also carried out on the level of domestic, family, and community units.[2] Benoît Garnot demonstrated that on most occasions the French settled their conflicts on their own, without the intervention of the authorities.[3] As was the case in Quito, French judges had to be just, not merely legal. They could make arbitrary decisions, yet their arbitrariness was structured. Judges were guided by customs, jurisprudence, and a value system that was receptive of public opinion. According to Richard J. Evans the early modern German state intervened only against deviants who could not be controlled within the community.[4] Evans reveals how the emergence of early modern judicial and penal institutions depended on implicit popular consent. Justice was not imposed by an absolutist state on a subjected people but was instead a multilayered, reciprocal, and negotiated system. In England, a number of scholars emphasize the use of law

1. S. Roberts, "The Study of Dispute: Anthropological Perspectives," *Disputes and Settlements. Law and Human Relations in the West,* ed. J. Bossy (Cambridge, 1983), 23.

2. T. A. Mantecón Movellán, *Conflictualidad y disciplinamiento,* 278–83; and idem, *La muerte de Antonia Isabel Sánchez. Tiranía y escándalo en una sociedad rural del norte español en el antiguo régimen* (Alcala de Henares, 1998), 14.

3. B. Garnot, *Crime et justice aux XVIIe et XVIIIe siècles* (Paris, 2000), 69–74, 100–104, 113–17, 121–29, 131–39, 183–94, and 186–87.

4. R. J. Evans, *Rituals of Retribution: Capital Punishment in Germany, 1600–1987* (London, 1996), 41–47 and 186–187.

by local communities.[5] They point out that many infractions were tolerated and that arbitration was very common. Sentences delivered by juries referred to the morality of the acts and the danger of criminals as much as to their legality. Courtrooms were sites of negotiations, not arenas of domination. The application of law was flexible and was a communal rather than a solitary act.

In many ways, we have reached the end of the Durkheimian road taken by Foucualt in the 1970s. We can no longer portray justice as a mechanism that enabled the growing intervention of the modern state. Nor can we claim that early modern justice was as exemplary and cruel as it was once attested or that this cruelty was necessary to disguise a practical inefficiency.[6] It is no longer possible to maintain that practices existing outside the state-run judicial system were deviant or popular. This said, we are still a long way from realizing that reading a division between early modern institutions and early modern society is a reflection of our own biases and is not necessarily the order of the past.

5. C. B. Herrup, *The Common Peace: Participation and the Criminal Law in Seventeenth-Century England* (Cambridge, 1987); idem, "Law and Morality in Seventeenth-Century England." *Past and Present* 106 (1985): 102–23; J. A. Sharpe, *Crime in Early Modern England;* J. H. Langbein, "Albion's Fatal Flaws," *Past and Present* 98 (1983): 113–14; and P. King, "Decision Makers and Decision Making in the English Criminal Law, 1750–1800," *Historical Journal* 27 (1984): 42–47.

6. Mantecón Movellán, *La muerte de Isabel,* 14; and R. Mowery Andrews, *Law, Magistracy, and Crime in Old Regime Paris, 1735–1789. The System of Criminal Justice* (Cambridge, 1994), 283.

Glossary

acuerdo	Plenary meeting of the **cabildo** or the **audiencia.**
alcabala	Sales tax.
alcalde de la Santa Hermandad	Judge of the **Santa Hermandad.**
alcalde ordinario	Ordinary municipal judge. A magistrate combining functions of mayor and judge.
alférez	Standard-bearer.
alguacil mayor	Chief constable. Officer charged with the execution of the orders of magistrates.
asesor letrado	Lawyer serving as a legal expert for judges who have no legal training.
asiento	Administrative and judicial center of a rural area.
audiencia	Royal court. High court of justice having some administrative functions. This term also refers to the territory under the jurisdiction of the court.
audiencia de relaciones	Similar to an **audiencia pública**. See chapter 1.
audiencia pública	Public hearing in the **audiencia.**
auto acordado	Decision voted on by a judicial or administrative body (**audiencia, cabildo,** etc.)
beneficio	Purchase of judicial office.
cabildo	Town council.
caja real	Royal treasury.
cargo	Accusation made against official in his **residencia** or **visita.**
causa de oficio	Penal case initiated by a judge or a **fiscal**
cédula	Edict or decree. A letter from the king containing a general law or a particular command.
ciudad	Town (in the legal sense of the term).

cojuez	Temporary judge.
Consejo de Indias	Royal council seated in Madrid charged with American affairs.
consulta	Opinion of a council formally submitted to the king in writing.
corregidor	Local governor also acting as a local judge.
corregimiento	Territory under the jurisdiction of a **corregidor.**
cuadrilla	Armed band.
descargos	Response to an accusation.
encomendero	Person in charge of an **encomienda**
encomienda	Profit drawn from the forced work of Native Americans in exchange for material and religious assistance.
escribanía	Workplace of an **escribano** or the office of one.
escribano	Public officer charged with the redaction of legal acts. A generic term used for notaries, secretaries, legal secretaries, and so forth.
escribano de cámara	Court notary. **Escribano** of the **audiencia** who acts as a secretary.
escribano de provincia	**Escribano** of the **juzgado de provincia.**
escribano público	Notary.
escribano receptor	See **receptor.**
escribiente	Employee charged with the physical writing of legal texts.
estado (estar en)	Status of a legal case when it is ready for the verdict.
excusa	Petition of an official not to take part in a specific legal process.
expediente	Legal file. Dossier.
fama	Renown or reputation
fiscal	Crown attorney. Representative of royal interests in an **audiencia** or a council.
futura	Right to exercise an office in the future.
gobernación	Term utilized in the eighteenth century for referring to a **gobierno.**
gobierno	District under the administration of a governor.

hidalgo	Gentry. Nobility.
juzgado de provincia	Section of the **audiencia** charged with reviewing civil demands proceeding from the province.
letrado	Person trained in law.
maestre de campo	Master of field.
mayorazgo	Entailed estate.
merced	Grant.
obraje	Textile mill. A clothing workshop.
oidor	Magistrate. Judge of the **audiencia.**
peso de-a-ocho	Local currency.
plaza mayor	Central town square.
pregón	Announcement by a town crier.
procurador	Procurator. A person charged with representing the parties in legal proceedings. Can also designate the representative of the interests of a body, such as the city council.
proprios	Property pertaining to a town.
protector de naturales	Magistrate of the **audiencia** charged with defending the interests of Indians.
provincial de la Santa Hermandad	Honorific title. In its origin, identical to the **alcalde de la Santa Hermandad.**
pulpería/pulpero	Food shop/owner of one.
real hacienda	Royal finances. The resources of the king, or the administration charged with their management.
receptor	Court clerk. An **escribano** of the **audiencia** charged with receiving evidence, testimonies, and petitions of the parties and collecting fines.
recogimiento	Women's prison. Also a place of reclusion for women at the request of their fathers or husbands.
recusación	Recusation. A demand that a certain person would not act as judge, expert, or notary because he is partial to the parties.
regidor	Alderman.
relator	Court recorder who renders accounts of the arguments and proofs in a legal proceeding.

residencia	Inspection. Judicial review of the activities of royal officials at the end of their terms in office.
ronda	Night patrol.
Santa Hermandad	Court charged with prosecuting crimes in uninhabited areas and on royal roads.
semanero/semanería	Magistrate "of the week." **Oidor** on guard.
Siete Partidas	Legal code of King Alfonso X of Castille (1252–84).
sumaria	Secret first phase of all criminal procedures. Similar to current-day pretrial investigation.
tacha	Complaint against the legal validity of a witness's testimony.
teniente	Lieutenant. Assistant to a **corregidor**.
togado	Literally man of the robe. A jurist judge.
vecino	Citizen. Person belonging to the local community.
visita	Inspection ordered by the king.
voz común	Rumor.

Bibliography

Archives and Libraries

Archivo de la Real Congregación de San Fermín de los Navarros (ARCSF), Madrid, sections: América, Arrendamientos, Cargos, Celebraciones, Congregantes, Constituciones, Contaduría, Edificios en que se hallaba la congregación y obras en ellos and venta de edificios, Inventarios (Obras de Arte, etc.).

Archivo General de Indias (AGI), Seville, sections: Escribanía de Cámara, Gobierno—Quito, Govierno-Lima, Indiferente General.

Archivo General del Palacio Real (AGPR), Madrid, section: Expedientes Personales.

Archivo Histórico de Protocolos de Madrid (AHPM), Madrid.

Archivo Histórico Nacional (AHN), Madrid, sections: Códices, Consejo de Indias (Consejos Suprimidos), Diversos.

Archivo Histórico Nacional (AHQ), Quito, sections: Autos Acordados, Cedulario, Criminales, Fondo Especial, Gobierno, Incorporación de Abogados, Matrimoniales, Milicias, Notarías 1 and 3–6 (juicios), Oficios, Pobreza, Prisiones, Reales provisiones y superiores ordenes, Real Hacienda, Rebeliones, Residencias, Testamentaría, Vínculos y mayorazgos.

Archivo Municipal (AMQ), Quito, Libros de Cabildo and sections: Cedularios, Miscelánea, Miscelánea—Museo de Historia de Quito.

Biblioteca de Jijón y Caamaño (BJC), Banco Central, Quito.

Biblioteca del Palacio Real (BPR), Madrid.

Biblioteca Nacional (BN), Madrid.

Manuscripts

"Apuntes de prácticas judiciales, vía ordinaria, ejecutivas y criminal . . . [18th c.]." MS 20.258(28). BN, Madrid.

Augustín de Riol, S. "Noticia general de todos los archivos y papeles pertenecientes a los consejos y audiencias de España, 1726." MS 5991. BN, Madrid.

Callejo y Urbino, F. V. "Apología legal de la verdad oprimida contra la calumnia exaltada . . . [1710]." MS 11391. BJC, Quito.

"Cartilla y examen de escribanos en que se contienen todo género de causas civiles y criminales, ordenanzas . . . que pueden servir para los que hablan de semejante asunto, . . . [n.d.]." MS 12.958(3). BN, Madrid.

Caxigal de la Vega, F. "Instrucciones para el trabajo en la secretaría del virreinato

de Nueva España que formó en México . . . [1760].” MS 2820, fol. 73. BPR, Madrid.
“Ceremonias y estilo de los tribunales del Reino de Navarra [18th c.?].” MS 9910. BN, Madrid.
Colón, M. “Disertaciones prácticas criminales en que con arreglo al derecho de España . . . [1778].” MS 2903. BN, Madrid.
“Consulta del Consejo de Castilla a Fernando IV sobre exceso de lujo y prágmatica de él motivada por la consulta.” MS 5563, BN, Madrid.
“Discurso con una breve idea de los estorbos que en la recta administración de justicia suelen poner los agentes subalternos de los tribunales [attributed to T. González, early 19th c.?].” MS 20.245(10). BN, Madrid.
“Discurso legal sobre la ley 1.9. de la visita que los del consejo y oidores . . . han de hacer de las cárceles [n.d.].” MS 2847, fols. 337–57. BPR, Madrid.
“Discurso sobre que los buenos ministros han de ser buscados y escogidos por más dignos que otros [1644].” MS 2848, fols. 1–26. BPR, Madrid.
“Disertación sobre la aplicación de la tortura a los reos [n.d.].” MS 2886, fol. 169. BPR, Madrid.
“Disertación sobre si las delaciones secretas son útiles o perjudiciales en una sociedad bien organizada [n.d.].” MS 2889, fol. 1. BPR, Madrid.
“Explicación teórica del rito y orden de proceder en los juicios [18th c.].” Misc. 001489. AMQ, Quito.
García de Samaniego, A. “Consultación jurídica en razón de la Real Pragmática sobre la reformación de los trajes . . . [1674].” MS 11396. BJC, Quito.
Gutiérrez, S. “Etiquetas generales que han de observar los criados de la casa de S.M. en el uso y ejercicio de sus oficios [1651].” MS 1041. BN, Madrid.
López, J.L. “Observaciones teo-políticas a ilustrar leyes recopiladas [1699].” MS 3013. BPR, Madrid.
“Memorial sobre el trabajo de relatores del Consejo de Castilla [n.d.].” MS 11.26(7). BN, Madrid.
Mora, P. “La ciencia vindicada escrita siendo abogado en favor de su profesión y contra los fulmanistas llamados comunalmente corbatas . . . [n.d.].” MS 11.038, fol. 79. BN, Madrid; MS 2828, fol. 295. BPR, Madrid.
Moriana, J. “Discursos penales y particulares del gobierno general y político del Consejo Supremo de Justicia de estos reinos de Castilla y León y ceremonial en él [1632].” MS 7467. BN, Madrid.
Moscoso y Córdoba, C. “Discurso en cuanto si es lícito a los reyes vender los oficios de la administración de justicia y qué sintió en esto Santo Tomás [n.d.].” MS 2843, fols. 32–53. BPR, Madrid.
“Notas sobre recusación de jueces [n.d.].” MS 13.297. BN, Madrid.
“Noticia de la Cámara de Indias [n.d.].” MS 2889, fol. 260. BPR, Madrid.
“Noticia del origen y principio del uso de las golillas en España . . . [n.d.].” MS 2850, fol. 241. BPR, Madrid.
“Ordenanzas de la Cámara de Indias de 1609.” MS 2987. BN, Madrid.
Peña, A. “Tratado de los juicios, jueces y orden de las penas criminales [16th c.].” MS 6379. BN, Madrid.

"Práctica de la Chancillería de Granada siglos XVII–XVIII [n.d.]." MS 309. BN, Madrid.
Rivera, D. "Primera parte de escrituras y orden de participación y de residencia judicial, civil y criminal con una instrucción a los escribanos del reino al principio y su arancel [1596]." MS 28.238. BN, Madrid.
Somoza, F. J. "La justicia vestida de todas sus autoridades . . . [n.d.]." MS 22.213. BN, Madrid.

Secondary Sources

La administración de justicia en la historia de España: Actas de las III jornadas de Castilla la Mancha sobre investigación en archivos, Guadalajarra, 11–14 noviembre 1997. Guadalajarra, 1999.
Aikin Araluce, S. *El recurso de apelación en el derecho castellano*. Madrid, 1982.
Alberto Garcés, C. *El cuerpo como texto: La problemática del castigo corporal en el siglo XVIII*. San Salvador de Jujuy, 1999.
Albi, F. *El corregidor en el municipio español bajo la monarquía absoluta*. Madrid, 1943.
Alcázar, B. *Crono-historia de la Compañía de Jesús en la provincia de Toledo y elogios de sus varones ilustres, fundadores, bienhechores, factores e hijos espirituales*. Madrid, 1710.
Alcedo Herrera, D. "Plano geográfico e hidrográfico del distrito de la real audiencia de Quito y descripciones de las provincias, gobiernos y corregimientos que se comprenden en su jurisdicción y las ciudades y villas, asientos y pueblos que ocupan sus territorios [signed Madrid, 30 May 1766]." In *Relaciones histórico-geográficas de la audiencia de Quito (siglo XVI–XIX)*, vol. 2, ed. P. Ponce Leiva, 418–65. Madrid, 1992.
Alessi Palazzolo, G. "Furto e pena: Aspetti del dibattito del tardo diritto comune." *Quaderni fiorentini* 2 (1973): 535–605.
Alonso Romero, M. P. *El proceso penal en Castilla (siglos XIII–XVIII)*. Salamanca, 1982.
———. "Aproximación al estudio de las penas pecunarias en Castilla (siglos XIII–XVIII)." *Anuario de historia del derecho español* 55 (1985): 9–94.
———. "El proceso penal en la Castilla Moderna," *Estudis* 22 (1996): 199–215.
Alonso Romero, M. P., and Hespanha, A. M. "Les peines dans les pays ibériques XVIIe–XIXe siècles." *Recueils de la société Jean Bodin* 3 (1989): 195–225.
Altamira y Crevea, R. *Manual de investigación de historia del derecho indiano*. Mexico, 1948.
Altolaguirre Duval, A. *Colección de documentos de Ultramar*. Madrid, 1930.
Alvarado Planas, J. "Del trifuncionalismo indoeuropeo y los tres estados: Derecho e ideología de las élites en la Edad Media española." *Anuario jurídico y económico escuriarense* 24 (1992): 393–490.
Álvarez, J. M. *Las instituciones de derecho real de Castilla y de Indias*. 1826. Reprint, Mexico, 1982.
Álvarez Alonso, C., "Tendencias en la investigación del derecho penal histórico: Los casos de Gran Bretaña, Francia e Italia como excusa." In *Sexo barroco y*

otras transgresiones premodernas, F. Tomás y Valiente, B. Clavero, A. M. Hespanha, J. L. Bermejo, E. Gacto, and C. Álvarez Alonso, 197–213. Madrid, 1990.

Álvarez-Coca González, M. J. "La concesión de hábitos de caballeros de las órdenes militares: Procedimiento y reflejo documental (siglos XVI–XIX)." *Cuadernos de historia moderna* 14 (1993): 277–97.

Amelang, J. "Barristers and Judges in Early Modern Barcelona: The Rise of a Legal Elite," *American Historical Review* 89 (1984): 1264–84.

Anda Aguirre, A. *Los marqueses de Solanda.* Quito, 1974.

Anderson, P. *Lineage of the Absolutist State.* London, 1974.

Andrien, K. J. "The Sale of Fiscal Offices and the Decline of Royal Authority in the Viceroyalty of Peru, 1633–1700." *Hispanic American Historical Review* 62 (1982): 49–71.

———. "Corruption, Inefficiency and Imperial Decline in the Seventeenth-Century Viceroyalty of Peru." *Americas* 41 (1984): 1–20.

———. "Economic Crisis, Taxes and the Quito Insurrection of 1765." *Past and Present* 129 (1990): 104–31.

———. "Corruption, Self Interest, and the Political Culture of Eighteenth-Century Quito." In *Virtue, Corruption and Self Interest. Political Values in the Eighteenth Century,* ed. R. K. Matthews, 270–96. Bethlehem, 1994.

———. *The Kingdom of Quito, 1690–1830: The State and Regional Development.* Cambridge, 1995.

Angeles, P. de los. *Compendio del orden judicial y práctica del tribunal de los religiosos en que se declara lo que deben hacer asi prelados como súbditos en causas criminales.* Madrid, 1643.

Arias, H. "La economía de la real audiencia de Quito y la crisis del siglo XVIII." In *Nueva historia del Ecuador,* vol. 4, *Epoca Colonia II,* ed. E. Ayala Mora, 187–229. Quito, 1983.

Arnold, L. J. "The Professionalization of the Bureaucracy in Late Colonial Mexico City." *New World* 1 (1986): 92–107.

Arron, S. M. "New Direction in Mexican Legal History." *Americas* 50/4 (1994): 461–65.

Asenjo Escudero, M. "Funcionamiento y organización de la Real Chancillería de Valladolid." *Hidalguía* 44 (1961): 397–647.

"Autos acordados de la Real Audiencia de Quito, 1578–1722." *Anuario histórico jurídico ecuatoriano* 2 (1971).

Autrand, F., ed. *Prosopographie et genèse de l'État moderne.* Paris, 1986.

Ávila Martel, A. *Aspectos del derecho penal indiano.* Buenos Aires, 1946.

Ayala Mora, E., ed. *Nueva historia del Ecuador.* Vol. 4, *Epoca Colonia II.* Quito, 1983.

———. *Resúmen de historia del Ecuador.* Quito, 1994.

Bacharach, S., and Lawler, E. J. *Power and Politics in Organizations.* San Francisco, 1980.

Baeza Martín, A. "La condena de españoles a obrajes en Nueva España en 1721: su secuela en la provisión de oficios de las audiencias indianas." *Anuario de estudios americanos* 57/2 (2000): 449–74.

Barbier, J. A. "Elite and Cadres in Bourbon Chile." *Hispanic American Historical Review* 52 (1972): 416–35.

———. *Reform and Politics in Bourbon Chile, 1755–1769*. Ottawa, 1980.

Barrientos García, A. *El tratado "De iustitia et jure" (1590) de Pedro de Aragón*. Salamanca, 1978.

Barrientos Grandón, J. *La cultura jurídica en el Reino de Chile: Bibliotecas de ministros de la real audiencia de Santiago (siglos XVII–XVIII)*. Santiago de Chile, 1992.

Bayle, C. *Los cabildos seculares en la América española*. Madrid, 1952.

———. "Vida social en la colonia según los libros de cabildo de Quito." *Arnahis* 11 (1968): 29–40.

Bazan Alarcón, A. "El tribunal de la acordada y la delincuencia en la Nueva España." *Historia Mexicana* 13 (1964): 317–46.

Bée, M. "Le spectacle de l'exécution dans la France d'Ancien Régime." *Annales ESC* 38 (1983): 843–59.

Beik, W. *Absolutism and Society in Seventeenth-Century France: State, Power, and Provincial Aristocracy in Languedoc*. Cambridge, 1985.

Benavides, C. *Les femmes délinquantes à Madrid: Justice et Société en Espagne au XVIIIe siècle*. Vol. 2. Toulouse, 2000.

Benavides Vega, C. "Sinópsis histórica del siglo XVII." In *Nueva historia del Ecuador*, vol. 4, *Epoca Colonia II*, ed. E. Ayala Mora, 105–37. Quito, 1983.

Beneyto Pérez, J. *Historia de la administración española e hispanoamericana*. Madrid, 1958.

Benveniste, H. "Le système des amendes pénales en France à la fin du moyen âge: Une première mise en perspective." *Revue historique de droit français et étranger* 70/1 (1992): 1–28.

Bermejo Cabrero, J. L. *Máximas, principios y símbolos políticos*. Madrid, 1986.

———. *Derecho y administración pública en la España del Antiguo Régimen*. Madrid, 1987.

Bernaldo de Quirós, C. *La picota y figuras de delincuentes*. 1907. Reprint, Madrid, 1975.

Bernal Gómez, B. "Un aspecto más del régimen carcelario novohispano: la visita de cárcel." In *Poder y presión fiscal en la América española (siglos XVI, XVII, XVIII): Actas del VI Congreso Internacional del Instituto de Historia del Derecho Indiano*, 255–79. Valladolid, 1986.

Bertrand, M. "L'état espagnol et ses officiers aux Indes: Le recrutement de la Cour des Comptes de Mexico (1680–1770)." *Mélanges de la Casa de Velázquez* 25 (1989): 119–220.

———. "Du bon usage des solidarités: Étude du facteur familial dans l'administration des finances de la Nouvelle Espagne, XVIIème–XVIIIème siècle." In *Les figures historiques de l'administrateur: Institutions, réseaux, pouvoirs en Espagne, en France et au Portugal, 16e–19e siècle*, ed. R. Descimon, J. F. Schaub, and B. Vincent, 43–58. Paris, 1997.

———. "La élite colonial en la Nueva España del siglo XVIII: un planteamiento en términos de redes socials." In *Beneméritos, aristócratas y empresarios:*

Identidades y estructuras sociales de las capas altas urbanas en América hispánica, ed. B. Schröter and C. Büschges, 35–51. Frankfurt, 1999.

———. "De la familia a la red de sociabilidad." *Revista mexicana de sociología* 61/2 (1999): 107–35.

———. *Grandeur et misère de l'office: Les officiers de finances de la Nouvelle-Espagne, XVIIe–XXVIIIe siècle*. Paris, 1999.

Blank, S. "Patron, Clients and Kin in Seventeenth-Century Caracas: A Methodological Essay in Colonial American Social History." *Hispanic American Historical Review* 54 (1979): 260–83.

Boissevain, J. *Friends of Friends. Networks, Manipulators and Coalitions*. Oxford, 1974.

Boltanski, L. *L'amour et la justice comme compétences: trois essais de sociologie de l'action*. Paris, 1990.

Bonnet, D. *El protector de naturales en la Audiencia de Quito siglos XVII–XVIII*. Quito, 1992.

Borah, W. *El Juzgado General de Indios en la Nueva España*. Mexico, 1985.

Borchart de Moreno, C. "Capital commercial y producción agrícola: Nueva España y la audiencia de Quito en el siglo XVIII." *Anuario de estudios americanos* 46 (1989): 131–72.

———. "Beyond the Obraje: Handicraft Production in Quito toward the End of the Colonial Period." *Americas* 21/1 (1995): 1–24.

Borchart de Moreno, C., and Moreno Yáñez, S. E. "La historia socioeconómica ecuatoriana del siglo XVIII. Análisis y tendencias." *Revista de Indias* 49 (1989): 379–409.

Bourdieu, P. "Sur le pouvoir symbolique." *Annales ESC* 32 (1977): 405–11.

———. "Le capital social: Notes provisoires." *Actes de la recherche en Sciences Sociales* 31 (1980): 2–3.

Boureau, A. "Les cérémonies royales françaises entre performance juridique et compétence liturgique." *Annales ESC* 46 (1991): 1253–64.

———. "Droit et théologie au XIIIe siècle" *Annales ESC* 47 (1992): 1113–25.

Boyer, R. "People, Places and Gossip: The Flow of Information in Colonial Mexico." In *La ciudad y el campo en la historia de México: Memoria de la VII reunión de historiadores mexicanos y norteamericanos*, 143–50. Mexico, 1992.

Brackett, J. K. *Criminal Justice and Crime in Late Renaissance Florence, 1537–1609*. Cambridge, 1992.

Braudel, F. "Unité et diversité des sciences de l'homme." In *Ecrits sur l'histoire*, 85–96. Paris, 1969.

Bravo Lira, B. "Vigencia de las partidas en Chile." *Revista de estudios histórico jurídicos* 10 (1985): 43–105.

———. "Símbolos de la función judicial en el Derecho Indiano." In *Poder y presión fiscal en la América española (siglos XVI, XVII, XVIII): Actas del VI congreso del instituto internacional de historia del Derecho Indiano*, 235–54. Valladolid, 1986.

———. "La noción del estado en la recopilación de 1680." In *La recopilación de leyes de los reinos de las Indias: Estudios históricos-jurídicos*, ed. J. Icaza Dafur, 145–60. Mexico, 1987.

Brennot, A. M. *Pouvoir et profits au Pérou colonial au XVIIIe siècle: Gouverneurs, clientèles et ventes forcées.* Paris, 1989.

Brewer, J. "Law and Disorder in Stuart and Hanoverian England." *History Today* 30 (1980): 18–27.

Brines Tyrer, R. *Historia demográfica y económica de la Audiencia de Quito: Población indígena e industria textil, 1600–1800.* Quito, 1988.

Bromley, R. D. F. "Urban Growth and Decline in the Central Sierra of Ecuador, 1698–1940." Ph.D. diss., University of Wales, 1977.

Bromley, R. J. "El comercio precolonial y la transición a un sistema de mercando colonial en la audiencia de Quito." *Revista ecuatoriana de historia económica* 1 (1987): 41–58.

Bronner, F. "Church, Crown and Commerce in Seventeenth-Century Lima: A Synoptic Interpretation." *Jahrbuch für geschichte von staat wirtschaft und gesellschaft lateinamerikas* 29 (1992): 75–89.

Brunner, O. *Land and Lordship. Structures of Governance in Medieval Austria.* Trans. J. Kaminsky and J. Von Horn Melton. Philadelphia, 1992; originally published in German in 1939.

Burkholder, M. A. "From Creole to Peninsular: The Transformation of the Audiencia of Lima." *Hispanic American Historical Review* 52 (1972): 395–415.

———. *Biographical Dictionary of Councilors of the Indies, 1717–1808.* New York, 1986.

———. "Honest Judges Leave Destitute Heirs: The Price of Integrity in Eighteenth Century Spain." In *Virtue, Corruption and Self Interest. Political Values in the Eighteenth Century,* ed. R. K. Matthews, 247–69. Bethlehem, 1994.

Burkholder, M. A., and Chandler, D. S. "Creole Appointment and the Sale of Audiencia Positions in the Spanish Empire under the Early Bourbons, 1701–1750." *Journal of Latin American Studies* 4 (1972): 187–206.

———. *De la impotencia a la autoridad. La corona española y las audiencias en América, 1687–1808.* Mexico, 1977.

———. *Biographical Dictionary of Audiencia Ministers in the Americas, 1687–1821.* Westpoint, CT, 1982.

Burns, R. I., ed. *Las siete partidas.* Trans. S. P. Scott, 5 vols. Philadelphia, 2001.

Büschges, C. "Crisis y reestructuración: La industria textil de la real audiencia de Quito al final del período colonial." *Anuario de estudios americanos* 53/2 (1995): 75–98.

———. " 'Las leyes del honor': Honor y estratificación social en el distrito de la audiencia de Quito (siglo XVIII)." *Revista de Indias* 52/209 (1997): 55–84.

Calvo, T. "Les réalités du pouvoir aux confins de l'empire: Le cas de la Nouvelle Galice au XVIIe siècle." In *Les élites locales et l'état dans l'Espagne moderne du XVIe au XIX siècle: Table ronde internationale (Talence 13–15 décembre 1990),* ed. M. Lambert-Gorges, 145–64. Paris, 1993.

Cameron, I. A. *Crime and Repression in the Auvergne and the Guyenne, 1720–1790.* Cambridge, 1981.

Campanella, T. *La monarquía hispánica.* 1620. Reprint, Madrid, 1982.

Campbell, L. G. "A Colonial Establishment: Creole Domination of the *Audiencia*

of Lima during the Late Eighteenth Century." *Hispanic American Historical Review* 52 (1972): 1–25.
Carboni, A. "La notorietà del delitto nelle riforme eclesiastiche medioevali." Parts 1 and 2. *Studi sassaresi* 27 (1957): 5–55; 28 (1959): 49–99.
Caro Baroja, J. "Honor and Shame: A Historical Account of Several Conflicts." In *Honour and Shame: The Values of Mediterranean Society,* ed J. G. Peristany, 81–137. London, 1965.
———. *La hora Navarra del XVIII (personas, familias, negocios e ideas).* Navarre, 1969. Reprint, 1985.
Caro Costas, A. R. *El juicio de residencia a los gobernadores de Puerto Rico en el siglo XVIII.* San Juan, 1978.
Carpintero, F. "En torno al método de los juristas medievales," *Anuario de historia del derecho español* 52 (1982): 617–26.
Carrancá y Rivas, R. "Las penas y las leyes de Indias." In *Recopilación de Leyes de los Reinos de las Indias: Estudios histórico jurídicos,* ed. F. Icaza Dafur, 433–49. Mexico, 1985.
Casado Fernández, F. "El tribunal de la Acordada de Nueva España." *Anuario de estudios americanos* 7 (1950): 279–323.
Castan, N. "Crime and Justice in Languedoc: The Critical Years (1750–1790)." *Criminal Justice History* 1 (1980): 175–84.
———. *Les criminels de Languedoc: Les exigences d'ordre et les voies du ressentiment dans une société pré-révolutionnaire, 1750–1790.* Toulouse, 1980.
Castan, Y. "Mentalités rurale et urbaine à la fin de l'Ancien Régime dans le ressort du parlement de Toulouse d'après les sacs à procès criminels, 1730–1790." In *Crimes et criminalité en France 17e–18e siècles,* ed. A. Abbiateci, F. Billacois, Y. Castan, P. Petrovitch, Y. Bongert, and N. Castan. *Cahiers des Annales* 33 (1971): 109–80.
———. *Honnêteté et relations sociales en Languedoc, 1715–1780.* Paris, 1974.
———. "Gestion du criminel et protectorat judiciaire dans la France d'ancien régime." *Estudis* 22 (1996): 53–69.
Castañeda, C. E. "The Corregidor in Spanish Colonial Administration." *Hispanic American Historical Review* 9 (1929): 446–70.
Castellano Castellano, J. L., and I. Gómez González. "Reflexiones sobre la justicia en el antiguo régimen a propósito de unas cartas a Villena." *Chronica nova* 22 (1995): 11–28.
Céspedes del Castillo, G. "La visita como institución indiana." *Anuario de estudios americanos* 3 (1946): 984–1025.
Chabod, F. "Was There a Renaissance State?" In *The Development of the Modern State,* ed. H. Lubasz, 26–42. New York, 1964.
Chamberlain, R. S. "The Corregidor in Castille in the Sixteenth Century and the Residencia as Applied to the Corregidor." *Hispanic American Historical Review* 23 (1943): 222–57.
Chauchadis, C. *Honneur, morale et société dans l'Espagne de Philippe II.* Paris, 1984.
———. *La loi du duel: Le code du point d'honneur dans l'Espagne des XVIe–XVIIe siècles.* Toulouse, 1997.

Chevalier, L. *Classes laborieuses et classes dangereuses*. Paris, 1978.
Chittolini, G. "The 'Private,' the 'Public,' the State." In *The Origins of the State in Italy, 1300–1600*, ed. J. Kirshner, 34–61. Chicago, 1996.
Cicala, M. *Descripción histórico topográfica de la provincia de Quito de la Compañía de Jesús*. 1770. Reprint, Quito, 1994.
Civil, P. "Corps, vêtement et société: Le costume aristocratique espagnol dans la deuxième moitié du XVIe siècle." In *Le corps dans la société espagnole des XVIe et XVIIe siècles*, ed. A. Redondo, 307–19. Paris, 1990.
Clavero, B. "Institución política y derecho: acerca del concepto historiográfico de 'estado moderno.'" *Revista de estudios políticos* 19 (1981): 43–57.
———. "*Hispanus fiscus, persona ficta:* Concepción del sujeto político en el ius commune moderno." *Quaderni fiorentini* 11–12 (1982–83): 95–167.
———. "Del pensamiento jurídico en el estudio de la historia." *Cuaderni fiorentini* 13 (1984): 561–77.
———. *Antidora: Antropología católica de la economía moderna*. Milan, 1991.
Clayton, L. A. *Los astilleros de Guayaquil colonial*. Guayaquil, 1978.
Cockburn, J. S. *Crime in England, 1500–1800*. London, 1977.
———. "Trial by the Book? Fact and Theory in the Criminal Process, 1558–1625." In *The Legal Records and the Historian*, ed. J. H. Baker, 60–79. London, 1978.
Cohen, S. *Visiones de control social. Delitos, castigos y clasificaciones*. Barcelona, 1988.
———. *Folk Devils and Moral Panics: The Creation of the Mods and Rockers*. Oxford, 1972. Reprint, 1990.
Colmenares, G. "Factores de la vida política colonial. El Nuevo Reino de Granada en el siglo XVIII (1713–1740)." In *Manual de historia de Colombia*, vol. 1, ed. J. Jaramillo Uribe, 386–415. Bogota, 1989.
Congrès National des Sociétés Savantes. *La tact, la répression et le pardon: Philologie et histoire jusqu'à 1610. 107 Congrès National des Sociétés Savantes*. Brest, 1982.
Congreso del Instituto Internacional de Historia del Derecho Indiano. *Ordenanzas de la Real Audiencia de Quito: V Congreso del Instituto Internacional de Historia del Derecho Indiano*. Quito-Guayaquil, 1978.
Copete, M. L. "Criminalidad y espacio carcelario en una cárcel del Antiguo Régimen: La cárcel real de Sevilla a fines del siglo XVI." *Historia social* 6 (1990): 105–25.
Cornblit, O. *Power and Violence in the Colonial City: Oruro from the Mining Renaissance to the Rebellion of Tupac Amaru (1740–1782)*. Trans. E. Ladd Glick. Cambridge, 1995.
Coronas González, S. M. "La recusación judicial en el derecho histórico español." *Anuario de historia del derecho español* 52 (1982): 511–615.
Corral García, E. *El escribano de consejo en la Corona de Castilla (siglos XVI al XVII)*. With an introduction by J. M. Pérez Prendes y Muñoz de Arraco. Burgos, 1987.
Corteguera, L. R. "The Painter Who Lost His Hat: Artisans and Justice in Early Modern Barcelona." *Sixteenth Century Journal* 29/4 (1998): 1023–42.

Corvalán Meléndez, J., and Castillo Fernández, V. *Derecho procesal indiano.* Santiago, Chile, 1951.

Costa, J. *Gobierno del ciudadano.* Ed. A. Ubach Medina, 245–395. 1575. Reprint, Zaragoza, 1998.

Costales, P., and Costales, A. *Nos la plebe.* Quito, 1986.

Cotterrel, R. *The Sociology of Law. An Introduction.* London, 1984.

Crozier, M. *Le phénomène bureaucratique: Essai sur les tendances bureaucratiques des systèmes d'organisations modernes et sur leurs relations en France avec le système social et culturel.* Paris, 1963.

Crozier, M., and Friedberg, E. *L'acteur et le système.* Paris, 1977.

Cunningham, C. H. *The Audiencia in the Spanish Colonies as Illustrated by the Audiencia of Manila.* New York, 1971.

Cushner, N. P. *Farm and Factory: The Jesuits and the Development of Agrarian Capitalism in Colonial Quito, 1600–1767.* Albany, 1982.

Cust, R. "News and Politics in Early Seventeenth-Century England." *Past and Present* 112 (1986): 60–90.

Cutter, C. "Community and the Law in Northern New Spain." *Americas* 50/4 (1994): 467–80.

———. *The Legal Culture of Northern New Spain, 1700–1810.* Albuquerque, 1995.

Dabhoiwala, F. "The Construction of Honor, Reputation and Status in Late Seventeenth- and Eighteenth-Century England." *Transactions of the Royal Historical Society* 6 (1996): 201–13.

Dalla Corte, G. "La red social frente a la crisis del orden colonial: Compensación judicial y vínculos de parentesco entre Buenos Aires y Cataluña." *Colonial Latin American Historical Review* 9/3 (2000): 347–77.

———. *Vida i mort d'una aventura al Riu de La Plata, Jaime Alsina i Verjés, 1770–1836.* Barcelona, 2000.

Dammert Bellido, J. "Soluciones inmediatas: Notas de derecho indiano." *Revista española de derecho canónico* 32 (1976): 111–22.

Davis, J. "The London Garoting Panic of 1862: A Moral Panic and the Creation of a Criminal Class in Mid-Victorian England." In *Crime and the Law: The Social History of Crime in Western Europe since 1500*, ed. V. A. C. Gatrrel, B. Lenman, and G. Parker, 190–213. London, 1980.

Daza Palacios, S., and Prieto Corbalán, M. R. *Proceso criminal contra fray Pablo de San Benito de San Lúcar de Barrameda (1774): Clérigo homocida en el siglo XVIII.* Seville, 1998.

D'Cruze, S. "The Middling Sort in Eighteenth Century Colchester: Independence, Social Relations and the Community Broker." In *The Middling Sort of People: Culture, Society and Politics in England, 1550–1800*, ed. J. Barry and C. Brooks, 181–207. New York, 1994.

De Benedictis, A. "Stato, comunità, dimensione guiridica: una riflessione su recenti dibattiti." *Società e storia* 40 (1988): 379–93.

Debuyst, C. *Dangerosité et justice pénale. Ambigüité d'une pratique.* Geneva, 1981.

Dedieu, J. P. *L'administration de la foi: L'inquisition de Tolède (XV–XVIIIe siècle)*. Madrid, 1989.

———. "Procès et interactions: L'analyse des relations interpersonnelles dans les groupes restreints à partir des documents judiciaires." In *Solidarités et sociabilités en Espagne (XVI–XXe siècles): Annales de l'Université de Besançon*, ed. R. Carrasco, 119–39. Besançon, 1991.

———. "Une approche 'fine' à la prosopography." In *Les figures historiques de l'administrateur: Institutions, réseaux, pouvoirs en Espagne, en France et au Portugal, 16e–19e siècle*, ed. R. Descimon, J. F. Schaub, and B. Vincent, 235–42. Paris, 1997.

———. "Procesos y redes: La historia de las instituciones administrativas de la época moderna, hoy." In *La pluma, la mitra y la espada: Estudios de historia institucional en la edad moderna*, ed. J. L. Castellano, J. P. Dedieu, and M. V. López Cordón, 13–30. Madrid, 2000.

Dedieu, J. P., and Windler, C. "La familia: ¿Una clave para entender la historia política? El ejemplo de la España moderna." *Studia historica—historia moderna* 18 (1998): 201–33.

De Dios, S. "Sobre la génesis y los carácteres del estado absolutista en Castilla." *Studia histórica-historia moderna* 3/3 (1985): 11–46.

———. "El estado moderno, un cadáver historiográfico?" In *Realidad e imagenes del poder: España a fines de la edad media*, ed. A. Rucquoi, 389–408. Valladolid, 1988.

Deler, J. P. *Ecuador: Del espacio al estado nacional*. Quito, 1987.

Dibble, K. "The Organization of Traditional Authority: English County Government, 1558–1640." In *Handbook on Organizations*, ed. J. G. March, 879–909. Chicago, 1965.

Dolan, C. "Entre les familles et l'état: Les procureurs et la procedure au XVIe siècle, " *Journal of the Canadian Historical Association* 10 (1999): 19–36.

Domengue, L., and Risco, A. *L'alcalde et le malandrin: Justice et société en Espagne au XVIIIe siècle*. Vol. 1. Toulouse, 2001.

Domínguez Ortiz, A. "La venta de cargos y oficios públicos en Castilla y sus consecuencias económicas y sociales." *Anuario de historia económica y social* 3 (1970): 105–37.

———. *Sociedad y estado en el siglo XVIII español*. Barcelona, 1976.

Domínguez Zoila, G. "Delito y sociedad en el Nuevo Reino de Granada período virreinal, 1740–1810." *Universitas Humanistica* 8/9 (1974–75): 281–398.

Doppagne, A. "La expresión de la cortesía." In *Actas del III congreso internacional de hispanistas*, 285–91. Mexico, 1970.

Durand, B. "La détermination de la peine chez les criminalistes catalans du XVIe au XVIIIe siècle: Logique juridique ou effet de mentalités?" *Recueil de mémoires et travaux* 15 (1991): 1–25.

Durand, Y., ed. *Clientèles et fidélités en Europe à l'époque moderne. Hommage à Roland Mousnier*. Paris, 1981.

Dyson, K. H. F. *The State Tradition in Western Europe: A Study of an Idea and Institution*. New York, 1980.

Eisenstadt, S. N. *The Political System of Empires*. London, 1963.
———. *Essays on Comparative Institutions*. New York, 1965.
Eisenstadt, S. N., and Roniger, L. "Patron-Client Relations as a Model of Structuring Social Exchange." *Comparative Studies in Society and History* 22 (1980): 42–77.
Eisenstadt, S. N., and Shachar, A. *Culture and Urbanization*. Beverly Hills, CA, 1987.
Elias, N. *La société de la cour*. Paris, 1969. Reprint, 1985.
Elliott, J. H. "España y América en los siglos XVI y XVII." In *Historia de América Latina*, vol. 2, *America Colonia*, ed. L . Bethell, 3–44. Barcelona, 1990.
———. "A Europe of Composite Monarchies." *Past and Present* 137 (1992): 48–71.
Enríquez, E. B. *Quito a través de los siglos*. Quito, 1938.
Ertman, T. *Birth of the Leviathan: Building States and Regimes in Medieval and Early Modern Europe*. Cambridge, 1997.
Escudero, J. A. "Un 'proyecto de estado' en el siglo XVI y la cuestión indiana." In *Administración y estado en le España moderna*, ed. J. A. Escudero, 591–96. Valladolid, 1991.
Estrada Icaza, J. *El puerto de Guayaquil*. Guayaquil, 1972.
Etzioni, A. "Organizational Control Structure." In *Handbook on Organizations*, ed. J. G. March, 650–72. Chicago, 1965.
———. "Organizational Dimensions and Their Interrelationships: A Theory of Compliance." In *People, Groups and Organizations*, ed. B. P. Indik and F. K. Benien, 94–109. New York, 1968.
Eugenios Martín, T. *La santa hermandad vieja de Talavera: Una institución tradicional de vigilancia y justicia en despoblado*. Toledo, 1992.
Evans, R. J. *Rituals of Retribution: Capital Punishment in Germany, 1600–1987*. London, 1996.
Fasano Guarini, E. "'État modern' et anciens états italiens: Éléments d'histoire comparée." *Revue d'histoire moderne et contemporaine* 45/1 (1998): 15–41.
Fernández Albaladejo, P. "Imperio y administración bajo Carlos V: una reevaluación." In *Hernán Cortés y su tiempo: Actas del congreso Hernán Cortés y su tiempo*, vol. 2, 520–27. Mérida, 1987.
———. *Fragmentos de monarquía: Trabajos de historia política*. Madrid, 1992.
———. "Les traditions nationales d'historiographie de l'état: l'Espagne." In *Visions sur le développement des états européens: théories et historiographies de l'état Moderne*, ed. W. Blockmans and J. P. Genet, 219–33. Rome, 1993.
Fernández Martínez, M. *La alcabala en la audiencia de Quito, 1765–1810*. Cuenca-Seville, 1984.
Fernández Santamaría, J. A. *The State, War and Peace: Spanish Political Thought in the Renaissance (1519–1559)*. Cambridge, 1977.
Fiorelli, P. *La tortura guidiziaria nel diritto commune*. Milan, 1953.
Flinchpaugh, S. G. "Economic Aspects of the Viceregal Entrance to Mexico City." *Americas* 52/3 (1996): 345–65.

Flory, T. *El juez de paz y el jurado en el Brasil imperial.* 1981. Reprint, Mexico, 1986.

Fogel, M. "Modèle d'Etat et modèle social de dépenses: Les lois somptuaires en France de 1485 à 1660." In *Prélèvement et redistribution dans la genèse de l'État moderne: Actes du colloque, 1984.* Fontevrault, 1987.

———. *Les cérémonies de l'information dans la France du XVIe au XVIII siècle.* Paris, 1989.

Foucault, M. *Surveiller et punir: naissance de la prison.* Paris, 1975.

Friedrich, C. J. "Corruption Concepts in Historical Perspective." In *Political Corruption: A Handbook,* ed. A. J. Heidenheimer, 15–24. New York, 1990.

Frye, D. "Telling Histories: A Late Colonial Encounter of 'Spanish' and 'Indian' in Rural Mexico and in the Archives." *Colonial Latin American Review* 3/1–2 (1994): 115–38.

Gacto, E. "Aproximación a la historia del derecho penal español." In *Hispania entre derechos propios y derechos nacionales: Atti dell'incontro di studio Firenze-Lucca, 25–27 de mayo 1989,* vol. 1, ed. B. Clavero, P. Grossi, and F. Tomás y Valiente, 501–30. Milan, 1990.

Gálvez Montero, J. F. "La Real Audiencia y su configuración en el virreinato." *Boletín del Instituto Riva Agüero* 17 (1990): 325–46.

Gangotena y Jijón, C. "Cómo era la sala de la Real Audiencia de Quito." *Revista del Museo Histórico* (1945–46): 72–74.

Garapon, A. "Justice rituelle el justice bureaucratique," *Annales de Vaucresson* 29 (1988): 103–15.

Garcés, J. A., ed. *Libros de cabildo de la ciudad de Quito, 1638–1646.* Quito, 1960.

García Gallo, A. "Jueces populares y jueces técnicos en la historia del derecho español." In *Justicia municipal y sus aspectos históricos y científicos: Ciclo de conferencias,* 57–61. Madrid, 1946.

———. "Alcaldes mayores y corregidores en Indias." In *Memoria del I congreso venezolano de historia,* vol. 1, 247–310. Caracas, 1972.

———. *Estudios de historia del derecho indiano.* Madrid, 1972.

García Marín, J. M. *La burocracia castellana bajo los Austrias.* Seville, 1976.

———. "El dilema ciencia-experiencia en la selección del oficial público de la España de los Austrias." In *Actas del IV symposium de historia de la administración,* 261–80. Madrid, 1983.

———. "Magia e inquisición. Derecho penal y proceso inquisitorial, siglo XVII." In *Perfiles jurídicos de la Inquisición Española,* 205–79. Madrid, 1989.

———. *Monarquía católica en Italia. Burocracia imperial y privilegios constitucionales.* Madrid, 1992.

———. *Teoría política y gobierno en la Monarquía Hispánica.* Madrid, 1998.

García Pelayo, M. *Del mito y de la razón en la historia del pensamiento político.* Madrid, 1968.

García Valdeavellano, L. "Las Partidas y los orígenes medievales del juicio de residencia." *Boletín de la Real Academia de la Historia*153 (1963): 205–46.

Garnot, B. "Une illusion historiographique: justice et criminalité au XVIIIe siècle." *Revue historique* 570 (1989): 361–80.

———. "La législation de la répression des crimes dans la France moderne (XVIe–XVIIIe siècle)." *Revue historique* 593 (1995): 75–90.

———. "L'ampleur et les limites de l'infrajudiciaire dans la France d'ancien régime." In *L'infrajudiciaire du moyen âge à l'époque contemporaine: Actes du colloque du Dijon, 5–6 octobre 1995*, ed. B. Garnot, 69–76. Dijon, 1996.

———. *Crime et justice aux XVIIe et XVIIIe siècles*. Paris, 2000.

———. "Justice, infrajustice, parajustice et extrajustice dans la France d'ancien régime." *Crime, histoire, société* 4/1 (2000): 103–20.

———, ed. *Histoire et criminalité de l'Antiquité au XXe siècle. Nouvelles approches*. Dijon, 1992.

Garriga, C. "La expansión de la visita castellana a Indias: presupuestos, alcance y significado." In *Actas y Estudios: XI Congreso del Instituto Internacional de Historia del Derecho Indiano. Buenos Aires, 4 a 9 de septiembre de 1995*, 51–79. Buenos Aires, 1997.

Gatrell V. A. C., Lenman, B., and Parker, G., eds. *Crime and the Law: The Social History of Crime in Western Europe since 1500*. London, 1980.

Gautheron, M., ed. *L'honneur. Image de soi ou don de soi: Un idéal équivoque*. Paris, 1991.

Genet, J. P. "Introduction: Which State Rises?" *Historical Research* 65/157 (1992): 119–33.

———, ed. *L'État moderne. Genèse. Bilans et perspectives: Actes du colloque tenu au CNRS (Paris, 19–20 Septembre 1989)*. Paris, 1990.

Gerardo Suárez, S. *Los fiscales indianos: Orígen y evolución del ministerio público*. Caracas, 1995.

Ghisalberti, C. "La teoría del notorio nel diritto commune." *Annali di storia del diritto* 1 (1957): 403–51.

Gibert y Sánchez de la Vega, R. "El funcionario español en la época austríaca." In *Actas del I symposium de historia de la administración*, 257–91. Madrid, 1970.

Gibson, C. *Spain in America*. New York, 1966.

Giesey, R. E. *Cérémonial et puissance souveraine: France XVe–XVIIe siècles*. Paris, 1987.

Gil-Bermejo García, J. "La casa de contratación de Sevilla (algunos apsectos de su historia)." *Anuario de estudios americanos* 30 (1973): 679–761.

Gilmore, D., ed. *Honor and Shame and the Unity of the Mediterranean*. Washington, D.C., 1987.

Gil Pujol, J. "Culturas políticas y clases dirigentes regionales en la formación del estado moderno: Un balance y varias cuestiones." In *Les élites locales et l'état dans l'Espagne moderne du XVIe au XIX siècle: Table ronde internationale (Talence, 13–15 décembre 1990)*, ed. M. Lambert-Gorges, 171–92. Paris, 1993.

Giraud, F. "Viol et société coloniale: Le cas de la Nouvelle Espagne au XVIIIe siècle." *Annales ESC* 41 (1986): 625–37.

Gómez, N. *La misión geodésica y la cultura de Quito*. Quito, 1987.

Gómez González, I. "La visualización de la justicia en el antiguo régimen: El ejemplo de la chancillería de Granada." *Hispania* 53/2 (1998): 559–74.

Gómez Vozmediano, M. F. "Una corte rural de justicia: la santa hermandad vieja de Almodóvar del campo." *Cuadernos de historia moderna* 22 (1998): 107–35.
Góngora, M. *El estado en el Derecho Indiano: Época de fundación, 1492–1570.* Santiago, Chile, 1951.
———. "Urban Social Stratification in Colonial Chile." *Hispanic American Historical Review* 55 (1975): 421–48.
González Alonso, B. *El corregidor castellano (1348–1804).* Madrid, 1970.
———. "El juicio de residencia en Castilla I: Origen y evolución hasta 1480." *Anuario de historia del derecho español* 48 (1978): 193–247.
———. *Sobre el estado y la administración de la Corona de Castilla en el Antiguo Régimen: Las comunidades de Castilla y otros estudios.* Madrid, 1981.
González Blanco, A. *Horcas y picotas en La Rioja.* La Rioja, 1984.
González Cruz, D. *Escribanos y notarios en Huelva durante el Antiguo Régimen (1700–1801).* Huelva, 1991.
González Jiménez, M. "Corrupciones municipales en Castilla a finales de la edad media." In *Instituciones y corrupción en la historia,* ed. M. González Jiménez, H. Pietschmann, F. Comín, and J. Perez, 7–30. Valladolid, 1998.
González Muñoz, V. *Cabildo y groups de poder en Yucatán (siglo XVII).* Seville, 1994.
González Suárez, F. *Historia general de la República del Ecuador.* 1890–1903. Reprint, Quito, 1970.
Greene, J. P. *Peripheries and Center: Constitutional Development in the Extended Polities of the British Empire and the United States, 1607–1788.* Athens, GA, 1986.
———. "Negotiated Authorities: The Problem of Governance in the Extended Polities of the Early Modern Atlantic World." In *Negotiated Authorities: Essays in the Colonial Political and Constitutional History,* ed. J. P. Greene, 1–24. Charlottesville, 1994.
Greengrass, M. "Conquest and Coalescence." In *Conquest and Coalescence: The Shaping of the State in Early Modern Europe,* ed. M. Greengrass, 1–24. London, 1991.
Gudmundson, L. "Aspectos socioeconómicos del delito en Costa Rica, 1725–1850." *Revista de historia* 3 (1977): 101–48.
Guerrero Mayllo, A. *Familia y vida cotidiana de una élite de poder: Los regidores madrileños en tiempos de Felipe II.* Madrid, 1993.
Guery, A. "L 'historien, la crise et l'état." *Annales ESC* 52/2 (1997): 233–56.
Guillamon Álvarez, F. J. "El concepto de la honra legal durante el reinado de Carlos III." *Cuadernos de historia* 9 (1978): 457–91.
Guillaume Alonso, A. *Una institución del antiguo régimen: la santa hermandad vieja de Talavera la Reina (siglos XVI y XVII).* Talavera, 1995.
Hamerly, M. *Historia social y económica de la antigua provincia de Guayaquil, 1763–1842.* Guayaquil, 1973.
———. *El comercio del cacao en Guayaquil durante el período colonial: Un estudio cuantitativo.* Quito, 1976.
Hampe Martínez, T. "Los funcionarios de la monarquía española en América:

Notas para su caracterización política, económica y social." *Histórica* 16 (1992): 89–118.
Hanson, E. "Torture and Truth in Renaissance England." *Representations* 34 (1991): 53–84.
Haslip-Viera, G. *Crime and Punishment in Late Colonial Mexico, 1692–1810*. Albuquerque, 1999.
Hay, D. "War, Death and Theft in the Eighteenth Century: The Records of the English Courts." *Past and Present* 95 (1982): 117–60.
Hay, D., Linebaugh, P., Rule, J. G., Tompson, E. P., and Witislow, C., ed. *Albion's Fatal Tree: Crime and Society in Eighteenth-Century England*. London, 1975.
Heidenheimer, A. J., ed. *Political Corruption: A Handbook*. New York, 1990.
Heras Santos, J. L. "Indultos concedidos por la Cámara de Castilla en tiempos de los Austria." *Studia histórica* 1 (1983): 115–41.
———. "Los galeotas de los Austrias, la penalidad al servicio de la armada." *Historia social* 6 (1990): 127–40.
———. *La justicia penal de los Austrias en la corona de Castilla*. Salamanca, 1991.
Herman, A. L. "The Language of Fidelity in Early Modern France." *Journal of Modern History* 67 (1995): 1–24.
Hernández, M. "¿Y después de las ventas de oficio qué? (Transmisiones privadas de regimientos en el Madrid moderno, 1606–1808)." *Anuario de historia del derecho español* 65 (1995): 705–48.
Herrera Puga, P. *Sociedad y delincuencia en el siglo de oro*. Granada, 1971.
Herrero García, M. *Ideas de los españoles del siglo XVII*. Madrid, 1966.
Herrero Herrero, C. *La justicia penal española en la crisis del poder absoluto*. Madrid, 1989.
Herrup, C. B. "Law and Morality in Seventeenth-Century England." *Past and Present* 106 (1985): 102–23.
———. *The Common Peace: Participation and the Criminal Law in Seventeenth-Century England*. Cambridge, 1987.
Herzog, T. "The Recopilación de Indias and Its Discourse: The Spanish Monarchy, the Indies and the Seventeenth Century." *Ius commune* 20 (1993): 143–63.
———. "¿Letrado o teólogo? Sobre el oficio de Justicia a mediados del siglo XVIII." In *Fallstudien zur spanischen und portugiesischen Justiz 16.–20. Jahrhundert*, ed. J. M. Scholz, 697–714. Frankfurt, 1994.
———. "Centro, periferia e integración política: el eje Quito-Madrid (siglo XVIII)." *Interpretatio: Revista de historia del derecho* 3 (1995): 139–48.
———. *Los ministros de la audiencia de Quito (1650–1750)*. Quito, 1995.
———. "El rescate de una fuente histórica: Los libros de visita de cárcel (el caso de Quito, 1738–1750)." *Anuario de estudios americanos* 52/2 (1995): 251–61.
———. "Sobre Justicia, honor y grado militar en la Audiencia de Quito durante el siglo XVIII." *Procesos* 6/2 (1995): 49–57.
———. "Sobre la cultura jurídica en la América colonial (siglos XVI–XVIII)." *Anuario de historia del derecho español* 65 (1995): 903–12.
———. "De la autoridad al poder: Quito, los Larrea y la herencia inmaterial (sig-

los XVII y XVIII)." In *Emigración y redes sociales de vascos en América,* ed. R. Escobedo Mansilla, A. de Zaballa Reascoechea, and O. Álvarez Gila, 373–83. Vitoria, 1996.

———. "La empresa administrativa y el capital social: los Sánchez de Orellana (Quito, siglo XVIII)." In *Sociedad, administración y poder en el siglo XVIII. Hacia una nueva historia institucional,* ed. J. L. Castellano, 381–96. Granada, 1996.

———. *Mediación, archivos y ejercicio: los escribanos de Quito (siglos XVII–XVIII).* Frankfurt, 1996.

———. "Las reformas borbónicas a escala humana: la extinción y el restablecimiento de la Audiencia de Quito, 1718–1721." *E.I.A.L.* 7/2 (1996): 133–45.

———. "Identidades colectivas, fronteras comunitarias y derecho: La domiciliación de mujeres de oidores quiteños durante el siglo XVII." *Anuario de historia del derecho español* 67/2 (1997): 1423–31.

———. "La presencia ausente: El virrey desde la perspectiva de las élites locales (Audiencia de Quito, 1670–1747)." In *Monarquía, imperio y pueblos en la España moderna, Actas de la IV reunión científica de la Asociación Española de Historia Moderna, Alicante, 27–30 de mayo de 1996,* ed. P. Fernández Albadalejo, 819–26. Alicante, 1997.

———. "Reglas jurídicas e integración social: el comercio (Quito, primera mitad del siglo XVIII)." In *Actas del XI congreso del Instituto Internacional de Historia del Derecho Indiano, Buenos Aires, 4–9 de septiembre de 1995,* 379–96. Buenos Aires, 1997.

———. "La configuración histórica del espacio: caminos y correos en la Audiencia de Quito (siglos XVII y XVIII)." In *Actas del XI congreso internacional de Ahila (Liverpool 17–22 de septiembre de 1996),* vol. 1, 413–27. Liverpool, 1998.

———. "De la historia y el mito: Las rebeliones de Quito (1592–1765)." *Reflejos* 7 (1998): 72–80.

———. "Private Organizations as Global Networks in Early Modern Spain and Spanish America." In *The Collective and the Public in Latin America: Cultural Identities and Political Order,* ed. L. Roniger and T. Herzog, 117–33. Brighton, 2000.

———. "Redes personales y capitales institucionales: la real hacienda y el cabildo de Quito a mediados del siglo XVIII." *Fronteras* 4/4 (2000): 113–26.

———. *Ritos de control, prácticas de negociación: Pesquisas, visitas y residencias y las relaciones entre Quito y Madrid (1650–1750).* In *Nuevas Aportaciones a la historia jurídica de Iberoamérica,* ed. J. A. Gallego [CD-ROM]. Madrid, 2000.

Hespanha, A. M. "A historiografia juridico-institucional e 'a morte do estado.'" *Anuario de filosofia del derecho,* n.s. 3 (1986):191–227.

———. "Une nouvelle histoire du droit?" In *Storia sociale e dimensione giuridica. Istrumenti d'indagine e ipotesi di lavoro. Atti dell'incontro di studio Firenze, 16–27 Abril 1985,* ed. P. Grossi, 315–40. Milan, 1986.

———. *A história do direito na história social.* Lisbon, 1987.

———. *Vísperas del leviatán: Instituciones y poder político (Portugal, siglo XVII).* Madrid, 1989.

———. "Justiça e administração entre o antigo regime e a revolução." In *Hispania entre derechos propios y derechos nacionales: Atti dell'incontro di studio Firenze-Lucca, 25–27 de mayo 1989*, vol. 1, ed. B. Clavero, P. Grossi, and F. Tomás y Valiente, 135–204. Milan, 1990.

———. "L'étude prosopographique des juristes: Entre les 'pratiques' et leurs 'représentations.'" In *El tercer poder. Hacia una comprensión histórica de la justicia contemporánea en España*, ed. J. M. Scholz, 93–101. Frankfurt, 1992.

———. *Poder e instituições no antigo regime: Guia de estudo*. Lisbon, 1992.

———. "La economía de la gracia." In *La gracia del derecho: Economía de la cultura en la edad moderna*, 151–76. Madrid, 1993.

———. "Da iustitia a disciplina: Texto, poder e politica no antiguo regime." In *Estudios em homenagem ao Prof. Pouter Eduardo Correia*, 3–98. Coimbra, 1986. Spanish translation in *La gracia del derecho: Economía de la cultura en la edad moderna*, 203–73. Madrid, 1993.

———. "Sabios e rusticos. A violência doce da razão juridica." Parts 1 and 2. *Crítica de ciencias sociais* 25 (1988): 31–60; 26 (1988): 3–98. Spanish translation in *La gracia del derecho: Economía de la cultura en la edad moderna*, 17–60. Madrid, 1993.

Hickson, D. J., Hinnings, C. R., Lee, C. A., Schneck, R. E., and Pennings, J. M. "A Strategic Contingencies' Theory of Intraorganizational Power." *Administrative Science Quarterly* 16 (1971): 216–28.

Hilaire, J. "'Supplier le roi': Les voies de recours extraordinaires aux XIIIe et XIV siècles." *Revue historique de droit français et étranger* 74/1 (1998): 73–81.

Hintze, O. "Esencia y transformación del estado moderno." In *Historia de las formas políticas*. 1931. Reprint, Madrid, 1968.

———. "The Formation of States and Constitutional Development: A Study in History and Politics." In *The Historical Essays of Otto Hintze*, ed. F. Gilbert and assisted by R. M. Berdahl, 157–77. 1902. Reprint, New York, 1975.

Hoberman, L. "Bureaucracy and Disaster: Mexico City and the Floods of 1629." *Journal of Latin American Studies* 6 (1974): 211–30.

Hobsbawm, E. *Social Bandits and Primitive Rebels: Studies in Archaic Forms of Social Movement in the Nineteenth and Twentieth Century*. Clencoe, 1959.

Hoock, J. "Dimensions analytiques et herméneutiques d'une histoire historienne du droit." *Annales ESC* 44 (1989): 1479–90.

Hurstfield, J. *Freedom, Corruption and Government in Elizabethan England*. Cambridge, MA, 1973.

Imizcoz Beunza, J. M. "De la comunidad a la nación: Élites locales, carreras y redes sociales en la España moderna (siglos XVIII–XIX)." In *Élites, poder y red social: Las élites del país vasco y Navarra en la edad moderna*, ed. J. M. Imizcoz Beunza, 193–210. Vitoria, 1996.

El innovador: Juan de Goyeneche. El señorío de la Olmeda y el conjunto arquitectónico de Nuevo Baztan. Madrid, 1991.

Israel, J. I. *Race, Class and Politics in Colonial Mexico, 1610–1670*. Oxford, 1975.

Jaque Martínez, E., and Salas Ausens, J. M. "El '*cursus honorum*' de los letrados aragoneses en los siglos XVI y XVII." *Studia storica* 6 (1988): 411–22.

Juan, J., and Ulloa, A. *Relación histórica del viaje a la América meridional.* Madrid, 1978.
———. *Noticias secretas de América.* 1826. Reprint, Madrid, 1988.
Jurado Noboa, F. *Los Larrea: Burocracia, tenencia de la tierra, poder político, crísis, retorno al poder y papel de la cultura.* Quito, 1986.
Kagan, R. *Students and Society in Early Modern Spain.* Baltimore, 1974.
———. *Pleitos y pleiteantes en Castilla, 1500–1700.* Salamanca, 1991.
Kagan, S. "Penal Servitude in Nueva España: The Colonial Textile Industry." Ph.D. diss., New York University, 1977.
Kamen, H. *Spain in the Later Seventeenth Century, 1665–1700.* London, 1980.
Kantorowicz, E. H. *The King's Two Bodies: A Study in Medieval Political Theology.* Princeton, 1957.
Kerr, D. N. *Petty Felony, Slave Defiance and Frontier Villainy. Crime and Criminal Justice in Spanish Louisiana, 1770–1803.* New York, 1993.
Kettering, S. *Judicial Politics and Urban Revolt in Seventeenth-Century France: The Parlement of Aix, 1629–1659.* Princeton, 1978.
———. "The Historical Development of Political Clientalism." *Journal of Interdisciplinary History* 18/3 (1988): 419–47.
———. "Patronage and Kingship in Early Modern France." *French Historical Studies* 16/2 (1989): 408–35.
———. "Friendship and Clientelage in Early Modern France." *French History* 6/2 (1992): 139–58.
Kettering, S., Major, J. R., and Jouanna, A. "Patronage, Language and Political Culture." *French Historical Studies* 17/4 (1992): 839–81.
Kicza, J. "The Legal Community of Late Colonial Mexico." In *Five Centuries of Law and Politics in Central Mexico,* ed. R. Spores and R. Hassig, 114–27. Tennessee, 1984.
King, P. "Decision Makers and Decision Making in the English Criminal Law, 1750–1800." *Historical Journal* 27 (1984): 25–58.
———. "Newspaper Reporting, Prosecution Practice, and the Perceptions of Urban Crime: The Colchester Crime Wave of 1765." *Continuity and Change* 2 (1987): 423–54.
Kirshner, J. "Introduction: The State is 'Back In.'" In *The Origins of the State in Italy, 1300–1600,* ed. J. Kirshner, 1–10. Chicago, 1996.
Klapisch-Zuber, C. *La maison et le nom: Stragégies et rituels dans l'Italie de la Renaissance.* Paris, 1990.
Koenigsberger, H. G. *La práctica del imperio.* 1696. Reprint, Madrid, 1975.
Konetzke, R. *Colección de documentos para la historia de la formación social de Hispanoamérica, 1493–1810.* Madrid, 1953.
———. "La literatura económica: Así se escribe la historia." *Moneda y crédito* 81 (1962): 67–77.
Kramnick, I. "Corruption in Eighteenth-Century English and American Political Discourse." In *Virtue, Corruption and Self Interest. Political Values in the Eighteenth Century,* ed. R. K. Matthews, 55–75. Bethlehem, 1994.
Lafuente, A., and Mazuecos, A. *Los caballeros del punto fijo: Ciencia, política y*

aventura en la expedición geodésica hispanofrancesa al virreinato del Perú en el siglo XVIII. Quito, 1992.

Lalinde Abadía, J. "Los gastos del proceso en el derecho histórico español." *Anuario de historia del derecho español* 34 (1964): 249–416.

———. *Iniciación histórica al derecho español*. Barcelona, 1970.

———. "Depuración histórica del concepto de estado." In *El estado español en su dimensión histórica*, ed. J. Lalinde Abadía, M. J. Peláez, A. Pérez Martín, E. Rotelli, I. Sánchez Bella, J. Tomás Villarroya, and E. Zurawka, 17–58. Malaga, 1984.

———. "España y la monarquía universal (en torno al concepto de 'estado moderno')." *Quaderni fiorentini* 15 (1986): 109–66.

Landau, N. *The Justices of Peace, 1676–1769*. Berkeley, 1984.

Landázurri Camacho, C. "Estructura y funcionamiento del cabildo de Quito, 1534–1551." *Anuario hístorico jurídico ecuatoriano* 6 (1980): 565–91.

Langbein, J. H. *Torture and the Law of Proof: England and the Ancient Regime*. Chicago, 1977.

———. "Albion's Fatal Flaws." *Past and Present* 98 (1983): 96–120.

Larrea, C. M. *El presidente de la Real Audiencia de Quito don Dionisio de Alcedo y Herrera*. Quito, 1961.

Larrea, G. C. *Genealogías quiteñas: la casa de Ontañón y sus enlazados*. Quito, 1994.

Lavallé, B. "La rebelión de las Alcabalas (Quito, julio 1592–abril 1593), ensayo de interpretación." *Revista de Indias* 44 (1984): 141–202.

———. *Quito et la crise de l'alcabala (1580–1600)*. Paris, 1992.

Laviana Cuetos, M. L. *Guayaquil en el siglo XVIII: recursos naturales y desarrollo económico*. Seville, 1987.

Leal Curiel, C. *El discurso de la fidelidad: Construcción social del espacio como símbolo de poder regio (Venezuela siglo XVIII)*. Caracas, 1990.

Lebigre, A. *La justice du roi. La vie judiciaire dans l'ancienne France*. Paris, 1988.

León Borja, D. "Los alcaldes ordinarios de Guayaquil y Puerto Viejo en el siglo XVI." *Anuario histórico jurídico ecuatoriano* 6 (1980): 531–61.

León Coloma, M. A. *El programa iconográfico de la real chancillería de Granada*. Granada, 1988.

León Pinelo, A. *Tratado de confirmaciones reales de encomiendas, oficios y casos en que se requieren para las Indias Occidentales*. Madrid, 1630.

Levaggi, A. "El delito de abigeato en los siglos XVII–XIX." *Revista del Instituto de Historia el Derecho Ricardo Levene* 24 (1978): 107–77.

———. "El concepto de derecho según los fiscales de la Segunda audiencia de Buenos Aires (1784–1810)." *Revista chilena de historia del derecho* 13 (1987): 245–59.

Levene, R. *Obras de Ricardo Levene*. Buenos Aires, 1962.

Levi, G. *Le pouvoir au village. Histoire d'un exorciste dans le Piémont du XVIIe siècle*. Paris, 1989. Originally published as *L'eredità immateriale: carriera di un esorcista nel Piemonte del Seicento*. Torino, 1985.

———. "Reciprocidad mediterránea," *Hispania* 60/1 (2000): 103–26.

Lévy, J. P. *La hiérarchie des preuves dans le droit savant du Moyen Age depuis la renaissance du droit romain jusqu'à la fin du XIVe siècle.* Paris, 1939.
Lévy, R., and Robert, P. "Le sociologue et l'histoire pénale." *Annales ESC* 39 (1984): 400–422.
Levy Peck, L. *Court Patronage and Corruption in Early Stuart England.* London, 1990. Reprint, 1993.
"Libro de matrícula de abogados (1733–1829)." *Boletín de la Academia Nacional de Historia* 8/13 (1964): 29–45.
Lisón Tolosana, C. *La imagen del rey: Monarquía, realeza y poder ritual en la Casa de los Austrias.* Madrid, 1991.
Lohmann Villena, G. *Los americanos en las órdenes nobiliarias (1529–1900).* Madrid, 1947.
———. *Los ministros de la Audiencia de Lima (1700–1821).* Seville, 1974.
Londoño, J. *Entre la sumisión y la resistencia: Las mujeres en la audiencia de Quito.* Quito, 1997.
López Bohórquez, A. *Los ministros de la Audiencia de Caracas (1786–1810): Caracterización de una élite burocrática del poder en Venezuela.* Caracas, 1984.
López Gómez, M. A. "Los fiscales del Consejo Real." *Hidalguía* 218 (1990): 81–114.
López Ruiz, S. J. *Discurso doctrinal sobre la obediencia y lealtad debida al soberano y a sus magistrados.* Lima, 1785.
Lozano Armendares, T. *La criminalidad en la ciudad de México, 1800–1821.* Mexico, 1987.
Lozano Castro, A. *Quito. Ciudad milenaria, fama y símbolo.* Quito, 1991.
Lucena Salmoral, M. "La población del reino de Quito en la época de reformismo borbónico: circa 1784." *Revista de Indias* 54/200 (1994): 33–81.
Luján Muñoz, J. *Los escribanos en las Indias Occidentales y en particular en el Reino de Guatemala.* Guatemala, 1977.
Lynch, J. "The Institutional Framework of Colonial Spanish America." *Journal of Latin American Studies: Supplement* 24 (1992): 69–81.
———. "Introduction." In *Latin American Revolutions, 1808–1826: Old and New World Origins,* ed. J. Lynch, 5–38. Norman, OK: 1994.
MacLachlan, C. M. *Criminal Justice in Eighteenth-Century Mexico: A Study of the Tribunal of the Acordada.* Berkeley, 1974.
———. *Spain's Empire in the New World: The Role of Ideas in Institutional and Social Change.* Berkeley, 1988.
Maddicott, J. R. "Law and Lordship. Royal Justices as Retainers in Thirteenth-Century England." *Past and Present* supp. 4 (1978): 635–57.
Madero, M. *Manos violentas, palabras vedadas. La injuria en Castilla y León (siglos XIII–XV).* Madrid, 1992.
Major, J. R., Kettering, S., and Schalk, E. "Forum: Fidelity and Clientelage in Seventeenth Century France." *French Historical Studies* 14/3 (1986): 391–446.
Malagón, J. *Teoría general del derecho procesal en las leyes indianas: Bases para su estudio.* Madrid, 1936.
Mantecón Movellán, T. A. "Desviación, disciplina social e intervenciones judi-

ciales en el antiguo régimen." *Studia historica-historia moderna* 14 (1996): 223–43.

———. *Conflictualidad y disciplinamiento social en la Cantabria rural del antiguo régimen.* Santander, 1997.

———. "Meaning and Social Context of Crime in Preindustrial Times: Rural Society in the North of Spain, Seventeenth and Eighteenth Centuries." *Crime, histoire et sociétés* 2/1 (1998): 49–73.

———. *La muerte de Antonia Isabel Sánchez. Tiranía y escándalo en una sociedad rural del norte español en el antiguo régimen.* Alcala de Henares, 1998.

Maravall, J. A. *La teoría española del estado en el siglo XVII.* Madrid, 1954.

———. "The Origins of the Modern State." *Cahiers d'histoire mondiale* 6/4 (1961): 789–808.

———. *Estado moderno y mentalidad social (siglos XV a XVII).* Madrid, 1972.

———. *Poder, honor y élites en el siglo XVII.* Madrid, 1979.

———. *La cultura del Barroco: Análisis de una estructura histórica.* Barcelona, 1975. Reprint, 1983.

———. *Estudios de historia del pensamiento español. Edad media.* Madrid, 1985.

Marchena Fernández, J. *Oficiales y soldados en el ejercito de América.* Seville, 1983.

———. "The Social World of the Military in Peru and Nueva Granada: The Colonial Oligarchies in Conflict, 1750–1810." In *Reform and Insurrection in Bourbon Nueva Granada and Peru,* ed. J. R. Fisher, A. J. Kuethe, and A. McFarlane, 54–95. Baton Rouge–London, 1990.

Mariana, J. de. *Del rey y de la institución real.* 1598. Reprint, Madrid, 1854.

Mariluz Urquijo, J. M. *Ensayo sobre los juicios de residencia indianos.* Seville, 1952.

———. *Orígenes de la burocracia rioplatense.* Buenos Aires, 1974.

———. "El asesor letrado del virreinato del Río de la Plata." *Revista de historia del derecho* 3 (1975): 165–228.

———. "El saber profesional de los agentes de la administración pública en Indias." In *Estructuras, gobierno y agentes de la administración en la América española (siglos XVI–XVIII), Actas del VI congreso del Instituto Internacional de Historia del Derecho Indiano,* 251–79. Valladolid, 1984.

Marin, L. *Le portrait du roi.* Paris, 1981.

———. "Logiques du secret." *Traverses* 30–31 (1984): 60–69.

Martínez Diez, G. "La tortura judicial en la legislación histórica española." *Anuario de historia del derecho español* 32 (1962): 223–300.

Martínez Millán, J., ed. *Instituciones y élites de poder en la Monarquía Hispana durante el siglo XVI.* Madrid, 1992.

———. "Las investigacione sobre patronazgo y clientelismo en la administración de la monarquía hispana durante la edad moderna." *Studia storica-historia moderna* 15 (1996): 83–106.

Martire, E. "La visita de cárcel en Buenos Aires durante el virreinato." *Revista chilena de historia del derecho* 13 (1987): 39–60.

———. "Las relaciones entre el rey y sus súbditos americanos (siglos XVI–XVIII)." *Receuils de la Société Jean Bodin* 47 (1988): 343–53.
Marzahl, P. "Creoles and Government: The Cabildo of Popayan." *Hispanic American Historical Review* 54 (1974): 636–56.
———. *Town in the Empire. Government, Politics and Society in Seventeenth-Century Popayan.* Austin, TX, 1978.
Masur, L. *Rites of Execution: Capital Punishment and the Transformation of American Culture, 1776–1865.* New York, 1989.
McFarlane, A. "Civil Disorders and Popular Protests in Late Colonial New Granada." *Hispanic American Historical Review* 64 (1984): 17–54.
———. "The 'Rebellion of the Barrios.' Urban Insurrection in Bourbon Quito." *Hispanic American Historical Review* 69 (1989): 283–330.
———. "Political Corruption and Reform in Bourbon Spanish America." In *Political Corruption in Europe and Latin America,* 41–63. London, 1996.
Meccarelli, M. *Arbitrium. Un aspetto sistematico degli ordinamenti giuridici in età di diritto comune.* Milan, 1998.
Mechanic, D. "Sources of Power of Lower Participants in Complex Organizations." In *Organizational Systems: A Text Reader in the Sociology of Organizations,* ed. K. Azumi and J. Hage, 281–93. Lexington, MA, 1972.
Mendiburu, M. *Diccionario histórico biográfico del Perú.* Lima, 1931.
Menzies, K. *Talcott Parsons and the Social Image of Man.* London, 1976.
Merchán, A. *El arbitraje: Estudio histórico-jurídico.* Seville, 1981.
Meyer, J. W., and Rowan, B. "Institutionalized Organizations: Formal Structure as Myth and Ceremony." *American Journal of Sociology* 83 (1977): 340–63.
Miller, H. *Informatique et prosopographie.* Paris, 1985.
Minchom, M. "La evolución demográfica del Ecuador en el siglo XVIII." *Cultura* 8/24B (1986): 459–80.
———. *The People of Quito, 1690–1810: Change and Unrest in the Underclass.* Syracuse, 1994.
Miño Grijalva, M. "La economía de la real audiencia de Quito: siglo XVII." In *Nueva historia del Ecuador,* vol. 4, *Epoca Colonia II,* ed. E. Ayala Mora, 47–103. Quito, 1983.
———. *La economia colonial. Relaciones socio-económicas de la real audiencia de Quito.* Quito, 1984.
Mitchell, J. C. *Networks in Urban Situations.* Manchester, 1969.
Molas Ribalta, P. *Consejos y audiencias durante el reinado de Felipe II.* Valladolid, 1984.
Monsalvo Antón, J. M. "Historia de los poderes medievales, del derecho a la antropología (el ejemplo castellano: monarquía, concejos y señoríos en los siglos XII–XV)." In *Historia a debate: medieval,* ed. C. Barros, 81–149. Santiago de Compostela, 1995.
Montúfar y Fraso, J. P. "Razón sobre el estado y gobernación política y militar de las provincias, ciudades, villas y lugares que contiene la jurisdicción de la real audiencia de Quito [13 Septembre 1754]." In *Relaciones histórico-geográficas de la audiencia de Quito (siglo XVI–XIX),* vol. 2, ed. P. Ponce Leiva, 323–52. Madrid, 1992.

Moore, J. P. *The Cabildo in Peru under the Habsburgs: A Study in the Origins and Powers of the Town Council in the Viceroyalty of Peru.* Durham, 1954.

———. *The Cabildo in Peru under the Bourbons: A Study in the Decline and Resurgence of Local Government in the Audiencia of Lima, 1700–1824.* Durham, 1966.

Morales Moya, A. "Milicias y nobleza en el siglo XVIII: Apuntes para una sociología de las armas y de la nobleza en España." *Cuadernos de historia moderna* 9 (1988): 121–37.

Morellet, A. *Abrégé du manuel des inquisiteurs, 1762.* Ed. J. P. Giucciardi. Grenoble, 1990.

Moreno, S. *Sublevaciones indígenas en la Audiencia de Quito: Desde comienzos del siglo XVIII hasta finales de la colonia.* Quito, 1985.

———. *Alzamientos indígenas en la audiencia de Quito, 1534–1803.* Quito, 1989.

Moreno Cebrián, A. "Venta y beneficios de los corregidores peruanos." *Revista de Indias* 36/143–44 (1976): 213–46.

Moreyra y Paz Soldán, M. "El limeño don José de Araujo y Río presidente de la audiencia de Quito y capitán general de Guatemala." *Mercurio peruano* 26/250 (1945): 506–29.

Morgan, G., and Rushton, P. *Rogues, Thieves and the Rule of Law: The Problem of Law Enforcement in North-East England, 1718–1800.* London, 1998.

Morse, R. M. "The Heritage of Latin America." In *The Founding of New Societies: Studies in the History of United States, Latin America, South Africa, Canada, and Australia,* ed. L. Hartz, 123–77. New York, 1964.

Mousnier, R. *La venalité des offices sous Henri IV et Louis XVII.* Rouen, 1945.

———. *Les institutions de la France sous la monarchie absolue, 1598–1789.* Paris, 1974.

Moutoukias, Z. "Power, Corruption, and Commerce: The Making of the Local Administrative Structure in Seventeenth-Century Buenos Aires." *Hispanic American Historical Review* 68 (1988): 771–801.

———. "Réseaux personnels et autorité coloniale: Les négociants de Buenos Aires au XVIIIe siècle." *Annales ESC* 47 (1992): 889–915.

———. "Negocios y redes sociales: modelo interpretativo a partir de un caso rioplatense (siglo XVIII)." *Caravelle* 67 (1997): 37–55.

———. "La notion de réseau en histoire social: Un instrument d'analyse de l'action collective." In *Résaux, familles et pouvoirs dans le monde ibérique à la fin de l'ancien régime,* ed. J. L. Castellano and J. P. Dedieu, 231–45. Paris, 1998.

———. "Familia patriarcal y redes sociales. Balance de una imagen de la estratificación social," *Anuario IEHS* 15 (2000): 133–51.

Mowery Andrews, R. *Law, Magistracy, and Crime in Old Regime Paris, 1735–1789. The System of Criminal Justice.* Cambridge, 1994.

Mozzarelli, C. "Introduzione." In *L'amministrazione nella storia moderna,* vol. 1, 5–20. Milan, 1985.

Muchembled, R. *Sorcières, justice et société aux 16e et 17e siècles.* Paris, 1987.

———. *L'invention de l'homme moderne: Sensibilités, moeurs et comportements collectifs sous l'Ancien Régime.* Paris, 1988.

———. *Le temps des supplices: De l'obéissance sous les rois absolus XVe–XVIIe siècle.* Paris, 1992.

Muriel, J. *Los recogimientos de mujeres: Respuesta a una problemática social Novohispana.* Mexico, 1974.

Muro Orejón, A. *Cedulario americano del siglo XVIII.* Seville, 1956.

Muro Romero, F. "El beneficio de oficios públicos con jurisdicción en Indias: Notas sobre sus orígenes." *Anuario de estudios americanos* 35 (1978): 1–67.

———. "La reforma del pacto colonial en Indias: Notas sobre instituciones de gobierno y sociedad en el siglo XVII." *Jahrbuch für geschichte von staat, wirtschaft und gesellschaft lateinamerikas* 19 (1982): 47–68.

———. "Instituciones de gobierno y sociedad en Indias, 1700–1760." In *Estructuras de gobierno agentes de administración en la América española (siglos XVI, XVII, XVIII), VI congreso del Instituto Internacional de Historia del Derecho Indiano,* 163–231. Valladolid, 1984.

Musi, A. "La storiografia politico-amministrativa sull'età moderna: tendenze e metodi degli ultimi trent'anni." In *Stato e pubblica amministrazione nell'Ancien Régime,* ed. A. Musi, 11–40. Naples, 1979.

———. "La storiografia spagnola." In *Stato e pubblica amministrazione nell'Ancien Régime,* ed. A. Musi, 102–20. Naples, 1979.

Nava Rodríguez, T., and Franco Rubio, G. "Venalité et futuras dans l'administration espagnole au XVIIIe siècle." In *Les figures historiques de l'administrateur: Institutions, réseaux, pouvoirs en Espagne, en France et au Portugal, 16e–19e siècle,* ed. R. Descimon, J. F. Schaub, and B. Vincent, 95–105. Paris, 1997.

Navarro García, L. "Los oficios vendibles en Nueva España durante la guerra de sucesión." *Anuario de estudios americanos* 32 (1975): 133–54.

———. "Honra, pobreza y aislamiento de los oidores indianos." *Temas americanistas* 1 (1982): 11–15.

Newson, L. A. *Life and Death in Early Colonial Ecuador.* Norman, OK: 1995.

Nicoli, O. "Rinuncia, pace, perdono, rituali di pacificazione della prima età moderna." *Studi storici* 40/1 (1999): 219–61.

Nieto Soria, J. M. *Fundamentos ideológicos del poder real en Castilla siglos XIII–XVI.* Madrid, 1988.

Nuñez Cabezas de Herrera, L. "El oficio de oidor en las Audiencias americanas durante el periodo hispano-colonial." In *Reseña y trabajos científicos del XXVI congreso internacional de americanistas, Sevilla 1935,* vol. 2, 181–98. Madrid, 1948.

Oberwittler, D. "Crime and Authority in Eighteenth Century England: Law Enforcement on the Local Level." *Historical Social Research* 15/2 (1990): 2–34.

Ortega Gil, P. "Apercibimientos penales en la práctica criminal de la real audiencia de Galicia (siglos XVII y XVIII)." *Cuadernos de historia del derecho* 3 (1996): 11–41.

Ortiz Crespo, A., and Terrán Najas, R. "Las reducciones de indios en la zona interandina de la real audiencia de Quito." In *Pueblos de otro urbanismo en la región andina,* ed. R. Gutiérrez, 205–61. Quito, 1993.

Ortiz de la Tabla, J. "Panorama económico y social del corregimiento de Quito (1768–1775)." *Revista de Indias* 36 (1976): 83–98.
———. "La población ecuatoriana en la época colonial: Cuestiones y cálculos." *Anuario de estudios americanos* 37 (1980): 235–77.
———. "Obrajes y obrajeros del Quito colonial." *Anuario de estudios americanos* 39 (1982): 341–65.
———. "Modelos peninsulares en la estratificación social del Perú." In *Europa e Iberoamérica: Cinco siglos de intercambio, IX congreso del Instituto de Historia de América (AHILA)*, vol. 1, 99–105. Cadiz, 1992.
———. *Los encomenderos de Quito, 1534–1660: Origen y evolución de una élite colonial.* Seville, 1993.
Ots Capdequi, J. M. *Historia del derecho español en América y del derecho indiano.* Madrid, 1967.
———. *El estado español en las Indias.* 1941. Reprint, Mexico, 1986.
Parker, D. "Sovereignty, Absolutism, and the Function of the Law in Seventeenth-Century France." *Past and Present* 122 (1989): 36–74.
Parry, J. H. "The Sale of Public Office in the Spanish Indies under the Habsburgs." *Iberoamericana* 37 (1935): 74–158.
———. *The Sale of Public Office in the Spanish Indies under the Habsburgs.* Berkeley, 1953.
Parsons, T. "Suggestions for a Sociological Approach to the Theory of Organizations." Parts 1 and 2. *Administrative Science Quarterly* 1 (1956/1957): 63–85 and 225–39.
Pelorson, J. M. *Les letrados. Juristes castillans sous Philippe III: Recherches sur leur place dans la société, la culture et l'état.* Poitiers, 1980.
———. "L'État et ses cadres dans la société espagnole (XVIe–XVIIIe siècles)." *Bulletin hispanique* 84 (1982): 454–66.
Peña-Peñaloza, R. I. "Principios doctrinarios del derecho penal castellano-indiano: la jurisprudencia." *Revista de estudios histórico-jurídicos* 16 (1994): 87–94.
Perez, J. "La Couronne de Castille." In *Le premier âge de l'État en Espagne (1450–1700)*, ed. C. Hermann, 108–9. Paris, 1989.
———. "El estado moderno y la corrupción." In *Instituciones y corrupción en la historia*, ed. M. González Jiménez, H. Pietschmann, F. Comín, and J. Perez, 111–29. Valladolid, 1998.
Pérez Baltazar, M. D. "Orígenes de los recogimientos de mujeres." *Cuadernos de historia moderna y contemporánea* 9 (1985): 13–23.
Pérez García, P. "Origen y configuración de una magistratura urbana de la Valencia Foral. La justicia criminal." *Estudis* 13 (1987): 21–73.
———. *La justicia criminal de Valencia.* Valencia, 1991.
Pérez Martín, A. "La protección del honor y de la fama en el derecho histórico español." *Anales de derecho* 11 (1991): 117–56.
Pérez Prendes y Muñoz de Arraco, J. M. *La Monarquía indiana y el estado de derecho.* Valencia, 1989.
Peristany, J. G., ed. *El concepto del honor en la sociedad mediterránea.* Barcelona, 1968.

Perry, M. E. *Crime and Society in Early Modern Seville.* Hanover, 1980.

Peveri, P. "'Cette ville était alors comme un bois . . .' Criminalité et opinion publique à Paris dans les années qui precèdent l'affaire Cartouche (1715–1721)." *Crime, histoire et sociétés* 1/2 (1997): 51–73.

Peytavin, M. "Naple 1610: Comment peut-on être officier?" *Annales ESC* 52/2 (1997): 265–91.

Phelan, J. L. "Authority and Flexibility in the Spanish Imperial Bureaucracy." *Administrative Science Quaterly* 5 (1960): 47–65.

———. *The Kingdom of Quito in the Seventeenth Century: Bureaucratic Politics in the Spanish Empire.* Madison, 1967.

———. *The People and the King: The Comunero Revolution in Colombia, 1781.* Madison, 1978.

Piasenza, P. "Opinion publique, identité des institutions, 'absolutism': Le problème de la légalité à Paris entre le XVIIe et le XVIIIe siècle." *Revue historique* 587 (1993): 97–142.

Pietschmann, H. "Burocracia y corrupción en Hispanoamérica colonial: Una aproximación tentativa." *Nova americana* 5 (1982): 11–37.

———. "Estado colonial y mentalidad social: El ejercicio del poder frente a distintos sistemas de valores, siglo XVIII." In *America latina dallo stato coloniale allo stato nazione (1740–1940),* ed. A. Annino, M. Carmagnani, et al., 427–47. Milan, 1987.

———. "El desarrollo estatal de hispanoamérica: enfoques metodológicos." *Chronica Nova* 21 (1993–94): 469–92.

———. "Corrupción en las indias españolas: Revisión de un debate en la historiografía sobre Hispanoamérica colonial." In *Instituciones y corrupción en la historia,* ed. M. González Jiménez, H. Pietschmann, F. Comín, and J. Perez, 31–52. Valladolid, 1998.

Pike, F. B. "The Municipality and the System of Checks and Balances in Spanish American Colonial Administration." *Americas* 15 (1958–59): 139–58.

Pinson Ramin, V. "La torture judiciaire en Bretagne au XVIIe siècle." *Revue historique de droit français et étranger* 72/4 (1994): 549–68.

Polanco Alcántara, T. *Las Reales Audiencias en las provincias americanas de España.* Madrid, 1992.

Ponce, M. *El control de la gestión administrativa en el juicio de residencia al gobernador Manuel González Torres de Navarra.* 2 vols. Caracas, 1985.

Ponce Leiva, P., ed. *Relaciones histórico-geográficas de la Audiencia de Quito (siglo XVI–XIX).* 2 vols. Madrid, 1992.

———. "El poder informal. Mujeres de Quito en el siglo XVII." *Revista complutense de historia de América* 23 (1997): 98–111.

———. *Certezas ante la incertidumbre: Élite y cabildo de Quito en el siglo XVII.* Quito, 1998.

Poole, S. "Institutionalized Corruption in the Letrado Bureaucracy. The Case of Pedro Farján (1568–1588)." *Americas* 38 (1981): 149–71.

Porras, M. E. "La élite quiteña en el cabildo, 1763–1805." M.A. thesis, Facultad Iberoamericana de Ciencias Sociales (FLACSO). Quito, 1987.

———. "La élite quiteña a mediados del siglo XVIII." *AFESE* 88/14 (1988): 43–55.

Portillo Valdés, J. M. "La administración en la reciente historiografía italiana (tema y variaciones)." *Anuario de historia del derecho español* 62 (1992): 633–74.

Powers Viera, K. *Prendas con pies: Migraciones indígenas y supervivencia cultural en la audiencia de Quito.* Quito, 1994.

Pradilla, F. De la. *Suma de las leyes penales.* Madrid, 1639.

Prest, W. "Judicial Corruption in Early Modern England." *Past and Present* 133 (1991): 67–95.

Priotti, J. P. "Emigración, redes vascas de negocios y poder en el imperio español (1500–1630): un punto de partida." Trans. A. Rodríguez Tomp. *Historias* 42 (1999): 103–13.

Pro Ruiz, J. "Las élites de la España liberal. Clases y redes en la definición del espacio social (1808–1931)." *Historia social* 21 (1995): 47–69.

Puente Brunke, J. "Los oidores en la sociedad limeña: Notas para su estudio (siglo XVII)." *Temas americanistas* 7 (1990): 8–13.

Puy Muñoz, F. *Las ideas jurídicas de la España del siglo XVIII (1700–1760).* Granada, 1962.

Quatrefages, R. "Le système militaire des Habsbourgs." In *Le premier âge de l'État en Espagne (1450–1700),* ed. C. Hermann, 341–79. Paris, 1989.

Quevedo y Hoyos, A. *Libro de indicios y tormentos que contiene toda la práctica criminal y modo de sustanciar el proceso.* Madrid, 1632.

Quintana Tonet, F. J. "De los delitos y las penas: La criminalidad en Málaga y su tierra durante el siglo de oro." *Estudis* 15 (1989): 245–69.

Ramos, G. "La privatización del poder: Inquisición y sociedad colonial en el Perú." In *Poder y violencia en los Andes,* ed. E. Urbano, 75–92. Cuzco, 1991.

Ramos Gómez, L. *Época, génesis y texto de las Noticias Secretas de América de Jorge Juan y Antonio de Ulloa.* Madrid, 1985.

———. "Un ejemplo de la lucha por el poder en Quito." *Cultura* 8 (1986): 117–32.

———. "La estructura social quiteña entre 1737 y 1745 según el proceso contra José de Araujo." *Revista de Indias* 51 (1991): 25–56.

———. "La pugna por el poder local en Quito entre 1737 y 1745 según el proceso contra el presidente de la audiencia José de Araujo y Río." *Revista complutense de historia de América* 18 (1992): 179–96.

———. "El 'bien común' como pretexto del presidente José de Araujo para crear una compañía de soldados y prohibir el aguardiente de caña en Quito en 1737." *Revista andina* 11/2 (1993): 381–401.

———. "Algunos datos sobre los abusos e injusticias padecidas en 1737 por los indios de los obrajes de la ciudad de Quito." *Revista española de antropología americana* 27 (1997): 153–66.

Ramos Gómez, L., and Ruigómez Gómez, C. "La entrada en religión (1739) de Pedro Martínez de Arizala, oidor de la Audiencia de Quito y sus consecuencias." *Revista complutense de historia de América* 22 (1996): 209–37.

Rawlings, P. *Crime and Power. A History of Criminal Justice, 1688–1998.* London, 1999.

Real Académia Española. Diccionario de la lengua Castellana. 6 vols. Madrid, 1726–39.

Redondo, A. "Mutilations et marques corporelles d'infamie dans la Castille du XVIe siècle." In *Le corps dans la société espagnole des XVIe et XVIIe siècles,* ed. A. Redondo, 185–99. Paris, 1990.

Reig Satorres, J. "Reales Audiencias." *Anuario histórico jurídico ecuatoriano* 2 (1971): 525–77.

———. "Precisiones sobre la Audiencia y la Presidencia de Quito." *Revista chilena de historia del derecho* 11 (1985): 377–403.

Restrepo Sáenz, J. M. *Biografías de los mandatarios y ministros de la Real Audiencia, 1671–1819.* Bogota, 1952.

Reumaux, F. "Traits invariants de la rumeur." In *Rumeurs et légendes contemporaines,* ed. V. Campion-Vincent and J. B. Renard. *Communications* 52 (1990): 141–59.

Revel, J., and Farge, A. *Logiques de la foule: L'affaire des enlèvements d'enfants Paris, 1750.* Paris, 1988.

Ripodas de Ardanaz, D. *El matrimonio en Indias: Realidad social y regulación jurídica.* Buenos Aires, 1971.

Rizo Patrón, P. "La nobleza en Lima en tiempos de los Borbones." *Boletín del Instituto Francés de Estudios Andinos* 19 (1990): 129–63.

Robert, P., and Lévy, R. "Histoire et question pénale." *Revue d'histoire moderne et contemporaine* 32 (1985): 481–526.

Roberts, S. "The Study of Dispute: Anthropological Perspectives." In *Disputes and Settlements. Law and Human Relations in the West,* ed. J. Bossy, 1–24. Cambridge, 1983.

Roche, D. *La culture des apparences: Une histoire du vêtement XVIIe–XVIIIe siècle.* Paris, 1989.

Rodríguez Crespo, P. "Sobre parentesco de los oidores con los grupos superiores de la sociedad limeña (a comienzos del siglo XVII)." *Mercurio peruano* 447–50 (1964): 49–61.

Rodríguez Docampo, D. "Descripción y relación del estado eclesiástico del obispado de San Francisco de Quito . . . [1650]." In *Relaciones histórico-geográficas de la audiencia de Quito (siglo XVI–XIX),* vol. 2, ed. P. Ponce Leiva, 211–22. Madrid, 1992.

Rodríguez Flores, M. I. *El perdón real en Castilla siglos XIII–XVIII.* Salamanca, 1971.

Rodríguez Sánchez, A. "La soga y el fuego: La pena de muerte en España de los siglos XVI y XVII." *Cuadernos de historia moderna* 15 (1994): 13–39.

Roldán Verdejo, R. *Los jueces de la monarquía absoluta, su estatuto y actividad judicial: La corona de Castilla siglos XIV–XVIII.* Laguna, 1989.

Rosnow, R. L., and Fire, G. A. *Rumor and Gossip: The Social Psychology of Hearsay.* New York, 1976.

Rovito, P. L. *Respublica dei togati: Giuristi e società nella Napoli del Seicento.* Naples, 1981.

Rueda Novoa, R. *El obraje de San Joseph de Peguchi.* Quito, 1988.

Ruiz Giñazú, E. *La magistratura indiana.* Buenos Aires, 1916.

Ruiz Medrano, E. *Gobierno y sociedad en Nueva España: Segunda Audiencia y Antonio de Mendoza.* Mexico, 1991.

Ruiz Rodríguez, A. A. *La Real Chancillería de Granada en el siglo XVI.* Granada, 1987.

Rumazo, J. *Documentos para la historia de la Audiencia de Quito.* Madrid, 1948.

Sabean, D. "La conscience et la peur: qui a tué le pasteur?" *Actes de la recherche en sciences sociales* 51 (1984): 41–54.

Sagués Azcona, P. *La Real Congregación de San Fermín de los Navarros de Madrid (1683–1691): Estudio histórico.* Madrid, 1963.

Saguier, E. R. "La corrupción administrativa como mecanismo de accumulación y engendrador de una burguesía comercial local." *Anuario de estudios americanos* 46 (1989): 269–303.

Sánchez Bella, I. *Derecho Indiano. Estudios.* Pamplona, 1991.

Sánchez Bella, I., Hera, A. De la, and Díaz Rementería, C. *Historia del Derecho Indiano.* Madrid, 1992.

Sánchez Gómez, R. I. *Delincuencia y seguridad en el Madrid de carlos II.* Madrid, 1994.

San Cristóbal, A. *Apéndice al diccionario histórico biográfico del Perú.* Lima, 1935.

Santos Pérez, J. M. "La práctica del autogobierno en centroamērica: conflictos entre la audiencia de Guatemala y el cabildo de Santiago en el siglo XVIII," *Mesoamérica* 21/40 (2000): 69–94.

Sarfatti, M. *Spanish Bureaucratic Patrimonialism in America.* Berkeley, 1966.

Scardaville, M. C. "Crime and the Urban Poor: Mexico City in the Late Colonial Period." Ph.D. diss., University of Florida, 1977.

———. "Habsburg Law and Bourbon Order: State Authority, Popular Unrest, and the Criminal Justice System in Bourbon Mexico City." *Americas* 50/4 (1994): 501–25.

Schaffer, E. *El Consejo Real y Supremo de las Indias, su historia, organización y labor administrativo hasta la terminación de la Casa de Austria.* Seville, 1935.

Schaub, J. F. "La penisola iberica nei secoli XVI e XVII: la questione dello stato." *Quaderni storici* 36/1 (1995): 9–49.

———. "Le Temps de l'ētat: Vers un nouveau régime historiographique de l'ancien régime français." *Quaderni fiorentini* 25 (1996): 127–81.

Scheffer, *Thesis inauguralis de fama.* Altdorff, 1662.

Schiera, P. "Legitimacy, Discipline, and Institutions: Three Necessary Conditions for the Birth of the Modern State." In *The Origins of the State in Italy, 1300–1600,* ed J. Kirshner, 10–33. Chicago, 1996.

Schmidt, J. C. *La raison des gestes dans l'occident médiéval.* Paris, 1990.

Schofield, P. R. "Peasants and the Manor Court: Gossip and Litigation in a Suffolk Village at the Close of the Thirteenth Century." *Past and Present* 159 (1998): 3–42.

Scholz, J. M. "L'obstacle épistémologique premier de l'historien du droit." In *Storia sociale e dimensione giuridica: Strumenti d'indagine e ipotesi di lavoro. Atti dell'incontro di studio Firenze, 16–17 aprile 1985*, ed. P. Grossi, 275–312. Milan, 1986.

———. "Rendre justice. Éléments pour une histoire contemporaine de l'espace judiciaire espagnol." *Mélanges de la Casa de Velázquez* 25 (1989): 355–79.

———. "Relatores y magistrados. De la naissance du juge modern au XIX siècle espagnol." In *Les figures historiques de l'administrateur: Institutions, réseaux, pouvoirs en Espagne, en France et au Portugal, 16e–19e siècle*, ed. R. Descimon, J. F. Schaub, and B. Vincent, 151–64. Paris, 1997.

Schulze, H. *States, Nations, and Nationalism: From the Middle Ages to the Present.* Trans. William E. Yuill. Cambridge, 1996.

Schwartz, S. B. "Magistracy and Society in Colonial Brazil." *Hispanic American Historical Review* 50 (1970): 713–30.

———. *Sovereignty and Society in Colonial Brazil: The High Court of Bahia and Its Judges, 1609–1715.* Berkeley, 1973.

———. "State and Society in Colonial Spanish America: An Opportunity for Prosopography," In *New Approaches to Latin American History,* ed. R. Grahan and P. H. Smith, 3–35. Austin, 1974.

Serra Ruiz, R. *Honor, honra e injuria en el derecho medieval español.* Murcia, 1969.

Sharpe, J. A. "Last Dying Speeches. Religion, Ideology and Public Execution in Seventeenth-Century England." *Past and Present* 107 (1985): 144–67.

———. *Crime in Early Modern England, 1550–1750.* London, 1984. Reprint, 1999.

Shaskolsky-Sheleff, L. "The Illusions of Law: Psychoanalysis and Jurisprudence in Historical Perspective." *International Journal of Law and Psychiatry* 9 (1986): 143–58.

Shoemaker, R. B. "The 'Crime Wave' Revisited: Crime, Law Enforcement and Punishment in Britain, 1650–1900," *Historical Journal* 34/3 (1991): 763–68.

———. *Prosecution and Punishment: Petty Crime and the Law in London and Rural Middlesex, c.1660–1725.* Cambridge, 1991.

———. "The Decline of Public Insult in London, 1660–1800," *Past and Present* 169 (2000): 97– 131.

Siebzehner, B. "Hacia la homogeneidad cultural entre España y América: la creación de la universidad de México." *E.I.A.L.* 2/2 (1991): 87–102.

Smith, J. M. "No More Language Games: Words, Beliefs and the Political Culture in Early Modern France." *American Historical Review* 102/5 (1997): 1413–40.

Soasti, G. "Mercaderes y tratantes en Quito durante el siglo XVII." In *Enfoques y estudios históricos: Quito a través de la historia,* ed. P. Aguilar, 87–106. Quito, 1992.

Soberanes Fernández, J. L. "La administración superior de justicia en Nueva España." *Boletin mexicano de derecho comparado* 12 (1980): 143–200.

———. "La administración de justicia en la recopilación de 1680." In *Recopi-*

lación de Leyes de los Reinos de las Indias: Estudios histórico jurídicos, ed. F. Icaza Dufor, 165–76. Mexico, 1985.

Socolow, S. M. "Women and Crime: Buenos Aires, 1757–1797." *Journal of Latin American Studies* 12 (1980): 39–54.

———. *The Bureaucrats of Buenos Aires, 1769–1810: Amor al Servicio Real.* Durham, 1987.

Solórzano y Pereira, J. *Política Indiana.* 1674. Reprint, Madrid, 1972.

Soman, A. "Deviance and Criminal Justice in West Europe, 1300–1800." *Criminal Justice History* 1 (1980): 3–28.

———. "L'infra-justice à Paris d'après les archives notariales." *Histoire, économie et société* 3 (1982): 369–75.

Songer, S., ed. *Fact, Fiction and Forensic Evidence: The Potential of Judicial Sources for Historical Research in the Early Modern Period.* Oslo, 1997.

Spierenburg, P. *The Spectacle of Suffering: Execution and the Evolution of Repression from a Pre-Industrial Metropolis to the European Experience.* Cambridge, 1984.

Stein, S. J., and Stein, B. H. *The Colonial Heritage of Latin America.* New York, 1970.

Strayer, J. *On the Medieval Origins of the Modern State.* Princeton, 1970.

Suárez, S. G. *Las milicias. Instituciones militares hispanoamericanas.* Caracas, 1984.

Sueiro, D. *La pena de muerte, ceremonial, historia, procedimiento.* Madrid, 1974.

Super, J. C. "Partnership and Profit in the Early Andean Trade: The Experience of Quito Merchants, 1580–1610." *Journal of Latin American Studies* 2/2 (1979): 265–81. Spanish translation in "Compañía y utilidades en el comercio andino temprano: la práctica de los comerciantes de Quito, 1580–1610." *Revista ecuatoriana de historia economica* 1 (1987): 59–79.

Tandeter, E. "La producción como actividad popular: Ladrones de minas en Potosí." *Nova America* 4 (1981): 42–65.

Tau Anzoátegui, V. "El abogado del cabildo de Buenos Aires durante el virreinato." In *Bicentenario del Virreinato del Río de la Plata,* vol. 1, 85–104. Buenos Aires, 1977.

———. "La ley 'se obedece pero no se cumple': En torno a la suplicación en las leyes del derecho indiano." *Anuario histórico jurídico ecuatoriano* 6 (1980): 55–110.

———. "Consideraciones sobre la aplicación de la recopilación de 1680." In *Recopilación de Leyes de los Reinos de las Indias: Estudios histórico jurídicos,* ed. F. Icaza Dafur, 55–82. Mexico, 1985.

———. "La noción de ley en América hispana durante los siglos XVI a XVIII." *Anuario de filosofía jurídica y social* 6 (1986): 192–232.

———. "La doctrina de los autores como fuente del derecho castellano-indiano." *Revista de historia del derecho* 17 (1989): 169–285.

Tauro, A. *Diccionario enciclopédico del Perú, ilustrado.* Lima, 1966.

TePaske, J. J. "La crisis del siglo XVIII en el virreinato del Perú." In *Historia y sociedad en el mundo de habla española: Homenaje a José Miranda,* 263–79. Mexico, 1970.

Terrán Najas, R. "Sinopsis histórica del siglo XVIII." In *Nueva historia del Ecuador,* vol. 4, *Epoca Colonia II,* ed. E. Ayala Mora, 263–300. Quito, 1983.

———. *Los proyectos del imperio borbónico en la Real Audiencia.* Quito, 1988.

———. "La ciudad colonial y sus símbolos: Una aproximación a la historia de Quito en el siglo XVII." In *Ciudades de los Andes: Visión histórica y contemporánea,* ed. E. Kingman Garcés, 153–71. Quito, 1992.

———. "Factores dinámicos en el desarrollo urbano del Quito colonial." In *Enfoques y estudios históricos-Quito através de la historia,* ed. P. Aguilar, 67–86. Quito, 1992.

———. "La historia económica y social sobre la época colonial ecuatoriana: Un balance de la producción historiográfica en los últimos 25 años." *Procesos* 5/2 (1993): 29–52.

Thompson, E. P. "Christianity, Sociology, and Historical Relevance." *British Journal of Sociology* 27 (1976): 387–402.

Thompson, I. A. A. "A Map of Crime in Sixteenth-Century Spain." *Economic History Review* 21 (1986): 244–67.

Tilly, C. "Reflections on the History of European State-Making." In *The Formation of National States in Western-Europe,* ed. C. Tilly. Princeton, 1975.

Tomás y Valiente, F. "El perdón de la parte ofendida en el derecho penal castellano." *Anuario de historia del derecho español* 21 (1961): 55–114.

———. *El derecho penal de la monarquía absoluta (siglos XVI–XVIII).* Madrid, 1969.

———. "Teoría y práctica de la tortura judicial en las obras de Lorenzo Matheu y Sanz (1618–1680)." *Anuario de historia del derecho español* 41 (1971): 439–85.

———. *La Tortura en España.* Barcelona, 1973.

———. "Ventas y renuncias de oficios públicos a mediados del siglo XVII." In *IV Congreso del Instituto Internacional de Historia del Derecho Indiano,* 725–53. Mexico, 1976.

———. "Opiniones de algunos juristas clásicos españoles sobre la venta de oficios públicos." In *Filosofía y derecho: Estudios en homenaje a José Corts Grau,* 627–49. Valencia, 1977.

———. *Gobierno e instituciones en la España del Antiguo Régimen.* Madrid, 1982.

———. *La venta de oficios en Indias (1493–1606).* Madrid, 1972. Reprint, 1982.

———. "El derecho penal como instrumento de gobierno." *Estudis* 22 (1996): 249–62.

Tomás y Valiente, F., Clavero, B., Hespanha, A. M., Bermejo, J. L., Gacto, E., and Álvarez Alonso, C., eds. *Sexo barroco y otras transgresiones premodernas.* Madrid, 1990.

Trinidad Fernández, P. "La inclusión de lo excluido: La historia de la delincuencia y de las instituciones penales." *Historia social* 4 (1989): 149–58.

Troconis de Veracoechea, E. *Historia de las cárceles en Venezuela (1600–1890).* Caracas, 1983.

Uribe, V. M. "The Lawyers and New Granada's Late Colonial State." *Journal of Latin American Studies* 27/3 (1995): 517–49.

———. "Colonial *Baracunatanas* and Their Nasty Men: Spousal Homicides and the Law in Late Colonial New Granada," *Journal of Social History* 35/1 (2001): 43–72.

Vallejo, J. "Historia del proceso, procedimiento de la historia: Diez años de historiografía procesal en España (1979–1988)." In *Hispania entre derechos propios y derechos nacionales: Atti dell'incontro di studio Firenze-Lucca, 25–27 maggio 1989*, vol. 2, ed. B. Clavero, P. Grossi, and F. Tomás y Valiente, 885–921. Milan, 1990.

———. "Amor de árbitros: Episodio de la sucesión de Per Afán de Ribera el viejo." In *Fallstudien zur spanischen und portugiesischen Justiz 15. bis 20. jahrhundert*, ed. J. M. Scholz, 212–69. Frankfurt, 1994.

Vanderwood, P. *Desorden y progreso: Bandidos, policías y desarrollo mexicano.* Mexico, 1981. Reprint, 1986.

Van Gennep, A. *The Rites of Passage.* Chicago, 1908; reprint, 1960.

Velasco, J. *Historia del Reino de Quito en la América meridional.* 1789. Reprint, Caracas, 1981.

Vericat, J. "La organizatoriedad del saber en la España del siglo XVI." *Revista internacional de sociología* 38 (1980): 261–92.

Viforcos Marinas, M. I. "Los recogimientos de centros de integración social a cárceles privadas: Santa Marta de Quito." *Anuario de estudios americanos* 50/2 (1993): 59–92.

Vigil, R. "*Oidores, Letrados* and the Idea of Justice, 1480–1570." *Americas* 47 (1990): 39–47.

Vincent, C. "Justice Criminelle et supplices sous l'ancien régime." *Gavroche* 67 (1993): 11–16.

Viqueira Albán, J. P. *¿Relajados o reprimidos? Diversiones públicas y vida social en la ciudad de México durante el siglo de las luces.* Mexico, 1987.

Waquet, J. C. *Corruption, Ethics and Power in Florence, 1600–1770.* Trans. L. McCall. Paris, 1984. Trans. University Park, PA, 1992.

———. "Some Considerations on Corruption, Politics, and Society in Sixteenth and Seventeenth Century Italy," In *Political Corruption in Europe and Latin America*, ed. W. Little and E. Posada-Carbó, 21–40. London, 1996.

Washburn, D. A. "The Bourbon Reforms: A Social and Economic History of the Audiencia of Quito, 1760–1810." Ph.D. diss., University of Texas at Austin, 1984.

Weisser, M. R. *Crime and Punishment in Early Modern Europe.* Sussex, 1979.

———. "Crime and Punishment in Early Modern Spain" In *The Social History of Crime in Western Europe since 1500*, ed. V. A. C. Gatrrel, B. Lenman, and G. Parker, 76–96. London, 1980.

Wellman, B., and Wetherell, C. "Social Network Analysis of Historical Communities. Some Questions from the Present for the Past." *History of the Family* 1/1 (1996): 97–121.

Wickham, C. "Gossip and Resistance among Medieval Peasantry." *Past and Present* 160 (1998): 3–24.

Williams, R. "Some Aspects of Summary Justice in Eighteenth Century Rural Berkshire," *Archives* 26/104 (2001): 41–53.

Windler, C. "Clientèles royales et clientèles seigneuriales vers la fin de l'ancien régime. Un dossier espagnol." *Annales ESC* 52 (1997): 293–310.

Wright, L. P. "Las órdenes militares en la sociedad española de los siglos XVII y XVIII: La encarnación institucional de una tradición histórica." In *Poder y sociedad en la España de los Austrias*, ed. J. H. Elliott, 15–56. Barcelona, 1982.

Xristóbal Martín, A. "Amistad, parentesco y patronazgo: Redes vinculares y servidores inquisitoriales en el tribunal de Logroño (siglo XVII)." *Historia social* 17 (1993): 21–31.

Zarazaga, L. "Recusación y excusación en el Derecho Indiano." *Revista chilena de historia del derecho* 13 (1987): 117–28.

Zaruma: cuatro siglos de peregrinaje histórico, 1560–1992 (Memoria XIV Jornadas de Historia Social: Zaruma 27–29.8.1992). Quito, 1992.

Zemon Davis, N. *Fiction in the Archives: Pardon Tales and Their Tellers in Sixteenth-Century France.* Stanford, 1987.

Zorraquín Becú, R. *La justicia capitular durante la dominación española.* Buenos Aires, 1947.

———. *La organización judicial argentina en el periodo hispánico.* Buenos Aires, 1952.

———. "El adelantado indiano: título honorífico." In *Memoria del Congreso Venezolano de Historia*, vol. 3, 551–78. Caracas, 1977.

Zorzi, A. "Control social, ordre public et répression judiciaire à Florence à l'epoque communale: éléments et problèmes." *Annales ESC* 45/5 (1990): 1169–88.

Zumalacarregui, L. "Visitas y residencias en el siglo XVI: Unos textos para su distinción." *Revista de Indias* 7 (1946): 917–21.

Zuniga, J. P. "Cabildo colonial et formation de l'élite: Le cas de Santiago du Chili (1655–1675)." In *Recherche sur l'histoire de l'État dans le monde ibérique*, ed. J. F. Schaub, 51–63. Paris, 1993.

Index